THE CONCISE ENCYCLOPEDIA OF THE GREAT RECESSION 2007–2010

Jerry M. Rosenberg

The Scarecrow Press, Inc.
Lanham • Toronto • Plymouth, UK
2010

Published by Scarecrow Press, Inc.
A wholly owned subsidary of The Rowman & Littlefield Publishing Group, Inc.
4501 Forbes Boulevard, Suite 200, Lanham, Maryland 20706
http://www.scarecrowpress.com

Estover Road, Plymouth PL6 7PY, United Kingdom

British Library Cataloguing in Publication Information Available

Library of Congress Cataloging-in-Publication Data
Rosenberg, Jerry Martin.
  The concise encyclopedia of the great recession 2007–2010 / Jerry M. Rosenberg.
      p. cm.
  Includes bibliographical references and index.
  ISBN 978-0-8108-7660-6 (hardback : alk. paper) — ISBN 978-0-8108-7691-0 (ebook)
  1. Financial crises—United States—History—21st century—Dictionaries. 2.
Recessions—United States—History—21st century—Dictionaries. 3. Financial
institutions—United States—History—21st century—Dictionaries. I. Title.
  HB3743.R67 2010
  330.9'051103—dc22   2010004133

For Ellen

Celebrating fifty years of love and adventure.
She is my primary motivation.
As a lifelong partner, Ellen
keeps me spirited and vibrant.

Listen less to those whose judgments brought us this crisis. Listen less to those who told us all they were the masters of noble financial innovation and sophisticated risk management. Listen less to those who complain about the burdens of living with smarter regulation or who oppose having to pay a few for the costs of this or future crises. . . . Risk will build up again . . . and future governments will have to act again to socialize private losses in the interest of preventing catastrophic damage. — U.S. Treasury Secretary Timothy Geithner, March 22, 2010

CONTENTS

PREFACE

It seemed to be a calm and typical summer. In mid-2008, the American economy was in a strong position as its gross domestic product grew by an annualized 3.3 percent, in part reflecting a strong trade performance. U.S. wealth had reached $14 trillion annually. Despite rising unemployment, soaring fuel prices, and constricting credit, consumer spending managed to grow at a 1.7 percent annual rate. President George W. Bush introduced a fiscal stimulus package that included $110 billion in tax rebates, of which $92 billion had been disbursed by early July. Then, the second half of the year began to look weaker. Real consumer spending tumbled at a 0.4 percent monthly rate.

By the end of 2008, the S&P 500 had declined 38 percent, jobs lost came to 1.9 million, and the U.S. government owned stock in 206 banks. The $700 billion bank bailout plan—the Troubled Asset Relief Program (TARP)—was passed by Congress on October 3, 2008, yet failed to fulfill the needs of the nation. And 2009 looked worse. Moving quickly, once he was inaugurated in January, President Barack Obama succeeded in getting a complex, expensive, and lengthy economic stimulus package passed by Congress in February, followed by the new Treasury secretary's plans for ways to effectively use the unspent $350 billion of TARP funds. The next day, the Dow Jones Industrial Average plummeted nearly 5 percent in response to what was considered to be the administration's lack of clarity; specifics were missing.

As the rescue tab rose, taxpayers were not being "adequately informed or protected." These gambles are the reason the government should have attached more strings to its help, including a say in how the money was used. To finance the bailouts, the U.S. Treasury was borrowing money and the Federal Reserve Bank was printing it. That bodes ill for a heavily indebted nation, presaging higher interest rates and higher prices—perhaps sharply higher. By mid-February, the president had signed into law the American Recovery and Reinvestment Act, followed by a housing plan to help nearly 10 million homeowners avoid foreclosure, with promises of more funds to come as needed.

By the summer 2009, there were more than five unemployed American workers for every job opening. The ranks of the poor continued to escalate, welfare rolls were rising, and those under thirty years of age had sustained nearly half the job losses since November 2007. A month before the melt-down began there were about 7 million Americans counted as unemployed; today there are about 15 million. By the end of 2009, there were six times as many Americans seeking work as there were job openings, and the average duration of unemployment—the time the average job seeker spends looking for work—was more than six months, the highest level since the 1930s. As promised by the government, new regulators and complicated federal regula-tions are appearing, all purporting to stop the leakage and misuse of the public trust. On Wall Street, 2010 will likely be known as the year of the regulator, with the most significant overhaul in seventy-five years.

This recession has touched Americans across incomes and races. It has slashed family earnings, increased poverty, created increased anxieties and emotional depression, and left more people without health insurance. Median household income fell 3.6 percent to just over $50,000, the steepest year-over-year fall in forty years. The poverty rate, at 13.2 percent, was the highest since 1997. And about 700,000 more people didn't have health insurance in 2008 than twelve months prior.

One year following the collapse of Lehman Brothers on September 15, 2008, few of the numerous government proposals to reshape the banking and financial industries were in place. Today, most of the institutions that received government funds are doing well. In mid-September 2009, the chairman of the Federal Reserve declared that it appeared that the recession had come to an end and that the economy was turning upward, while at the same time, housing foreclosures and unemployment continued to climb. The jobless rate then hit 10.2 percent in October, the highest since 1982; more than one out of every six workers—17.5 percent—were unemployed or underemployed. Of-ficially, the Great Recession began in December 2007; unofficially it ended in the early fall 2009. However, for the 15 million unemployed and for those experiencing the meltdown, the year 2010 was part of their nightmare.

GOALS

Global understanding is a major part of the new world economic order. This volume attempts to spell out the activities and events of the past two years and to be a guide to help navigate the reader through this economic downturn. With current, accurate, and sufficiently detailed explanations of the economic seesaw of 2008–2009 and into 2010, this book should help readers to better understand the reasoning, motives, hidden agendas, and power plays of those who are responsible for this debacle and, most important, what the govern-ment has done to try to overcome it. At the same time, this historical and factual encyclopedia, based on daily reports from the media and from specialists in the field, will provide readers with the necessary resources for planning future moves for themselves and their families, friends, and colleagues.

To the user of this volume, it is my hope that this volume will prove to be a rewarding learning experience. I look forward to receiving your comments and suggestions that may assist me in the continuous upgrading of this book. **Email: ejrosenber@aol.com**

ACKNOWLEDGMENTS

No work of this nature can be the exclusive product of one person's effort. Even when written by one individual, such a work requires the tapping of many sources, which is especially true of this book. By the very nature of the subjects and fields included, I have had to rely on the able and extensive efforts of others, especially writers, practitioners, and specialists. I have not deliberately quoted from any copyrighted source. Any apparent similarity to existing, unreleased explanations in these cases is purely accidental and the result of the limitations of language. Various organizations have aided me directly by providing informative sources. Some government agencies and nonprofit associations have provided a considerable amount of usable information. In addition, being, according to the *New York Times*, "the leading business and technical lexicographer in the nation" has allowed me to borrow entries from my eight business dictionaries.

During the preparation of this book, beginning in fall 2007 until the end of 2009, numerous reliable sources have been tapped. The *Wall Street Journal*, the *International Herald Tribune*, and the *New York Times* have been particularly useful tools. To a lesser extent the *Economist* and the *Financial Times* of London were helpful in presenting a needed global perspective. In addition, most of the country introduction write-ups are drawn extensively from information provided by the Organization for Economic Cooperation and Development (OECD). I acknowledge these print sources for this data in each country's entry. I could not have achieved my goals without their professional wisdom and input.

On a personal level, I thank the many professionals and specialists whom I used as a sounding board to clarify my ideas and approach; they offered valuable suggestions and insight and encouraged me to move ahead. A special thanks to Gregory Henderson, a former MBA student, who is currently vice president in a major finance company in New York City. He has devoted an enormous amount of hours and talent to reviewing my listings and correcting errors, thereby validating many of the entries. To my publisher, Ed Kurdyla, senior editor Stephen Ryan, and production editor Jessica McCleary at Scarecrow Press, I add my appreciation for their willingness and encouragement to proceed with this project.

Then, there are those who have been closest to me. Nothing has been more fulfilling than sharing an adult lifetime, first with my wife, Ellen, who for fifty years has contributed immensely to my limited talents by providing her gifts of charm, responsibility, orientation to family, and intellect, and as a partner sharing adventure. Lauren and Bob, Liz and Jon are the next generation, and they appear already in place as contributors to their communities and chosen areas of work. Of course, four grandchildren—Bess, Ella, Celia, and Rita—make this all come full circle, with the delights of just watching and being fascinated by the ever-changing rainbow in their lives.

READER'S NOTE

The Concise Encyclopedia of the Great Recession 2007–2010 has been prepared with the hope that the reader's understanding of the entries will help
in the sharing of information and ideas. Hopefully, the confusion about the
events that have occurred during this difficult time will be reduced, and this
record will serve as a consistent, accurate, and informative resource. Most
importantly, it should help people gain clarity about the significant economic
issues of the past several years. Entries can take on different meanings in
different contexts and situations, and a goal of this encyclopedia is to be
inclusive and to present all the key elements for each entry. I have organized
this work to provide these elements easily and rapidly.

DATES

Some entries provide dates that are essential to understanding the sequence of
events. At the first appearance, a date is given by month, day, and year; the
year may not be repeated when placed alongside different months and days
within the same year. It should be assumed that the year remains constant
until the next year appears. For example, January 8, 2008, is given, followed
by February 5, March 14, and so on, all in 2008. When the next full date is
given, for example, January 12, 2009, that triggers a new year for the subsequent months and days.

ALPHABETIZATION

Entries are presented alphabetically. The listings are alphabetized up to the
first comma and then by words following the comma, thus establishing clus-
ters of related terms. Entries with numerals are listed according to the spelling
of the number.

ENTRIES

The current most common entry is usually given as the principal one, with others cross-referenced to it. Some terms have been included for historical significance only; some entries are given as background to enhance the user's understanding of the recent meltdown events; others are included to assure the smoothness of transition from the past one hundred years of political and economic institutions, regulations, and rules.

CROSS-REFERENCES

"See" and "See also" references are suggested to provide the reader with additional, often related, and significant information. Utilizing these listings will provide a deeper and expanded sense of the entry. The use of "Cf." suggests entries to be compared with the original one. "Synonymous with" following a description does not imply that the entry is exactly equivalent to the principal title under which it appears. Usually the entry only approximates the primary sense of the original term.

FEEDBACK

Major entries have been reviewed by bank/finance/legal specialists and educators. However, I am solely responsible for including the entries and descriptions. I welcome suggestions and critical comments bringing errors to my attention.

A

ABA. *See* AMERICAN BANKERS ASSOCIATION.

ABC. The television division of the Walt Disney Company announced on January 29, 2009, that it would eliminate about 400 jobs from its work force of 6,500 to 7,000 because of the weakening economy.

First-quarter profit dropped 46 percent. Ongoing promotion helped increase its hotel occupancy to 89 percent, up slightly from the previous year in their Florida resort. Its theme division shed about 1,900 jobs through a combination of layoffs and buyouts and restructured many of its behind-the-scenes operations.

Profit declined in the second quarter 2009 by 26 percent. Net income fell to $954 million from $1.28 billion the year earlier.

Fourth-quarter 2009 profit at Walt Disney rose 18 percent, with an $895 million profit. ABC profit climbed 26 percent on a 14 percent revenue gain.

ABERCROMBIE & FITCH CO. Reported a 68 percent drop in its fiscal fourth-quarter earnings of 2008. The firm expected deep losses into 2009. Abercrombie lowered prices as much as 90 percent over the Christmas 2008 buying season.

After reporting a larger-than-expected fiscal first-quarter 2009 loss in May the firm had a 24 percent decline in revenue for the quarter ending May 2, while sales at stores open for more than a year fell a sharper 30 percent.

Abercrombie & Fitch posted a quarterly loss of $26.7 million on August 14, 2000. Sales fell 23 percent to $648.5 million; revenue decreased 15 percent to $765.4 million.

ABU DHABI. *See* BARCLAYS; DAIMLER; DUBAI; UNITED ARAB EMIRATES.

AB VOLVO. *See* FORD; VOLVO.

ACCOR. The global hotel company announced on July 16, 2009, that its second-quarter sales fell 9 percent.
Cf. MARRIOTT.

ACCOUNTABILITY. The quality or state of being accountable; an obligation or willingness to accept responsibility or to account for one's actions. Becoming more important since the Great Recession took hold.

See also EMERGENCY ECONOMIC STABILIZATION ACT OF 2008; FINANCIAL STABILITY OVERSIGHT BOARD; REGULATION; TRANSPARENCY.

ACCOUNTANTS. Accountants have been accused of failing to protect the public interest before, during, and following the Great Recession. Questions remain—why didn't they know that the major banks were hiding assets off their balance sheets and stretching regulations, if not outright breaking them?

ACCOUNTING RULES. *See* FINANCIAL CRISIS ADVISORY GROUP.

ACQUISITIONS. *See* MERGERS AND ACQUISITIONS.

ADB. *See* ASIAN DEVELOPMENT BANK.

ADIDAS. Reported a 93 percent fall in second-quarter 2009 net profit. Adidas's total quarterly sales fell 2.5 percent.
   See also RETAILING.

ADMINISTRATION. In the United Kingdom, a term synonymous with bankruptcy protection.

ADVANCED MICRO DEVICES INC. Reported in January 2009, a $1.42 billion fourth-quarter loss, resulting from a rapidly deteriorating environment for computer sales as well as big write-offs.

ADVERSE FEEDBACK LOOP. The combination of job losses and falling corporate profits that creates new loan defaults, which hurt banks beyond the original mortgage problems that began the 2008–2009 economic collapse.

ADVERTISING. Worldwide, in 2009, spending for advertising slipped 0.2 percent to $490.5 billion, led by a 6.2 percent drop in the United States, the first decline since 2001. Advertising spending in the United States fell 2 percent in the third quarter 2008 as the recession prompted cutbacks, with the steepest toll on national spot radio spending, which dropped 18 percent from 2007. Most forecasts for 2009 predicted general advertising to fall by 5 percent or more, and 9 percent specifically on television. The fate of the car industry is critical, as it spends around $20 billion a year on advertising. Car ads contribute up to 25 percent of advertising revenues for local television channels. Assuredly, advertising agencies will suffer.

   U.S. advertising spending on media such as TV, print, and online display ads dropped 14 percent to $30.18 billion in the first quarter 2009 from a year earlier. The top ten advertisers for the first quarter 2009, by ad spending, in millions were:

a. Procter & Gamble—$674.1
b. Verizon Communications—$577.1
c. AT&T—$459.4
d. General Motors—$424.2
e. Johnson & Johnson—$397.2
f. News Corporation—$341.2
g. Sprint Nextel—$317.7
h. Walt Disney—$303.7
i. Time Warner—$263.4
j. General Electric—$261.4

See also INTERNET ADVERTISING; LUXURY GOODS; RETAILING.

AER LINGUS. In November 2009, the airline reported that revenue for the three months ending September 30 fell 9.7 percent from the year before, slowing from a 12 percent year-to-year decline in the first half.
See also AIRLINES.

AFGHANISTAN. *See* WARS IN AFGHANISTAN AND IRAQ.

AFRICA. At first minimally affected by 2008 meltdown, South Africa, the region's largest economy, closely linked to the outside world, was the first to feel the impact of the global meltdown.

By November 1, 2008, its currency, the rand, lost about 30 percent of its value against the U.S. dollar; its stock market also fell significantly. Nevertheless, South Africa was in good shape with capital controls, financial-sector regulations, and sound banking practices. Most of sub-Saharan Africa was minimally affected, except for Nigeria and Lagos, where their stock markets declined abruptly. Plunging commodity prices and lower overseas demand will also impact this region, as will the drop in oil prices and demand. In Zambia, there has been a 25 percent drop in their currency against the dollar as copper prices tumbled.
See also AUTOMOBILE INDUSTRY; SOUTH AFRICA.

AFRICAN AMERICANS. Historically, the automobile industry employed blacks when many industries would not. For many, jobs at car factories were the route to a better life for several generations, but those gains have been threatened since 2008.

African Americans were the most likely to get higher-priced subprime loans, leading to higher foreclosure rates, and have replaced Hispanics as the group with the lowest homeownership rates. The unemployment rate for African Americans is nearly twice that of whites. And nearly half of young black men without a high school diploma have no job. Black workers are also unemployed for about five weeks longer, on average, than the rest of the population. Forty-five percent of unemployed blacks have been out of work for 27 weeks or longer, compared with just 36 percent of unemployed whites.

By October 2009, the unemployment rate for African American men reached 17.1 percent.

See also LIVING STANDARDS; MEN UNEMPLOYED; UNEMPLOYMENT; WOMEN UNEMPLOYED.

Cf. HISPANICS.

AGGREGATE DEMAND. *See* KEYNES, JOHN MAYNARD.

AGGREGATOR BANK. An institution where the private sector plays a role in pricing bad assets. Of major importance since 2008 meltdown.

Synonymous with "BAD BANKS."

AIG. *See* AMERICAN INTERNATIONAL GROUP.

AIR BAGS. *See* AUTOLIV.

AIRBUS. January 15, 2009, signaled the start of a "very soft year" as the global downturn cut demand for aircraft, and Airbus in turn cut its forecasts. The European aircraft maker held the top spot in global airliner production for the sixth year in a row in 2008, with a 7 percent rise in deliveries to a record 483 planes, compared with Boeing, its U.S. rival.

By April, Airbus trimmed its jumbo output as carriers deferred orders primarily based on the economic meltdown. Originally, Airbus planned to deliver more than 30 super-jumbos in 2010, carrying a catalog price of $327 million each. Airbus, which expects to sell about 300 planes in 2009, projected that sales would stabilize in 2010 and would rise by as much as 4.6 percent. The decline in 2009 traffic was 2 to 4 percent.

On November 16, 2009, Airbus reported a third-quarter net loss, posting a $129.9 million loss. Revenue also fell 1.8 percent.

See also AIRLINES.

Cf. BOEING.

AIR CARGO. *See* DHL.

AIR FRANCE-KLM. Warned on March 26, 2009, that it would have an operating loss of about $272 million for its fiscal year ending March 31 because of shrinking passenger traffic and cargo activity and the costs of fuel. It expected revenues to decline 6 percent for 2009. The airline had a net loss for its fiscal fourth quarter, of $684.5 million with revenue declining 12 percent. On July 30, Air France-KLM posted its fiscal first quarter with a net loss of $599 million, compared with a net profit of more than $200 million a year earlier. Its first-quarter 2009 revenue declined 21 percent to 5.17 billion euros.

Air France-KLM had a net loss for its fiscal second quarter 2009 of $218.6 million. Revenue dropped 19 percent.

See also AIRLINES.

AIRLINES. The upheaval of airlines in the world continued throughout the economic crisis of 2008–2009 as passenger volumes continued to decline, even though the price of fuel dropped. Lufthansa Airlines made a bid for Austrian Airlines; Iberia had a drop of 11 percent air travel in October; and British Airways' traffic fell 5.9 percent in November. Passenger travel worldwide declined 4.6 percent from a year earlier for a third straight month in 2008. Freight traffic dropped almost 14 percent.

Further hurting the industry, on December 10 the government of China urged its state-owned airlines to cancel or defer new aircraft purchases at a time of global economic turmoil, hurting American and European aircraft makers. State-owned airlines had total losses of $612 billion in the first ten months of 2008.

Losses for the world's airlines, announced on March 24, with its deepest crisis in sixty years, were projected to total nearly $5 billion for 2009, as passenger and freight traffic continued to fall. The loss forecast made in December 2008 was $2.5 billion. Projections for 2009 were for losses for global airlines of $9 billion because of low demand and poor yields in a global economic slump and the spread of H1N1 flu virus, double the $4.7 billion loss estimated in March 2009. In 2008, the loss was $10.4 billion. By summer 2009 it was clear that profits for airlines were down. In the first four months of the year, premium traffic dropped by 15 percent, while traffic within Europe dropped by 37 percent. The industry is expected to lose $9 billion in 2009.

The five largest hub-and-spoke carriers reported second-quarter 2009 losses, including AMR Corporation's American Airlines, Delta Air Lines, UAL Corporation's United Airlines, Continental Airlines, and US Airways Group. Passenger air-traffic, measured in revenue passengers per kilometer, fell 2.9 percent from a year earlier in July, an improvement from the 7.2 percent fall in June 2009 and the 6.8 percent decline for the first eight months of the year. Cargo volumes, measured in freight ton per kilometer, fell 11.3 percent in July, better than the 16.5 percent fall in June of 2009.

In September 2009 the global airline industry was facing $11 billion of losses for the year, $2 billion more than originally projected. Its trade association expects airlines to lose $3.8 billion worldwide in 2010, marking a third straight annual loss. The industry had lost $416.8 billion in 2008. The association representing airlines reported on September 17 that the world's airlines would lose a combined $411 billion in 2009, on top of a $16.8 billion loss in 2008.

The loss of $4.6 billion in 2010 is an improvement over the $11 billion loss in 2009.

By December 2009, business-class sales were up. The industry appeared to be headed toward a recovery as fuller planes, fewer discounted fares, lower fuel prices, and revenue from a variety of formerly free services started to pay off.

Although it is expected that air travel will expand in 2010, airlines will still have significant losses, perhaps $5.6 billion.

See also AER LINGUS; AIRBUS; AIR FRANCE-KLM; AIRTRAN; ALL NIPPON AIRWAYS; AMERICAN AIRLINES; AMERICAN INTERNATIONAL GROUP; AUSTRIAN AIRLINES; BOEING; BRITISH AIRWAYS; CATHAY PACIFIC AIRWAYS; DELTA AIR LINES; FINNAIR; IBERIA; JAPAN AIRLINES; LUFTHANSA; QUANTAS AIRWAYS; SCANDINAVIAN AIRLINES; SOUTHWEST AIRLINES; UNITED AIRLINES; US AIRWAYS.

AIR-TRAFFIC. *See* AIRLINES.

AIRTRAN. A Florida-based airline, it posted a profit of $78.4 million, with revenues falling in the second quarter 2009 by 13 percent to $603.7 million.

ALCATEL-LUCENT. The struggling French-American telecommunications equipment maker announced on December 11, 2008, that it would eliminate 1,000 management positions, or about 7 percent of its managers, in an austerity plan that aimed to save 750 million euros. The job cuts, about 1.3 percent of the global work force of 77,000, suggested more hard times ahead.

A fourth-quarter 2008 report indicated a net loss of $5.07 billion. Their first-quarter 2009's loss was $536 million.

On July 30, 2009, the company posted its first quarterly profit since its creation in 2006. Alcatel-Lucent had earnings of $19.6 million.

On October 30 it reported that its third-quarter loss more than quadrupled from a year earlier as demand dropped for older-generation wireless network gear. Its loss climbed to $270 million. Sales in the third quarter fell 9.8 percent from a year earlier.

ALCOA. Cut 13 percent of its workforce in early 2009, and 1,700 contractors were eliminated. Alcoa, the third-largest aluminum company in the world, and the largest U.S. aluminum producer, lost $1.19 billion during the fourth quarter 2008, as prices and demand for the metal plunged in the troubled global market.

Alcoa announced in mid-March 2009 that it would slash its dividend 82 percent. In addition to reducing operational expenses by $2.4 billion it would embark on a new round of cost cutting. These measures were in addition to the earlier cuts in 2009 that included 15,000 layoffs, asset sales, and plant closures. In the first quarter 2009, Alcoa revealed that it was significantly hit by falling aluminum prices and a 41 percent decline in sales; a loss of $497 million resulted. The price of its metal fell 26 percent, since January 1.

Alcoa, on July 8, became the first blue-chip company to report its second-quarter 2009 earnings, with a $454 million loss. Revenue fell 42 percent to $4.24 billion in the quarter, compared with $7.25 billion one year earlier. Meanwhile the price of aluminum fell 49 percent from the second quarter 2008 to $1,485 a metric ton.

On October 7, 2009, Alcoa posted a profit of $77 million in the third quarter. This was a 71 percent decline from a year before, but indicated a hopeful turnaround. By month's end Alcoa reported its first profitable quarter in a year.

ALDRICH-VREELAND ACT. A forerunner of the Federal Reserve Act. Congress in 1908 passed legislation as a temporary relief measure until such time as new banking rules could be formulated.

ALLIED IRISH BANKS. *See* IRELAND.

ALL NIPPON AIRWAYS. Reported a fiscal first-quarter 2009 net loss of $308.6 million in the three months ending June 30. Revenue dropped 22 percent.

ALTERNATIVE ENERGY. *See* EMERGENCY ECONOMIC STABILIZATION ACT OF 2008.

ALUMINUM. *See* ALCOA; RIO TINTO.

AMAZON.COM INC. Shares on October 23, 2009, surged 27 percent to $118.49, an all-time closing high following strong third-quarter results.

AMERICAN AIRLINES (AMR). Reported fourth-quarter 2008 losses, capping a miserable year that saw soaring fuel prices drop sharply, only to be replaced by a recession-induced drop in travel. Demand was off 2.5 percent from 2007, and international bookings were down about 8 percent. American Airlines would cut its mainline capacity by 6.5 percent in 2009, after trimming it by 8 percent in 2008. AMR lost $2.07 billion in 2008.

On April 15, it was announced that the airline lost $4,375 million in the first quarter, cutting the company's revenue by 15 percent. Prices of the average fare fell by 4.5 percent from a year earlier. Then, on July 15, American Airlines reported a $390 million second-quarter loss as collapsing travel demand continued to erase gains from lower fuel costs. Its second-quarter revenue fell 21 percent to $4.89 billion from a year before. Averages fares dropped 15 percent.

On September 1, AMR announced that it was cutting 921 flight-attendant positions taking effect on October 1. Two hundred twenty-eight employees would be furloughed, and 244 others placed on leave for two months. Another 449 would take voluntary options such as leave. AMR reported that its traffic fell 8.1 percent in August from a year before. The airline's capacity fell 9.4 percent.

AMR reported a loss of $359 million for the third quarter 2009, with revenue falling 20 percent from a year earlier.

By December 2009, AMR announced that it was prepared to invest $1.1 billion in Japan Airlines.

See also AIRLINES; JAPAN AIRLINES.

AMERICAN ASIATIC UNDERWRITERS. *See* AMERICAN INTERNATIONAL GROUP.

AMERICAN BANKERS ASSOCIATION (ABA). The national organization of banking formed in 1875 to "promote the general welfare and usefulness of banks and financial institutions." Critiques are that the ABA failed the public by not staying on top of the evolving banking crisis.

AMERICAN DREAM. *See* HOUSING BAILOUT PLAN; MODIFYING MORTGAGES.

AMERICAN EXPRESS (AMEX). In February 2009, the credit card company offered select customers a $300 AmEx prepaid gift card if they paid off their balances and closed their accounts. As the economic crisis widens and unemployment rises, there is growing concern that credit-card defaults will soar.

AmEx customers reduced spending by 16 percent in the first quarter 2009, sending the company's quarterly net income down 56 percent. The firm's three-month net income was $437 million, down from $991 million a year earlier. With customers reducing their spending by 16 percent in the second quarter, the company's quarterly net income fell 48 percent. Its net income was $337 million down from $653 million a year earlier.

See also CREDIT CARDS.

AMERICAN INTERNATIONAL GROUP (AIG). Founded in Shanghai in 1919 and called American Asiatic Underwriters.

The world's largest insurance company on May 9, 2008, announced a record $7.8 billion first-quarter loss. AIG provides insurance protection to more than 100,000 entities, including small businesses, municipalities, 401(k) plans, and *Fortune* 500 firms, who together employ over 100 million workers. AIG has over 375 million policyholders in the United States, with a face value of $19 trillion, and remains a major source of retirement insurance. On August 7, AIG announced a $5.4 billion second-quarter loss as the housing market continued to pose problems.

The U.S. government created an $85 billion emergency credit line in September to keep AIG, a ninety-year-old firm, from folding and added $38 billion more in early October when it became obvious that the initial amount was insufficient. As part of the revised plan, the Fed indicated that it would reduce that credit line to $60 billion. The government then announced on November 10, an overhaul of its rescue of the insurance giant, indicating it would purchase $40 billion of the firm's stock, after indications that the initial bailout was placing too much strain on AIG.

When the reorganized deal is finalized, taxpayers will have invested and lent a total of $150 billion to AIG, the most the government had ever invested in a single private enterprise. But Fed officials said the $40 billion investment would permit them to reduce their exposure of $112 billion from $152 billion, and improve the condition of the collateral for its loan. The government invested an additional $22.5 billion in AIG to help the firm buy residential mortgage-backed securities that it also insured. Treasury Department officials stated that the $40 billion AIG investment was separate from the $250 billion the Treasury had earmarked for buying stakes in banks. AIG reported a loss of $24.47 billion for the third quarter, compared with a profit of $3.09 billion a year earlier.

Together with the U.S. government, AIG on December 3, agreed to clear AIG of its obligations on about $53.5 billion in toxic mortgage debt. By December 31, AIG was prepared to ask the Federal Reserve to relax its rules on its $60 billion-plus disposal program to permit bidders to use a greater proportion of shares to pay for its assets. The government's $153 billion bailout of AIG had effectively made it a majority owner of the insurance group. By mid-February 2009 the staggering infusion had not been able to stem losses at the company, as it tried to raise as much as $60 billion in fresh capital to stay afloat.

At the beginning of March, the government overhauled its $150 billion bailout of AIG hoping to support the ailing insurers. The arrangement, the government's fourth, represented a near reversal of the one first given in mid-September. Going from the government serving as a demanding lender, thereby forcing AIG to pay a steep interest rate on an anticipated short-term loan, the government eliminated interest charges and is now acting as a majority shareholder. The focus was on splitting the firm, with businesses made into separate stock offerings. AIG would combine its giant property-casualty insurance activities into a new unit, with a different name and separate management, and sell nearly 20 percent of it to investors. Another $30 billion in new cash from TARP would cut the firm's $60 billion credit line with the Federal Reserve to between $20 billion and $25 billion.

Since the Federal Reserve first bailed out AIG in September 2008, government aid to the insurer has almost doubled, as follows:

a. September 16—Government seized AIG, exchanging an $85 billion loan for a 79.9 percent equity stake.

b. October 8—Fed increased its loan by $38 billion, for a total of $123 billion.
c. November 9—The government scrapped the original loan in favor of a new deal that included lending and an equity share, for a total of $150 billion.
d. March 1—The government made $30 billion of TARP money available and cut the loans by up to $25 billion.

By March, the government was resigned to a long stewardship after failing to sell the insurer into smaller units, with the government owning nearly 78 percent of the firm. The AIG bailout was now up to $173.3 billion in taxpayer assistance. On March 2, AIG reported a $61.7 billion fourth-quarter loss that brought their losses for 2008 to $99.3 billion. Its assets also dropped, from over $1 trillion as of September 30, to $860 billion at year end 2008.

In the fourth quarter 2008, the firm took $13 billion in charges on distressed investments, particularly related to commercial mortgages. Another $7 billion came from interest and other costs associated with a federal loan central to the bailout. On March 23, fifteen of the top twenty recipients of $165 million in bonuses to employees of the AIG Financial Products division (the division blamed for most of AIG's losses and woes) agreed to give back their bonuses—amounting in excess of $30 million in cash. A major portion of these monies would be returned, according to the New York attorney general, Andrew Cuomo. AIG reported the largest quarterly loss in history, around $62 billion. The quarterly losses suffered by Merrill Lynch and Citigroup, $15.4 billion and $8.3 billion, respectively, pale by comparison with AIG. The federal government would provide a third plan of assistance, on top of the $150 billion in loans, investments, and equity injections, to keep it afloat. Once again, in March, the government provided AIG with its fourth round of assistance. On March 17, the government sought to recoup from AIG the $165 million in bonuses paid to employees in the wake of a national furor over the payments.

AIG reported a roughly $5 billion first-quarter 2009 loss.

The first-quarter deficit is small in comparison to the $62 billion loss AIG reported for 2008's fourth quarter. AIG closed a deal with the Treasury Department on April 20 where the government will make new funds available to AIG. Subtracted from the new monies was an amount to offset the bonus payments AIG made in March to employees of its financial products unit. The arrangement was originally set at $30 billion, and now $165 million was subtracted leaving a total of $29.835 billion. In addition, the Treasury would invest in the company as long as AIG didn't file for Chapter 11 bankruptcy protection and the Treasury would hold more than 50 percent of the voting power. Then, on August 7, AIG reported a quarterly profit, its first since late 2007.

AIG's International Lease Finance Corporation, the largest airplane-finance firm in the world, was on the brink of collapse by mid-September 2009, unable to pay its coming debts. Over the coming three years, the company has about $18 billion of debt coming due, and $30 billion overall.

AIG reported its second consecutive quarterly profit on November 6, 2009, but about 15 percent lower than a year earlier. The company earned $455 million in the quarter, with $363 million allotted to the federal government, which owns about 80 percent of AIG.

See also FEDERAL RESERVE; GEITHNER, TIMOTHY F.; GREEN-BERG, MAURICE RAYMOND "HANK"; LEHMAN BROTHERS; "TOO BIG TO FAIL"; U.S. TREASURY.

AMERICAN INTERNATIONAL UNDERWRITERS (AIU). *See* AMER-ICAN INTERNATIONAL GROUP.

AMERICAN RECOVERY AND REINVESTMENT ACT (OF 2009). Originally suggested by president-elect Obama on January 3, 2009. This pro-posal would be combined with one-time measures that were more typical of federal stimulus packages to jump-start a weak economy, like spending for roads and other job-creating projects. President Obama's proposed $825 bil-lion act would be the largest stimulus measure ever. He urged $275 billion in tax cuts and credits to jump-start the economy and $550 billion in spending for clean energy, road construction, social welfare programs, and emergency assistance to states.

Then, on February 17, following two differing bills from the House of Rep-resentatives and the Senate, reconciliation negotiations were successful and the bill received the president's endorsement. The House of Representatives and the Senate on February 11 struck a deal on a $787.2 billion economic stimulus bill in just twenty-four hours of negotiations. Final congressional ac-tion occurred on February 13; the bill arrived on President Obama's desk for his signature on February 16. Conservatives and many other well-informed citizens believed that this piece of legislation would mark the largest single-year increase in domestic federal spending since World War II; it would send the budget deficit to heights not seen since the Great Depression; it would create a new and higher spending baseline for years to come. In the end, the concern was that the United States was about to test the outer limits of our national balance sheet.

The 407-page act included $507 billion in spending programs and $282 billion in tax relief, including a scaled-back version of the president's middle-class tax cut proposal, which gave credits of up to $400 for individuals and

12 • AMERICAN RECOVERY AND REINVESTMENT ACT

$800 for families within certain income limits. It provided a one-time payment of $250 to recipients of Social Security and government disability support. Selected programs include:

Spending

a. $30 billion—Modernization of the electric grid, advanced battery manufacturing, energy efficiency grants.
b. $19 billion—Payments to hospitals and physicians who computerize medical-records systems.
c. $8.5 billion—National Institutes of Health biomedical research into diseases, such as Alzheimer's, Parkinson's, cancer, and heart diseases.
d. $5 billion—Home weatherization grants to low- and middle-income families.
e. $6.3 billion—Energy efficiency upgrades to federally supported and public housing, including new insulation, windows, and frames.
f. $29 billion—Road and bridge infrastructure construction and modernization.
g. $8.4 billion—Public transit improvements and infrastructure investments.
h. $8 billion—High-speed rail investments.
i. $18 billion—Grants and loans for water infrastructure, flood prevention, and environmental cleanup.

Tax Cuts

j. $6.6 billion—Tax credit for first-time homeowners buying between April 2008 and June 2009 was raised from $7,500 to $8,000, and would not have to be repaid.
k. $116.2 billion—Workers earning less than $75,000 would get a payroll tax credit of up to $400; married couples filing jointly for less than $150,000 would get up to $800.
l. $69.8 billion—Middle-income taxpayers got an exemption from the alternative minimum tax of $46,700 for an individual and $70,950 for a married couple.
m. $5.1 billion—Businesses can more quickly deduct the cost of investment in plant and equipment from taxable income.

Aid

n. $40.6 billion—Aid to local school districts to balance educational budgets, to prevent cutbacks and modernize schools.

o. $87 billion—A temporary increase in federal funding for Medicaid to states.
p. $2 billion—Funds for communities to buy and rehabilitate foreclosed and vacant properties.
q. $8 billion—Aid to states for public safety and critical services.
r. $14 billion—Education tax credit, a partially refundable $2,500 credit or tuition and book expenses.
s. $17.2 billion—Increase in student aid, including raising maximum Pell Grant to $5,350 in 2009 and to $5,550 in 2010.
t. $200 million—Extra grants for colleges' work-study programs.
u. $27 billion—Jobless benefits extended to a total of twenty weeks on top of regular unemployment compensation, and thirty-three weeks in twenty-nine states with high unemployment.

Critically, the act gave states more than $150 billion over a period of two and a half years to help them balance their budget. Nevertheless, huge state deficits remained.

Six months after its passage the Recovery Act's single largest distribution of the entire $787 billion—more than one-third of it—was for tax cuts, with 95 percent of working citizen seeing their taxes lowered. The second-largest part—just under one-third—was for direct relief to state governments and individuals. The final third was for roads and construction projects. By mid-July 2009, more than 30,000 projects had been approved. Seventy percent of the funds were to be spent by September 2010.

On September 10, 2009, the White House estimated that 1 million more people would have been out of work in August without programs funded by the stimulus plan.

Recalling that the $787 billion stimulus package was expected to increase the nation's GDP by enough to create 3.6 million jobs, most economic experts concluded by mid-September 2009 that government transfers and rebates failed to increase consumption. Initially there were one-time payments of $250 to eligible individuals and temporary reductions in income-tax withholding for a refundable tax credit of up to $400 for individuals and $800 for families with incomes below certain thresholds. The government pointed to the sharp reduction in the decline in real GDP from the first to the second quarter 2009 as evidence that the stimulus program was succeeding. The growth improvement that followed in the second quarter was largely due to factors other than the stimulus program.

By the end of October 2009, the government's $787 billion stimulus program had created or saved 640,239 jobs. More than half—325,000—were in education, and only about 80,000 were in construction.

See also COBRA; EDUCATION; EXECUTIVE PAY; FIRST-TIME HOME BUYER CREDIT; HOME AFFORDABLE MODIFICATION PROGRAM; KEYNES, JOHN MAYNARD; MAKING WORK PAY; MASS TRANSIT; NATIONAL DEBT; PART-TIME WORKERS; PAYROLL TAX CUTS; "READY-TO-GO" PROJECTS; STIMULUS PLAN (EUROZONE); U.S. COMMERCE DEPARTMENT; U.S. ENERGY DEPARTMENT; U.S. TREASURY.

Cf. CITIGROUP; ECONOMIC STIMULUS PLAN (BILL FROM HOUSE OF REPRESENTATIVES); ECONOMIC STIMULUS PLAN (BILL FROM SENATE); ECONOMIC STIMULUS PLAN; EMERGENCY ECONOMIC STABILIZATION ACT OF 2008; FRAUD; MERRILL LYNCH.

Synonymous with RECOVERY ACT.

AMEX. *See* AMERICAN EXPRESS.

AMR. *See* AMERICAN AIRLINES.

ANDORRA. *See* TAX HAVENS.

ANGELIDES, PHIL. *See* FINANCIAL CRISIS INQUIRY COMMISSION.

ANGLO IRISH BANK. *See* IRELAND.

ANN TAYLOR STORES. On March 6, 2009, announced a wider fiscal fourth-quarter net loss and disclosed new cost-cutting plans as sales dropped nearly 20 percent. Ann Taylor posted a net loss of $375.6 million, or $6.66 a share, for the period ending January 31, compared with a year-earlier loss of $6.7 million, or 11 cents a share.

The company reported a sharp sales decline in its fiscal third quarter 2009 but went into profit on low inventory levels and fewer markdowns. Sales at stores open at least one year fell 26 percent with a profit of $2.1 million. Net sales fell 12 percent to $462.4 million.

ANTI-FORECLOSURE PLAN. *See* FORECLOSURE; MODIFYING MORTGAGES.

AOL. On January 28, 2009, announced that it was discharging around 700 workers, or 10 percent of its workforce, as a sharp decline in ad spending continued to pressure its transition from an Internet service provider to an advertising business.

On November 19, 2009, AOL announced further plans to cut about a third of its staff. The company would ask up to 2,500 people to take buyout packages, leaving the firm with about 4,400 workers.

See also ADVERTISING; TIME WARNER.

APARTMENT VACANCIES. By July 2009, the vacancy rate for U.S. apartments hit a twenty-two-year high in the second quarter. Rents fell sharpest in markets where white-collar workers lost their jobs. Of the 79 markets that were tracked, 45 showed an increase in vacancies.

In October 2009, the apartment vacancy rate hit its highest since 1986. The vacancy rate reached 7.8 percent, a twenty-three-year high. As a result, monthly rents continued to fall. Nearing 10 percent unemployment, more would-be renters were moving in with friends and families.

The collapse of the rental market in 2009 has benefited renters. In many cities, landlords are offering tenants up to six months of free rent, flat-screen TVs, and new appliances. At the same time, they are slashing monthly rates and easing application standards. Rents fell a record of 3.5 percent in 2009, with 2010 projections for another 2 percent decline. Nationwide, apartment vacancy is 7.8 percent, up from 4.8 percent at the end of 2007.

See also UNEMPLOYMENT.

A.P. MOLLER-MAERSK. *See* MOLLER-MAERSK; SHIPPING.

APPLE. Resisting the recession, Apple posted a 15 percent jump in second-quarter 2009 profit. Apple sold 5.2 million iPhones in the quarter, more than seven times what it sold a year earlier.

Throughout the meltdown Apple Inc. continued to prosper. The company posted a 47 percent quarterly profit as consumers continued to buy their iPhones and Macintosh computers. Apple sold 7.4 million iPhones in its quarter ending September 26, up 7 percent from the year before, and 41 percent more than the previous quarter. The company also sold 3.1 million Macintosh computers in the quarter, up 17 percent from the year before.

Cf. YAHOO!

APPLIANCES. Appliance manufacturers are counting on a similar "cash for clunkers" type of rebate program in the fall 2009. These rebates are expected to be for purchases of high-efficiency household appliances. Earlier in 2009, Congress had authorized $300 million for the program as part of the economic stimulus bill. Rebates are expected to range between $50 and $200 per appliance.

By year's end, the appliance rebate program was only available in Delaware and won't be available in many states until spring 2010. Delaware issued mail-in rebates in December 2009 for $25 to $200 allowing anyone to participate, and does not require that old appliances be turned in. The government allocated funds to states based on population.

See also CASH FOR CLUNKERS.

APPRAISALS. On May 1, 2009, under the Home Valuation Code of Conduct, a major change took effect meant to lower the conflicts of interest in home appraisals while safeguarding the independence of the people who do them. Brokers and real estate agent can no longer order appraisals. Lenders now control the entire process.

ARCANDOR. A German tourism and retailing giant that filed for insolvency on June 9, 2009.

ARCELORMITTAL. The world's largest steelmaker said on November 5, 2008, that it would cut output by about one-third amid deteriorating demand from automakers and the construction industry. Its net debt was $33 billion, and market capitalization was $35 billion. Nevertheless, the company had sufficient liquidity to cover maturing debts for 2009.

In South Africa alone, ArcelorMittal cut 1,000 contractor jobs and lowered 2009 capital spending by more than half as a plunge in steel prices pushed the firm to slow expansion. The steel giant had a $1.06 billion first-quarter loss. Sales declined 49 percent to $15.12 billion from $29.81 billion and its plants were slowed down to operate at about 50 percent capacity by the end of April 2009. The world's largest steelmaker swung to a $792 million loss in the second quarter 2009.

The company reported in fall 2009 a loss of $53 million, from a $3.82 billion profit in 2008. By year's end the company planned to eliminate about 10,000 jobs, or about 3.5 percent of its 287,000 employees.

ARGENTINA. Considered Latin America's most vulnerable country. Since 2008, Argentines were pulling money out of the country's banking system at an alarming pace, creating the potential for a crippling default on international debt that brought the country's seven-year expansion to a halt. The stock exchange tumbled to a five-year low in the fourth quarter of 2008. Its pension grab was seen as an admission that Argentina might not meet 2009's debt payments, approximately $20 billion.

By mid-December 2009 the government reported that it would set aside a portion of the central bank's foreign-currency reserves into a fund dedicated to debt service. Argentina moved to earmark $6.57 billion, of its total $47.54 billion, in reserves for debt service.

See also LATIN AMERICA; WORLD TRADE.

ARION. *See* ICELAND.

ARMENIA. A landlocked country of 3 million people in the Caucasus that has been dependent on the monies received from citizens living abroad. With the meltdown, many are returning to their birthplace and remittances that once contributed significantly to support relatives is quickly disappearing

It is also drawing $540 million from the IMF and $550 million from the World Bank. Exports accounted for only 10 percent of the nation's GDP.

ARTS, THE. Art organizations are pulling back as they are having increasing difficulty attracting support. About 10,000 art organizations, or 10 percent of the U.S. total are at risk of closing. Art groups get about 40 percent of their income, more than other nonprofits, from private donations, which are down considerably.

See also METROPOLITAN OPERA.

ASIA. Approximately $2 trillion of market value was lost in Asia in 2008.

See also AUTOMOBILE INDUSTRY; CHINA; FORMOSA; JAPAN; KOREA.

ASIAN DEVELOPMENT BANK (ADB). At their annual meeting on May 3, 2009, finance officials agreed to set up an emergency $120 billion liquidity fund that thirteen Asian nations could tap to help overcome the global financial meltdown. In addition, the Chiang Mai Initiative was created to become a network of bilateral currency-swap arrangements among the nations. Small Asian economies would be able to borrow larger amounts in proportion to their contributions than the more-developed economies.

See also GLOBAL ECONOMIC OUTPUT.

ASSET-BACKED SECURITIES. *See* FINANCIAL REGULATION PLAN (2009).

ASSET GUARANTEE PROGRAM. A 2008 government effort providing a U.S. government guarantee for assets held by firms that "face a high risk of losing market confidence due in large part to a portfolio of distressed or illiquid assets." This new insurance program of the U.S. Treasury was announced on January 2, 2009, for bad loans and other troubled assets that it could use to further help financial institutions.

See also U.S. TREASURY.

ASSET-MANAGEMENT FIRMS. Companies that specialize in taking over all or part of a firm's servicing activities and then running them more efficiently. BlackRock merged with Barclays Global Investors in mid-June 2009, making it the world's largest asset manager.

See also BLACKROCK; EMERGENCY ECONOMIC STABILIZATION ACT OF 2008.

ASSET PROTECTION SCHEME. Developed by the British Treasury, in which a bank's riskiest assets will be covered for up to 90 percent of future losses. The Royal Bank of Scotland was the first to participate, putting $430 billion of assets in the scheme.

See also BARCLAYS; UNITED KINGDOM.

AT&T. *See* UNEMPLOYMENT.

AT-RISK HOMEOWNERS. *See* HOUSING BAILOUT PLAN.

AUCTION HOUSES. *See* CHRISTIE'S INTERNATIONAL; SOTHE-BY'S.

AUDI. In mid-March 2009, announced that it expected a sharp decline in profits and its first such drop in sales in fourteen years. Sales declined around 11 percent to 63,400 cars.

Its first-quarter operating profit declined 29 percent amid waning demand for luxury cars.

See also AUTOMOBILE INDUSTRY.

AUDITORS. U.S. government auditors urged the Treasury Department in December 2008 to act quickly to develop internal controls to insure that its $700 billion financial rescue package was operating effectively and ethically. This was to fulfill the obligations of the Economic Stabilization Act passed on October 3.

AUSTRALIA. GDP growth weakened from 2.5 percent in 2008 to about 1.75 percent in 2009 before picking up, as forecast, to 2.75 percent in 2010. This would still imply that, despite the depressed international environment, the impact of the financial crisis and the fall in the terms of trade should be relatively contained. Unemployment is likely to increase, however, and inflation may dip below 3 percent in 2010. The expected reduction of inflation due to the current slowdown, along with the need to preserve the stability of the financial system, militates for looser monetary conditions. Budget measures, made possible by the significant fiscal leeway built in the previous years, will also support activity, although their effectiveness might be limited if confidence is not restored. It is important for the ongoing reform of industrial relations to preserve labor-market flexibility (OECD).

Australia's central bank cut the policy interest rate by a percentage point, to 4.25 percent on December 2, 2008.

The government announced at the outset of 2009 that it began a spending program of $11.8 billion to stimulate the economy. The program came after Australia's economy expanded at its weakest rate in eight years in the third quarter of 2008. The prime minister announced in early February that it would wipe US$73.37 billion from government revenues in the next four years. Analysts predicted a deficit equaling up to 4 percent of Australia's trillion-dollar-a-year economy.

The government also announced a stimulus package worth $27 billion to keep the economy growing. Growth predictions in 2009 were for a drop from 2.7 percent to 1 percent, and just 0.75 in the following year. That same day, the central bank cut interest rates by a percentage point to a cash rate of 3.25

percent, the lowest for forty-five years. In mid-March, the government said it planned to crack down on excessive executive-pay packages and curb so-called golden parachute termination payments, prompting an angry response from business groups. Shareholder approval will be required for any termination payments that exceed average annual base salary, which excluded additional compensation such as shares or stock options. On April 7, the Reserve Bank of Australia cut interest rates a further one-quarter of a percentage point to a forty-nine-year low.

Australia's economy grew in the first quarter 2009, defying a global slowdown to become one of the few developed nations to have sidestepped a technical recession. The nation's GDP rose 0.4 percent in the first quarter from the fourth quarter of 2008, and rose 0.4 percent from a year earlier. In the second quarter the nation's economy grew significantly, reducing any threat of recession. GDP grew at the fastest pace, 0.6 percent, among the globe's thirty-three advanced economies. The economy expanded 0.6 percent from the first quarter.

On October 6, 2009, Australia became the first G-20 nation to raise interest rates since the beginning of the Great Recession, setting a stage for further central banks increases. The Reserve Bank of Australia raised its main interest-rate target one-quarter of a percentage point to 3.25 percent.

See also G-20.

AUSTRIA. Former Communist countries of Europe contributed 42 percent of the Austrian financial sector's profit in 2007. In 2008, Austrian banks were owed $290 billion by borrowers from Russia to Albania. This exposure was much higher than that of Italy or Germany and is equal to Austria's gross domestic product.

On December 14, 2009, the government nationalized the local unit of a German bank, Hypo Group Alpe Adria, following huge losses. That bank had assets of about $58 billion. This was the second bank to be nationalized in Austria since the beginning of the Great Recession.

See also AIRLINES; TAX HAVENS.

AUSTRIAN AIRLINES. Lufthansa completed its takeover of the Austrian carrier on September 3, 2009. Austrian was 42 percent government owned before.

See also AIRLINES.

AUTO CZAR. *See* RATTNER, STEVEN.

AUTO DEALERS. During the January–March 2009 quarter, 271 auto dealers in the United States went out of business. At the end of the quarter there were 19,738 auto dealers in the United States, down from 20,009 at the end of

2008. Another 1,200 dealers were expected to permanently close their doors before the end of the year.

See also AUTOMOBILE INDUSTRY.

AUTOLIV. The world's largest maker of air bags for cars said in March 2009 that it would cut 3,000 jobs in the first two months of the year, eliminating 2,600 permanent positions. In June 2008, it further reduced its total work force by 20 percent, or 9,000 positions.

AUTOMATIC STABILIZERS. Known in Europe, barely used in the United States, where spending on unemployment benefits automatically rises further the longer a downturn lasts.

AUTOMOBILE CZAR. *See* RATTNER, STEVEN.

AUTOMOBILE INDUSTRY. The years 2008–2009 were the worst years for selling cars and trucks since 1992. The U.S. motor vehicles and parts manufacturing industries employed 703,900 people in 2008. The sector had shed 116,500 jobs since November. The Big Three carmakers employed about 201,000 workers. Indirectly the industry employed between 2.5 million and 3 million workers, who were usually employed by suppliers or in services such as warehousing and ports. As a whole, the industry accounted for 13 percent of U.S. manufacturing jobs. General Motors, Chrysler, Ford, and Toyota announced on April 2, 2008, that they had a double-digit drop in U.S. vehicle sales in March. Lenders were making fewer auto loans.

After rescuing the banks in October, governments on both sides of the Atlantic turned their attention to the ailing automobile industry. President George W. Bush sought help to spur a merger between General Motors and Chrysler.

In the first nine months of the year, GM earned nearly $2 billion in Latin America, Asia, the Middle East, and Africa, even as its North American operations recorded a $5.7 billion loss. Similarly, Ford earned more than $1 billion in Latin America, while it lost $4 billion in North America. Ford earned $1.4 billion in Europe in the first half of 2008, and nearly $1 billion in 2007. GM lost $18.8 billion in the first six months of 2008. A merger with Chrysler would give GM access to approximately $11.7 billion in cash that was on Chrysler's books as of June. New car sales fell across Europe in October, with sales down 40 percent in Spain, the worst hit among four countries publishing data. With 55,000 workers spread across twenty plants, GM's European workforce was now down 40 percent from a decade ago. But with market share shrinking to about 9.5 percent currently from roughly 12 percent, GM remained under pressure to cut overhead.

If the Big Three automobile firms were to collapse, 3 million people would potentially lose their jobs, counting autoworkers, suppliers, and the employees of a variety of businesses dependent on the companies. The cost to local, state, and federal governments could be as much as $156 billion over three years in lost taxes and higher outlays for such things as unemployment and health care assistance. The car and parts industries employed 732,800 workers directly in September and the three U.S. automobile carmakers, Ford, GM, and Chrysler, employed 239,341 workers at the end of 2007. Some 2 million present and former workers depend on carmakers for health care, a costly part of the automobile industries dilemma.

In Europe, car sales fell almost 15 percent in October, the sixth straight monthly decline. For example, Renault, the French carmaker, cut its output to reduce inventories by the end of 2008 to the same level as the end of 2007. For October 2008, its sales were down 14.1 percent from a year earlier. New car sales in the United States fell below 800,000 in November for the first time in decades. Sales of new luxury cars in the United States were 39 percent lower in November than a year before. For example, Mercedes-Benz saw American sales decline by 43 percent and Porsche by more than half. The same held true in Asia and Europe. This in great part is a result of the credit crunch and the lack of available financing.

In addition, the U.S. automakers owed more than $100 billion to their bankers and bondholders, and experts wondered how much of that would be repaid.

The proposed rescue bill of December 10 would have extended $14 billion in emergency loans to General Motors and Chrysler, the two most imperiled automakers, and subjected them to far-reaching government oversight at the direction of a so-called car czar. The czar (never appointed) would have been required by March 31, 2009, to certify that the automakers and their stakeholders—including creditors, labor unions, and dealers—had agreed to carry out a long-term viability plan and that they would have provided a hard economic definition of what it meant to be a viable firm. The proposed plan would give the government stock warrants in the automakers, allowing taxpayers to profit should share prices rise. It would also have prevented shareholder dividends, executive bonuses, and golden parachute severance packages. It would have required the car czar to call in the emergency loans for repayment should the auto firms fail to carry out an aggressive reorganization plan or meet other requirements found in the law.

The following day, December 11, prospects of the $14 billion rescue plan seemed to vaporize as Republican leaders spoke out forcefully against the bill. The Bush administration shifted position on December 12 and said it would dip into the money set aside for the $700 billion financial bailout to keep General Motors and Chrysler from going bankrupt. The Treasury Department promptly indicated that it would provide short-term relief to the automakers. By mid-December, there was increasing concern for the overseas operations of U.S. carmakers Ford and GM, which were profitable in the first half of the year. Ford earned $1.4 billion in Europe in the first half of the year, while GM earned nearly $300 million in the first half of the year, 2008. Their collapse could also imperil the survival of automobile manufacturers in both Asia and Europe, who are dependent on U.S. components. In addition, European car sales fell 26 percent in November, the biggest drop since 1999. Registrations declined to 932,537 from 1.26 million a year earlier.

With one month left in office, President George W. Bush announced on December 19 that he would extend up to $17.4 billion in emergency loans to prevent the collapse of General Motors and Chrysler. He then shifted onto the Obama administration, commencing on January 20, 2009, how to apply these funds and what sacrifices it would mean to the firms and workers. Ford Motor Company was excluded, as they were still able to fulfill their financial obligations and did not seek or require government assistance. The loans were considered to be critical, as the companies were already on the brink of insolvency and with taxpayers monies would now remain afloat until March 31, 2009. At that time, a decision would be made to determine if the conditions of the loans were met allowing them to receive additional monies or whether they would have to repay the loans and face bankruptcy. The events of rescue were:

September 2008—Auto executives began lobbying for U.S. loans.

November 18 and 19—CEOs of Big Three were grilled before Congress about their need for rescue.

November 20—Lawmakers turned down automakers' pleas, and told CEOs to return in December.

December 2—Automakers returned to Congress, this time with turnaround plans in hand.

December 11—In huge blow to industry, Senate relief effort collapsed amid partisan disputes.

December 19—White House agreed to $17.4 billion in bailout loans.

February 17—GM and Chrysler requested another $14 billion in bailout funds.

March 30—White House agreed to provide additional aid to GM and Chrysler on conditions of change, including fulfilling auto task force recommendations.

April 30—Chrysler Corporation declared bankruptcy.

June 1—General Motors declared bankruptcy.

June 10—Chrysler signed papers formally establishing relationship with Fiat.

The monies would come from the U.S. Treasury's $700 billion financial stabilization fund; Congress had released the second $350 billion for that program. The rescue of GM and Chrysler cost taxpayers more than $62 billion. January 2009 automobile sales were down, with an industry-wide 656,976 cars and light trucks sold, down 37 percent from January 2008. It was the lowest total since December 1981, and the first time U.S. sales were lower than in China, where about 790,000 cars were sold in January. On February 17, both Chrysler and General Motors requested $21.6 billion more to move them toward recovery, in addition to the $7.6 billion they had previously requested but not received. Deep cuts were promised.

Despite the offering of deep car discounts, vehicle sales in the United States still fell to their lowest level in twenty-eight years. Reported on March 3, industry sales declined 4.9 percent from January and plummeted 41 percent from February of 2008. It was equally sour for European car sales, shrinking 18 percent in February. Only Germany prospered, as sales rose 22 percent, following the government's offering of $3,230 to people who trade in their old cars for new ones. There was a bit of optimism. Despite major sales declines in March, the leaders of automakers saw signs of the industry's downturn bottoming out. All the big carmakers suffered sales declines of 36 percent or more compared to March 2008. U.S. sales industry-wide totaled 857,735 cars and trucks, down 37 percent from a year before. But that's up from 688,909 vehicles sold in February and was the highest total since September 2008. February's sales were down 41 percent from a year earlier.

On April 30, the Chrysler Corporation filed for bankruptcy, after months of negotiations with regulators, unions, and creditors. Meanwhile, car sales continued to plummet. April results indicated:

General Motors—down 33.2 percent retaining 21.0 percent of global sales.
Ford—down 31.5 percent retaining 16.3 percent of global sales.
Chrysler—down 48.1 percent retaining 9.4 percent of global sales.
Toyota—down 41.9 percent retaining 15.4 percent of global sales.
Honda—down 25.3 percent retaining 12.3 percent of global sales.
Nissan—down 37.8 percent retaining 5.8 percent of global sales.
Hyundai—down 13.6 percent retaining 4.1 percent of global sales.
KIA—down 14.8 percent retaining 3.1 percent of global sales.
Volkswagen—down 14.8 percent retaining 2.9 percent of global sales.
BMW—down 38.4 percent retaining 2.4 percent of global sales.

U.S. car sales fell 34 percent in May to 925,824 vehicles, but began to show some signs of improving.

By July, the three biggest carmakers in the United States envisioned a bottom to the long decline in auto sales as the industry reported its smallest monthly sales drop in 2009. New-vehicle sales in June declined 28 percent from a year earlier to 860,000 cars and light trucks, making it the smallest decline in any month of the year. U.S. carmakers sold 1,261,977 cars and pickup trucks industry-wide in August 2009, up about 1 percent from the year before, and up from July's 997,824. It was the highest total sales since May 2008 and the first time automobile executives saw a year-over-year increase since October 2007.

U.S. auto sales dropped 23 percent in September 2009 following the termination of the U.S. government's "cash for clunkers" incentive program. Car manufacturers sold 745,997 vehicles in September, compared with 964,783 in the same month one year earlier. GM's sales fell 45 percent in September, Chrysler's car sales dropped 42 percent, Honda's sales declined 20 percent, and Toyota's sales dropped 13 percent.

October 2009 auto sales were 838,052 new cars and light trucks, just 104 fewer than in the year before, with an increase of 12 percent from September. By mid-November 2009, the global automobile industry noted that it had sufficient capacity to produce 85.9 million cars and trucks each year, about 30 million more than it made in 2009. The manufacturers were only utilizing about 65 percent of their available production capacity. Global auto sales are projected to grow by 25 million vehicles over the next six years; however, the industry-wide capacity utilization will only reach 85 percent by 2015.

U.S. auto sales continued to improve, selling an estimated 750,000 cars and trucks in November 2009 compared with 746,789 in the same month in 2008.

See also ADVERTISING; AMERICAN RECOVERY AND REINVEST-MENT ACT; AUDI; AUTO DEALERS; AUTOLIV; AUTO PARTS; AUTO TASK FORCE; AVIS; BMW; CANADA; CAR CZAR; CASH FOR CLUNKERS; CHINA; CHRYSLER; CONTROLLED BANKRUPTCY; ENTERPRISE; EXPORTS (U.S.); FIAT; FORD; FRANCE; FUEL TAX; GENERAL MOTORS; GOLDEN PARACHUTE; GOODYEAR TIRE AND RUBBER COMPANY; HERTZ; HONDA; HUMMER; HYUNDAI MOTOR COMPANY; MAZDA MOTOR CORP; MITSUBISHI MOTORS; NISSAN; PEUGEOT-CITROEN; RATTNER, STEVEN; RENAULT; SAAB; SPAIN; SUBARU; SWEDEN; TATA MOTORS; TOYOTA; TRADE DEFICIT (U.S.); TRUCKING INDUSTRY; UNFAIR TRADE SUBSIDIES; U.S. TREASURY; VEBA; VOLKSWAGEN.

AUTO PARTS. By 2009, following the lead from the U.S. automobile industry, auto parts makers sought a bailout, asking the U.S. Treasury for $25.5 billion. Four hundred parts makers applied for Chapter 11 bankruptcy protection in 2008. By mid-February President Obama's auto task force met with senior procurement executives from GM, Chrysler, and Ford. Suppliers had raised concerns over their finances and submitted plans to the Treasury Department on February 13, arguing that 1 million jobs were at risk.

In mid-March the Treasury Department announced a $5 billion program to aid struggling auto parts suppliers drawing money from the bailout fund, the Troubled Asset Relief Program (TARP). It offered financing to help suppliers to bridge the gap between delivering parts to carmakers and receiving payment. The Treasury Department announced on April 8 a program to assist ailing auto parts makers, providing $3.5 billion in aid to be funneled to suppliers through GM and Chrysler. GM would oversee $2 billion and Chrysler $1.5 billion (Ford continued to claim that it could make supplier payments from its own funds). Auto parts firms announced in June 2009 that they would seek up to $10 billion in loan guarantees from the federal government. On June 16, the Obama administration rejected the request, concluding that the government shouldn't further interfere in the industry's contraction.

See also AUTOMOBILE INDUSTRY; DELPHI.

AUTO SUPPLIERS. *See* AUTO PARTS; DELPHI.

AUTO TASK FORCE. Before providing additional funding to General Motors and Chrysler, at the end of March 2009 the task force concluded that the firms' survival depended on greater concessions from the workers' union because the cost of funding retiree benefits had become unmanageable, especially given the economic meltdown. They called on President Obama to urge hourly workers and retirees to be ready to accept more sacrifices if they hoped to keep their employers afloat.

See also AUTOMOBILE INDUSTRY; AUTO PARTS; RATTNER, STEVEN.

AVIS. Congress was asked, in January 2009, to allow Avis and other car renters to use TARP funds to finance new auto purchases. As part of the car rental business, firms purchase as many as 1.8 million new vehicles each year, being the auto industry's largest customer.

Cf. ENTERPRISE; HERTZ.

AVON PRODUCTS. Reported on May 5, 2009, a 37 percent drop in first-quarter profit as beauty industry sales continued to sag. Profits fell to $117.3 million, down from $184.7 million.

B

BA. *See* BRITISH AIRWAYS.

BACK-TO-SCHOOL SALES. *See* RETAILING.

"BAD BANKS." Banks with troubled assets, where they could be held by the government and then sold over time when market and economic conditions improved. In the meantime, the government uses taxpayer money to provide enough capital to allow banks to resume normal lending. Bad banks could have troubled assets exceeding $5 trillion if defined as assets that could show a loss rate close to or above 10 percent, an amount that is just over 40 percent of the $12.3 trillion in total assets of U.S. commercial banks.

Sweden nationalized its bad banks in the early 1990s and a rapid recovery followed that led to taxpayers making money in the long run.

"Good banks" did not require nationalization.

Experts predicted that over five years, from 2009–2014, as many as one thousand banks could close, which is six times more than the Treasury Department placed on the regulatory problem list in 2009.

By March, the government considered creating multiple investment funds to purchase bad loans and other distressed assets that were at the center of the financial crisis. Obama's intention was for the government to partner with the private sector to purchase $500 billion to $1 trillion of distressed assets as part of its revamping of the $700 billion bank bailout plan. The administration is considering a private-public financing partnership to deal with troubled assets.

See also EUROPEAN UNION; IRELAND; "NEW BANKS"; "TOO BIG TO FAIL"; TOXIC MORTGAGE ASSETS.

Synonymous with AGGREGATOR BANK.

BAILOUT. The dictionary publisher Merriam-Webster chose "bailout" as its word of the year 2008.

See also PAULSON, HENRY; TOXIC MORTGAGE ASSETS.

BAILOUT FUND (PLAN) OF 2008 (U.S.). *See* BANK BAILOUT (PLAN) OF 2008; BANK RESCUE (PLAN) OF 2009; EMERGENCY ECONOMIC

STABILIZATION ACT OF 2008; TROUBLED ASSET RELIEF PRO-GRAM.

BAILOUT HOUSING PLAN. *See* HOUSING BAILOUT PLAN; MORT-GAGE BAILOUT.

BAILOUT RESCUE (PLAN) OF 2009 (U.S.). *See* BANK RESCUE (PLAN) OF 2009 (U.S.); TROUBLED ASSET RELIEF PROGRAM.

BAILOUT RESCUE PLAN (UK). *See* UNITED KINGDOM.

BAIR, SHEILA C. Chairwoman of the Federal Deposit Insurance Corporation.

BALL BEARINGS. *See* SKF.

BALTICS. The three Baltic countries were experiencing, in 2009, a spiraling economic downturn. Latvia, in December 2008, received a $10 billion bailout from the IMF and was facing a 13 percent decline in its GDP. Estonia and Lithuania expected a decline of a tenth.

All three Baltic states were facing double-digit economic declines in GDP throughout 2009, all following the collapse of credit bubbles created by reckless lending and spending.

See also ESTONIA; LATVIA.

BALTIMORE SUN. Maryland's largest newspaper discharged sixty-one people at the end of April 28, 2009. It represented about 27 percent of the newsroom staff.

See also NEWSPAPERS.

BANGLADESH. Since 2004 and ending in 2007, the economy of Bangladesh grew at more than 6 percent each year, with a falling poverty rate. With the recent global downturn, the country finds it harder to feed its people. According to the World Bank, nearly 56 million out of a total 147 million people found it difficult to feed themselves.

BANK AID (EU). *See* EUROPEAN UNION.

BANK BAILOUT (PLAN) OF 2008 (U.S.). The bailout plan, officially the "Troubled Asset Relief Program," was announced on Monday, October 27, 2008, when the U.S. government started doling out $125 billion to nine major banks to get credit flowing again. These deals were intended to bolster the banks' balance sheets so they would be able to commence more normal lending. This action marked the first deployment of resources from the government's $700 billion financial rescue package passed by Congress on October 3.

Treasury Secretary Paulson used $250 billion of the $700 billion to make direct purchases of bank stock, partly nationalizing the U.S. banking system, as a way to get money into the financial system more quickly. The plan aimed to clear banks' balance sheets of bad assets.

Then on November 12, Paulson announced a major shift in the thrust of the $700 billion financial rescue program. He stated that the funds would not be used to purchase up troubled mortgage-related securities, as the rescue effort was originally conceived, but would instead be used in a broader campaign to help financial markets and, in turn, make loans, including car and student loans, more accessible for creditworthy borrowers.

Of the initial $350 billion out of the $700 billion that Congress authorized, all but $60 billion had been committed the Treasury Department by early November 2008. By month's end, more than $1 trillion was allocated in giant bank rescues globally from governments in the United States, Europe, and Asia.

The Treasury Department concluded that there were some banks that were "too big to fail" out of fear that their collapse would severely damage the world's economy.

See also AUDITORS; BANK RESCUE (PLAN) OF 2009; BASEL 2 ACCORD; CITIGROUP; CREDIT UNIONS; EMERGENCY ECONOMIC STABILIZATION ACT OF 2008; FEDERAL DEPOSIT INSURANCE CORPORATION; FORECLOSURE; GINNIE MAE; LEHMAN BROTHERS; NATIONAL DEBT; PUBLIC-PRIVATE INVESTMENT FUND; TERM AUCTION FACILITY; "TOO BIG TO FAIL"; TROUBLED ASSET RELIEF PROGRAM.

Synonymous with TROUBLED ASSET RELIEF PROGRAM.

BANK BAILOUT (REPAYMENT). The U.S. government, and therefore the U.S. taxpayer, has profited from its investment to save the nation's banks.

See also TROUBLED ASSET RELIEF PROGRAM.

BANK BAILOUT FUND. *See* HOUSE (U.S.) FINANCIAL OVERHAUL PLAN. *Synonymous with* TROUBLED ASSET RELIEF PROGRAM.

BANK BONUSES. *See* TROUBLED ASSET RELIEF PROGRAM.

BANK BUYOUTS. At the end of August 2009, the five-member board of the FDIC voted for new rules that required buyout firms to hold on to failed banks they purchase for at least three years. Investors would also be required to maintain larger amounts of high-quality capital at their acquired banks.

See also FEDERAL DEPOSIT INSURANCE CORPORATION; MARKET CAPITALIZATION; "TOO BIG TO FAIL."

BANK CAPITAL. Proposal, not requiring legislative approval, that would increase the amount of capital banks must have as a percentage of their assets. By mid-September 2009, the Obama administration had proposed new principles for capital requirements, but does not plan to announce rules for some time.

See also STRESS TESTS.

BANK CREDIT CARDS. *See* CREDIT CARDS.

BANK DEPOSIT INSURANCE ACT OF 1934. Federal legislation to protect depositors, extended to June 1935 for bank deposit insurance, originally established by the Banking Act of 1933. This act eventually led to the creation of a permanent deposit insurance program in 1935.

BANK FAILURES. There were a total of 25 bank failures in 2008. By February 2009, of the nation's 8,300 banks, 83 had failed by the end of August 2009 and 252 banks were currently on the agency's watch list, meaning that they were at risk of failing. In September alone, regulators took over 11 banks in nine states that were saddled with soured commercial real estate loans.

By mid-October, as the 100th bank failed for the year, the rate further indicated a growing divide between the small and the large bank as the economy improved. The FDIC feared that hundreds of small lending institutions would fail over the coming years, pulling down the economy, as well as adding the strain on the FDIC.

By the end of October U.S. bank failures reached 105, the highest number since 1992.

See also CAPITALISM; COLONIAL BANCGROUP; FEDERAL DEPOSIT INSURANCE CORPORATION; MARKET CAPITALIZATION; STRESS TESTS; "TOO BIG TO FAIL."

BANK HOLDING COMPANY. Any company that owns or controls one or more banks. As defined in the Bank Holding Company Act of 1956, a company that controls two or more banks. Such companies must register with the Board of Governors of the Federal Reserve System and are commonly referred to as registered bank holding companies.

See also BANK HOLDING COMPANY ACT OF 1956; BANK HOLDING COMPANY ACT AMENDMENTS OF 1966; BANK HOLDING COMPANY ACT AMENDMENTS OF 1970.

BANK HOLDING COMPANY ACT OF 1956. Applied to any corporation controlling 25 percent or more of the voting shares of at least two banks, or otherwise controlling the election of a majority of the directors of two or more banks. The law formulated standards for the formation of bank holding companies. These firms were strictly limited to the business of banking, managing banks, and providing services to affiliated banks.

See also BANK HOLDING COMPANY; BANK HOLDING COMPANY ACT AMENDMENTS OF 1966; BANK HOLDING COMPANY ACT AMENDMENTS OF 1970.

BANK HOLDING COMPANY ACT AMENDMENTS OF 1966. Established uniform standards for bank agencies and the court in evaluating the legality of bank holding company acquisitions.

See also BANK HOLDING COMPANY; BANK HOLDING COMPANY ACT OF 1956; BANK HOLDING COMPANY ACT AMENDMENTS OF 1970.

BANK HOLDING COMPANY ACT AMENDMENTS OF 1970. Ended the exemption from the Bank Holding Company Act that one-bank holding companies had enjoyed since 1956. This amendment clearly regulated the ownership of bank shares and limited bank holding company entries into activities related only to the business of banking.

See also BANK HOLDING COMPANY; BANK HOLDING COMPANY ACT OF 1956; BANK HOLDING COMPANY ACT AMENDMENTS OF 1966.

BANKING. Primarily the business of receiving funds on deposit and making loans. Three decades ago, banks supplied three out of every four dollars worth of credit worldwide. In 2009, that share had dropped to about one in three dollars.

See also CANADA; CAPITALISM; CAPITAL ONE FINANCIAL CORPORATION; CITIGROUP; HSBC; INVESTMENT BANKING CHASE; JP MORGAN CHASE; US BANCORP.

BANKING ACT OF 1933. Created the Federal Deposit Insurance Corporation to insure deposits of member banks. Other sections, known as the Glass-Steagall Act, prevented national banks from most investment banking. The first major piece of banking legislation during the Roosevelt administration; it led to significant changes in banking laws.

See also PECORA COMMISSION.

BANKING REGULATIONS. *See* BANK HOLDING COMPANY ACT OF 1956; BANKING ACT OF 1933; BASEL 2 ACCORD; FEDERAL HOME LOAN BANK ACT OF 1932; FEDERAL RESERVE ACT; FINANCIAL INSTITUTIONS REFORM, RECOVERY AND ENFORCEMENT ACT OF 1989; GRAMM-LEACH-BILLEY ACT OF 1999; NATIONAL BANK ACT OF 1863; RIEGLE-NEAL INTERSTATE BANKING AND BRANCHING EFFICIENCY ACT OF 1994; SAVINGS AND LOAN HOLDING COMPANY ACT OF 1967.

BANK LENDING. *See* LENDING.

BANK LOSSES. *See* BASEL 2 ACCORD; EUROPEAN CENTRAL BANK.

BANK NATIONALIZATION. *See* NATIONALIZATION.

BANK OF AMERICA (BOFA). On January 12, 2008, it agreed to purchase the nation's largest mortgage lender, Countrywide Financial, for $4 billion in stock, protecting a casualty of the mortgage-default crisis from possible collapse. When the acquisition occurred in July, it was valued at only $2.5 billion.

In late 2008, management announced plans to cut 30,000 to 35,000 positions over the next three years as it completed its acquisition of Merrill Lynch. That was more than 11 percent of the combined firms' global work force of 308,000. The $19.36 billion purchase of Merrill Lynch & Company enabled Bank of America to announce that it was the largest U.S. bank by assets, with $2.7 trillion on its balance sheet.

Key dates in Bank of America's acquisition of Merrill Lynch were:

1. September 15, 2008—announced deal to buy Merrill for $50 billion in stock.
2. November 30—Merrill had accumulated $13.34 billion in pretax quarterly losses.
3. December 5—shareholders for both firms approved the deal. Nothing was said about Merrill's problems.
4. January 1, 2009—The Merrill–Bank of America deal closed on New Year's Day.
5. January 16—Bank of America announced the new bailout and a fourth-quarter net loss of $1.79 billion. Merrill reports a net loss of $15.31 billion for the fourth quarter.

The government extended a new multibillion-dollar lifeline on January 16, 2009, providing Bank of America with an additional $20 billion in support from the government's $700 billion financial rescue fund. Bank of America agreed to pay the government an 8 percent dividend on the $20 billion capital injection and restrict executive pay and benefits.

The January 2009 additional $20 billion that Bank of America received from the government was to help the bank, based in Charlotte, North Carolina, to absorb the losses at its just-acquired unit, Merrill Lynch. Bank of America had received a total of $45 billion in capital injections from TARP, including $10 billion originally given Merrill Lynch prior to its merger with Bank of America.

On April 20, Bank of America reported a $4.2 billion first-quarter 2009 profit. Shares of the bank fell 24 percent, to $8.02 on concerns that major banks could face more credit losses or write-downs or a need to secure further capital.

On April 29, during the huge criticism of the takeover procedures of Merrill Lynch, shareholders voted to strip Kenneth Lewis of his duties as chairman of the nation's largest bank, as measured in assets. He remains as president and CEO following a vote of 50.34 percent by the shareholders.

Bank of America reported a $3.2 billion profit for the second quarter 2009. BofA's chief executive announced at the end of July his intention to shrink the company's 6,100 branch network by about 10 percent.

On September 14, 2009, a federal judge threw out the SEC's proposed settlement with BofA over its disclosure of controversial bonuses paid to Merrill Lynch workers. On September 21, BofA announced it would soon reduce its dependence on federal assistance and repay its $45 billion loan; it would also hopefully convince U.S. regulators that the bank was sound enough by repaying billions in federal aid.

On September 30, 2009, Kenneth D. Lewis, Chief Executive of BofA re-signed, effective at the end of 2009, following criticism of his taking over of Merrill Lynch.

On October 16, 2009, Bank of America during the Merrill Lynch takeover reported a $1 billion net loss revealing continued exposure to bad loans and a weak U.S. consumer. The third-quarter results were down from a net profit of $1.18 billion a year before.

On December 2 Bank of America announced that they had reached an agreement to repay $45 billion in federal bailout funds and thus escape pay restrictions and other curbs imposed by the U.S. government. BofA becomes the first of several companies to return their taxpayer-funded TARP monies. The bank plans to raise about $18.8 billion in new equity through the sale of securities, a move required by federal regulators to ensure the bank has adequate capital reserves and would not find it necessary to come back to the government for further aid.

See also BERNANKE, BEN; MERRILL LYNCH; STRESS TESTS; "TOO BIG TO FAIL"; TROUBLED ASSET RELIEF PROGRAM; UNEM-PLOYMENT.

BANK OF CHINA. On March 24, 2009, Bank of China announced a 59 per-cent drop in fourth-quarter net profit as its overseas investments were hit by the global financial crisis. The bank's fourth-quarter net fell to $646.8 million (4.42 billion yuan) from 10.77 billion yuan a year earlier.

See also CHINA.

BANK OF ENGLAND. November 6, 2008, the central bank slashed the base rate by an astonishing one and a half percentage points, bringing it down from 4.5 percent to 3 percent, the lowest since early 1955.

It cut its policy rate to a record low of 1 percent on February 5, 2009. Then again, on March 5, the Bank of England cut key interest rates by a further half a percentage point, pushing the rate to their lowest levels ever. The benchmark rate, at the lowest in the bank's 315-year-old history, became 0.5 percent.

In August 2009, the Bank of England received permission from the government to inject an additional $85 billion into the economy.

On September 10, 2009, the Bank of England decided to leave its benchmark interest rate at a record low 0.5 percent, amid signs that the nation's economy was recovering more slowly than those in other parts of Europe. The central bank also left its $290 billion program of buying bonds intact.

See also UNEMPLOYMENT; UNITED KINGDOM.

BANK OF IRELAND. *See* IRELAND.

BANK OF NEW YORK MELLON. Posted a steeper-than-expected 51 percent decline in first quarter 2009, and net profit.

BANK OF WYOMING. FDIC regulators shut the Bank of Wyoming on July 10, making it the fifty-third failure of a federally insured bank in 2009.

BANK PAYBACK. *See* TROUBLED ASSET RELIEF PROGRAM.

BANK RESCUE (PLAN) OF 2009 (U.S.). Treasury Secretary Timothy Geithner's announcement on February 10, 2009, led to a near 400-point drop (almost 5 percent) in the Dow Jones Industrial Averages. The lack of clarity was given as the reason by many disappointed Wall Street traders.

The government's bank rescue plan, using $350 billion of the Troubled Asset Relief Program, described the Obama administration's roadmap to "financial stability and recovery," which included a fresh round of capital injections into banks, an expansion of a Federal Reserve lending program, and a public-private effort to relieve banks of toxic assets. These steps were aimed at getting $1 to $2 trillion in financing into the economy to kick-start both consumer and business lending.

The idea was to entice private capital to buy bad loans and derivatives in an effort to set the "market price."

The government would be committed to spend $50 billion to stem home foreclosures, and to create a Public-Private Investment Fund to remove bad assets off banks' books.

The goals were to encourage lending through a variety of efforts:

a. To stabilize banks with a fresh round of capital injections. It would provide a financial cushion for banks and encourage them to lend. Large banks would have to undergo "stress tests" to measure their capacity to absorb future losses. Investments could be converted into common equity if needed. Banks faced restrictions on dividends, stock repurchases, acquisitions, and executive compensation.
b. To stabilize banks by purchasing toxic assets. It would create a public-private investment fund to purchase bad loans that were causing bank losses and eroding confidence in the financial system. The fund was designed to attract capital for large-scale asset purchases and to allow the private sector to determine the price of current troubled and previously illiquid assets.
c. To unfreeze consumer lending by offering financing for loans. It would expand a Federal Reserve program designed to jump-start markets that provided funding for debt such as student loans and car loans. Investors would purchase newly packaged securitized loans with AAA ratings using attractive financing from the Fed.
d. To help homeowners by modifying home loans. Attempts would be made to halt the spiral of foreclosures and falling home prices, one of the root causes of the crisis. One option was committing funds for programs to reduce monthly payments and setting guidelines for loan modification.

President Obama's first budget, presented on February 26, 2009, included a $250 billion placeholder for government losses associated with further financial rescue efforts. Those losses would come from the possible deployment of an additional $750 billion, a sum that would double the size of the current bailout, and was based on estimates that the government would get back two-thirds of its investment.

The International Monetary Fund reported in April that U.S. banks had $510 billion in write-downs by the end of 2008, facing another $550 billion in 2009 and 2010.

One year following the collapse of Lehman Brothers on September 15, 2008, banks were returning to their normal way of conducting business.

2008

a. September 15—Lehman Brothers declares that it would file for bankruptcy.

b. September 16—U.S. officials agree to bail out American International Group.

c. September 22—The Federal Reserve approves emergency bank holding company applications for Goldman Sachs and Morgan Stanley.

d. September 25—Washington Mutual fails; largest bank failure in U.S. history.

e. September 29—FDIC agrees to help Citigroup acquire Wachovia; House defeats initial bank bailout proposal.

f. October 3—President Bush signs into law $700 billion financial market bailout package.

g. October 13—U.S. officials tell top bankers that government wants to buy stakes in their firms.

h. November 23—U.S. officials agree to purchase more stock in Citigroup and insures large chunks of assets.

2009

a. January 16—U.S. agrees to bolster Bank of America with more bailout funds and guaranteed assets.

b. March 22—Treasury Secretary Geithner details plans for a public-private investment structure to rid banks of bad assets.

c. May 7—Bank regulators release results of bank stress tests.

d. June 17—President Obama proposes overhaul of financial market rules.

e. July 15—U.S. rejects deal to save CIT Group.

f. August 25—Obama nominates Ben Bernanke to another four-year term as Fed chairman.

See also BANK BAILOUT (PLAN) OF 2008 (U.S.); FORECLOSURE; GEITHNER, TIMOTHY F.; PUBLIC-PRIVATE INVESTMENT FUND; STRESS TESTS; "TOO BIG TO FAIL"; ZOMBIE BANKS.
Synonymous with FINANCIAL STABILITY PLAN; TARP 2.0.

BANKRUPT. A person, corporation, or other legal entity that, being unable to meet its financial obligations, has been declared by a decree of the court to be insolvent, and whose property becomes liable to administration under the Bankruptcy Reform Act of 1978. Originally came from Italy, deriving from *banca rotta*, or "broken bench." When a medieval money lender could not pay his debts, his bench was broken in half.
See also BANKRUPTCY.

BANKRUPTCY. The conditions under which the financial position of an individual, corporation, or other legal entity are such as to cause actual or legal insolvency. Two types are: (a) involuntary bankruptcy—one or more creditors of an insolvent debtor file a petition having the debtor declared bankrupt; and (b) voluntary bankruptcy—the debtor files a petition claiming inability to meet debts and willingness to be declared a bankrupt. A court adjudges and declares a debtor bankrupt.

See also BANKRUPT; BANKRUPTCY FILINGS; CHRYSLER; CONTROLLED BANKRUPTCY; CRAMDOWN; GENERAL MOTORS.

BANKRUPTCY COURT. *See* BANKRUPTCY FILINGS; MODIFYING MORTGAGES.

BANKRUPTCY FILINGS. In the United States, filings rose 40 percent in October 2008, as home values sank and individual credit grew, with more than 880,000 bankruptcy petitions filed from January 1 through November 1, 2008, equal to the total for all of 2007.

However, the credit crisis of 2008–2009 had forced more firms that would have filed for bankruptcy protection to close down and liquidate rather than restructure, because they could not obtain enough financing to operate while they reorganized.

Filings jumped nearly 33 percent in 2008 and were expected to climb through 2009. Consumer filings reached 1,064,927 in 2008, up from 801,840 in 2007.

For many people, declaring personal bankruptcy could be the step needed to solvency. More than a million people filed for personal bankruptcy in one year, a staggering 30 percent increase from earlier years. In some cases, individual credit could emerge in better shape once debts are dealt with via bankruptcy. Chapter 7 or Chapter 13 is often used for personal bankruptcy filings.

An average of 5,945 bankruptcy petitions were filed each day in March 2009, up 9 percent from February and up 38 percent from one year earlier. A total of 130,793 people filed for bankruptcy in March. Experts believe it will rise to at least 1.4 million by the end of 2009, compared to 1.1 million at the end of 2008.

Consumer bankruptcies rose 27.9 percent in October 2009 from the year before. Filings rose to 135,913 in October, an 8.9 percent jump from September's 124,790. Businesses filing for bankruptcy protection in October numbered 7,771, compared to 7,271 in September, a 7 percent rise in commercial filings.

See also GENERAL GROWTH PROPERTIES; GENERAL MOTORS; LEHMAN BROTHERS.

BANKRUPTCY PROTECTION. A mechanism where each sovereign nation attempts to assure the public that funds in a bankrupt company will be secure and that regulations are in place to sustain the institution and/or that the government will, via its laws, guarantee procedures so that over time the bankrupt organization can pull out of bankruptcy and become viable again.

Synonymous with ADMINISTRATION, used in the United Kingdom.

BANK TURALEM. *See* KAZAKHSTAN.

BARCLAYS. The British bank raised nearly 10 billion U.S. dollars by selling shares to Abu Dhabi and Qatar to meet Britain's new capital requirements for banks seeking to avoid the government's help.

The UK's second-largest bank, founded more than 300 years ago, told the country's government not to forward them assistance. Instead of participating in a program in which the government injected $60 billion into other British banks, Barclays raised capital without state aid.

Barclays shareholders showed their displeasure with the British bank's fundraising even as they approved the plan. The issue revolved around the attractive investment terms that were granted to investors from several Middle East countries. Part of the funds carried a long-term interest rate of 14 percent.

On January 14, 2009, the bank announced that it was in the process of cutting an additional 2,100 jobs in its consumer and commercial banking business and at its credit card unit, bringing the total job cuts to 4,600, including 400 information-technology positions in Britain.

To deal with its credibility gap, Barclays announced on January 26 that it would write down an additional $11 billion for 2008, but wouldn't seek a bailout.

Barclays, in early April, chose not to participate in the British government's Asset Protection Scheme, where a bank's riskiest assets were surrounded and then protected against future losses.

In mid-June 2009, Barclays accepted BlackRock's offer to purchase Barclays Global Investors for $13.5 billion.

See also BLACKROCK; LEHMAN BROTHERS; SECURITIES AND EXCHANGE COMMISSION; UNITED KINGDOM.

BARCLAYS GLOBAL INVESTORS. *See* BLACKROCK.

BARNES & NOBLE. The world's largest chain of bookstores, it laid off 100 people in its New York headquarters on January 14, 2009. Its Christmas 2008 sales were down 5.2 percent from a year earlier. Online sales were down 11 percent. At that time there were no plans to close any of the 799 stores.

Its net income plummeted 29 percent for its fiscal fourth quarter, resulting from weak store traffic, poor holiday spending, and charges. It had a net income of $81.2 million down from $115 million in the quarter one year earlier.

Fourth-quarter losses at Barnes & Noble were announced on May 21. On-line sales fell 7 percent to $93 million in the quarter ended May 2. Revenue fell 4.4 percent to $1.11 billion, while sales at stores open at least a year fell 5.7 percent.

Barnes & Noble's sales fell five consecutive quarters. Revenue dropped 5.3 percent by August 2009, with earnings falling 20 percent to $12.3 million from $15.4 million a year before. Its loss widened to $24 million for its second quarter, compared to a loss of $18.4 million a year before. Revenue climbed 4.3 percent to $1.2 billion.

Cf. BORDERS GROUP.

BASEL 1 ACCORD. Its strength lay in being reasonably simple to negotiate and administer. Then, banks soon started to favor profitable businesses, which under Basel 1's crude definitions, escaped the appropriate capital charges. There was a need for Basel 2 during the meltdown of 2008.

Synonymous with BASEL STANDARDS.

Cf. BASEL 2 ACCORD.

BASEL STANDARDS. *Synonymous with* BASEL 1 ACCORD.

BASEL 2 ACCORD. A set of rules on banks' capital adequacy created in 1988.

Implemented in Europe in 2008, and expected to become a force in the United States in 2009.

Its objective is to align the amount of capital that banks set aside to absorb unexpected losses with the amount of risk that they are taking. Under Basel 2, banks will be rewarded if they take fewer risks with lower capital requirements.

It failed its first big test in part because global diplomatic initiatives were difficult to implement. A shortcoming of such models is that their risk projections come with a caveat that they are assumed to be accurate during normal market conditions. This often is not true.

See also BANK BAILOUT (PLAN) of 2008; BASEL 1 ACCORD.

BASF. A Germany-based global chemical company. It announced in November 2008 that it was temporarily shutting around 80 plants and reducing production at 100 factories around the world.

BASF's first-quarter 2009 net profit fell 68 percent, with sales falling 23 percent.

See also GERMANY.

BASIC-MATERIAL COMPANIES. *See* ARCELORMITTAL; CEMEX; LAFARGE; RIO TINTO; TATA STEEL; XSTRATA.

BAYERISCHE MOTOREN WERK. *See* BMW.

BEAR STEARNS. On March 16, 2008, the Federal Reserve came forward and rescued Bear Stearns, the country's fifth-largest investment bank, by guaranteeing a large portion of its assets against losses in order to get J.P. Morgan to agree to acquire the bank. By lending money to banks for longer against worse collateral, the Fed hoped to stem panic and buy time.

It was to be the first indication of how financial services were spreading, mostly without being regulated or checked upon. There were conflicts of interest and fraud in the sale of subprime mortgages, which significantly contributed to Bear Stearns's collapse becoming the first bank crisis of securitization in 2008. Bear Stearns was particularly active in the credit-default swaps market.

Eventually, JP Morgan Chase saved Bear Stearns and purchased the investment house. As recently as January 2007, Bear Stearns was worth $20 billion. However, due to risky business practices and massive exposure to subprime mortgages, its customers and investors lost confidence in the company and the value of Bear Stearns stock plummeted.

Cf. JP MORGAN CHASE; LEHMAN BROTHERS

BEER BREWERS. *See* CARLSBERG; SABMILLER.

BEGGAR THY NEIGHBOR. *See* BUY AMERICAN; PROTECTIONISM.

BEIGE BOOK. A survey from the twelve regional Fed banks.

BEIJING AUTOMOTIVE INDUSTRY HOLDING COMPANY. *See* SAAB.

BELARUS. The IMF loaned Belarus $2.5 billion in early 2009 to help the country cope with the global economic crisis. Belarus received access to about $800 million of the financing. Belarus's central bank sharply devalued the country's ruble, allowing the currency to plunge 20 percent. This action was a condition of the loan from the IMF.

BELGIUM. Activity is projected to contract slightly and, thereafter, growth may remain below potential well into 2010, before rebounding on the back of easier monetary conditions, renewed growth in real incomes, and a recovery in world trade. As a result, unemployment will increase over the projection period. Headline inflation should decline with the fall in energy and food prices, although core inflation should show more persistence. The automatic stabilizers should be allowed to work fully during the downswing, but securing fiscal sustainability over the longer term will at some point require long-term structural measures to achieve expenditure restraint at all levels of government (OECD).

See also BNP PARIBAS; FORTIS BANQUE; TAX HAVENS.

BENCHMARK INTEREST RATE. *See* FEDERAL RESERVE.

BENEFITS. *See* RETIREMENT BENEFITS; UNEMPLOYMENT.

BENETTON GROUP. In August 2009, Benetton posted a drop in first-half net profit, with revenue falling 11 percent.

BERKSHIRE HATHAWAY. In May 2009, Berkshire reported a loss of $1.53 billion in the three months ending March 31, its first unprofitable period since 2001. The company then returned to profitability in the second quarter 2009, with a net income of $3.3 billion.

Third-quarter 2009 profit tripled as the improving economy and stock market increased the value of its derivatives contracts. The investment company generated $3.2 billion in net income, up from $1.1 billion the year before.

Berkshire shed 8 percent of its workforce. It had 21,000 fewer employees than it had at the end of 2008, and today, along with its subsidiaries, has about 225,000 workers.

See also BUFFET, WARREN E.

BERNANKE, BEN. Was sworn in on February 1, 2006, as chairman and a member of the Board of Governors of the Federal Reserve System. Before his appointment as chairman, Dr. Bernanke was chairman of the president's Council of Economic Advisers, from June 2005 to January 2006. He had been a chaired professor of Economics and Public Affairs at Princeton University since 1985.

Bernanke was born in 1953 in Augusta, Georgia, growing up in Dillon, South Carolina. He received his BA in economics in 1975 from Harvard University and a PhD in economics in 1979 from the Massachusetts Institute of Technology.

Dr. Bernanke is one of the few government officials that had an active role through both the Bush and Obama administrations. His comments before congressional committees were powerful and had an enormous impact on government policy.

On March 5, 2008, Bernanke called on lenders to aid homeowners by reducing their principal to lessen the likelihood of foreclosure.

As U.S. Federal Reserve chairman, he authorized putting $800 billion into the financial system during the September–October 2008 meltdown.

On April 29, he announced that the Fed would hold official interest rates low and would continue to purchase government bonds and other debt, in an effort to pump credit into banks and companies. Also, he indicated plans to substantially increase the Fed's holdings of mortgage-backed securities and Treasury securities in the months to follow.

Bernanke announced at the same time that the Fed had purchased $74 billion of Treasury securities.

On June 25, Bernanke faced open hostility from lawmakers barraging him during a congressional hearing over his handling of the financial crisis and the Fed's role in reshaping the banking system. In particular, they focused on the aid package given to the Bank of America to complete its acquisition of Merrill Lynch in January 2009. It was clearly the harshest treatment of a Federal Reserve chairman in a decade.

During his July 22 presentation before the Senate Banking Committee stating that President Obama's call for a consumer protection agency for risky financial products was not needed, he argued that consumer oversight was part of the Fed's mission to oversee the safety and soundness of banks.

On August 25, President Obama, seeking continuity in U.S. economic policy, nominated Ben Bernanke for another four-year term as chairman of the Federal Reserve. As chairman, he will have to make decisions regarding how and when to withdraw federal support without undermining the recovery. Moving too slowly could lead to a period of inflation, as happened in the 1970s.

One year after the collapse of Lehman Brothers on September 15, 2008, Ben Bernanke stated that the recession was "very likely over. . . . At this point we are in a recovery." This confidence was in part based on the government's report that retail sales climbed 2.7 percent in August 2009 after falling 0.2 percent in July.

Bernanke warned the nation on November 28, 2009, that he opposed the revamping of the Fed's proposed financial legislation changes. He criticized a provision that he said "would strip the Fed of all its bank regulatory powers" and stated that he wants "to protect monetary policy from short-term political influence."

Time magazine announced on December 15, 2009, that Ben Bernanke was the Person of the Year 2009. And on December 17 the Senate Banking Committee backed Bernanke for a second term as chairman of the Federal Reserve by a vote of 16–7.

See also CONSUMER FINANCIAL PROTECTION AGENCY; DEPRESSION 2.0; EMERGENCY ECONOMIC STABILIZATION ACT OF 2008; FEDERAL RESERVE.

BEST BUY. Sales declined in same-store sales during the December 2008 peak holiday period. The company posted its fiscal fourth-quarter profit as declining 23 percent, compared to 2007. Earnings dropped 4.9 percent, with net earnings of $570 million.

The company said that its fiscal first-quarter earnings fell 15 percent, with sales falling 4.9 percent.

The government reported that sales at electronics and appliance stores had decreased 10.4 percent in August 2009, but that was a significant improvement from July when sales dropped 14.1 percent. Best Buy raised its annual revenue forecast to between $48 billion and $49 billion from September 2009 until February 2010, and forecast revenue of $46.5 billion to $48.5 billion, with sales falling as much as 5 percent. Revenue increased 12 percent to $11.02 billion.

On December 14, 2009, Best Buy reported that revenues grew and earnings quadrupled for its third quarter ending in November. However its fourth-quarter profits were lower than expected because purchasers sought less expensive electronics, offering smaller corporate profits. The company showed a 4.6 percent increase in revenue, with sales rising 1.7 percent following a 5.3 percent fall in 2008.

See also RETAILING.

BGI (BARCLAYS GLOBAL INVESTORS). *See* BLACKROCK.

BILLABLE HOUR. *See* LAW FIRMS.

BILLIONAIRES. *See* WEALTH.

BIRTHS. *See* ICELAND.

BLACKROCK. BlackRock purchased Barclays Global Investors for $13.5 billion. BGI, which is based in San Francisco, combined with BlackRock creates the globe's biggest money manager, with nearly $2.8 trillion in assets.

BlackRock's second-quarter 2009 net profit fell 20 percent from a year earlier, despite the money-management giant's cost controls and stronger stock and bond markets. The nation's largest publicly traded asset manager by market capitalization posted earnings of $218 million, down from $274 million the year before. Revenue fell 26 percent to $1.03 billion.

BLACKS. *See* AFRICAN AMERICANS.

BLACKSTONE GROUP. *See* CHINA.

BLAIR, DENNIS C. *See* GLOBAL UNEMPLOYMENT.

BLAIR, TONY. *See* FRANCE; UNITED KINGDOM.

BLANKFEIN, LLOYD. Born in the Bronx, New York City, Blankfein rose to the top position at Goldman Sachs.

See also GOLDMAN SACHS.

BLS. *See* BUREAU OF LABOR STATISTICS.

BLUE CHIP. A corporation maintaining a good dividend return and having sound management and good growth potential.

See also DOW JONES INDUSTRIAL AVERAGE; STOCK MARKET.

BMW (BAYERISCHE MOTOREN WERK). November 2008 sales were down 25 percent.

In January 2009, BMW announced that a total of 26,000 workers would move to shorter shifts on some days in February and March, with four plants affected. BMW employs about 75,000 people in Germany.

In February, BMW announced that it would eliminate 850 positions from its national responsibility.

BMW swung to a rare loss in the fourth quarter 2008, and its full-year net profit plunged 90 percent. It had sustained a net loss of $1.24 billion for the quarter. Revenue fell 18 percent as auto sales for the year dropped 30 percent.

The world's best-selling premium automaker by sales reported a loss of $204 million, compared with a year earlier net profit. BMW had a first-quarter 2009 net loss.

BMW posted a 76 percent fall in second-quarter net profit as demand for luxury cars sagged. Profit declined to $171.5 million, while revenue fell 11 percent. In August 2009, BMW indicated that sales for the month had fallen by 11 percent. Sales fell 18 percent in the year's first nine months.

In October 2009, BMW reported that monthly sales increased year-on-year for the first time in 2009. BMW's third-quarter profit slumped 74 percent from a year earlier. Quarterly sales fell 7.2 percent to 324,100 vehicles. With a sales rise in November, the automaker expects full-year sales to fall 10–15 percent lower than in 2008.

See also AUTOMOBILE INDUSTRY.

BNP PARIBAS. Its shares fell to a six-year low on December 23, 2008, resulting from its failure to purchase part of Fortis. BNP shares closed down 71 cents or 2.3 percent.

BNP Paribas, one of the largest French banks, had a fourth-quarter 2008 net loss of about €1.4 billion, but managed a net profit for the year of about €3 billion, helped by its retail banking, asset management, and services unit.

See also FORTIS BANQUE.

BOEING. The rival of Airbus delivered 375 planes in 2008, making it the second-largest producer of airplanes.

The company reported an unexpected fourth-quarter loss and forecast 2009 earnings well below Wall Street estimates. It expected delivery of 480 to 485 commercial planes in 2009.

The plane maker expected to cut a total of 10,000 jobs in 2009, about 6 percent of its work force. The number included 4,500 layoffs announced in January 2009 by Boeing's commercial plane unit.

Boeing announced in April that it would scale back production of some of its jetliners, along with job cuts. Orders for their commercial planes had declined. It reduced its monthly production of its twin-aisle 777 to five airplanes from seven, beginning in June 2010, and planned to cut a total of 10,000 positions after reporting a loss for the fourth quarter 2008.

Boeing cut its full-year earnings forecast as it reported in April a 50 percent drop in first-quarter profit. Earnings for the year were lowered to $4.70 to $5 a share.

Boeing is by far the largest beneficiary of the U.S. Ex-Im Bank financing, with $11.2 billion in the value of loans and guarantees.

See also AIRLINES; EXPORT-IMPORT BANK; TRADE DEFICIT (U.S.). *Cf.* AIRBUS.

BOFA. *See* BANK OF AMERICA.

BOLLYWOOD. *See* INDIA.

BOND BUYING. The Federal Reserve declared in mid-March 2009 that it would purchase as much as $300 billion of long-term U.S. Treasury securities in the coming months and hundreds of billions of dollars more in mortgage-backed securities. The Fed pumped as much as an extra $1.15 trillion into the economy via bond purchases.

See also FEDERAL RESERVE; MORTGAGE-BACKED SECURITIES; MUNICIPAL BONDS.

BONDS. *See* YIELD CURVE.

BONUSES. *See* AMERICAN INTERNATIONAL GROUP; BANK OF AMERICA; BONUS TAX BILL; GOLDMAN SACHS; RETENTION BONUS; WINDFALL TAX.

BONUS TAX BILL. The U.S. House of Representatives passed legislation on March 19, 2009, that would significantly curb Wall Street bonuses in 2009. The measure was approved on a 328–93 vote and imposed a 90 percent surtax on bonuses granted to employees who earn more than $250,000 at firms that have received at least $5 billion from the government's financial rescue program. If approved by the Senate and signed into law by President Obama, it would be retroactive to December 31, 2008.

On March 22, President Obama expressed doubt about the constitutionality of the Bonus Tax Bill.

BORDERS GROUP. The country's second-largest bookstore chain reported in May 2009 reported a 12 percent decline in revenue. Sales declined to $650.2 million from $735.8 million a year earlier. Sales at their superstores fell by 14 percent.

The Borders Group posted a wider loss for its fiscal second quarter 2009, with a loss of $45.6 million compared with a loss of $9.2 million one year earlier. Revenue fell 18 percent to $624.7 million.

Borders reported that it would close 200 of its mall stores in January 2010, discharging approximately 1,500 employees from its workforce of 25,000, many who work part-time.

For its fiscal third quarter 2009 the company reported a loss of $37.7 million compared to a loss of $175.4 million one year before. Revenue declined 13 percent to $602.5 million.

Cf. BARNES & NOBLE.

BOSTON GLOBE. *See* NEWSPAPERS; *NEW YORK TIMES.*

BOUND RATES. *See* WORLD TRADE ORGANIZATION.

BP. *See* BRITISH PETROLEUM.

BRANDEIS UNIVERSITY. On January 26, 2009, the trustees of Brandeis University voted unanimously to close the Rose Art Museum in order to sell its collection to help shore up the university's finances. Following outcries from the public, students, and alumni, the board cancelled this decision in February.

See also ENDOWMENTS.

BRAZIL. The expansion that gathered pace during 2007 was sustained in the first half of 2008, although activity appears to be slackening owing to a worsening of financial conditions. Domestic demand has been the main driver of growth. The trade surplus is shrinking, essentially due to buoyant demand for imports, and the current account has shifted into deficit. Dynamism in the labor market continued to deliver robust job creation. Inflation picked up considerably through mid-year. Further monetary tightening is expected in the near term, despite a falling out gap in 2009, to quell the inflationary pressures arising from a sharp exchange rate depreciation. The primary budget surplus target is expected to be met, although the 2009 draft budget law calls for further increases in expenditure. Reversing the trend of increased public spending is among Brazil's main macroeconomic policy challenges (OECD).

Brazil's currency fell as the nation's trade surplus narrowed to a six-year low in 2008, propelled by a deepening economic slowdown that curbed demand for their exports. The currency declined 0.1 percent to 2.3176 per dollar from 2.3145 at the start of 2009.

Brazil reported its first monthly trade deficit since 2001 as the global economic crisis cut exports. Exports fell 26 percent in January 2009 from a year earlier to $9.8 billion, while imports fell 17 percent, to $10.3 billion.

Brazil lowered interest rates below 10 percent, to 9.25 percent, on June 10, following two decades of double-digit levels. Its central bank lowered its 10.25 percent overnight-lending rate by more than half a percentage point, its fourth cut so far in 2009.

On September 11, Brazil reported that it had returned to growth after a short-lived recession with a 1.9 percent growth in its GDP in its second quarter 2009. Industrial production increased by 2.2 percent in October, but was still 3.2 percent lower than a year before.

Brazil's third-quarter GDP expanded 1.3 percent, but fell short of estimates for growth of 1.9 percent.

According to its fourth-quarter inflation report submitted on December 22, 2009, Brazil's growth could swell to 5.8 percent in 2010 from near zero in 2009, with the possibilities of a climb in the inflation rate to 4.6 percent.

See also WORLD TRADE.

BRETTON WOODS. In 1944, one year before the end of World War II, the focus of Bretton Woods was on creating a new system. It sought to avoid a repeat of the Great Depression of the 1930s by creating the World Bank to rebuild Europe after the war and the International Monetary Fund to oversee an economic system based on fixed exchange rates.

The three-week meeting took place at a time when trade and financial cooperation had virtually ceased.

The 700 representatives gathered at the luxury Mount Washington Hotel in New Hampshire. The meeting lasted three weeks and was preceded by more than two years of technical preparation.

Since the 2008–2009 meltdown many specialists and governments are urging a reexamination of the Bretton Woods concepts and outcome.

See also BRETTON WOODS II; HYUNDAI MOTOR COMPANY; LATIN AMERICA.

BRETTON WOODS II. Following the meltdown in the fall of 2008, there was a push to replace the original Bretton Woods concepts of a World Bank and IMF with a new, updated version.

Cf. BRETTON WOODS.

BRIC. Brazil, Russia, India, and China.

BRIDGES. *See* AMERICAN RECOVERY AND REINVESTMENT ACT (OF 2009).

BRITAIN. *See* UNITED KINGDOM.

BRITISH AIRWAYS (BA). In early April 2009, management announced that ongoing layoffs would mean a bigger-than-expected operating loss for the fiscal year, just ended. Ending March 31, operating losses amounted to $220.5 million.

On May 22, BA announced that it had a significant full-year loss. BA had a loss of $594.6 million for the twelve months ending March 31. Passenger and cargo volumes slumped and fuel costs climbed $45 percent.

To cut costs during the meltdown, in mid-June, BA asked its staff to voluntarily work for no pay or take an unpaid leave for up to one month to help the company "fight for its survival."

BA reported in July 2009 that it would further reduce summer and winter capacity and lay off another 3,700 jobs in its fiscal year through March. BA would cut capacity by 3.5 percent in the April–October period and would cut its winter schedule by 5 percent.

BA reported its first pretax loss for the fiscal first quarter since its shares were posted twenty-two years ago. Ending June 30, 2009, its quarter loss was $247.2 million. BA had lost $465 million in the six months to September 2009.

On November 6, 2009, BA announced that it would reduce an additional 1,200 jobs, raising the reductions to nearly 5,000. The cuts represent about 13 percent of its total staff of 39,000. Its net loss climbed to a record $345 million for the six months to September 30. Revenue during this period fell nearly 14 percent.

On November 12, BA and Iberia Lineas Aereas de Espana agreed to merge, creating a carrier with annual revenues of about $20 billion.

See also AIRLINES; IBERIA.

BRITISH PETROLEUM (BP). Adjusting to $50 a barrel of crude oil, BP's earnings dropped 64 percent by the end of April 2009.

On July 28, BP posted a 53 percent fall in profit for the second quarter. Profit was $4.39 billion for the three months ended June 30, from $9.36 billion a year before.

In October 2009, BP reported a decline in third-quarter results. The giant oil company expected to slash costs by $4 billion in 2009, twice its original forecast.

See also OIL COMPANIES.

BRITISH POUND. *See* POUND.

BROADBAND ACCESS. The economic stimulus package of 2009 gave $183 million in stimulus grants to expand broadband Internet service to rural areas in seventeen states. It was approved in late December 2009.

See also AMERICAN RECOVERY AND REINVESTMENT ACT (OF 2009).

BROKERS. *See* STOCK BROKERS.

BROWN, GORDON. Holding his first meeting in Washington, D.C., with President Obama on March 3, 2009, the prime minister of the United Kingdom called for a "global New Deal" to set common principles for regulation banks, declaring that the fiscal crisis could help to overcome past resistance to increased oversight across borders.

Prime Minister Brown urged and then hosted the April 2 economic summit in London.

See also BUSINESS 20; FINANCIAL PROTECTIONISM; G-20; UNITED KINGDOM.

BTA (BANK TURALEM). *See* KAZAKHSTAN.

BUDGET (CITY). *See* CITY BUDGETS.

BUDGET (U.S.) (FISCAL YEAR 2010). President Obama's proposed U.S. budget of $3.6 trillion for the fiscal year beginning October 1, 2009 marked the most significant change in nearly thirty years on the subjects of national health care, moving energy away from oil and gas, and boosting the federal role in education.

Federal outlays were to soar in fiscal 2009 to $4 trillion, or 27.7 percent of GDP, from $3 trillion or 21 percent of GDP in 2008, and 20 percent in 2007. This was higher as a share of the economy than any year since 1945. It is more spending by far than during the recessions of 1974–1975 or 1981–1982.

A 134-page booklet described the priorities of the Obama administration, with income tax rates sharply increasing. Rates would rise for single people earning $200,000 and for couples earning $250,000 beginning in 2011. Limits would be set on personal exemptions and itemized deductions, as well as higher capital-gains rates.

The president also called for an additional $75.5 billion for the wars in Iraq and Afghanistan for the remainder of 2009 and an additional $130 billion for 2010.

It set aside contingency funds of $250 billion in the event that more funds would be required to bail out teetering banks and other firms.

The president's plan indexed Pell Grants to inflation plus 1 percent, making it akin to Medicare and Social Security.

It envisioned raising $646 billion between 2012 and 2019 by capping carbon levels and auctioning off permits for the emission of greenhouse gases.

The government established a $630 billion reserve fund for the creation of a national health care plan to provide universal access to health insurance.

The deficit, which by 2009 was $1.75 trillion or 12.3 percent of the GDP is today the highest it has been since 1942, when World War II began. With a return to economic well-being the president looked forward to 2013 when stability will have returned.

The top tax rate for couples would rise to 39.6 percent from 35 percent to fund expanded benefits. Top earners would see mortgage deductions fall $70 for every $1,000 in deductions.

Programs of the proposed 2010 fiscal budget were:

a. Defense—includes war spending; shake-up in weapons-buying process: $663.7 billion, a 1.4 percent change from 2009.

b. Health and Human Services—$630 billion fund to finance health care overhaul; crackdown on fraud in Medicare and Medicaid: $78.7 billion.

c. Transportation—$5 billion to improve high-speed rail corridors; $800 million for satellite-based air-traffic control: $72.5 billion, change of 2.8 percent.

d. Veterans Affairs—boost spending by $25 billion; expand centers for prosthetics, mental health, and other medical needs: $52.5 billion, 10.3 percent change.

e. State and other international programs—expands Foreign Service positions; doubles spending on foreign aid: $51.7 billion, 40.9 percent change.

f. Housing and Urban Development—crackdown on mortgage fraud; $1 billion in funds for an affordable-housing trust fund: $47.5 billion, 18.5 percent change.

g. Education—removes private lenders from student-loan market: $46.7 billion, 12.8 percent change.

h. Homeland Security—deporting illegal immigrants who commit crimes; boosting airline-passenger screening: $42.7 billion, 1.2 percent change.

i. Energy—Seeks cap on U.S. carbon emission; companies would bid for right to pollute: $26.3 billion, minus 0.4 percent change.

j. Agriculture—cut subsidies to wealthiest farmers; reduced funding for overseas promotion of U.S. brand-name products: $26 billion, 8.8 percent change.

k. Justice—$8 billion for the FBI to combat financial fraud; funds for local governments to hire 50,000 police officers: $23.9 billion, minus 6.3 percent change.

l. Commerce—Boosts funding for research into climate change; $4 billion for 2010 census: $13.8 billion, 48.4 percent change.

m. Labor—"Green jobs" training; action to curb improper benefits mistakenly paid; targets employer tax evasion: $13.3 billion, 4.7 percent change.

n. Treasury—$250 billion placeholder for losses tied to more rescue efforts; funds for IRS enforcement: $13.3 billion, 4.7 percent change.

o. Interior—Excise tax on oil and gas output in the Gulf of Mexico; new fees on companies that drill on federal lands: $12 billion, 6.2 percent change.

p. Other—SEC would receive 13 percent funding boost; EPA's budget would jump nearly 35 percent, the largest in its history; new fund to finance infrastructure: $78.2 billion, 15 percent change.

Congress passed a $3.5 trillion budget for 2010 on April 29, by a vote of 233–193 without any Republicans voting for it, and 17 Democrats voting against it. The Senate vote was 53–43 with 4 Democratic defections. The budget outline includes $530 billion in basic spending for domestic programs.

See also DEFICIT (BUDGET); WARS IN AFGHANISTAN AND IRAQ.

BUDGET DEFICIT. *See* DEFICIT (BUDGET); FEDERAL RESERVE; WARS IN AFGHANISTAN AND IRAQ.

BUFFET, WARREN E. A renowned investor and one of the world's wealthiest people, Buffet's Berkshire Hathaway recorded a loss of $5.1 billion in 2008. The firm reported a 62 percent drop in net income for the year and posted negative results for only the second time since he took control in 1965.

Buffet said on March 9, 2009, that the U.S. economy was facing an economic Pearl Harbor and it had fallen off a cliff.

Moody's, on April 8, lowered the long-term issuer rating of Berkshire to Aa2 from its top Aaa rating, citing the weakening economy and "severe decline in equity markets." Berkshire has seen its shares decline by 33 percent over the past year.

Berkshire Hathaway had a loss of $1.5 billion in the first quarter 2009, compared with a profit of $940 million a year earlier.

See also BERKSHIRE HATHAWAY.

BULGARI. Sales dropped to $410.7 billion in the fourth quarter 2008, a 10 percent declined from a year earlier.

See also JEWELRY; LUXURY GOODS; RETAILING.

BULGARIA. Cut its forecast for economic growth in 2009 by nearly two percentage points, with the global financial crisis expected to hurt investments and exports. The current-account deficit was 24 percent in 2008.

By mid-September 2009, the government of Bulgaria reduced its budget deficit to $76.5 million. There is an 81 percent reduction in Bulgaria's budget.

BURBERRY. The British luxury-goods firm said on January 20, 2009, that it would cut 540 jobs in Britain and Spain as part of a plan to save about $49 million.

Burberry reported on July 15 a further drop in sales growth for its fiscal first quarter as the economic meltdown continued to hold back demand.

BUREAU OF LABOR STATISTICS (BLS). A research agency of the U.S. Department of Labor; it compiles statistics on hours of work, average hourly earnings, employment and unemployment, consumer prices, and many other variables.

BUSH, GEORGE W. President of the United States from 2001 to 2009. Between January 2001 and 2008, the U.S. economy under his watch added about 3 million nonfarm jobs, including 1.34 million in the private sector.

Bush outlined a sweeping plan on April 1, 2008, to streamline the U.S. financial-regulatory system, with proposals that consolidated bank regulation, created a new type of insurance charter, improved the oversight of mortgage lending, and allowed the Federal Reserve to peek into more corners of finance.

On July 31, President Bush signed a housing-rescue bill into law, completing Congress's ambitious legislative effort to head off foreclosures and stabilize jittery financial markets.

See also AUTOMOBILE INDUSTRY; OBAMA, BARACK; TAX BREAKS; TROUBLED ASSET RELIEF PROGRAM; UNFAIR TRADE SUBSIDIES.

BUSINESS BANKRUPTCY FILINGS. *See* BANKRUPTCY FILINGS.

BUSINESS STARTS. *See* NEW COMPANIES.

BUSINESS 20. Proposed by Gordon Brown, prime minister of the United Kingdom in January 2009, a group of multinational firms to work with leaders of G-20 nations to tackle the financial crisis.

See also BROWN, GORDON; G-20.

BUY AMERICAN. Legislation, originally adopted in 1933, setting up the basic principles of buying national. Amended in 1954, the scope of the act was expanded to allow procuring entities to set aside procurement for small businesses and firms in labor-surplus areas and to reject foreign bids either for national interest reasons or national security reasons.

A protectionist concept in the 2009 economic stimulus package that creates conflicts and reactions from other nations. This program is spreading protests against foreign workers, fuels a backlash on trade, and invites retaliation by other nations.

See also BUY LOCAL; PROTECTIONISM; SMOOT-HAWLEY ACT OF 1930.

BUYBACKS. *See* STOCK BUYBACKS.

BUY LOCAL. An argument made by some Americans since 2008–2009 to purchase goods and services from within the boundaries of a country, state, and/or community. Buy local is a policy purporting to protect local industries and stores against imports.

See also BUY AMERICAN.

BUYOUT FIRMS. These private-equity groups tapped the public markets for cash during the borrowing booms and are having increasing difficulty since summer 2008, with lower-reported values.

The American Recovery and Reinvestment Act (of 2009) allows firms to defer income taxes when they repurchase their own debt at a discount. This allows companies restructuring debt to defer possible taxes for as long as five years, and then to pay the taxes over the next five years.

See also BANK BUYOUTS.

BUYOUTS. *See* BANK BUYOUTS.

C

CADILLAC. *See* GENERAL MOTORS.

CALIFORNIA. *See* FURLOUGHS.

CANADA. Canada had run a surplus since 1997, but in 2009 it was expected that a deficit was inevitable as the country moved to weather the global financial and economic storms.

In December 2008, the Bank of Canada cut its benchmark interest rate three-quarters of a percentage point to 1.5 percent, a fifty-year low. The lack of a mortgage and banking crisis in Canada did shield the country from the economic downturn to a certain extent. However, a drop in exports, like car and auto parts to the United States, as well as a collapse in energy and commodity prices, brought an end to the nation's privileged isolation.

Also in December, moving to preempt a possible shift of auto production back to the United States, the governments of Canada and the Ontario province offered the auto industry Can$4 billion in emergency loans. The Canadian auto industry exported about 90 percent of its production, employing about 400,000 people.

The Bank of Canada revised downward its economic forecast for the first quarter of 2009, saying it expected growth to shrink 4.8 percent.

In January 2009, employers cut 129,000 jobs, more than in any single month during earlier downturns. Canada's jobless rate climbed from 6.6 percent to 7.2 percent. Canada remains uncomfortably dependent on the United States as a market, with 76 percent of its exports coming into its southern neighbor.

Canadian output fell in the last three months of 2008 at the sharpest rate since 1991 as the nation entered its first recession in almost twenty years. GDP contracted at a 0.8 percent quarterly rate as exports, capital investment, and personal spending all fell.

The Bank of Canada announced on April 21 that it cut its interest rates by a quarter-percentage point to a historic low of 0.25 percent, and that it would maintain its benchmark overnight-lending rate for fourteen months.

The April stress-test program in the United States of its largest nineteen banks could be turned onto the Canadian banking system. Canada's five largest banks would have passed the U.S. government stress test brilliantly. They were profitable in the fourth quarter 2008, are adequately capitalized, and have had no difficulty securing additional private capital. On average, only 7 percent of their mortgage portfolios consisted of subprime loans (versus 20 percent in the United States). And no major Canadian bank has required direct government infusions of capital.

Canada's economy improved with 27,000 new jobs in August 2009, climbing to 16.8 million. However, unemployment rose slightly to 8.7 percent and Canada's economy shrank unexpectedly in August. Its GDP contracted 0.1 percent to US$1.11 trillion. By December 2009, Canada's GDP grew by 0.1 percent, the first quarter of economic growth since the third quarter of 2008.

See also AUTOMOBILE INDUSTRY; MAGNA.

CANON. In January 2009, reported a 91 percent tumble in its fourth-quarter 2008 net profit, caused primarily by plummeting overseas demand. The Tokyo-based maker of digital cameras and precision electronics, which generates about 80 percent of its total revenue outside of Japan, projected a poor 2009.

Canon's first-quarter 2009 net profit fell 83 percent, with revenues dropping 32 percent.

Canon reported weaker third-quarter 2009 results as profits fell 56 percent to $398.3 million and revenue slipped 22 percent.

See also JAPAN.

CAPITAL ASSISTANCE PROGRAM. *See* STRESS TESTS.

CAPITALISM. Accused by some governments and individuals as a primary contributor to the 2008 meltdown. It is usually defined as an economic system based on freedom of ownership, production, exchange, acquisition, work, and movement and open competition.

The 2008-and-beyond economic meltdown has, not for the first time, but acutely because of its gravity, introduced the huge question of capitalism's survival and value. The capitalist economy, while dynamic and productive, is presently unstable. At its core is a banking system that allows large-scale borrowing and lending. Without this procedure, the majority of businesses cannot deal effectively with incurring costs and receiving revenues, and most consumers cannot achieve their level of consumption. When the banking system collapses, and credit consequently seizes up, economic activity falls.

Capitalism has created its own rules, in and outside the boundaries of government. Business people want to maximize profits within a framework created by the government. Once it is determined what people want to purchase, firms generate profits, which induces competitors to enter the market until excess profit is eliminated and resources are allocated more efficiently.

It appears that greater regulation, not less, is needed within the banking industry, and to pull the nation out of its present recession. The failure that drove the nation into its present predicament can be blamed on both the banks and on the U.S. government regulators. The government, as it is argued, failed to develop contingency plans to deal with future concerns that most experts believed were on the horizon. Others, including professional economists, are to be included in their judgment calls as to the future of our traditional capitalist system.

CAPITAL ONE FINANCIAL CORPORATION. Wrote off an additional $1 billion for bad loans and posted a worse-than-expected loss in the fourth quarter 2008 due to a rising default rate. The bank expected losses to worsen in 2009 based on estimates that the unemployment rate would hit 8.7 percent and home prices would drop another 10 percent.

Capital One Financial posted a loss of $275.5 million in July, compared with a profit of $452.9 million.

CAPITAL REQUIREMENTS DIRECTIVE. A requirement for financial institutions to retain at least the equivalent of 5 percent of the capital value of an asset that they securitize. Introduced as part of the 2008 bailout fund.

See also BANK BAILOUT (PLAN) OF 2008; TROUBLED ASSET RELIEF PROGRAM.

CAPITAL RESERVES. *See* FEDERAL HOUSING ADMINISTRATION.

CAR ALLOWANCE REBATE SYSTEM (CARS). *See* CASH FOR CLUNKERS.

CAR CZAR. Would help press the automakers as well as their various constituents, employees and unions, creditors, and suppliers to make concessions to reorganize the businesses to become profitable.

On February 15, the president announced that he would drop the idea of appointing a single, powerful "car czar" to oversee the revamping and restructuring of GM and Chrysler. Instead he will keep the task in the hands of his senior economic advisers.

The president created a panel—the Presidential Task Force on Autos—drawing officials from several federal agencies and being led by his senior economic advisers. A few days later, GM and Chrysler placed on file with the Treasury Department their plans for a complete restructuring of their companies.

See also AUTOMOBILE INDUSTRY; AUTO TASK FORCE; PRESIDENTIAL TASK FORCE ON AUTOS; RATTNER, STEVEN.

CAR-INDUSTRY SUPPLIERS. *See* AUTO PARTS.

CAR LEASING. *See* GENERAL MOTORS.

CARLSBERG. The beer producing company Carlsberg of Denmark, based in Copenhagen, said on January 15, 2009, that it would cut 270 jobs in the face of an uncertain market.

CARLYLE CAPITAL. Mortgage-securities hedge fund that on March 11, 2008, sought a moratorium on more forced sales of assets after about $5 billion of their $21 billion in holdings were liquidated.

CARMAKERS. *See* AUTOMOBILE INDUSTRY.

CARNEGIE BANK (OF SWEDEN). *See* SWEDEN.

CARNIVAL. A major cruise-ship operator, it reported its earnings in mid-June 2009, which fell 33 percent. For its fiscal second quarter, ending May 31, Carnival reported a profit of $264 million, down from $390 million a year earlier. Revenue fell 12 percent to $2.95 billion.
    At the end of July, Carnival posted its second consecutive quarterly loss. *Cf.* ROYAL CARIBBEAN CRUISES.

CAR-PARTS MAKERS. *See* AUTO PARTS.

CARREFOUR. A French firm, the world's second-largest retailer announced on December 18, 2008, that its net income fell 7.4 percent. The group, with more than 15,000 stores in thirty countries, blamed a downturn in consumer spending across its markets and the cost of promotions to maintain market share in the face of competition from discounters.
    See also RETAILING.

CARRIER AIR CONDITIONERS. *See* UNITED TECHNOLOGIES.

CARRY TRADE. Any investment that appears suspiciously profitable. A foreign-exchange trading of borrowing cheaply in a funding currency to exploit high interest rates in a target currency.

CARS. Official name for Car Allowance Rebate System.
    See also AUTOMOBILE INDUSTRY; CASH FOR CLUNKERS.

CASH FOR CLUNKERS. A 2009 government proposal to give money to consumers who trade in their old car for a new one. Used extensively in Europe to encourage car sales. July 24 was the first day of the federal government program to purchase more fuel-efficient cars.
    Officially, the Car Allowance Rebate System (CARS) provided up to $4,500 for a traded-in vehicle. It was aimed at lifting sales for the automobile industry and taking gas-guzzlers off the road.

To qualify, buyers had to turn in a car or light truck that gets no more than 18 miles per gallon and purchase or lease one that gets at least 22 miles per gallon. The vehicle also had to be less than twenty-five years old.

The program was federally funded by $1 billion and was to terminate on November 1, 2009. The program was so popular that by August 19, 435,000 vouchers worth either $3,500 or $4,500 had been distributed to consumers. The government then added another $2 billion to the $1 billion and announced that the program would be terminated at 8:00 PM, Monday, August 24.

On August 27, 2009, the government reported that buyers bought 690,000 new vehicles under the program. U.S. automakers accounted for 38.6 percent, while Japan's largest carmakers sold 41 percent.

While the program was terminated at the end of August 2009, European automakers in September were urging their governments to continue the cash-for-clunkers program out of fear that car sales would plunge if programs ended abruptly.

Cf. APPLIANCES; TOYOTA.

CATERPILLAR. The maker of heavy equipment announced in January 2009 that it would cut 20,000 jobs after it forecast that this would be one of its worst years in decades and would slash its payroll by 16 percent.

In March, Caterpillar announced it would lay off nearly 2,500 U.S. workers and close a plant in Georgia. The cuts were in addition to the 22,100 layoffs that were announced in January. Buyouts were offered to about 25,000 U.S.-based employees.

On April 21, Caterpillar moved into a first-quarter 2009 loss and cut its full-year sales and profit forecasts, underestimating the severity of the global economic slump. Caterpillar reported a first-quarter net loss of $112 million, compared with a year-earlier profit of $922 million.

On July 21, Caterpillar reported a 66 percent drop in second-quarter profit. The company's second-quarter profits were $371 million, down from $1.106 billion a year before. By mid-July Caterpillar's layoffs approached 15 percent of total workforce.

On October 26, 2009, Caterpillar management announced that it would recall 550 laid-off workers by the end of 2010 but would permanently trim about 2,500 idle workers. The company had already laid off more than 30,000 permanent and temporary workers.

CATHAY PACIFIC AIRWAYS. Announced in April 2009 that it would reduce passenger and cargo capacity, delay new aircraft deliveries, and ask staff to accept unpaid leaves, following a dramatic drop in first-quarter revenue. Passenger capacity would fall by 8 percent and the airline asked its 17,000 workers to take unpaid leaves of one to four months.

See also AIRLINES.

CDS. *See* CREDIT-DEFAULT SWAP.

CDX. *See* CREDIT-DEFAULT SWAP.

CEA. *See* COUNCIL OF ECONOMIC ADVISORS.

CELL PHONES. *See* MOTOROLA; NOKIA CORPORATION; VODA-FONE.

CEMEX. Mexico's Cemex had in November 2008 a net debt of $16 billion, with $8 billion of that debt maturing by the middle of 2010, but only $560 million in cash.

In mid-December, shares of Cemex, the largest cement maker in the Americas, rose sharply after it reached an agreement with lenders that cleared the way for the company to refinance $6 billion in debt coming due in 2009. Shares had plunged 24 percent in two days on concern that it might fall short in efforts to refinance its debt.

CENSUS (U.S.). *See* U.S. CENSUS.

CENTRAL ASIA. Kazakhstan's annual average GDP growth since 2000 was 10 percent; in 2008 it dropped to 5 percent. Predictions were for a national insolvency, even with its $48.4 billion in foreign reserves. The government injected 15 percent of its GDP into the economy, including a $5 billion bailout for local banks.

See also KAZAKHSTAN.

CENTRAL BANK. The national bank of a sovereign nation. A bank holding institution that maintains the bank reserves of a nation and is the prime reservoir of credit. It impacts on monetary policy, regulates not just banking but a whole range of financial services and markets, encourages economic innovation and legal infrastructure, and possesses proper links with other global financial centers. Central banks played a major role in the 2008 meltdown and in nations' futures.

See also "TOO BIG TO FAIL."

CENTRAL BANK (U.S.). *See* FEDERAL RESERVE.

CENTRAL BANKERS. Meeting at the end of August 2009 in Jackson Hole, Wyoming, central bankers from around the globe expressed growing confidence that the worst of the financial crisis was over and that a global economic recovery was moving forward.

CENTRAL EUROPE. *See* EASTERN EUROPE.

CERBERUS. Cerberus Capital Management bought Chrysler from the German automaker Daimler in August 2007. Chrysler then cut 33,000 jobs and reduced its production capacity by 1.2 million units a year.

By the end of March 2009, Cerberus was expected to lose its entire stake in Chrysler under the latest bailout offer to the automaker.

By the summer's end 2009, investors in Cerberus had withdrawn more than $5.5 billion, or nearly 71 percent of the hedge fund's assets, responding to the significant investment losses and their own personal requirement for cash.

See also AUTOMOBILE INDUSTRY; CHRYSLER; DAIMLER; FIAT; GMAC.

CFPA. *See* CONSUMER FINANCIAL PROTECTION AGENCY.

CHAMPAGNE. Indicating the sharp decline in consumer spending in the recession, champagne producers agreed in the summer 2009 to pick 32 percent fewer grapes for the year. Champagne sales throughout the world are expected to fall as low as 260 million bottles in 2009, compared to 339 million bottles in 2007. In 2008, as the meltdown hit hardest, sales fell to 322 million bottles, the first decline since 2000.

CHAPTER 7. *See* BANKRUPTCY FILINGS.

CHAPTER 11. *See* BANKRUPTCY FILINGS; LEHMAN BROTHERS.

CHAPTER 13. *See* BANKRUPTCY FILINGS.

CHARITY. *See* FOUNDATIONS.

CHARLES SCHWAB. Discount brokerage firm; its stock declined 8.2 percent after it announced that its earnings were crimped by a slowdown in the retail business, expected to continue in both 2009 and 2010.

Charles Schwab's third-quarter 2009 profit fell 34 percent with its net income declining to $200 million.

The largest discount broker by market capitalization projected fourth-quarter 2009 profit below estimates. Schwab expects fourth-quarter earnings would be two to four cents a share lower than the third quarter's 17 cents.

CHARTER SCHOOLS. In order to tap the $5 billion in federal stimulus funds, charter schools are expanding. Typically they are nonunionized, publicly funded alternative schools.

See also EDUCATION.

CHAVEZ, HUGO. President of Venezuela.

See also VENEZUELA.

"CHEAP MONEY." *See* FEDERAL RESERVE.

CHEVROLET. *See* GENERAL MOTORS.

CHEVRON. On July 31, 2009, Chevron announced that its profit fell 71 percent in the second quarter. Net income amounted to $1.75 billion, compared with $5.98 billion one year earlier. Revenue fell 51 percent to $4.2 billion from $81 billion.

CHIANG MAI INITIATIVE. *See* ASIAN DEVELOPMENT BANK.

CHICO'S FAS INC. The women's apparel retailer said in January 2009 that it would cut about 180 jobs or about 11 percent of its headquarters staff and planned to close as many as twenty-five stores. The company aimed to reduce expenses by approximately $15 million in 2009.

CHILDREN IN POVERTY. *See* POVERTY.

CHILE. After several years of robust expansion, activity is projected to moderate and inflation to recede. The slowing world economy, tighter financial conditions and lower investments in mining and energy will all slow growth. Inflation will decline gradually as second-round wage increases from high commodity prices wear off and expectations are re-anchored to the central bank's target. Past current account surpluses have disappeared as copper prices have retreated from high levels. To ensure an orderly decline in inflation, policies should remain prudent. Depending on world macroeconomic and financial developments, a gradual loosening of the monetary policy stance may be warranted unless the recent depreciation of the peso revives inflationary pressures. The fiscal rule provides an appropriate mild counter-cyclical cushion to activity (OECD).

See also WORLD TRADE.

CHIMERICA. Term coined by Niall Ferguson, the financial historian, describing the significant trade and financial relationship between China and the United States.

CHINA. Thirty years after the official beginning of economic reform in China, 200 million fewer people live in poverty, and the country had a 6 percent share of global GDP compared with 1.8 percent in 1978. Importantly, to feed its people there had been a nearly 70 percent increase in grain production in the thirty years since reform took hold.

In 2000, China's reserves were less than $200 billion; today China has a $2 trillion arsenal of reserves, a current-account surplus, little connection to foreign banks, and a budget surplus that offers lots of room to increase spending.

In the past decade, China invested more than $1 trillion, mostly earnings from manufacturing exports, in U.S. government bonds and government-backed mortgage debt. That helped lower U.S. interest rates and fuel the consumption binge and housing bubble.

Low-cost Chinese goods helped to keep a lid on U.S. inflation, while the flood of Chinese investment helped the U.S. government finance mortgage and a public debt of nearly $11 trillion.

China's $3.3 trillion economy accounted for about a quarter of the world's economic growth in 2007. Its GDP growth rate slowed to 9 percent in the third quarter in 2008, year-on-year the lowest in five years, creating worries. Most experts believe that China needs a minimum 7 percent growth each year to contain social unrest.

China, in 2008, held $652 billion in Treasury debt, up from $459 billion a year ago. China owns $1 out of every $10 of America's public debt.

The slowdown in exports contributed to the closing of at least 67,000 factories across China in the first half of 2008. Middle-class homeowners were having their first housing downturn in 2009 after years of boom, with earlier buyers wanting their money back.

On November 9, China announced a huge economic stimulus package aimed at bolstering its weakening economy. Beijing said it would spend an estimated $586 billion by 2010 on a wide array of national infrastructure and social welfare projects. China's central bank cut interest rates by more than a full percentage point, the largest Chinese rate reduction since the Asian financial crisis of a decade ago, amid signs of existing slowdowns.

Exports, which make up 40 percent of GDP, slipped toward the end of November, sliding 2.2 percent and marking the first fall in seven years. In October, by contrast, exports had surged 19.2 percent. The sudden shift provided clear evidence that the global financial crisis had arrived. Exports to all of China's trading partners suffered, with those to the United States down 6.1 percent. Additionally, the stock market was in the doldrums and property values in many cities were off by 30 to 40 percent.

Power generation, a reliable tool for measurement in China, fell by 7 percent. Growth in industrial production slowed to 5.4 percent in November from 8.2 percent in October.

Since ascending to membership in the World Trade Organization in 2001, China's exports had quadrupled, helping transform it into the world's fourth-largest economy after the United States, Japan, and Germany. Converting the export figures into China's own currency, a better measure of the effect on China's economy, exports plunged 9.6 percent.

As reported by the government on December 10, imports also plunged sharply in November, falling 17.9 percent, which widened the trade surplus to $40 billion from $35.2 billion in October.

Household consumption in 2007 made up just 35.3 percent of China's GDP, a record low for a major country in peacetime. In the 1980s it was over

50 percent. (In the United States it was 72 percent of GDP in 2007.) China clearly had taken savings to an extreme.

The International Monetary Fund cut its 2009 forecast for Chinese economic growth to around 5 percent in its revision as the global economy continued to decline.The central bank cut interest rates for the fifth time in four months, effective the end of December, in a new effort to revive economic growth as the government worried about spreading job losses and worker protests. The one-year lending rate fell by 0.27 percentage points to 2.24 percent. The reduction came just four weeks after China's biggest rate cut in eleven years.

The gap between average urban and rural incomes expanded to about $1,600 in 2008, with the ratio between the richer city residents to those in the countryside rising to 3.36 to 1.

China's urban incomes had increased much more quickly, with average annual income jumping 74 percent since 2003, while rural incomes rose only 31 percent. The official urban unemployment rate for the end of 2008 was 4.2 percent, up from 4 percent in 2007, the first time the official rate had risen after five consecutive years of decline. Some studies show as large as a 9.4 percent urban unemployment rate.

About 670,000 businesses shut down and 6.7 million jobs evaporated in 2008. The government announced in January 2009 that it would dole out $1.3 billion to 74 million people as a one-time living subsidy.

In January 2009, the government said that its economy expanded 6.8 percent in the fourth quarter of 2008 from a year earlier, confirming a dramatic slowdown that cut growth rates. This downturn marked the first time since 2002 that China's economy had expanded by less than 10 percent annually.

The current growth rate puts China in danger of falling below the government's longstanding annual target of 8 percent.

On January 14 China revised upward its gross domestic product growth for 2007 to 13 percent from 11.9 percent, which meant that it had passed Germany to become the third-largest economy in the world.

The Chinese premier, Wen Jiabao, on January 28 blamed the U.S.-led financial system for the world's deepening economic slump.

China had $2 trillion in foreign exchange reserves, and continued to buy U.S. government debt, surpassing Japan in September 2008 as the biggest foreign holder of the Treasury.

By January 2009, an estimated 20 million migrant workers were out of work, with another 5 million expected to be searching for jobs.

The consumer price index rose 1 percent in January from a year earlier, the ninth straight month the rate of increase had slowed.

The year 2009 saw China surpassing the United States in auto sales: 790,000 vehicles were bought by Chinese consumers in January compared with 656,976 vehicles sold in the United States.

On February 9, the government announced plans to create jobs, lower distribution costs, and improve the quality and availability of products sold in rural areas. The government planned to establish 150,000 stores in the countryside in 2009 to offer rural residents easy access to safe consumer goods. These stores were expected to create 775,000 new jobs by 2010.

China's exports plummeted in January, with exports falling 17.5 percent from a year earlier. The decline was far worse than the 2.8 percent fall recorded in December 2008.

The U.S. trade deficit with China narrowed sharply in December 2008 to $19.9 billion from $23.1 billion in November, but left China reeling amid lower demand for its goods.

Chinese bank lending more than doubled in January 2009 as the government pushed banks to free up credit to hard-hit sectors of the economy.

Foreign direct investment in China plunged 33 percent in January compared to a year before. The government reported on February 16 that the fourth consecutive monthly decline is indicative of the dire situation in China.

The nation's manufacturing sector declined in February 2009 for the seventh straight month. A sharp drop in its trade surplus in February signaled a shift in the nation's financial balance with the rest of the world and lowered the speed with which it piled up foreign-currency assets such as U.S. Treasury bonds.

Once a year, China's parliament convenes. On March 4, 2009, Premier Wen Jiabao promised to bolster the economy and reaffirmed an economic growth forecast of 8 percent for the year.

China moved to minimize the sale of state-owned stakes in financial firms at below-market prices. New rules took place on May 1, 2009, requiring that state-owned shares of listed financial firms be sold through stock exchanges and further stated that sale prices in block trades should be no lower than the average weighted stock price on the trading day closest to the date of transaction.

Meanwhile, the World Bank on March 18 lowered its forecast for economic growth in China to 6.5 percent in 2009. This figure was down from the bank's earlier forecast of 7.5 percent, and was well below the 8 percent projected by Chinese officials.

China called for the establishment of a new currency on March 23 to replace the U.S. dollar as the world's standard, proposing a major overhaul of global finance, which reflects developing nations' growing displeasure with the U.S. role in world economics.

More than 40 percent of China's GDP was traced to factory construction and other kinds of fixed-asset investment. Over the past decade entrepreneurs created five million businesses of at least eight employees each. They spawned about 75 million jobs for China's university graduates, workers discarded from state firms, and streams of people from the countryside. The output of China's private firms and their investment spending made up half of 2008's $4.42 trillion GDP.

China is preparing to become the world leader in the making and selling of the electric cars. The government plans to raise its annual production capacity to half a million all-electric cars and hybrids by the end of 2011, from 2,100 in 2008.

To the dismay of the government, it was announced on April 15 that the country had its worst quarterly economic growth in nearly two decades. China's GDP in the first quarter of 2009 rose 6.1 percent from the same period one year earlier. That was lower than the 6.8 percent from the fourth quarter of 2008, and a dramatic slowdown from the past growth hitting 13 percent for the year 2007.

Although economic growth slowed to 6.1 percent in the first quarter 2009, the retail sales, after adjusting for price changes, rose 15.9 percent for the same time frame.

While that was slower than the 17.7 percent rise in spending in the fourth quarter 2008, it indicated that growth in consumption was encouraging compared to other major economies.

China's exports fell 22.6 percent from a year earlier to $91.94 billion in April, deeper than March's 17.1 percent decline.

Beijing's stimulus spending was expected to aid China's economy to grow 7.5 percent in 2009 and 9 percent in 2010.

The World Bank raised its forecast in mid-June for China's economic growth in 2009 to 7.2 percent (in March it was predicted to be as low as 6.5 percent).

China's government had turned its economy around far faster than expected. On July 15, it was announced the growth accelerated to 7.9 percent in the second quarter 2009.

On September 11, 2009, the government issued data showing that industrial expansion accelerated in August, with output rising 12.3 percent from a year before. By mid-September, China's economy roared back, following its stimulus plan. The central bank said that the nation's economy surged at an annualized rate of 14.9 percent at the second quarter, compared to the U.S. economy which shrank at an annualized rate of 1 percent in the same period.

Government data released on October 22 showed China's GDP grew by 8.9 percent in the third quarter from a year before. Industrial output accelerated further to 13.9 percent in September. China allowed the yuan to rise by 21 percent against the dollar in the three years to July 2008, but since then it has more or less kept the rate fixed.

China's industrial output grew 16.1 percent in October, the fastest in over one year. The increase accounts for two-thirds of China's economic output.

By November 2009, China had transformed itself from a global font of low-price items fueled by cheap labor, creating significant disparities of wealth. Today, there are billionaires—the fastest growing in the world—and a lot of poverty in China. Per capita income is small, roughly $3,200, which is less than 10 percent of the United States, with many farmers earning as little as $1 a day. China provides multibillion-dollar loans to other developing countries, and retains large holdings in Wall Street giants, such as Morgan Stanley and the Blackstone Group. China is poised to eclipse the United States by selling nearly 15 million cars in one year. No nation has ever acquired larger foreign exchange reserves ($2.2 trillion). The country leads the world in initial public stock offerings.

By the end of 2009 China was rapidly moving out of deflation after nearly a year of falling consumer prices. The return of inflation highlights the recovering economy, with prices rising for a range of items. For example, gasoline prices are up 50 percent since the beginning of the year.

By November, China's imports increased 26.7 percent from the year before, to $94.56 billion, countering the October fall of 6.4 percent. It was the first increase in 13 months.

China purports to have an industrial-production growth in 2010 at about 11 percent, to help fulfill its economic-growth target of 8 percent.

See also AIRLINES; AUTOMOBILE INDUSTRY; BANK OF CHINA; CHIMERICA; EXPORTS (U.S.); GENERAL MOTORS; INDUSTRIAL & COMMERCIAL BANK OF CHINA; INTERNATIONAL MONETARY FUND; JAPAN; LENOVO; TRADE DEFICIT (U.S.); U.S.-CHINA TRADE; WORLD TRADE.

Cf. INDIA.

CHINA CERAMICS AND POTTERY. *See* WATERFORD WEDGWOOD.

CHIP SALES. In November 2008 global semiconductor sales fell almost 10 percent from a year earlier to $20.8 billion. November sales were 7.2 percent lower than the $22.4 billion in October 2008.

By January 2009, chip sales plunged by almost a third from a year earlier, to $15.3 billion.

CHRISTIE'S INTERNATIONAL. Sold $1.8 billion of fine and decorative arts in the first half of 2009, falling nearly 49 percent from one year earlier. In the United States, sales fell by half, to $462.9 million.

Cf. SOTHEBY'S.

CHRISTMAS SALES. Holiday sales in 2008 in the United States plummeted 2.2 percent. November and December sales accounted for 25 to 40 percent of many retailers' annual sales.

CHRYSLER. On December 11, 2008, during congressional debates it appeared that Chrysler's demise was all but inevitable, regardless of whether it received government aid.

The automaker warned that it could soon run out of money without a $7 billion loan, and would be forced to sell off its parts or merge with a foreign automaker. By the end of the month, President Bush came forward and announced a rescue plan. Chrysler was owned by Cerberus Capital Management in 2008–2009, but the federal government may change this relationship.

Chrysler received $4 billion in emergency loans at the end of 2008, and planned to submit a restructuring plan by March 2009 showing how the carmaker would shrink in response to the sharp decline in auto sales. The company needs $7 billion every 45 days in order to pay parts suppliers.

Predictions were that by 2010 Chrysler would be acquired by another automaker or sold in pieces by its majority owner.

The Treasury Department announced on January 14, 2009 that a $1.5 billion, five-year loan would be given to Chrysler Financial, enabling the firm to offer 0 percent financing on select 2008 and 2009 vehicles.

In January 2009, Chrysler's U.S. sales fell 55 percent compared with a year earlier, to 62,157 vehicles.

On February 17, the automaker requested another $5 billion from the government to survive through 2009 (Chrysler had already received $4 billion in loans). On the same day, Chrysler announced that it was cutting another 3,000 jobs and discontinuing three of its models. Without this funding, management would likely be forced to declare bankruptcy.

On March 30, President Obama made a speech saying Chrysler could file for bankruptcy, giving it until April 30 to complete a deal.

By April 1, it was clear that Cerberus would lose its entire stake in Chrysler auto division, but would continue to control its finance arm. The Treasury was pressing the Italian automaker Fiat to take 20 percent ownership initially of Chrysler. The Treasury on April 2, made opening offers of $1 billion to lenders at a meeting in Washington, D.C. On April 20 the banks made their first offer to Treasury, proposing $4.5 billion in new debt, a 40 percent equity stake, a $1 billion investment from Fiat, and $1 billion in preferred equity and a board seat. In rapid succession:

On April 22, the Treasury proposes bank group take $1.5 billion in new debt and 5 percent equity.

On April 26, the UAW and the Treasury agree to labor-contract deal and it is announced. UAW-Chrysler members begin voting the next day.

On April 28, lead banks agree to back $2 billion cash offer. Other lenders do not.

On April 29, the government makes last offer of $2.25 billion. Lenders are informed on a 4:30 PM call and told they have ninety minutes to vote on the offer. It fails. New UAW deal is ratified by Chrysler workers.

As the April 30 Treasury deadline approached for Chrysler to seal an agreement with Fiat of Italy, a group of large banks and other lenders rebuffed a Treasury Department request that they slash 85 percent of Chrysler's secured debt, proposing instead to eliminate about 35 percent in exchange for a minority stake in the restructured car market and get a seat on its board.

Under the government plan, a restructured Chrysler would be owned by Fiat, the lenders, the United Auto Workers (UAW), and the Treasury. Under the agreement, the Treasury or Chrysler, if it returned to profitability would pay in cash half the $10.6 billion the company owed a retiree health care fund. The remainder would be paid in an undetermined amount of Chrysler equity.

Chapter 11 bankruptcy protection was nearing even as a deal was struck with Chrysler's lenders or an alliance forged with Fiat. Even with an agreement with its lenders, bankruptcy protection would permit Fiat to pick and choose which operations it wanted, and the U.S. government would provide bankruptcy financing while the reorganization played out.

The UAW union was on board with the plan and would end up owning a significant stake in the restructured automaker. The union would eventually own 55 percent of a restructured Chrysler, as announced on April 27, with Fiat owning another 35 percent. Chrysler's secured lenders together would end up owning 10 percent of the firm once it was reorganized.

Chrysler would also issue a $4.59 billion note to the health care trust fund of the union for retired workers. Chrysler would pay $300 million in cash into the trust fund in 2010 and 2011, with increasing amounts up to $823 million in the years 2019 and 2023.

Daimler would surrender its remaining 19.9 percent stake in Chrysler and pay as much as $600 million into the carmaker's pension fund. Fiat, on the other hand, would produce at least one small car in a Chrysler plant in the United States and permit Chrysler to use a 3.0 liter diesel engine and a 1.4 liter gasoline engine in its cars. Fiat's investment was estimated to be worth $8 billion, and would create 4,000 union jobs for Chrysler.

Key lenders agreed, by the end of April, to Chrysler's debt swap, allowing movement toward reorganization. Lenders would accept $2 billion in cash in exchange for the $6.9 billion in secured debt they now hold. Meanwhile, adding to the plight of the carmaker, sales fell 48 percent in April, which was considerably worse than the industry average of 34 percent compared to a year ago.

On April 30, Chrysler filed for bankruptcy protection.

The eighty-four-year-old firm will have new owners. The UAW union's retirees will own 55 percent, Fiat up to 35 percent, the U.S. government 8 percent, and the Canadian government 2 percent.

On May 3, a bankruptcy judge said that the automaker could use $4.5 billion in government loans for bankruptcy financing while attempting to win court approval for a sale of its assets to Fiat. Also, after losing nearly $17 billion in 2008, Chrysler projected a return to profitability by 2012.

Chrysler plans to close 789 dealerships, almost one-quarter of its retail stores.

On June 6, a group of pension funds opposed to the sale of Chrysler to Fiat asked the U.S. Supreme Court to put the deal on hold while they continued their attempt to block it. Then, on June 9 the Court cleared the way for Chrysler to exit bankruptcy court, lifting a stay on its proposed sales to a group including Fiat.

On June 10, with a wire transfer from the federal government, Chrysler both received $6.6 billion in exit financing and cemented its alliance with Fiat, thus ending its forty-two days of bankruptcy.

Chrysler announced on June 17 that it will restart production in June 2009 at seven of its twelve assembly plants.

Chrysler Financial, in mid-July, reimbursed the U.S. government with $1.5 billion, becoming the first auto-sector company to pay off the loans provided by the Treasury Department.

Even during the cash-for-clunkers program in August 2009, Chrysler sales dropped by 15 percent.

Chrysler's sales have fallen significantly over the past two years. In November 2009, cars and light trucks were down from 11.4 percent for the same month a year before. Five years ago, it had 14 percent of the market.

See also AUTOMOBILE INDUSTRY; AUTO TASK FORCE; CERBERUS; DAIMLER; FIAT; GENERAL MOTORS; GMAC; JOB BANKS; MARCHIONNE, SERGIO; U.S. TREASURY; VEBA.

CHRYSLER FINANCIAL. *See* CHRYSLER; FIAT.

CIRCUIT CITY STORES. Filed for bankruptcy-court protection on November 11, 2008, amid a worsening financial state and store closings.

On Friday, January 16, 2009, Circuit City became the first major post-holiday casualty of the retail slump and announced that it would close all of its 567 stores and begin selling off its assets. More than 30,000 employees would lose their jobs and no value would remain in the firm for shareholders. Circuit City officially closed its stores on Sunday, March 8. The company initially filed for restructuring and then later switched to liquidation.

CISCO SYSTEMS. A giant networking-equipment company, it reported a 24 percent drop in profit and a 17 percent drop in revenue for its fiscal quarter ending April 25. Revenue for the quarter fell to $8.16 billion from $9.79 from a year earlier. Profit was $1.35 billion down from $1.77 billion a year earlier. Over the past three quarters Cisco eliminated nearly $1.5 billion in costs and planned to cut up to 2,000 positions in its current fiscal year.

Cisco Systems laid off several hundred workers on July 16, 2009, as its sales continued to decline. Between 600 and 700 workers were laid off out of its total 66,558 employees. By August 2009, Cisco posted a 46 percent fall in quarterly profit.

Cisco reported a 19 percent profit decline and a 13 percent revenue fall for its fiscal first quarter 2009. Profit fell to $41.8 billion and revenue declined to $9 billion from $10.3 billion the year before.

CITADEL BROADCASTING. The nation's third-largest radio broadcaster, it filed for bankruptcy on December 20, 2009. Owning 224 stations, the bankruptcy reflects the troubles plaguing radio shows and significant declines in advertising revenue during the meltdown period.

CIT GROUP. A lender to almost a million mostly small and midsize businesses across the United States, CIT was narrowly saved from bankruptcy on July 19, 2009. The 101-year-old company had $68 billion of liabilities as of March 31, 2009. CIT is registered as a bank holding company; the twenty-sixth-largest bank holding company in the country. It received $2.33 billion from the federal TARP in December 2008, after winning approval to become a bank holding firm.

On July 15, the U.S. government rebuffed pleas to rescue the struggling company a second time. Should CIT fail, it would be the largest American bank to fall since Lehman Brothers collapsed in 2008.

CIT avoided imminent bankruptcy protection when on July 19 its bondholders rescued the company through a $3 billion emergency loan. It gave CIT time to restructure its business model and reduce its voluminous debt load, even if only temporarily. Another $1.7 billion in debt payments was due by the end of 2009 and CIT must pay off an additional $8 billion in 2010.

CIT was charged high interest rates (10.5 percentage points above the London Interbank Offered Rate) but avoided the pressure to pay down $1 billion in debt that came due in August. It also preserved the U.S. Treasury's $2.33 billion investment made as part of TARP.

By the end of September 2009 CIT had readied a plan to hand over control of the company to its bondholders. By doing this, CIT would eliminate 30 to 40 percent of its more than $30 billion in outstanding debt. The plan offered bondholders new debt secured by CIT assets and nearly all of the equity in a restructured firm.

Then, on October 30, CIT decided it would declare an abbreviated bankruptcy filing to relieve its debilitating debt burden. With its $71 billion in assets, its bankruptcy filing would be the fifth largest in U.S. history. The U.S. Treasury, which in 2008 injected $2.33 billion of funds from TARP to help stabilize the company, became a major loser from the bankruptcy. The result is that CIT's lending capacity could fall to less than 20 percent of what it was two years before. CIT lends about $60 billion to retailers and small firms, providing capital for operations, purchases, and other expenses.

On November 1, 2009, CIT filed for bankruptcy protection, creating problems for nearly 1 million small and midsize firms. CIT gained support from about 90 percent of voting debt holders for a prepackaged reorganization plan that would permit the lender to speed through Chapter 11 and emerge with a new business model by the end of the year. At this time, CIT's assets were about $71 billion and nearly $65 billion in liabilities.

On December 8, 2009, CIT listed liability of nearly $65 billion in its bankruptcy filing. A restructuring plan took effect on December 10 giving creditors new debt aid.

CIT's major history is:

1908—founded in St. Louis by Henry Ittleson.
1916—works with Studebaker to provide financing to car buyers.
1924—first listed on the New York Stock Exchange.
1930s—signs contract with Sears Roebuck for purchases of refrigerators.
1941—during World War II, acquires two manufacturing companies and sends 2,000 employees to war.
1958—purchases Bank of North America.
1965—merges two banks to create The National Bank of North America.
1980—acquired by RCA, which sells CIT's four manufacturing businesses.
1986—transfers its consumer loan portfolio to Manufacturers Hanover Trust.
1997—holds its IPO, posts earnings of $300 million.

Cf. LEHMAN BROTHERS.

CITIBANK. *See* CITIGROUP.

CITIGROUP. On January 16, 2008, this financial services company wrote down certain assets by $18.1 billion as it showed fourth-quarter 2007 losses of about $10 billion that were linked to the subprime-mortgage crisis. Then on April 19, Citigroup posted a $5.1 billion quarterly loss.

Citigroup announced on November 17, 2008 that it would cut 50,000 jobs, from investment bankers to the back office. Investment bankers would bear the brunt of the losses because senior managers were asked to reduce expenses significantly. In addition, the bank would trim expenses by 16 to 19 percent, to about $50 billion in 2009.

Citigroup reported four consecutive quarterly losses, including $2.8 billion in the third quarter 2008. Its share price continued to fall in November. On November 21, it dropped 20 percent, after falling 26 percent the day before and 23 percent the previous day. For the week, Citigroup plummeted 60 percent.

Citigroup, once the largest and mightiest U.S. financial institution, was brought to its knees by more than $65 billion in losses, write-downs for troubled assets, and charges to account for expected future losses. More than half of that amount stemmed from mortgage-related securities.

Its stock had fallen to its lowest price in more than a decade, closing on November 21, at $3.77. At that price the company was worth just $20.5 billion, down from $244 billion two years before. Waves of layoffs accompanied that slide, with about 75,000 jobs lost or soon to disappear from a workforce that number about 375,000 in 2007.

On Monday, November 24, Citigroup agreed to halt dividend payments for the next three years and to restrictions on executive compensation under terms of the U.S. government rescue of the struggling bank.

These concessions were made in return for the U.S. government's direct investment of about $20 billion in the bank and an agreement to back about $306 billion in loans and securities, largely residential and commercial real estate loans and certain other assets, which remained on the bank's balance sheet. Citigroup would shoulder losses on the first $29 billion of that portfolio.

Any remaining losses would be split unequally between Citigroup and the government, with the bank absorbing 10 percent and the government absorbing 90 percent. The Treasury Department would use its bailout fund to assume up to $5 billion of losses. If necessary, the Federal Deposit Insurance Corporation would bear the next $10 billion of losses. Beyond that, the Federal Reserve would guarantee any additional losses.

In exchange, Citigroup would issue $7 billion of preferred stock to government regulators. In addition, the government bought $20 billion of preferred stock in Citigroup. The preferred shares would pay an 8 percent dividend and only slightly erode the value of shares held by investors. Citigroup lost 77 percent of its stock value in 2008.

On December 31, Citigroup's chief executive and chairman announced that senior staff would forgo their 2008 bonuses.

Citigroup posted an $8.29 billion loss, twice as much as analysts estimated. Events since the government got involved with Citigroup were:

a. October 14, 2008—Treasury Department announced plans to inject $125 billion into eight banks, including $25 billion into Citigroup.
b. November 23—The United States pumped another $20 billion into Citigroup, but demanded that the company revamp its strategy and shrink.
c. January 13, 2009—Under federal pressure, Citigroup announced a deal to spin off Smith Barney into a joint venture with Morgan Stanley.
d. January 16—Citigroup reported an $8.3 billion fourth-quarter loss.
e. January 21—The company named a new CEO, Vikrim Pandit, handing him responsibility for pushing out more directors and recruiting fresh blood.
f. January 27—After being publicly scolded by President Obama, Citigroup reneged on its plans to buy a luxury corporate jet.
g. February 11—Citigroup's CEO testified before a congressional committee, saying he would get paid $1 a year until Citigroup returns to profitability.
h. February 21—Negotiations intensified about expanding the government's stake in Citigroup to as much as 40 percent.
i. February 27—Treasury Department announced that it would increase its ownership in Citigroup to 36 percent from 8 percent.
j. July 16—Citigroup said it earned a $4.3 billion profit.

Taxpayers had already put more than $50 billion in capital into the bank, while guaranteeing $301 billion of its bad assets. Still Citigroup remains unable to stop its slide.

Citigroup announced on March 3 a new plan to aid unemployed homeowners. Citigroup would temporarily lower mortgage payments to an average of $500 per month for some borrowers who have recently lost their positions and were at least sixty days behind on their mortgage payments. Borrowers would then be permitted to make the lower payments for three months and the bank would waive interest and penalties during this time period. Citigroup holds in excess of 1.4 million mortgages.

To qualify, borrowers had to have loans of no more than $417,500; they had to live in their home and possess a mortgage serviced by CitiMortgage.

In mid-April, Citigroup reported a $1.6 billion first-quarter 2009 profit by the way it accounted for the decline in the value of its own debt.

By the end of April, Citigroup, soon to be one-third owned by the U.S. government, asked permission to pay special bonuses to key workers. Pay restrictions imposed on banks receiving bailout funds were resulting in the threat of important employees finding work elsewhere, and receiving significantly higher incomes. Citigroup referred to these bonuses as "retention awards." The U.S. government now has a 33.6 percent stake in Citigroup.

Following results of the stress test, Citigroup will need to raise as much as $10 billion in new capital.

Citigroup made a $101 million profit in the third quarter 2009 on revenue of about $20.4 billion.

On December 14, 2009, Citigroup announced that it would repay $20 billion that had been given to them under TARP. Hours later Wells Fargo, the last of the big banks, announced that it would repay its loans to the government. The U.S. Treasury could earn a profit of nearly $14 billion on its Citigroup investment.

See also BANK BAILOUT (PLAN) OF 2008 (U.S.); STRESS TESTS; "TOO BIG TO FAIL."

Cf. AMERICAN INTERNATIONAL GROUP; MERRILL LYNCH; WELLS FARGO BANK.

CITIMORTGAGE. *See* CITIGROUP.

CITY BUDGETS. By the end of the summer 2009, the recession hit city budgets hard, with overall city revenues down for the year for the first time in seven years. In 379 cities studied it was found that revenues declined by 0.4 percent, as expenses climbed 2.5 percent. It was the worst outlook in twenty-four years.

CITY UNEMPLOYMENT. *See* UNEMPLOYMENT.

CIVILIAN CONSERVATION CORPS. *See* ROOSEVELT, FRANKLIN DELANO.

CLARIANT. In January 2009, the chemical giant posted a 5 percent drop in full-year sales, cut a further 1,000 jobs, and cancelled its dividend in the face of the global economic slump.

CLARITY. *See* TRANSPARENCY.

CLASSICAL ECONOMICS. *See* KEYNES, JOHN MAYNARD.

CLAWBACKS. Payments that are given back due to unfulfilled promises or other circumstances. President Obama, on February 4, 2009, placed limits on severance packages for dismissed employees whose firm received government funds, allowing for clawbacks of such payments.

Many allege that the current financial collapse was caused by employees in the mortgage and financial products industries pursuing short-term gains without regard for long-term losses and/or consequences.

Prior to the financial crisis of 2008–2009, clawback provisions were rare or nonexistent, so an employee's only incentive was to work to make the current year's bonus as large as possible.

See also EXECUTIVE PAY; GOLDEN PARACHUTE; G-20; NAME AND SHAME; UNEMPLOYMENT.

CLINTON, HILLARY. President Obama's secretary of state, starting in January 2009.

CLUB MED (MEDITERRANEE) (MEDITERRANEAN). The largest European resort company, it lowered planned spending for 2009 by almost half to €50 million and set a goal of lowering costs by €31 million following a travel slump that cut into bookings.

CLUNKERS. *See* CASH FOR CLUNKERS.

COACH. This upscale company operated 324 full-priced stores and 106 factory outlets in North America and another 158 locations in Japan. Profits fell 14 percent in the fourth quarter 2008.

Coach posted net income of $216.9 million, down from $252.3 million in 2007. Coach fired off 150 employees (10 percent of workforce).

Coach's profit, ending the quarter of June 27, fell to $145.8 million. Sales declined less than 1 percent.

The company reported a 3.4 percent fall in its fiscal first-quarter 2009 earnings, as sales rose slightly by 1.2 percent to $761.4 million. For the quarter ending September 26, earnings were $140.8 million.

COAL USAGE. *See* ENERGY EFFICIENCY.

COBRA. A law—the Consolidated Omnibus Budget Reconciliation Act— under which severed employees can remain on their employer's group health plan for a limited time. On December 21, 2009, President Obama signed a measure to extend the federal subsidy for continued health-insurance coverage for involuntarily terminated workers under employer group programs. The stimulus package provided a federal subsidy for 65 percent of the COBRA premium for nine months for workers who qualify. The subsidy applies to workers who lost their jobs between September 1, 2008 and December 31,

2009. Workers who may have preexisting conditions must maintain coverage to protect insurability. An estimated 14 million people will be eligible for the subsidy.

See also AMERICAN RECOVERY AND REINVESTMENT ACT (OF 2009).

COLGATE-PALMOLIVE COMPANY. At the end of October 2009, Colgate reported profit of $590 million up 18 percent from $500 million a year earlier. Revenue was flat at $3.99 billion.

Cf. KELLOGG COMPANY; PROCTER & GAMBLE.

COLLEGE ENDOWMENTS. *See* ENDOWMENTS.

COLOMBIA. Colombia's peso fell the most in one week (January 2009) on concern of a deepening global recession. The currency declined as much as 1.4 percent.

The central bank cut its key rate on March 21, to 7 percent from 8 percent.

See also LATIN AMERICA.

COLONIAL BANCGROUP. A Southern-based large lender, on August 14, 2009, it was seized by federal regulators, making it the largest bank failure of the total of seventy-seven banks in 2009.

Cf. INDYMAC BANK.

COLUMBIA UNIVERSITY. The university's endowment investments lost 16.1 percent in the year ending June 30, 2009, with a value of about $5.7 billion. On June 30, 2008, the endowment fund was valued at $7.1 billion.

Cf. HARVARD UNIVERSITY; PRINCETON UNIVERSITY; STANFORD UNIVERSITY; YALE UNIVERSITY.

COMCAST CORPORATION. The largest U.S. cable operator by subscribers, it posted a 22 percent third-quarterly profit 2009.

COMMERCE DEPARTMENT. *See* U.S. COMMERCE DEPARTMENT.

COMMERCIAL PAPER. *See* CONSUMER CREDIT.

COMMERCIAL REAL ESTATE. One thousand large commercial properties in the United States, representing $25.7 billion, were already bank-owned or the landlord was in default by the end of 2008. Possibly another $80.9 billion, more than 3,700 properties, faced a similar situation in 2009. Retail vacancy rates were expected to climb to 11 percent in 2009, and rents declined between 4 and 6 percent as property owners contended with more tenant bankruptcies, store closures, and fewer retailer expansions.

Commercial real estate debt could be more dangerous to a financial system than debt classes such as credit card and student loans, as $6.5 trillion was invested in such holdings, and financed by about $3.1 trillion in debt.

See also COMMERCIAL REAL ESTATE LOANS; GENERAL GROWTH PROPERTIES.

COMMERCIAL REAL ESTATE DEBT. *See* COMMERCIAL REAL ESTATE.

COMMERCIAL REAL ESTATE LOANS. By March 2009, commercial real estate loans were delinquent at an accelerating pace, possibly threatening additional losses to banks of tens of billions of dollars. The delinquency rate on about $700 billion in securitized loans from office buildings, hotels, stores, and other investment properties had more than doubled since September 2008, to 1.8 percent in March 2009. It had been estimated that as much as $250 billion in commercial real estate losses could occur during the meltdown period, with as many as 700 banks failing as a result of their involvement with commercial real estate.

See also COMMERCIAL REAL ESTATE.

COMMERZBANK. *See* GERMANY; UNEMPLOYMENT.

COMMODITIES. Commodities were strong at the beginning of 2008 and then dropped in 2009.

See also DOW JONES-AIG COMMODITY INDEX; OIL.

COMMODITIES REGULATIONS. *See* COMMODITY EXCHANGE ACT OF 1936; COMMODITY FUTURES MODERNIZATION ACT OF 2000; COMMODITY FUTURES TRADING COMMISSION ACT OF 1974; FUTURES TRADING PRACTICES ACT OF 1992.

COMMODITY EXCHANGE ACT OF 1936. Broadened the types of agricultural commodities that can trade through futures contracts on an organized exchange.

COMMODITY FUTURES MODERNIZATION ACT OF 2000. Allowed trading of over-the-counter financial derivatives between certain sophisticated counterparties, such as regulated financial institutions and pension funds, to be exempted from being executed on an exchange.

COMMODITY FUTURES TRADING COMMISSION ACT OF 1974. Transferred authority over futures markets from the secretary of agriculture to the new Commodity Futures Trading Commission; gave the CFTC jurisdiction over nonagricultural futures and options on those contracts.

See also DERIVATIVES LEGISLATION; FINANCIAL REGULATION PLAN (2009).

COMMUNITY BANKS. *Synonymous with* SMALL BANKS.

COMPENSATION. Major banks and securities firms planned to pay their workers about $140 billion in 2009, a record high. Employees at the top twenty-three investment banks, hedge funds, asset managers, and stock and commodities exchanges expect to earn more than they did the peak year of 2007. Total compensation and benefits at publicly traded companies are expected to increase 20 percent from 2008's $117 billion, and to top 2007's $130 billion payout. That translates into $143,400 on average, up almost $2,000 from 2007 levels.
See also PAY CZAR.

COMPENSATION CZAR. *See* PAY CZAR.

COMPTROLLER OF THE CURRENCY. A federal office created in 1863 to oversee the chartering and regulation of national banks.
See also NATIONAL BANK SUPERVISOR.

COMPUTERS. Following a difficult period, computer sales and home-office equipment rose in the summer 2009, up 7.3 percent from a year before.
See also APPLE; DELL INC.; GOOGLE; INTERNATIONAL BUSINESS MACHINES CORPORATION; YAHOO!

CONFERENCE BOARD. An organization supported by business executives that conducts research. By the end of November 2008, the Conference Board, with a financial-industry research study, concluded that its confidence index was 44.9 in November, up from a revised 38.8 the month before. The October reading was the lowest since the index was established in 1967. By March 2009, the index was flat, with slight indications of a positive turn.

In early April, the Conference Board found that confidence among chief executives improved in the first quarter 2009. Its index rose to 30 from 24 in the fourth quarter of 2008, though well below the 50 mark reflecting a positive position.

In a sign of economic recovery, the Conference Board said its index of leading economic indicators rose 1 percent in April, after seven straight monthly declines. It was the largest gain in nearly four years.

On September 21, 2009, the Conference Board index rose 0.6 percent, indicating the public's expectation that there are signs of recovery ahead.

In late December 2009 the Conference Board's consumer-confidence index rose to 52.9 from 50.6 in November. That was up from the 25.3 showing in February, which was the lowest level in its forty-two-year history. The index remains below pre-meltdown levels.

See also CONSUMER CONFIDENCE; RECESSION.

CONFIDENCE. *See* CONFERENCE BOARD; CONSUMER CONFIDENCE.

CONGRESSIONAL BUDGET OFFICE. *See* DEFICIT (BUDGET).

CONOCOPHILLIPS. The third-largest U.S. oil company, it announced in January 2009 that it would cut its workforce 4 percent, slashing capital spending by 18 percent and writing off $34 billion in noncash assets because of plummeting energy prices.

ConocoPhillips reported on April 23 its first-quarter profit fell 80 percent from the year before.

Conoco lost money in the second quarter 2009, with profit down 76 percent. The company earned $1.3 billion in the quarter, down from $5.4 billion a year earlier.

On October 28, 2009, the company reported a 71 percent decline in third-quarter earnings because of lower commodity prices and a weak environment for refining operations. A profit of $1.5 billion was announced from $5.19 billion from the year before. Revenue fell 42 percent to $41.31 billion.

See also COMMODITIES; OIL; OIL COMPANIES.

CONSOLIDATED OMNIBUS BUDGET RECONCILIATION ACT. *See* COBRA.

CONSTRUCTION. By December 2009, construction industry jobs had fallen by 1.6 million since the recession began. In October unemployment climbed to 19.1 percent, up from 10.7 percent the year before. The transportation and material-moving sector had a rise in unemployment to 11.6 percent from 7.9 percent over the same time frame.

CONSTRUCTION SPENDING. *See* CONSUMER SPENDING.

CONSUMER AND BUSINESS LENDING INITIATIVE. A 2009 administration plan, designed to finance lending to consumers and higher spending. Purports to help increases in spending and reduce trillion-dollar deficits.

CONSUMER CONFIDENCE. The U.S. government reported at the end of October 2008 that consumers sharply cut their spending during the summer months, causing the longest American shopping spree on record to come to an end. The U.S. economy contracted at an annual rate of 0.3 percent in the third quarter of 2008.

The housing bust, the resulting credit crunch, and the deteriorating job market had pushed most Americans to cut back. Personal consumption fell at an annual rate of 3.1 percent in the third quarter of 2008, its biggest drop since the spring of 1980. Disposable personal income dropped at an 8.7 percent rate in the third quarter, the biggest decline since the quarterly data was first recorded in 1947.

At the same time, the U.S. Conference Board found that consumer confidence had plunged to the lowest point on record in October 2008, as Americans complained about fewer jobs, lower net worth, and smaller incomes.

Citizens also believed that the economy would worsen before it improved, a sign of deep pessimism that reflected a year of painful declines in stocks, jobs, and home values.

The survey's confidence index with 5,000 households fell to 38 in October from 61.4 in September. In October, consumer prices tumbled by a record amount, carried lower by skidding energy and transportation prices, while new home construction continued to fall.

Consumer spending was expected to decrease in 2009, the first time since 1980 and perhaps by the largest amount since 1942.

By the end of 2008, gloom over the state of the economy had led to a huge disappointment around the world. Five out of six people surveyed in France expressed pessimism. The average was seven in ten in many other European nations, with the most optimistic European country, Germany, with only 37 percent expressing pessimism. The negative response compared to two years earlier was about 25 percent, except for Spain, which was even more optimistic. In December 2006, only 15 percent of Spaniards were pessimistic; now the number was 59 percent.

A year earlier the Conference Board index was at 90.6.

In February, the confidence of the U.S. consumer tumbled to its lowest level in more than forty-one years, with home prices continuing to decline accompanied by bank-loan delinquencies, and a worsening consumer market.

In August 2009, consumer confidence climbed more than expected, rising to an index of 54.1 from a July level of 47.4.

See also CONFERENCE BOARD; CONSUMER PRICES; CONSUMER SPENDING; FEAR GAUGE; FEDERAL RESERVE; FRANCE; RECESSION; RETIREMENT.

CONSUMER CREDIT. In August 2009, consumer credit by commercial banks stood at $834 billion, about $45 billion less than at the end of 2008. Banks' outstanding commercial and industrial loans fell to $1.411 trillion in September 2009, $170 billion lower than a year before. Commercial paper issued by nonfinancial businesses fell 40 percent from the year before.

Consumer lending shrank at an annual rate of 1.7 percent in October, its ninth consecutive fall. The $3.5 billion decline caps a 4 percent drop in consumer lending from its July 2008 peak. By December, lending to consumers continued to shrink as the credit squeeze dragged on.

See also CREDIT CARDS.

CONSUMER FINANCIAL PROTECTION AGENCY (CFPA). Proposed by President Obama as a new regulatory agency to assist consumers to make informed decisions about financial products, save for retirement, and receive improved investment guidance. Under this plan, firms will be given the option of offering products such as credit cards without hidden fees or penalty interest rates, without having to maneuver regulatory hurdles.

The agency, if approved by Congress, would have the authority to write regulations and require upgraded disclosure, with enforcement capability. Ben Bernanke, chairman of the Fed, argued before the Senate Banking Committee that this proposed agency was not needed and that the Fed had a sound handle on consumer protection. By mid-September 2009, the Obama administration had submitted draft legislation, and the House Financial Services Committee had drafted a bill under the chairmanship of Barney Frank.

See also BERNANKE, BEN; FEDERAL RESERVE; FINANCIAL REGULATION PLAN (2009); HOUSE (U.S.) FINANCIAL OVERHAUL PLAN.

CONSUMER GOODS. *See* PROCTER & GAMBLE; UNILEVER.

CONSUMER LENDING. *See* CONSUMER CREDIT.

CONSUMER PRICE INDEX. *See* CONSUMER PRICES.

CONSUMER PRICE INFLATION (EUROZONE). Fell from 3.2 percent to 2.1 percent in November 2008.

CONSUMER PRICES. In the United States, consumer prices dropped by 1.7 percent in November 2008, the largest one-month decline on record. Prices were only 1.1 percent higher than one year before.

The consumer price index, the broadest measure of product and service costs across the country, fell 0.4 percent in March 2009, compared to the year earlier, the first time since August 1955 that prices declined over the year.

Consumer prices posted their largest annual decline in fifty-nine years. The consumer price index rose 0.1 percent in May from April.

Consumer prices held steady in July 2009, with prices 2.1 percent lower than the previous July 2008.

Consumer prices rose in August 2009. The consumer price index rose 0.4 percent from July. Over the past year consumer prices declined 1.5 percent, the largest declines in any twelve-month period since February 2004.

Consumer prices rose modestly in September by 0.2 percent.
See also CONSUMER CONFIDENCE; DEFLATION.

CONSUMER PROTECTION. *See* HOUSE (U.S.) FINANCIAL OVER-HAUL PLAN.

CONSUMER SPENDING. Rose just 0.1 percent in February 2008, before inflation, continuing months of lethargic activity. Consumer spending, which accounts for more than two-thirds of U.S. economic activity, fell 1 percent in December 2008, for the fifth month in a row. Residential spending slumped by about 27 percent for all of 2008, and total construction spending dropped 5.1 percent to $1.08 trillion, the biggest annual drop since records began in 1993.

For a second consecutive month in February 2009, consumer spending climbed. It rose at a seasonally adjusted annual rate of 0.2 percent.

Consumers cut their spending in March as incomes dropped, leading to a 0.2 percent fall from February. The drop in consumer spending, the first since December 2008, showed that a recovery was short-lived.

On August 4, 2009, the government indicated that consumer spending rose 0.4 percent in June. But adjusted for inflation, it fell 0.1 percent. Personal income also declined 13 percent in June, the largest single-month drop in four years.

By the end of September 2009, consumer spending was showing growth. Personal income climbed 0.2 percent in August compared with July, and spending increased 1.3 percent. Personal savings as a percentage of disposable income was 3 percent, compared with 4 percent in July. However, GDP growth forecast to 3.1 percent from 2.7 percent.

Consumer spending climbed modestly, 0.5 percent for the sixth time in seven months. Adjusted for inflation, spending increased 0.2 percent in November 2009.

See also CONSUMER CONFIDENCE; FOOD SPENDING.

CONSUMPTION. *See* CONSUMER CONFIDENCE.

CONTAINER SHIPPING. *See* SHIPPING.

CONTINENTAL. German tire maker, it reported on April 29 that it had a net loss of $350.9 million, compared with a year-earlier net profit. In the first quarter 2009 revenue fell 35 percent.

CONTROLLED BANKRUPTCY. By March 2009, the government reintroduced controlled bankruptcy for General Motors, which attempts to persuade some creditors to agree to a plan that would divide the company into two pieces.

See also CHRYSLER; GENERAL MOTORS.

CONVERTIBLE-ARBITRAGE FUNDS. Funds that attempt to exploit price anomalies among corporate bonds. These funds lost 46 percent of their value in 2008.

CONVERTIBLE WRAPAROUND MORTGAGE. *See* FLEXIBLE-PAYMENT MORTGAGE; RENEGOTIABLE-RATE MORTGAGE; VARIABLE-RATE MORTGAGE.

CORNING. A maker of specialty glass, it announced in January 2009 that it would cut 3,500 jobs, or 13 percent of its work force, as well as an additional 1,400 temporary workers, in order to brace for declining demand for its liquid-crystal-display (LCD) glass. The world's largest maker of LCD glass by revenue saw 2008 fourth-quarter profit plunge 65 percent.

At the beginning of the meltdown, Corning shifted many employees to four-day workweeks and began eliminating 1,400 temporary and contract workers.

Corning's first-quarter 2009 profits allowed the firm to rehire some of its laid-off staff.

Corning reported on July 27 that its second-quarter earnings fell 81 percent, to $611 million. Sales dropped 18 percent to $1.4 billion from $1.69 billion.

The company's management reported that third-quarter 2009 profit declined 16 percent. Earnings were $643 million, down from $768 million a year earlier. Revenue fell 4.9 percent to $1.48 billion.

CORPORATE CREDIT UNIONS. *See* CREDIT UNIONS.

CORPORATE PROFITS. *See* PROFITS.

CORUS BANKSHARES. On September 11, 2009, the FDIC closed this Chicago-based bank (the ninety-first bank failure in 2009), whose loan portfolio tripled to $4.5 billion in the four years from 2001 to 2005.

COSTCO WHOLESALE. Earnings at this retailer known for selling household goods in bulk dropped 29 percent for its fiscal third quarter 2008. For the period ending May 10, 2009, Costco posted net income of $209.6 million. Sales at stores open at least a year fell 7 percent.

The company reported on December 10 that it had flat fiscal first-quarter earnings with a profit of $266 million, compared to $263 million one year before. Total revenue increased 7.9 percent to $17.3 billion from $16.4 billion, with sales increased 5.5 percent to $16.92 billion.

COST CUTTING. By mid-November 2009 many companies were reporting strong earnings. However a large portion of their profits came from cost cutting, not from hoped-for revenue growth. Revenue fell by 10 percent.

COSTS OF WAR. *See* WARS IN AFGHANISTAN AND IRAQ.

COUNCIL OF ECONOMIC ADVISORS (CEA). A group of economists charged with advising the U.S. president on a variety of matters, including the preparation of the budget message to Congress and the American people.

COUNTER-CYCLICAL POLICIES. Lower interest rates and undiminished public spending often created by fiscal austerity and tight money.

COUNTERFEITING. *See* EUROPEAN CENTRAL BANK.

COUNTERPARTY RISK. *See* CREDIT-DEFAULT SWAP.

COUNTRYWIDE FINANCIAL. Mortgage lender that posted an $893 million loss in April 2008, as a federal probe found that sales executives at the company deliberately overlooked inflated income figures for borrowers.
See also BANK OF AMERICA.

COX, CHARLES CHRISTOPHER. Chairman of the Securities and Exchange Commission.
See also SECURITIES AND EXCHANGE COMMISSION.

CRABTREE & EVELYN. The purveyors of specialty soaps, fragrances, and lotions filed Chapter 11 bankruptcy protection on July 1, 2009. It operated 126 stores in thirty-four states and employed 950 people. The retailer lost $13.3 million on revenue of about $100 million in the current fiscal year.

CRAMDOWN. A measure by which should the mortgage industry fail to modify mortgage loans, bankruptcy judges could cut payments more sharply by cramming down mortgage loan balances on primary residences for people filing for bankruptcy protection.
The cramdown would have allowed bankruptcy judges to rewrite contracts to reduce the amount that people owe on their mortgages.
President Obama's hope for a mortgage cramdown passage in Congress failed.
See also BANKRUPTCY PROTECTION; MODIFYING MORTGAGES; OBAMA, BARACK.

CREDIT. *See* EXPORTS; G-20.

CREDIT CARD ACT OF 2009. *See* CREDIT CARDS.

CREDIT CARD LEGISLATION. *See* CREDIT CARDS.

CREDIT CARDS. Toward the end of April 2009, the Obama administration turned attention to high credit card rates in order to put limits on the industry. Banks had come under considerable pressure over raising their credit card rates during the meltdown.

Congress was determined to minimize the rising costs of credit cards, from higher interest rates on past balances to fees for paying by phone or online. The president threw his support behind legislation moving through Congress that would restrict the ability of banks to impose higher fees and interest rates on consumers.

Credit card delinquencies increased in the first quarter 2009 from a year earlier. The delinquency rate rose to 1.32 percent for consumers who were three months or more behind in payments on their cards, up 11 percent from 1.19 percent a year earlier.

Banks always tighten credit standards in an economic slowdown. By the summer 2009, many banks were tightening things up before many of the restrictions of Congress were to go into effect. Banks had until February 2010 to comply with the government's key provisions. Their responses to legislative and economic changes included:

a. Tightening standards for credit card applicants, rejecting more people, and offering smaller credit lines.
b. Raising interest rates and fees and switching customers with fixed rates to variable ones.
c. Enhancing rewards programs for a few customers but adding more fees.

On August 20, 2009, banks, as stated in the Credit Card Act of 2009, are required to mail bills at least twenty-one days before their due dates and provide at least forty-five days' notice before making a significant change to their rates or fees. The new rules bar banks from increasing fees and rates without warning when a consumer misses a payment or exceeds a credit limit. Consumers will also be permitted to avoid future interest-rate increases and pay off any outstanding balance over time under the original rate terms. The bulk of the legislation's key provisions took effect in February 2010, including limits on interest-rate increases on existing balances. Then in July 2010, new disclosure rules will be introduced.

See also AMERICAN EXPRESS; REGULATION; TALF.

CREDIT-DEFAULT SWAP (CDS). Insurance-like contracts that Wall Street created in the early 1990s allowing bondholders to protect themselves against losses if a company or a debt issuer defaults.

A way for market participants to bet on the likelihood that a firm or other debt issuer will default on its obligation.

There is a viable and legitimate use for CDSs, especially when they permit bondholders and firms to limit their risks to actual economic exposure.

Recently, they became a haven for speculators who were doing nothing more than betting on whether a debt issuer would survive.

Buyers of CDSs pay premiums to firms issuing the contract. If a debt default occurs, the party providing the credit protection has to make the buyer whole on the amount of insurance bought. It is similar to payments that insurers pay to homeowners if their houses burn down.

CDSs provide insurance against an organization defaulting on its debt, by providing a real-time gauge of credit risk. They permit the investor to purchase insurance against a firm defaulting on its debt payments.

CDS made many firms and investors feel comfortable owning corporate debt because they could eliminate the risk of the issuer failing, which helped lower the cost of capital.

The value of outstanding CDSs exploded from nearly zero a decade ago to $62 trillion at the end of 2007, and fell back to $55 trillion in 2008.

The collapse of Lehman Brothers in September 2008 indicated that the main systematic risk posed by CDSs came not from widespread losses on underlying debts but from the demise of a major dealer.

See also BEAR STEARNS; DERIVATIVES LEGISLATION; EMPTY CREDITOR; HEDGE.

CREDIT RATING. *See* RATERS; STANDARD & POOR'S.

CREDIT RATING AGENCY REFORM ACT OF 2006. Empowered the SEC to register nationally recognized statistical rating organizations and imposed disclosure and record-keeping requirements.

CREDIT SUISSE. One of Europe's strongest banks, in December 2008, it announced a cut of about 5,300 jobs, or 11 percent of its workforce. Its top executives would not receive any bonuses for 2008. For the third quarter 2008, the bank posted a loss of 1.26 Swiss francs, worth about $1 billion.

On July 23, 2009, Credit Suisse's second-quarter profit rose 29 percent.

See also UNEMPLOYMENT.

CREDIT UNIONS. Federal regulators announced on January 28, 2009, that they would guarantee $80 billion in uninsured deposits at credit unions. Regulators also injected $1 billion of new capital into the largest of the wholesale credit unions.

A federal plan, introduced in February 2009 to rescue troubled wholesale credit unions, had a provision requiring credit unions to pay an extra $4.7 billion into a government insurance fund.

On March 20, federal authorities took control of the two largest wholesale credit unions after learning that their losses on mortgage-related securities were larger than originally believed. These institutions do not impact on the general public in that they provide critical financing, check clearing, and other tasks for the retail institutions. They are referred to as "corporate credit unions" that are owned by their retail credit-union members.

CREDIT-WORTHY BORROWERS. *See* SUBPRIME.

CRIME. *See* HACKING.

CROATIA. Its government, rejected in December 2008, planned to run a balanced budget in 2009. In 2008, Croatia's economy expanded at the slowest pace in eight years. GDP climbed at an annual rate of 1.6 percent, compared with 3.4 percent earlier.

CROSS-BORDER INVESTMENT FLOWS. Investments between nations collapsed in 2009, with the value of mergers and acquisitions likely to be 56 percent lower than in 2008. Foreign direct investment will fall to $600 billion in 2009 from $1.02 trillion.

CRUDE OIL. *See* OIL.

CRUISE LINE. In 2009, projections showed a 2.3 percent drop in travelers to 13.5 million people.
   See also CARNIVAL.

CUBA. See VENEZUELA.

CUOMO, ANDREW. The New York State attorney general.
   See also AMERICAN INTERNATIONAL GROUP.

CURRENCY-SWAP ARRANGEMENTS. *See* ASIAN DEVELOPMENT BANK.

CURRENT RECESSION. *See* RECESSION.

CYBER MONDAY. *See* RETAILING.

CZECH REPUBLIC. By mid-January 2009, unemployment rose to 6.8 percent compared with 6 percent a year before. After growing about 4 percent in 2008, its economy contracted by 2 percent in 2009, a sharp decline from a growth peak around 7 percent in 2006.

Until the meltdown of 2008, nearly 40 percent of new jobs in the Czech Republic were filled by foreigners. By the end of 2008, more than 360,000 foreigners were working there. By the end of April, the economy having soured, the Czech government announced in February that it would pay $660 and provide one-way plane tickets to its citizens who wanted to return home.
   See also EASTERN EUROPE; MIGRANT WORKERS ; SPAIN.

D

DAIMLER. The German maker of luxury cars announced in December 2008 that it would cut working hours at Mercedes-Benz plants in Stuttgart and Berlin as the recession in Europe and the United States continued to hurt car sales. (Daimler sold an 80.1 percent stake in Chrysler to Cerberus in August 2007.)

On February 17, 2009, Daimler reported a net loss of €1.53 billion, or $1.93 billion, for the fourth quarter 2008, as the economic slowdown intensified. This net loss compared with a profit of €1.7 billion in the quarter a year earlier indicated the depths of the fallout.

In a deal worth $2.65 billion announced in mid-March, Daimler ceded a 9.1 percent stake in the company to an Abu Dhabi investment firm.

Daimler planned to cut labor costs in Germany by $2.66 billion in 2009, with measures including salary reductions. It was announced on April 1 that its vehicle sales had dropped 40 percent in February.

Daimler said on April 8 that it expected a significant decline for the first quarter 2009, resulting in company-wide cost-cutting and efficiency programs in response to the downturn in auto markets worldwide. Labor savings would be $2.68 billion in Germany, with other reductions possible.

On April 27, Daimler agreed to give up its remaining 19.9 percent stake in Chrysler and pay as much as $600 million into the automaker's pension fund. This stake would be turned over to Chrysler's parent, Cerberus Capital Management. The following day, Daimler posted a worse-than-expected net loss of €1.29 billion for the first quarter as revenue fell 22 percent. In the first three months of the year sales were down 34 percent from the previous year.

Daimler, the number two master luxury carmaker, indicated that their sales had dropped 12 percent in August.

Daimler's third-quarter 2009 earnings before interest and tax were about $700 million.

See also AUTOMOBILE INDUSTRY; CERBERUS; CHRYSLER; GERMANY.

DARK POOLS. Trading venues that match buyers and sellers anonymously. By hiding identities, in addition to the quantity of shares bought or sold, dark pools help institutional investors avoid price movements as the wider market reacts to their trades. Stock quotes aren't displayed until after the trade is completed.

Synonymous with TRADING DESKS.

DEBT. Money, services, or materials owed to another person as the result of a previous agreement.

DEBT, FEDERAL (U.S.). In the past two years the portion of U.S. debt maturing in less than a year has climbed from 30 percent to over 40 percent, the most since the early 1980s. Just 37 percent of GDP two years ago, the federal debt has climbed to 56 percent, and rising.

See also CHINA; DEFICIT (BUDGET, U.S.).

DEBT-BUYBACK. *See* BUYOUT FIRMS.

DEBT CEILING. The limit that the U.S. government can borrow. The debt cap's legal limit is presently $12.1 trillion. On December 24, 2009, the government approved a short-term increase in federal borrowing authority of $290 billion, fearful of it exceeding the legal limit and not having the ability to pay its debts.

DEBT MONETIZATION. The process by which the national debt is used to increase currency in circulation. Essentially, this is carried out by the purchase of government bonds, thus releasing Federal Reserve notes into circulation. These purchases may be effected through member banks.

DEBT PAYBACK. Companies worldwide had $4 trillion in debt due to be repaired or renewed before the end of 2010. That sum, roughly equivalent to Japan's annual economic output, could be the next phase of the global financial crisis.

Synonymous with REFINANCE.

DECEMBER 2007. The government's official date for the beginning of the recession in the United States.

See also RECESSION.

DECLINING GROWTH. With a $14.4 trillion U.S. economy, the output of goods and services had been declining by nearly $50 billion a month since September 2008.

DEED. A formal, written agreement of transfer by which title to an estate or other real property is transmitted from one person to another.

DEED-FOR-LEASE PROGRAM. *See* FANNIE MAE.

DEED IN LIEU OF FORECLOSURE. A mortgagor's way of presenting title to the mortgagee to prevent foreclosure of property.
See also FORECLOSURE.

DEERE & CO. The manufacturer of agricultural equipment posted a 27 percent fall in its fiscal third-quarter 2009 profit. Net sales fell 24 percent.

DEFERRAL. *See* PROMOTE AMERICA'S COMPETITIVE EDGE (PACE).

DEFICIT (BUDGET, U.S.). Between 2004 and 2007 the budget deficit narrowed from $413 billion to $162 billion thanks to rapid growth in tax revenue. Before the 2008 meltdown the Congressional Budget Office projected the 2009 deficit at $438 billion, now expected to be at least $750 billion. At 5 percent of GDP, that would be the highest level since 1986.

In February 2009, several weeks after passage of the American Recovery and Investment Act, President Obama set a goal to cut the annual deficit at least in half by the end of his term. The reduction would come in large part through Iraq troop withdrawals and higher taxes on the rich.

For 2009, the deficit was about $1.2 trillion, which could reach more than $1.5 trillion. Starting in fiscal year 2010, the ten-year program would result in an annual deficit declining to $33 billion in 2013. Measured against the size of the economy, the projected $533 billion shortfall for 2013 would mean a reduction from a deficit equal to more than 10 percent of the GDP—larger than any deficit since World War II—to 3 percent.

To implement slashing the deficit, President Obama would tax the investment income of hedge funds and private-equity partners at ordinary income tax rates.

The Congressional Budget Office presented on March 20 a forecast that President Obama's spending program would produce significantly deeper long-run deficits. Summarizing, the deficits would average nearly $1 trillion a year over the coming decade. The cumulative deficit from 2010–2019 would total about $9.3 trillion, $2.3 trillion more than President Obama's original forecast.

The Treasury Department reported on April 10 that the deficit had reached nearly $1 trillion—$956.8 billion—for the first half of the 2009 fiscal year. In the first six months of fiscal 2008, the government ran a deficit of $312.75 billion. For the entire fiscal 2008, it ran a deficit of $454.8 billion.

Spending on government bailouts combined to widen the deficit in the fiscal year that began on October 1, 2008. Gross spending through the Troubled Asset Relief Program was $2.89 billion for March 2009. Another $46 billion went to mortgage firms. For the first six months of the fiscal year, government receipts were down about 13.6 percent to $990 billion compared with the first half of fiscal 2008. Government expenditures grew by some 33.5 percent compared with a year earlier, to $1.95 trillion.

The U.S. federal budget deficit broke through the $1 trillion mark in June.

By August 2009, with falling tax receipts, soaring spending, and a sluggish recovery, the country's deficit was predicted to rise higher over the next decade. The White House Office of Management and Budget forecast a $9 trillion debt over the coming 10 years, $2 trillion more than it had previously projected.

On October 7, 2009 the Congressional Budget Office and the Treasury estimated that the federal deficit for fiscal 2009 would be $1.4 trillion, or about 10 percent of the U.S. GDP.

The issue is increasingly controversial. In 2009 the U.S. debt rose from 41 percent of the nation's output of goods and services, the GDP, to 53 percent. Without changes in taxes or spending, it will climb to 85 percent of GDP by 2018, 100 percent by 2022 and 200 percent by 2038.

See also DEBT, FEDERAL; FEDERAL RESERVE; MISERY INDEX; TROUBLED ASSET RELIEF PROGRAM; U.S. DEFICIT.

DEFLATION. Symptoms occur when goods pile up without buyers and prices steadily fall, suffocating new investment and worsening joblessness. Deflation accompanied the Great Depression of the 1930s. The decline in the general price level results in an increase in the purchase power of money.

Consumers and businesses worldwide lose their ability to purchase and prices for many goods fall. Production is slowed and layoffs are accelerated, taking more paychecks out of the economy, further weakening demand for products and services. Dropping profits reduce opportunities for profit, making firms reluctant to invest even when they can borrow money for free. From 1929 to 1933 prices fell by 27 percent.

As prices of consumer goods continued to fall in 2009, projected to be 1 percent, it brought the total drop from summer 2008 to the end of 2009 to about 4 percent.

Twenty-two percent of U.S. consumers expected deflation during 2009, the highest proportion to anticipate declining prices in the past half a century.

Consumer prices in the U.S. advanced at their slowest pace in fifty years in 2008, raising concerns about deflation as the weakening economy suppressed demand for cars, clothing, electronics, and a host of goods and services. The consumer price index fell by a seasonally adjusted 0.7 percent in December 2008, its third consecutive monthly decline, after sliding 1.7 percent in November.

In July 2009, the annual contraction in eurozone consumer prices increased the risk of deflation. The rate fell 0.6 percent from a year earlier.

See also EUROZONE; FRUGALITY; JAPAN; SPAIN; SWITZERLAND.

Cf. INFLATION; REFLATION; STAGFLATION.

Synonymous with FALLING PRICES.

DELEVERAGE. A company's attempt to decrease its financial leverage, a leading issue in the Great Recession meltdown. The best way for a firm to deleverage is to immediately pay off an existing debt on its balance sheet; otherwise there is the significant risk of defaulting.

DELEVERAGING. *See* DELEVERAGE.

DELINQUENCY RATES. On February 23, 2009, the Federal Reserve announced that delinquency rates on consumer and business loans at large banks were higher in the fourth quarter 2008, led by increases in residential-mortgage delinquencies, which neared 7 percent of outstanding mortgages.

See also COMMERCIAL REAL ESTATE LOANS.

DELINQUENT TAXPAYERS. *See* TAXPAYERS.

DELL INC. On May 28, 2009, the computer maker announced that it had a 63 percent drop in quarterly profit amid a 23 percent decline in revenue. This marked the third consecutive quarter of shrinking sales and profit at the company. Dell reported a 20 percent decline in laptop revenue and a 34 percent drop in desktop PCs for the quarter. The division that sells to large firms posted a 31 percent revenue slide.

In August 2009, Dell reported that its revenue from consumers had climbed 2 percent in the second quarter, while revenue from large businesses fell 3 percent over the same time period.

Cf. HEWLETT-PACKARD COMPANY; INTEL.

DELPHI. The Pension Benefit Guaranty Corporation (PBGC) agreed on July 22, 2009. to take on $6.2 billion in pension liabilities from the bankrupt auto supplier Delphi Corporation. The $6.2 billion rescue is PBGC's second largest ranked by dollar.

On July 30, Delphi won court approval to sell its assets to its lenders and General Motors, allowing the auto parts supplier to end its four-year stay in bankruptcy.

DELTA AIR LINES. Delta Air Lines reported in January 2009 a wider fourth-quarter loss. The world's largest carrier by traffic expected a 4 percent decline in passenger revenue in 2009. It was reducing its capacity by 6 to 8 percent to match the weaker demand.

Delta stated on April 6 that its international passenger traffic declined 15.1 percent in March. Business fell 13.9 percent in March, measured in revenue passenger miles.

Delta posted a loss of $257 million for the second quarter 2009, compared with a loss of $1.04 billion a year before. Seat capacity was expected to decline 9 percent in 2009.

In mid-September 2009 the airline projected an operating margin of 3 to 4 percent, while its passenger capacity would drop 5 to 6 percent from a year before.

Delta projected revenue growth in 2010 at 5 percent on a roughly 15 percent increase in ticket sales.

See also AIRLINES.

DENMARK. After years of strong expansion, the construction boom is now over and falling house prices have put an end to debt-financed consumption growth. As the impact of global financial turmoil materialized, forecasts remained weak during 2009, leading businesses to cut back investment. Denmark entered the slowdown with severe capacity pressures and wages rising much faster than warranted by productivity growth. There is thus little need presently for fiscal demand stimulus, especially since monetary conditions are set to ease along with those of the euro area. Aggressive fiscal stimulus to keep unemployment at recent record-low levels would magnify the loss of competitiveness and, ultimately, challenge the stability of the fixed exchange rate regime. This would make it difficult to lower interest rates in line with cuts in the eurozone (OECD).

Economy was expected to shrink 0.5 percent in 2009. Unemployment was 1.6 percent. Denmark announced on December 8, 2008, a bank support plan aimed at allaying the worst global credit crunch since the Great Depression.

On February 23, Denmark seized control of Fionia Bank, a bank of 90,000 customers, by injecting about 1 billion Danish kroner, or about $172 million, in a deal that took away shareholder control and split the bank into two parts until a sale could be found.

See also FLEXICURITY; ICELAND.

DEPOSIT INSURANCE. *See* FEDERAL DEPOSIT INSURANCE CORPORATION.

DEPOSITORY AGREEMENT. *See* MORTGAGE CERTIFICATE.

DEPOSITORY INSTITUTIONS DEREGULATION AND MONETARY CONTROL ACT. Legislation passed in the spring of 1980, the act committed the government to deregulate the banking system. It provided for the elimination of interest-rate controls for banks and savings institutions within six years, and it authorized them to offer interest-bearing accounts beginning in 1981 anywhere in the country.

The act also wiped out all state usury laws on home mortgages above $25,000. It also modernized the mortgage instrument by repealing dollar limits, thus permitting second mortgages.

DEPRESSION (OF THE 1930S). *See* GREAT DEPRESSION (OF THE 1930S).

DEPRESSION 2.0. Federal Reserve Chairman Bernanke's description for the Great Recession.

DERIVATIVE(S). A financial contract that specifies the terms of a future transaction (or set of transactions) in some underlying assets. Its origin is from "derived" from the underlying asset price. A derivative is a powerful and mostly unregulated investment that became a primary source of controversy before and following the meltdown. It is a security whose price is dependent upon or derived from one or more underlying assets. Derivatives enable people and companies to insure themselves against risk, allowing them to lower that risk. The derivative itself is merely a contract between two or more parties. Its value is determined by the fluctuations in the underlying asset. The most common underlying assets include stocks, bonds, commodities, currencies, interest rates, and market indexes. Most derivatives are characterized by high leverage.

European regulators proposed new measures in July 2009, fueling concern that trading of these exotic contracts could be pushed onto exchanges, crimping the profits of banks that currently handle such transactions. The measures of the European Commission include expanding collection of trading information and broadening efforts to standardize the market.

See also BEAR STEARNS; COMMODITY FUTURES MODERNIZATION ACT OF 2000; CREDIT-DEFAULT SWAP; DERIVATIVES LEGISLATION; FINANCIAL REGULATION PLAN (2009); HOUSE (U.S.) FINANCIAL OVERHAUL PLAN; LEHMAN BROTHERS; LONG-TERM CAPITAL MANAGEMENT; SUMMERS, LAWRENCE; SWAP CONTRACT.

Synonymous with DERIVATIVE CONTRACT.

DERIVATIVE CONTRACT. *Synonymous with* DERIVATIVE.

DERIVATIVE DEPOSIT. A deposit that is created when a person borrows money from a bank. A customer is lent a sum, not in money but by credit to his or her account, against which he or she may draw checks as required.

DERIVATIVE MARKET. The manipulation of options and futures stemming partly from the huge leverage they afford.

Synonymous with SHADOW MARKET.

DERIVATIVES LEGISLATION. Proposals in Congress that would have these products, which have not been regulated, fall under the jurisdiction of the Securities and Exchange Commission and the Commodities Future Trading Commission. Credit-default swaps would also be regulated. By mid-September 2009, the House of Representatives was considering several bills.

DEUTSCHE BANK. German bank that has kept itself from resorting to public bailouts but now has the German government as an indirect shareholder. The state owns 30 percent of Deutsche Post, which on January 14, 2009, agreed to take an 8 percent stake in Deutsche Bank.

Deutsche Bank reported in late October 2009 that its third-quarter profit would be about €1.4 billion.

See also GERMANY.

DEUTSCHE POST. *See* DEUTSCHE BANK; DHL.

DEVELOPING ECONOMIES. *See* WORLD BANK.

DEVELOPMENTALLY CHALLENGED POPULATION. *See* UNEMPLOYMENT.

DHL. Owned by Deutsche Post of Germany, the package delivery company cut 9,500 jobs at its U.S. unit on November 10, 2008, and effectively conceded the American domestic market to its rivals, FedEx and United Parcel Service.

DIAMOND SALES. *See* TIFFANY.

DISCLOSURE REQUIREMENTS. *See* REGULATORS; SECURITIES AND EXCHANGE COMMISSION.

DISNEY. *See* ABC.

DISPLAY ADVERTISING. *See NEW YORK TIMES.*

DISPOSABLE INCOME. *See* SAVINGS RATE.

DISTRESSED ASSETS. *See* "BAD BANKS."

DISTRESSED SALES. In the housing industry, a situation when sellers face foreclosure or are forced to sell their home for less than the value of the mortgage.

See also HOUSING.

DIVORCE. *See* MARRIAGE.

DODD, CHRISTOPHER J. The head of the U.S. Senate Banking Committee, Senator Dodd of Connecticut wanted in fall 2009 to merge four agencies and diminish the role of the Federal Reserve as a systemwide overseer, a plan significantly different from President Obama's position.

DOLLAR (U.S.). On February 29, 2008, the dollar hit a record low against the euro, deepening a six-year slide in which it is off more than 40 percent against the currency amid a softening U.S. labor market, weak housing, and slowing growth.

As the economic crisis unfolded during the third quarter, into the fourth of 2008, the dollar strengthened against the euro, the British pound, and the Swiss franc. The dollar remained the world's reserve currency.

By December 15, the dollar had commenced a downward trajectory as the world digested the implications of a difficult recession in the United States. The euro soared past $1.44 in its sharpest daily movement ever. The euro gained 15 percent against the dollar after it hit a low for the year of $1.2453 on November 20.

The dollar's December performance was good, as the currency emerged from a seven-year downtrend in 2008. The dollar had fallen against the yen, but ended 2008 higher against the sterling (pound) and the euro.

For the year 2008, the dollar strengthened 4.5 percent against the euro, 36 percent against the British pound, and 22 percent against the Canadian dollar. It also jumped 30 percent or more against the Brazilian real, the South Korean won, and the Turkish lira, and strengthened 24 percent against the Russian ruble.

The year 2009 began with a three-week high against the yen.

On March 23, China proposed a replacement of the U.S. dollar as the world's standard.

On October 8, 2009, the U.S. dollar fell to a 14-month low against other world currencies. The dollar is down 11.9 percent against a basket of currencies since President Obama's administration took office in January.

See also CHINA; EURO; POUND.

DOUBLE-DIP RECESSION. *See* RECESSION.

DOW. *See* DOW JONES INDUSTRIAL AVERAGE.

DOW CHEMICAL. On December 8, 2008, it announced that 5,000 jobs would be cut due to the economic slowdown. It would close twenty facilities and cut 11 percent of its global workforce, in light of the global economic slump. On December 10, Dow forecast fourth-quarter earnings of thirty cents a share.

Then, on February 3, 2009, it reported a loss before exceptional items of sixty-two cents a share. Dow cut operating capacity in the face of slumping demand but couldn't cut fast enough; utilization slumped to 44 percent in December.

On July 30 the company reported a quarterly loss of $435 million.

DOW JONES-AIG COMMODITY INDEX. A broad benchmark, it finished 2008 with a 37 percent loss, the worst year since the index began in 1998.

DOW JONES INDUSTRIAL AVERAGE (DOW). The averages of closing prices of thirty representative industrial stocks, fifteen public utility stocks, twenty transportation stocks, and an average of the sixty-five computers at the end of a trading day on the New York Stock Exchange.

On January 3, 2008, the Dow fell 220.86 points, or 1.7 percent in the first trading session of the year. Twelve months later, on January 2, 2009, it rose 258.3 points, or 2.94 percent, to 9,034.69. It ended at 8,000.86, down 148.15, 8.84 percent for the month, making January 2009 the worst January in its 113-year history.

On February 20, the Dow lost nearly half its value, or 47 percent, since its record close sixteen months earlier.

The Dow Jones Industrial Average tumbled on March 2, below 7,000 for the first time in twelve years, as investors appeared to be giving up hope and girding for a prolonged recession. The Dow fell 4.2 percent to 6,763.29, its lowest close since April 1997, thus losing almost one-quarter of its value in 2009, and more than half since its high in October 2007.

On March 23, in reaction to the Treasury secretary's announcement of the Public-Private Investment Program, the Dow soared 6.8 percent or 497.48 points, to 7,775.86, in its biggest gain since October 2008. It finished the first quarter 2009 at 7,608.92, down 13 percent. The string of quarterly declines was the longest stretch since the six quarters that ended in June 1970, and the worst first quarter in percentage terms since 1939.

By the end of April, the Dow was up 24 percent from its March low.

On October 15, 2009, the Dow Jones Industrial Average surged to 10,015.86, passing the symbolic 10,000 level, leaving a 53 percent gain in just seven months. By the end of December 2009 the Dow had risen 61 percent from March and 20 percent for the year. It is the Dow's largest annual gain since 2003, when it rose 25 percent.

See also GENERAL MOTORS; PUBLIC-PRIVATE INVESTMENT FUND; STOCK MARKET.

D.R. HORTON. One of the two largest home builders in the United States, it reported on August 4, 2009, its ninth consecutive quarterly loss, where revenue fell 36 percent to $914.1 million and orders fell 7.5 percent to 5,089.

Cf. PULTE.

DUBAI. By November 2008, the world financial crisis hit Dubai, slamming the door nearly shut on its galloping development. Projects were delayed as tourism was declining and the government explored ways to collect taxes.

Life in the United Arab Emirates changed rapidly. Before 2008, a typical government position paid $3,600 a month; marriage prospects were supported with a free piece of land and about $200,000 to build a house, plus access to a ten- to twenty-year interest-free loan.

Dubai's debt was $50 billion more than the GDP of the entire Emirates in 2006.

On November 24, the UAE began to bail out rattled lenders, consolidated the financial sector, and capped a building spree as it moved to cut spending in the face of the credit crisis.

Dubai's sovereign debt stood at $10 billion, while the debts of state-affiliated companies amounted to $70 billion. By December, Dubai held $90 billion in government assets and $260 billion in assets.

While Dubai started 2008 on a high, it ended the year with the Emirates economic model unraveling. Its problems could mean a drastic change in economic power within the United Arab Emirates.

The United Arab Emirates announced on February 22, 2009, that it would spend $10 billion to bail out the once-highflying emirate of Dubai.

A debt crisis in Dubai in November 2009 brought a stock market tumble throughout Europe and Asia, creating the largest one-day fall in values since April. The sprawling conglomerate—the state-owned Dubai World—sought on November 25 a six-month standstill on interest payments tied to roughly $60 billion in debts.

Dubai gorged on debt and borrowed too much to finance a building boom that went bust in the global meltdown. Dubai's debt debacle has created a new fear that government default by heavily indebted nations is spreading around the globe.

Dubai's stock market fell 6.4 percent as their debt concerns continued to spin downward by 27 percent since November 25, 2009.

Throughout 2009 Abu Dhabi has committed $25 billion to Dubai in subordinated loans yielding a mere 4 percent.

See also MIDDLE EAST.

DUBAI WORLD. *See* DUBAI.

DUNCAN, ARNE. Secretary of the Department of Education in the Obama administration.

See also EDUCATION.

DUPONT. The chemical company posted a fourth-quarter 2008 net loss on a $500 million restructuring charge and cut its 2009 earning guidance amid slowing global chemical demand.

Sales fell 17 percent in its first quarter 2009, and DuPont reported on April 21 that profits fell 59 percent in their product sales volume. First-quarter net income fell to $488 million from $1.2 billion a year before. DuPont expects to cut an additional 2,000 jobs in a restructuring plan announced in April.

DuPont Company's second-quarter profit plunged 61 percent as the meltdown continued for its products. The company reported earnings of $417 million, down from the $10.08 billion a year earlier.

The company's third-quarter 2009 earnings rose 11 percent from a year before to $409 million. Sales declined 18 percent to $5.96 billion.

See also UNEMPLOYMENT.

DURABLE GOODS. Durable goods orders rose 3.4 percent in February 2009, following a 7.3 percent decline in January. There was a 2.1 percent increase in February.

Orders for durable goods fell 0.8 percent in March.

In July 2009, new orders for durable goods increased 4.9 percent from their level in June, suggesting that companies' inventory levels had reached the point where they needed to increase orders to keep pace with demand.

Durable goods were up 2.9 percent in November 2009 with orders up 0.2 percent to a seasonally adjusted $166.87 billion.

DUTCH. *See* NETHERLANDS, THE.

E

EARMARKS. President Obama signed a $410 billion spending bill on March 11, 2009, that included thousands of pet projects inserted by lawmakers, even as he unveiled regulations to restrict such activity.

EARNED INCOME TAX CREDIT. The 2009 economic stimulus plan sought to expand the Earned Income Tax Credit temporarily in order to raise the pay of the working poor.

EARNINGS. *See* COST CUTTING.

EASTERN EUROPE. By the end of November 2008, the European Bank for Reconstruction and Development cut its growth forecast for the region by half. The future appeared to include several years of low or no growth.

On February 17, 2009, the region's currencies were shaken fearing an economic collapse. Nowhere did the economic downfall appear more dangerous than in Eastern Europe.

The average growth among countries of Eastern Europe dropped to 3.2 percent in 2008, from 5.4 percent in 2007.

Since peaking in the summer 2008, Poland's currency slumped 48 percent against the euro; Hungary's had fallen 30 percent, and the Czech Republic's is off 21 percent.

On February 26, 2009, the World Bank, European Bank for Reconstruction and Development (EBRD), and the European Investment Bank announced the offer of $31 billion for struggling banks in Eastern Europe to help head off a precipitous slide in the economies of these nations.

In response to a call for assistance, European Union leaders rejected on March 1, a call for a sweeping bailout, further straining the bonds holding together the twenty-seven EU nations. A special EU fund of up to $241 billion to protect the weakest members was requested.

Governments of the EU had by March already spent $380 billion in bank recapitalizations and put up $3.17 trillion to guarantee banks' loans and try to get credit moving again.

By mid-March the recession hit consumers with higher food prices. In Hungary, monthly food inflation had jumped 2.7 percent in January, as well as in many other Eastern European nations.

In both Slovakia and Latvia, GDP dropped 11.2 percent in the first quarter. Hungary's economy would contract by 2.3 percent.

The IMF forecast a 4.9 percent average decline in GDP, while the EBRD projected a 5.2 percent drop. By June, the biggest concern was the Baltic three, which saw the sharpest falls in GDP. Estonia's first-quarter figures indicated a decline of 15.6 percent, Latvia's drop was 18 percent, and in Lithuania 12.6 percent.

See also CZECH REPUBLIC; EUROPEAN BANK FOR RECONSTRUCTION AND DEVELOPMENT; EUROPEAN UNION; HUNGARY; INTERNATIONAL MONETARY FUND; POLAND; ROMANIA; RUSSIA.

EASTMAN KODAK. The 130-year-old company planned 3,500 to 4,500 more layoffs in 2009, or 14 to 18 percent of its workforce, and disclosed on February 4 that it anticipated a loss from continuing operations of $400 million to $600 million. Sales in 2008 fell 24 percent to $2.43 billion, with film down 27 percent and digital products such as cameras, printers, and picture frames down 30 percent.

The company's first-quarter net loss widened to about triple last year's level. Kodak's cash shrank 40 percent to $1.3 billion.

On July 30, Eastman Kodak posted a second-quarter 2009 loss of $189 million; its gross profit margin fell to 18.5 percent, and revenue declined by 29 percent.

On October 29, 2009, the company announced that it had lost $111 million in the third quarter, as sales fell 26 percent. Sales dropped to $1.78 billion from $2.41 billion.

EATON CORPORATION. A diversified manufacturer in Cleveland, Ohio, it announced on January 20, 2009, that it planned to cut 5,200 jobs, or about 6 percent of its workforce. This figure was in addition to the 3,400 layoffs announced in the second half of 2008, bringing the total to 10 percent.

Eaton posted a 39 percent decline in third-quarter 2009 profit, declining to $193 million from $315 million a year before. The firm's net sales in the quarter dropped 26 percent to $3.03 billion.

EBAY. First-quarter profit in 2009 dropped 22 percent amid consumer reluctance to spend in the meltdown economy. EBay's revenue fell 8 percent from a year before, to $2.02 billion.

EBRD. *See* EUROPEAN BANK FOR RECONSTRUCTION AND DEVELOPMENT.

EC. *See* EUROPEAN COMMISSION.

ECB. *See* EUROPEAN CENTRAL BANK.

ECONOMIC NATIONALISM. The urge to keep jobs and capital at home. This urges banks to support businesses and jobs within their boundaries, not abroad.
See also NATIONALIZATION; PROTECTIONISM.

ECONOMIC OUTPUT. *See* GLOBAL ECONOMIC OUTPUT.

ECONOMIC PEARL HARBOR. *See* BUFFET, WARREN E.

ECONOMIC RECOVERY ADVISORY BOARD. *See* VOLCKER, PAUL.

ECONOMIC STIMULUS PLAN. Final bill following negotiations between members of the U.S. House of Representatives and the U.S. Senate. Signed into law by President Obama on February 17, 2009, as the American Recovery and Reinvestment Act (of 2009).
See also AMERICAN RECOVERY AND REINVESTMENT ACT (OF 2009).
Cf. ECONOMIC STIMULUS PLAN (BILL FROM HOUSE OF REPRESENTATIVES); ECONOMIC STIMULUS PLAN (BILL FROM SENATE).

ECONOMIC STIMULUS PLAN (BILL FROM HOUSE OF REPRESENTATIVES). The House passed an $819 billion tax-and-spending bill on Wednesday, January 28, 2009, to reshape policies on energy, education, health care, and social programs. Major goals included:

- doubling generating capacity for renewable energy over three years.
- undertaking a program to weatherize 75 percent of federal buildings and 2 million homes.
- computerize every American's health record within five years.
- launch a school-modernization program, sufficient to upgrade 10,000 schools.
- enact a large investment increase in roads, bridges, and major transit systems.

The Senate measure, to come to a vote in early February, was valued at nearly $900 billion. Not a single Republican voted for the House bill. The act, signed by the president, would be called the American Recovery and Reinvestment Act (of 2009).

See also AMERICAN RECOVERY AND REINVESTMENT ACT (OF 2009); EARNED INCOME TAX CREDIT; MAKING WORK PAY; STIMULUS PLAN (EUROZONE).

Cf. ECONOMIC STIMULUS PLAN (BILL FROM SENATE).

ECONOMIC STIMULUS PLAN (BILL FROM SENATE). On February 6, 2009, the U.S. Senate completed what became an $827 billion stimulus bill, only slightly more than the $820 billion cost of the measure adopted by the House.

The plan, as with the House plan, was intended to blunt the recession with a combination of tax cuts and government spending on public works and other programs to create more than 3 million jobs.

The Senate bill cut $40 billion of aid to help states and localities and created $30 billion in tax incentives to encourage people to buy homes and cars within 2009.

Another significant difference between the House and Senate bill was the Senate's inclusion of nearly $70 billion to protect thousands of middle-class Americans from paying the alternative minimum tax in 2009, sparing them from a system originally intended to prevent the wealthy from claiming too many tax deductions.

The Senate version also eliminated $19.5 billion in construction aid for schools and colleges and sliced proposed new aid for the Head Start program.

On Tuesday, February 10, the Senate passed the $838 billion stimulus bill, beginning the process. The act, signed by the president, would be called the American Recovery and Reinvestment Act (of 2009).

See also AMERICAN RECOVERY AND REINVESTMENT ACT (OF 2009).

Cf. ECONOMIC STIMULUS PLAN (BILL FROM HOUSE OF REPRESENTATIVES).

ECONOMY (U.S.). On August 1, 2009, the American economy's decline of 1 percent indicated that there would be a turnaround in the second half of the year. On October 29, the government unofficially announced that the country had emerged from the longest economic contraction since World War II. The GDP grew at an annual rate of 3.5 percent in the quarter ending in September 2009, matching its average growth rate of the last 80 years.

See also GROSS DOMESTIC PRODUCT; RECESSION OF 2007–2010.

ECUADOR. Borrowed $2.58 billion in 2009 from regional lenders after defaulting on its international debt for the second time in a decade.

Ecuador made a $30.9 million interest payment on its Global 2015 bonds, despite vowing to stop paying some other debts.

See also LATIN AMERICA.

EDDIE BAUER HOLDINGS. A specialty retailer, it announced in January 2009 that it was eliminating 193 jobs, or about 15 percent of its nonretail staff.

The company filed for Chapter 11 bankruptcy protection on June 17. With 371 stores in North America, it is seeking to sell the company.

On July 17 Eddie Bauer Holdings was successfully auctioned for a purchase price of $286 million. Initially, it would keep the majority of the retailer's stores open.

EDUCATION. The American Recovery and Reinvestment Act (of 2009) provided $100 billion in emergency aid for public schools and colleges. With the stimulus program, the budget of the department doubled. The bill, signed by President Obama on February 18, 2009, doubled federal spending on disadvantaged and disabled children, for Head Start, and school renovation.

Most of the funds, $54 billion, would be used to prevent public-sector layoffs, mostly in schools. Another $5 billion was for setting high standards and narrowing achievement gaps between poor and affluent students.

See also AMERICAN RECOVERY AND REINVESTMENT ACT (OF 2009); CHARTER SCHOOLS; HARVARD UNIVERSITY; PREP SCHOOLS; RACE TO THE TOP PROGRAM; YALE UNIVERSITY.

EDUCATION JOBS. *See* UNEMPLOYMENT.

EGYPT. *See* MIDDLE EAST.

EISENHOWER, DWIGHT DAVID. *See* FEDERAL AID HIGHWAY ACT (OF 1956); OBAMA, BARACK.

EL CENTRO, CALIFORNIA. See UNEMPLOYMENT.

ELDERLY, THE. The number of unemployed workers seventy-five and older increased to more than 73,000 in January 2009, up 46 percent from the prior January. Among workers sixty-five and older, the jobless rate stood at 5.7 percent. Although below the national average, it was well above what it was in previous recessions, including the recession of 1981, when it reached 4.3 percent.

The percentage of people sixty-five and older who are in the workforce rose to 16.8 percent at year-end, from 11.9 percent a decade earlier. Among those who are seventy-five and older, the increase was even greater, to 7.3 percent from 4.7 percent.

See also UNEMPLOYMENT.

ELECTRIC CARS. *See* AUTOMOBILE INDUSTRY; CHINA.

ELECTRIC GRID. *See* AMERICAN RECOVERY AND REINVESTMENT ACT (OF 2009).

ELECTRICITY. The recession sent demand and rates for electricity lower. By August 2009 it was clear that electricity demand had fallen 4.4 percent in the first half of the year.

Electricity sales remained sluggish in the third quarter 2009. Overall electricity sales declined 3.3 percent in the year.

ELECTROLUX. The largest European appliance maker, based in Sweden, it announced on December 15, 2008, that it would fall short of its yearly earnings forecast and cut more than 3,000 jobs globally as a result of an abrupt slowdown in demand. On October 26, 2009, it posted a 93 percent rise in third-quarter net profit amid cost cuts, higher prices, and lower raw-material costs, a net profit of $239.9 million.

See also SWEDEN.

ELECTRONIC HEALTH RECORDS. Under the $787 billion stimulus package, approved in February 2009, more than $20 billion was set aside for health-information technology. Doctors using electronic records would be eligible for more than $40,000 each in incentive payments over several years beginning in 2011. Hospitals would also qualify for millions of dollars in incentive payments. Doctors and hospitals not going electronic by 2015 would be subject to penalties.

Synonymous with ELECTRONIC MEDICAL RECORDS.

ELECTRONIC MEDICAL RECORDS. *Synonymous with* ELECTRONIC HEALTH RECORDS.

EMERGENCY ECONOMIC STABILIZATION ACT OF 2008. Signed into law by President George W. Bush on October 3, 2008. It was a $700 billion bailout package to minimize the impact of a financial meltdown. Initially rejected by the House of Representatives, the Senate version approved the funds with a higher limit for insured bank deposits and tax breaks for businesses and alternative energy. The Treasury secretary, Henry Paulson Jr., was given access of up to $700 billion to purchase and later resell troubled securities clogging the financial system. Needed support was also given by the Federal Reserve chairman, Ben Bernanke.

The bailout plan attempted to place a dollar value on mortgage-related assets that no one appeared to want in order to move them off the books of ailing banks and unlock the frozen credit markets. The U.S. Treasury would not manage the mortgage assets alone. Instead, they outsourced nearly all the work to professionals, who oversaw huge portfolios of bonds and other securities for management fees.

The asset-management firms received a portion of the $250 billion that Congress allowed the Treasury to spend in the first phase of the bailout. Some of the funds were used to help restructure many subprime mortgages in the hopes of enabling troubling homeowners to avoid foreclosure.

The 2008 federal deficit was $455 billion, or about 3.3 percent of gross domestic product.

The government said it would temporarily guarantee $1.5 trillion worth of new senior debt issued by banks, as well as insuring $500 billion in deposits in noninterest-bearing accounts. The potential cost of the bailout package might be $2.25 trillion, triple the size of the original bailout rescue plan.

See also AUDITORS; BERNANKE, BEN; BRETTON WOODS II; CAPITAL REQUIREMENTS DIRECTIVE; FINANCIAL STABILITY OVERSIGHT BOARD; GREENSPAN, ALAN; RESOLUTION TRUST CORPORATION; REVULSION STAGE; SUBPRIME; TROUBLED ASSET RELIEF PROGRAM.

Cf. AMERICAN RECOVERY AND REINVESTMENT ACT (OF 2009).

EMERGING MARKETS. At first these economies (including Poland, Hungary, Ukraine) seemed healthy, even thriving, but they were swept up in global financial panic by the end of October 2008.

Of the four biggest emerging markets, Brazil, Russia, India, and China, India has the largest current-account deficit, which widened to 3.6 percent of GDP in the second quarter of 2008.

See also BRAZIL; CHINA; INDIA; RUSSIA; WORLD BANK.

EMERSON ELECTRIC. A maker of industrial-automation equipment, power systems, and heating and cooling gear, it reported on May 5, 2009, a 32 percent drop in fiscal second-quarter earnings. Revenue fell 16 percent to $5.09 billion. Sales for 2010 were estimated to decline by 10 percent.

EMPLOYEE FREE CHOICE ACT. Supported by union leaders in March 2009, the bill would make it easier for unions to recruit workers because it would permit them to join unions merely by signing cards rather than through secret-ballot elections where firms can campaign against the union.

EMPLOYMENT. *See* UNEMPLOYMENT.

EMPTY CREDITOR. A hypothesis that purchasers of credit insurance can profit by permitting, or even encouraging, firms to file for bankruptcy. Used by credit-default swaps where traders insure themselves against a firm's default. Empty creditors are investors who hedge with credit-default swaps and benefit if firms fail because the payout on the swap would make them whole on the value of their debt.

See also CREDIT-DEFAULT SWAP.

ENDOWMENTS. The value of university endowments fell about 23 percent on average in the four months ending on November 2008. Many universities were predicting layoffs following the stock market decline, the worst since the 1970s.

By the end of June 2009 when the fiscal year ends for endowments, the five largest single-school endowments acknowledged a decline of 25 to 30 percent. Specifically, by the end of June the two largest higher education endowments lost 30 percent in their value. Combined, Yale and Harvard lost a staggering $17.8 billion.

See also BRANDEIS UNIVERSITY; COLUMBIA UNIVERSITY; HARVARD UNIVERSITY; STANFORD UNIVERSITY; YALE UNIVERSITY.

ENERGY. *See* ELECTRICITY.

ENERGY DEPARTMENT. *See* U.S. ENERGY DEPARTMENT.

ENERGY EFFICIENCY. The American Recovery and Reinvestment Act, signed by President Obama on February 17, 2009, called for $80 billion to be used to promote energy efficiency, renewable energy sources, higher-mileage cars, and coal technology that is cleaner.

Of the $25 billion provided for energy efficiency, more than half was aimed at helping low-income households weatherize 1 million homes and helping governments at all levels retrofit public buildings.

Tax incentives of $20 billion were offered for wind, solar, hydroelectric, and other renewable power sources; $11 billion in grants and $6 billion in loans would help modernize the electric grid and increase its capacity to deliver power generated by renewable sources. In addition, $2 billion was made available for research into advanced car batteries and $3.4 billion to develop coal-fired power plants that could capture and store greenhouse gases.

See also AMERICAN RECOVERY AND REINVESTMENT ACT (OF 2009).

ENFORCEMENT. *See* REGULATION.

ENTERPRISE. A car-rental firm, it laid off 2,000 employees, about 3 percent of its workforce in November 2008 to trim about $200 million from its overall cost structure. Enterprise sought TARP funds.

Cf. AVIS; HERTZ.

ENTITLEMENTS. A guarantee of access to benefits because of rights, or by agreement through law. Often refers to a person's belief that one is deserving of some particular reward or benefit.

ENVIRONMENT. *See* GREEN ENVIRONMENT.

ENVIRONMENTAL CLEANUP. *See* AMERICAN RECOVERY AND REINVESTMENT ACT (OF 2009).

EQUITY BUYOUT. The purchase of a company without using any borrowed money, the "leveraged" portion of a leveraged buyout.
See also LEVERAGED BUYOUT FIRMS.

ERICSSON. The world's largest telecommunications-network company by sales, it posted a 31 percent drop in fourth-quarter 2008 net profits. It had already cut 4,000 workers in 2008 and projected another 5,000 people would be released, or about 6.4 percent of its work force.

Ericsson reported a first-quarter 2009 profit drop of 35 percent, falling to $212.9 million, and a 56 percent drop to $111.3 million in the second quarter.
See also SONY CORPORATION.

ESCADA. An international women's luxury fashion company. On August 13, 2009, Escada filed for bankruptcy protection.

ESPRIT HOLDINGS. Manufacturer of apparel, accessories, and housewares. In February 2009, it reported a 13 percent decline in first-half net profit, its first earnings decline since 1998. The company noted that the global economic downturn had squeezed its operating profit margin.

ESTEE LAUDER. Beauty brand and perfume maker, it reported in February 2009 sharply lower sales and a 30 percent drop in profit for its fiscal second quarter, ending December 31.

Reported on May 3, a fiscal third-quarter 70 percent drop in profits. Posted sales of $1.7 billion were down 9.8 percent from a year earlier. Profit was $27.2 million, down from $90.1 million the year before.

ESTONIA. GDP fell by 3.5 percent in the third quarter of 2008. There were concerns that without an improved social safety net, the public would suffer greatly, as unemployment could hit 20 percent during the meltdown.

By the end of October 2009 Estonia set its 2010 budget with a deficit of 2.95 percent.
See also BALTICS; LATVIA.

ETF. *See* EXCHANGE-TRADED FUND.

EU. *See* EUROPEAN UNION.

EURO. The single currency of most European Union nations designed to replace the currencies of individual nations. There are seven euro-denominated notes and eight coins. Starting January 2002, the euro became the official legal tender of these countries (the eurozone).

On February 13, 2009, figures showed that the eurozone GDP shrank at an annualized rate of around 5 percent in the fourth quarter of 2008. GDP was projected by the IMF to decline by 2 percent in 2009, and then barely recover in 2010. By year's end 2009 the euro was considered overvalued by between 7 and 8 percent relative to other major currencies.

See also DOLLAR (U.S.); EUROPEAN CENTRAL BANK; EURO-ZONE; EXCHANGE RATES; ICELAND.

EURODOLLARS. Dollar balances held by private people or firms in European banks. They provide a stock of international currency not appearing in governmental returns. Traffic is not confined to dollars. It is also a fund of international short-term capital that usually flows to those nations offering the highest interest rates. The system came into being in 1957.

See also LIBOR.

EUROFIRST. *See* FTSE.

EUROPEAN AERONAUTIC DEFENSE AND SPACE. *See* AIRBUS.

EUROPEAN BANK. *Synonymous with* EUROPEAN BANK FOR RECONSTRUCTION AND DEVELOPMENT.

EUROPEAN BANK FOR RECONSTRUCTION AND DEVELOPMENT (EBRD). Commenced operations in April 1991 to help former Soviet-bloc nations make the transition to market economies.

The bank forecast in November 2008 that Eastern Europe's economic growth would fall by half in 2009, to 3 percent, as a result of declining consumption and rising unemployment.

In February 2009, the bank warned that the economic crisis "is threatening to throw nearly two decades of economic reform into reverse."

In its annual report 2009 EBRD reported that the combined GDP of the 29 nations in which it invests would shrink 6.3 percent for the year, with the region hit harder than other emerging markets.

See also EASTERN EUROPE.

Synonymous with EUROPEAN BANK; EUROPEAN DEVELOPMENT BANK.

EUROPEAN CAR SALES. *See* AUTOMOBILE INDUSTRY.

EUROPEAN CENTRAL BANK (ECB). Inaugurated in Frankfurt, Germany, on June 1, 1998, and became operational on January 1, 1999. It set interest rates along with the participating member national central bank chiefs in the eurozone.

On November 6, 2008, the ECB reduced its main borrowing gauge by a half percentage point, to 3.25 percent. In Britain, the Bank of England cut its benchmark interest rate by 1.5 percentage points. The new rate, at 3 percent, was the lowest the country had seen since 1954.

On December 18, the central bank reduced the return it gave banks to deposit money with it overnight and lifted its emergency lending rate in an effort to jolt banks into lending more to one another.

In mid-January 2009, the ECB slashed its main interest rate by a half percentage point to 2 percent as it sought to protect the 330 million people in the sixteen countries that use the euro against a deepening recession.

The ECB said in January that the number of counterfeit euro bank notes it removed from circulation rose 19 percent in 2008 to 666,000. The twenty-euro bill was most popular among forgers, accounting for 43 percent of notes taken from circulation.

The ECB developed guidelines to prevent bailout plans from one country being significantly more generous than plans from another.

On March 5, the ECB cut its main interest rate by a half point to 1.5 percent, the lowest since the creation of the euro and the bank itself ten years earlier.

The president of ECB said in mid-March that Europe didn't need to boost spending more to combat the global financial crisis, giving the bank's support in Europe's battle with the United States over how to overcome the economic recession.

On April 2, the ECB cut its key rate by a quarter percentage point to 1.25 percent.

The ECB forecast further financial-sector weakness restraining countries from expanding their economies before mid-2010.

By the end of June, the ECB pumped $622 billion into its lenders to revive the sagging eurozone economy.

On July 2, the bank left its main interest rate steady for the second consecutive month.

On October 8, 2009, the ECB left its key interest rate unchanged at 1 percent, indicating concerns for growth in the future.

On December 3, the ECB took steps to absorb some of the hundreds of billions of euros it gave to banks. Now the ECB is planning to pull back some of its stimulus aid as inflation remained just under 2 percent, considered low.

By year's end 2009 the ECB reported that banks in the eurozone faced higher losses than earlier thought. Updated losses for all loans and securities were $796.57 billion for 2007 to 2010.

On December 30, 2009 the ECB reported lending to the private sector was down 0.7 percent from November 2008, the third straight month of decline, reflecting a lower demand for credit.

See also EUROZONE; EUROZONE LENDING; FINANCIAL PROTEC-TIONISM; SWITZERLAND.

EUROPEAN CLEAN URBAN TRANSPORTATION INITIATIVE. *See* EUROPEAN COMMISSION.

EUROPEAN COMMISSION (EC). The European Commission is the driving force of EU policy and the starting point for every European Union action, presenting proposals and drafts for legislation. It is obliged to act in behalf of its members. The EC has law-making powers and is the guardian of its treaties. It monitors applications for new members and institutes infringement proceedings in the event of any violation of its laws.

The EC announced at the end of November 2008 a stimulus package worth 130 billion euros aimed at bolstering the bloc's economy.

On November 24, the EC outlined a €200 billion (US$254 billion) wish list of measures for Europe to spend its way out of recession and gave national capitals permission to temporarily break budget-deficit ceilings if required. This amounted to 1.5 percent of the EU's GDP, calling for the twenty-seven member governments to provide €170 billion of the total. The remaining €30 billion would come from the EU budget and the European Investment Bank.

The bank also announced that it would provide the automobile industry of Europe with €4 billion in low-interest loans in both 2009 and 2010, as part of the European Clean Urban Transportation Initiative. The European Commission would spend €5 billion over two years for the same ends.

The EC agreed in mid-December to loosen rules on state subsidies to allow governments to double the amount of money, to $720,000, that they could pump into cash-strapped firms without first checking with regulators.

On December 19, the EC declared that there were "substantial downward risks regarding economic prospects for 2009 as well as 2010. The euro-area economy has entered into recession territory."

See also AUTOMOBILE INDUSTRY; DERIVATIVE(S); STIMULUS PLAN (EUROZONE); and individual countries.

EUROPEAN DEVELOPMENT BANK. *Synonymous with* EUROPEAN BANK FOR RECONSTRUCTION AND DEVELOPMENT.

EUROPEAN INVESTMENT BANK. Authorized by the Treaty of Rome in 1957, the bank provides loans and guarantees in all economic sectors of the EU, especially to promote the development of less-developed regions, to modernize or convert undertakings or create new jobs, and to assist projects of common interest to several member states.

On March 12, 2009, the European Investment Bank approved €3 billion in loans to the European automotive industry.

See also EUROPEAN COMMISSION (EC); KOENIGSEGG; UNITED KINGDOM.

EUROPEAN PARLIAMENT. Although the Parliament cannot enact laws, it has a co-decision procedure that empowers it to veto legislation in certain policy areas. It can question the European Commission, amend or reject the EU budget, and dismiss the entire Commission through a vote of censure.

A law was passed on January 13, 2009, to help mutual funds expand abroad. The bill lets funds regulated by the European Union attract investors anywhere in the region with a harmonized, two-page offering document.

It has now made it easier for mutual funds to merge and allows asset managers to manage funds more easily across the EU. Management firms can easily notify regulators when they want to offer new products across the EU. It was estimated that fund managers could save €6 billion to €8 billion each year.

EUROPEAN SYSTEMIC RISK COUNCIL (PROPOSED). *See* EUROPEAN UNION.

EUROPEAN TOURISM. *See* TOURISM.

EUROPEAN UNION (EU). The twenty-seven nations of western and central Europe. The EU was created by means of the Treaty of Maastricht, signed on February 7, 1992. The EU is governed by five institutions.

On December 2, 2008, finance ministers called for EU member states to inject an average of 1.3 percent of their own GDP into the economy.

At the end of December, the EU approved bank rescue measures for many of the continent's major economic powers, clearing the way for cash injections and loan guarantees expected to help lenders through the financial crisis.

The EU announced in mid-January 2009 that the economy in the sixteen nations that use the euro would shrink by 1.9 percent in 2009, with the entire EU contracting 1.8 percent, and that 3.5 million jobs would disappear in 2009. At the same time, the EU predicted a moderate recovery in 2010, when the EU could grow 0.5 percent.

Finance ministers of the EU agreed on February 10 to guidelines for handling bad assets on banks' balance sheets. Principles for governments helping resuscitate banks hurt by nonperforming loans and other impaired assets were spelled out. Remedies included the formation of a so-called bad bank or series of bad banks to hold troubled assets. The guidelines call for a "correct and consistent approach of valuation" for these assets selected. The goal was to restore bank lending while preserving a level playing field across the EU.

On February 27, unemployment rose in the EU to 8.2 percent, up from 8 percent in December. Inflation slowed to 1.1 percent from 1.6 percent in December 2008 as businesses cut costs across the board.

By March the EU feared that the jobless rate would increase to 10 percent, but its governments continued to argue that there was no immediate need for further fiscal stimulus measures. While the unemployment rate in the twenty-seven nations had dipped below 7 percent in 2008, it rose to 7.6 percent in January 2009. Spain had the highest at 14.8 percent in January, while the Netherlands the lowest at 2.8 percent.

The EU reversed course on assistance to Eastern Europe's troubled nations, by doubling a fund to €50 billion. On March 21, the twenty-seven countries put aside funds by offering $102.55 billion for the IMF to rescue economies.

The International Monetary Fund estimated in April that nations of the EU would have to write down $1.19 trillion in loans and securities.

The EU announced on May 3 that the ongoing recession would last at least six months longer than originally expected and predicted a 4 percent contraction for the EU economy in 2009, more than double its earlier forecast.

EU economies contracted sharply in the first quarter. The economy in every major European nation fell. For the EU as a whole including the sixteen countries that use the euro, GDP shrank by 2.5 percent in the first quarter, or at a 10 percent annual rate.

Meeting on June 18, EU leaders agreed to broad principles for forming new supranational financial supervisors, stopping short of giving those regulators the power to force national governments to bail out firms. The Brussels two-day summit meeting concluded its session by endorsing the creation of a European Systemic Risk Council to track the financial system for stability. A second group would set standards for governments to supervise banks, insurers, and other financial firms.

The EU bounced back with strength in the second quarter 2009. A significant improvement from the first quarter with rebounds primarily in France and Germany. Their economies both grew following four negative quarters.

On October 1, 2009, the EU declared that their largest twenty-two banks would survive a potential $485 billion in credit losses in 2009.

See also EUROPEAN PARLIAMENT; EUROZONE; ICELAND; STRESS TESTS.

EUROZONE. In 2003, twelve EU nations adopted a cooperative single-currency effort, now extended to most of the twenty-seven countries of the EU. In 2008, sixteen of the European Union countries were part of the eurozone.

The eurozone slipped into a recession during the third quarter of 2008. The figures pointed to the region's first recession since the inception of the euro in 1999.

There was a sharp increase in imports into the eurozone compared with a surplus in 2007. Statistics of the EU indicated that the external trade deficit of the countries using the euro totaled $7.1 billion.

Following concerns of increased inflation, with the economic crisis in the fall 2008, eurozone inflation declined in November. Evidence of a slowdown showed that consumer price inflation in the eurozone fell by 1.1 percentage points to 2.1 percent. It was expected that the inflation rates would fall below 1 percent in 2009 and might even turn negative.

The economies of nations sharing the euro had their worst performance in three decades. GDP shrank an annualized 5.9 percent in the fourth quarter.

The eurozone's manufacturing sector had its worst month in more than 10 years in February, the ninth consecutive month of contraction.

In the final three months of 2008, the number of people at work in the then fifteen countries that used the euro plummeted by 453,000, an acceleration from the 80,000 jobs lost in the third quarter. This represented a drop in employment of 0.3 percent in the fourth quarter, compared with a fall of 0.1 percent in the prior period.

In February, eurozone industrial producer prices posted their biggest year-on-year decline since 1999, while retail sales had their largest drop since 2000, when records were first kept.

The International Monetary Fund reported in April that their bank reported just $154 billion in write-downs by the end of 2008, and in 2009 still faced $750 billion in projected write-downs.

The inflation rate across the eurozone dropped to zero in May, its lowest in thirteen years of records, underlining the increasing risk of deflation—a damaging decline in wages and prices that could dampen recovery prospects worldwide. Prices are declining in six of the nations that share the euro.

The eurozone reported a trade surplus in May. Non-seasonally adjusted figures indicated that the surplus narrowed to $2.7 billion in May.

Consumer prices in the eurozone fell for the first time ever in June, while an index of producer prices fell by 6.6 percent in June from a year before, the sharpest fall since records began in 1982.

Unemployment in the eurozone nations rose in July 2009 to the highest level in more than ten years. The jobless rate rose to 9.5 percent, the highest reading since May 1999. Nearly 22 million people in the EU were out of work. The EC estimated that the nations of the eurozone would see their economies stop contracting in the third quarter 2009.

The eurozone had its fourth straight monthly increase in industrial output in August 2009. Industrial output in the sixteen countries increased 0.9 percent that month from July. Output growth was greatest in Germany, up 1.5 percent from July, France grew 1.5 percent, and Italy's factory output rose 7 percent.

The eurozone's trade balance swung to a deficit in August 2009, from a surplus in July after exports declined to their lowest level in four and a half years. The nations of the eurozone reported a combined trade deficit of $5.97 billion. Unemployed rose to 9.6 percent in August and 9.7 percent in September 2009.

In the third quarter 2009, the eurozone economy returned to modest growth, marking the end of five months of recession. Economic activity expanded at an annualized rate of 1.5 percent in the period from July to September.

Eurozone producer prices rose 0.2 percent in October from September. Producer prices fell 6.7 percent from October 2008.

Bank lending fell in October 2009 and at the fastest rate on record. Credit to the private sector was down 0.8 percent from a year before.

By November the pace of economic recovery gained momentum, with economic activity increasing 0.55 in November from 0.33 in October. Industrial producer prices rose by 0.2 percent but was still 6.7 percent lower than a year before.

See also CONSUMER-PRICE INFLATION; DEFLATION; EUROPEAN CENTRAL BANK; EUROPEAN COMMISSION; EUROPEAN UNION; EUROZONE LENDING; ICELAND; IRELAND; UNITED KINGDOM.

EUROZONE LENDING. In 2008, eurozone loans stagnated as the economy slumped and lenders tightened credit standards. Lending had expanded at the slowest rate in seventeen years. The annual growth of lending to the private sector slowed to 7.1 percent in November, from a rate of 7.8 percent in October. The annual growth rate of loans to households fell to a low of 2.5 percent in November, from 3.3 percent in October.

See also AMERICAN RECOVERY AND REINVESTMENT ACT (OF 2009); EUROPEAN CENTRAL BANK; EUROZONE.

EVERGREENING. *See* ZOMBIES.

EXCHANGE RATES. Most major currencies have weakened against the dollar since the end of 2008. By April 22, 2009, the biggest loser has been the Swiss franc, which fell by 8.4 percent in 2009. The euro, the Korean won, and the Swedish krona also weakened by more than 6 percent against the U.S. dollar, and the yen has fallen by 7.6 percent. The British pound has risen by 1.1 percent against the dollar, but only after collapsing against the dollar in 2008.

EXCHANGE-TRADED FUND (ETF). An investment that uses futures to hedge against broad market declines instead of shorting individual stocks. ETF fees are small compared with management charges by many hedge funds. ETFs did not exist more than a decade ago; today there are nearly 1,000 U.S. listings. Originally ETFs dealt with passive investments in specific securities.

Cf. HEDGE FUNDS.

EXECUTIVE COMPENSATION LEGISLATION. Proposal to give shareholders the right to vote on compensation and require that independent directors sit on compensation committees. If enacted it would allow regulators to prohibit inappropriate or risky compensation practices for banks and other financial institutions.

By mid-September 2009, this legislation had passed the House of Representatives, but had yet to be considered by the Senate.

See also EXECUTIVE PAY; HOUSE (U.S.) FINANCIAL OVERHAUL PLAN.

EXECUTIVE PAY. Many have criticized the six- and seven-figure paychecks that Wall Street's top brass collected in pre-2008 years while driving their companies—and the entire financial system—into the ground.

President Obama, on February 4, 2009, laid out a plan for executive compensation, with a cap of $500,000 for top executives at firms that accepted "extraordinary assistance" from the government, except for restricted stock. The pay would be disclosed to shareholders for a nonbinding vote. Bonuses would be clawed back if they provided misleading information. No golden parachutes would be permitted upon severance, and the board would decide policies on luxuries such as airplanes and entertainment. The rules were not retroactive to firms that had already been bailed out.

A provision of the $787 billion economic stimulus plan imposes restrictions on executive bonuses at financial institutions. The restriction prevented top executives from receiving bonuses that exceed one-third of their annual pay. Any bonus would have to be in the form of long-term incentives, like restricted stocks, which would not be cashed out until the TARP money was paid back in full.

On March 22, the president called for increased oversight of executive pay at all Wall Street institutions, as part of a sweeping plan to overhaul financial regulations. The president was seeking a broader new role for the Federal Reserve to oversee large firms, including major hedge funds, proposing that numerous derivatives and other exotic financial instruments that contributed to the crisis be traded on exchanges or through clearinghouses so they are more transparent and can be more rigorously regulated. It also called for federal standards for mortgage lenders beyond what the Federal Reserve adopted in 2008, as well as greater enforcement of mortgage regulations.

See also AUSTRALIA; CLAWBACKS; COMPENSATION; EXECUTIVE COMPENSATION LEGISLATION; FEDERAL RESERVE; FINANCIAL REGULATION PLAN (2009); GOLDEN PARACHUTE; HOUSE (U.S.) FINANCIAL OVERHAUL PLAN; NAME AND SHAME.

EX-IM BANK. *See* EXPORT-IMPORT BANK.

EXPAND REGULATORY POWERS LEGISLATION. Proposal that would give the FDIC the power to seize and liquidate any troubled financial institution; it would require hedge funds to register with the SEC and to open their books. The legislation gives the Federal Reserve the power to regulate and oversee any large financial institution, whose failure would threaten the economy.

By mid-September 2009, there had been no action in either the House or Senate committees. There has been much disagreement over whether the Fed should be a systematic regulator.

EXPORT-IMPORT BANK (EX-IM BANK). Created in 1934 to help fight the Great Depression.

See also BOEING.

EXPORTS (U.S.). The spiraling financial crisis severely affected the U.S. export market. The trade deficit widened in October 2008 for the first time in three months as exports dropped 2.2 percent, with large declines in sales of American-made products like automobiles and consumer goods. China, one of the larger sources of export demand, had cut back sharply.

October exports totaled $151.7 billion. Sales of U.S.-made cars and car parts fell $236 million, consumer goods exports dropped $156 million, and industrial supply sales fell $1.4 billion.

Export by the end of 2008 and into 2009 declined in almost every country as the world endured a recession. The decline began in the summer of 2008 after Lehman Brothers failed. Credit became harder to obtain for importers and confidence waned among would-be buyers of many products. Overall, the total reported exports from 43 countries peaked in July 2008 at $1.03 trillion. By November, it was down 26 percent to $766 billion.

In February 2009, U.S. exports rose by 1.6 percent to $126.8 billion, the first gain since July 2008.

Farming exports, once a major source of income for U.S. farmers, declined during the meltdown. Developing nations were slowing their food imports, the price of dairy products was slumping, and the strengthening U.S. dollar made imports more costly. Farm commodities fell 40 to 50 percent from six months before. Farm exports, which account for about 20 percent of the value of farm production, dropped to $96 billion in 2009, from $117 billion in 2008.

By the end of the first quarter, exports from the United States declined 30 percent from the previous three months.

The dollar value of exports, which surged in July 2009, rose another 0.2 percent in August. That put exports at their highest gain since December 2008, but still 21 percent below the same time one year earlier.

See also AUTOMOBILE INDUSTRY; TRADE DEFICIT.
Cf. IMPORTS.

EXXON (EXXON-MOBIL). The energy company reported on July 30 that its second-quarter 2009 profit tumbled 66 percent. Its net income fell to $3.95 billion from $11.68 billion one year before.

F

FACTORY ORDERS. Factory orders declined 0.8 percent in August 2009 from a month before, following four months of increases. Orders rose 0.6 percent in October, the sixth gain in seven months. Durable goods orders rose 0.6 percent, and nondurable goods 1.6 percent.

See also DURABLE GOODS.

FAILED BANKS. By August 1, 2009, regulators, usually the Federal Deposit Insurance Corporation, had closed 68 failed banks nationwide in 2009, compared with 25 in 2008 and 3 in 2007. It would reach 100 by mid-October 2009. By mid-November the FDIC had taken over 150 failed banks.

See also BANK FAILURES; COLONIAL BANCGROUP; MARKET CAPITALIZATION.

FALLEN ANGELS. Blue-chip companies at risk of losing investment-grade ratings. A cut to junk status invariably adds to financing risks. Before the meltdown, banks were healthy enough and provided alternative funding. And high-yield investors were keen to purchase bonds from large firms as the bank debt was refinanced.

Today, a downgrade to junk may be just the start of a firm's problems. If financing is unavailable, and raising equity proves troublesome, management can be forced into disposals or spending cuts that further harm credit quality. This could lead fallen angels to continue their fall.

FALLING PRICES. *Synonymous with* DEFLATION.

FANNIE MAE (FEDERAL NATIONAL MORTGAGE ASSOCIATION) (FNMA). An independent, government-sponsored enterprise (GSE) agency originally chartered in 1938 and reconstituted in 1954. Its major function is to purchase mortgages from banks, trust companies, mortgage companies, savings and loan associations, and insurance companies to help these institutions with their distribution of funds for home mortgages.

Nicknamed Fannie Mae, the mortgage finance company is now under government control. On March 20, 2008, federal regulators eased Fannie Mae's capital requirements, a move that allowed the agency to buy an additional billion dollars of mortgage securities.

The U.S. mortgage financial company announced on November 10 a $29 billion loss for the third quarter and that it was losing money so fast that it would have to tap the federal government for cash to avoid shutting down. Along with Freddie Mac, Fannie Mae owns or guarantees about half of all mortgages in the United States. Credit expenses soared to $9.2 billion in the quarter as mortgage credit conditions deteriorated and as home prices declined.

On November 11, both Freddie Mac and Fannie Mae announced that they planned a broad new effort to reduce the loan burdens of homeowners facing foreclosure. The program was offered to people who are at least ninety days behind on their payments. The goal was to modify the mortgage—most likely by reducing the interest rate—so that the monthly loan payment would be no higher than 38 percent of the borrower's monthly income. The plan would help as many as 300,000 families that are delinquent in their mortgage payments.

Borrowers would have to provide evidence that they had suffered a hardship, such as losing a job. They would have to be occupying the home, and they would have to go through a ninety-day trial period before the loan modification became final.

On February 26, 2009, Fannie Mae reported a $25.2 billion loss for the fourth quarter 2008, with homeowner defaults continuing to increase even as the government redirected the company to focus its attention on preventing foreclosures and propping up the housing market. For the entire 2008, Fannie had a loss of $58.7 billion, compared with a year-earlier loss of $2.1 billion. The loss for 2008 exceeded net income for the preceding seventeen years. The "Deed for Lease" program permits borrowers who don't qualify for loan modifications to transfer their property to Fannie Mae for a lease. Fannie Mae acquired 57,000 properties through foreclosures during the first half of 2009.

On December 24, 2009, the government announced significant new financial support for Fannie Mae, no matter how poorly it performs in the coming two years. The U.S. government already owns 79.9 percent of Fannie Mae and permitted its chief executive to receive up to $6 million in compensation for two years. The pay package includes a $900,000 salary, $3.1 million in deferred payments in 2010 that are not dependent on performance, and an additional $2 million to meeting certain goals.

See also FEDERAL RESERVE; FORECLOSURE; FREDDIE MAC; GINNIE MAE; HOUSING BAILOUT PLAN; MODIFYING MORTGAGES; MORTGAGE-BACKED SECURITY; SECURITIES AND EXCHANGE COMMISSION; UNDERWATER; U.S. TREASURY.

FARM EXPORTS. *See* EXPORTS (U.S.).

FARMING. The Agriculture Department forecast on August 27, 2009, that U.S. farm profits would fall 38 percent for the year. Net farm income was expected to drop to $54 billion, down $33.2 billion from a year earlier.

See also UNEMPLOYMENT.

FARM REAL ESTATE. Values of farm real estate fell for the first time in more than twenty years, according to the U.S. Agriculture Department. The value of all land and buildings on U.S. farms averaged $2,100 an acre January 1, 2009, down 3.2 percent from a year before. The decline was the first since 1987.

FASB. *See* FINANCIAL ACCOUNTING STANDARDS BOARD.

FDIC. *See* FEDERAL DEPOSIT INSURANCE CORPORATION.

FEAR GAUGE. Prices investors are willing to pay to buy and sell stocks or options.

See also CONSUMER CONFIDENCE.

FED. Short for Federal Reserve (System).

See also FEDERAL RESERVE.

FEDERAL ADVISORY COUNCIL. A committee of the Federal Reserve System that advises the Board of Governors on major developments and activities.

FEDERAL AID HIGHWAY ACT (OF 1956). Signed by President Dwight David Eisenhower, ultimately resulting in the construction of 42,795 miles of roads, dramatically improving highway travel. In 1991, the government concluded that the total cost of the act was $128.9 billion. Eisenhower's interstate highway system, at $400 billion in today's dollars, cost four times as much and took three times as long as planned.

In September 2008, the nonpartisan Congressional Budget Office estimated it would take two years to spend just 60 percent of $37 billion in infrastructure funds in a stimulus bill. President Obama was considering spending taxpayers' monies to rebuild U.S. infrastructures, including roads and highways.

FEDERAL CREDIT UNION. A cooperative association organized under the Federal Credit Union Act for the purpose of accepting savings from people, making loans to them at low interest rates, and rendering other financial services to members.

FEDERAL DEBT. *See* AMERICAN RECOVERY AND REINVESTMENT ACT (OF 2009); DEBT, FEDERAL.

FEDERAL DEFICIT. A public or federal debt; the difference that exists between revenue and government expenditures. The deficit hit a record $311 billion for the first half of fiscal 2008 as corporate tax revenue fell.

See also DEFICIT (U.S.); EMERGENCY ECONOMIC STABILIZATION ACT OF 2008; FEDERAL RESERVE.

FEDERAL DEPOSIT INSURANCE CORPORATION (FDIC). A government corporation that insures the deposits of all banks that are entitled to the benefits of insurance under the Federal Reserve Act. The FDIC was created through the Banking Act of 1933 and was affected by amendments of 1935. All national banks and all state banks that are members of the Federal Reserve System are required by law to be members of the FDIC. Mutual savings banks are also encouraged to join.

In January 2009, the FDIC began asking banks getting capital injections from the $700 billion financial rescue program to report how they were using the funds to support consumer lending and foreclosure relief.

The FDIC, which insures deposits on accounts worth up to $250,000, estimated that it would lose $65 billion through 2013 as a result of bank failures.

On February 27, its board imposed a one-time $15 billion increase in insurance premiums on the nation's 8,300 banks. Banks were required to pay $27 billion to replenish the insurance funds in 2009, nine times more than in 2008.

A three-page bill to give greater clout to the FDIC in March 2009, would temporarily allow the FDIC to borrow $500 billion to replenish the fund it employed to guarantee bank deposits. The Fed and Treasury Department must support this presidential request, which would permanently raise the level that the FDIC could borrow from the Treasury, now $30 billion, to $100 billion, and the FDIC could use these funds without prior approval from the Fed and the Treasury.

Banks that have benefited from the purchase of FDIC-backed bonds (in billions):

Bank of America	$44.0
JP Morgan Chase	$45.0
General Electric	$37.7
Citigroup	$27.6
Morgan Stanley	$23.8
Goldman Sachs	$21.1
Wells Fargo	$9.5
American Express	$5.6
State Street	$3.9
PNC Financial Services	$3.9

On August 27, 2009, the FDIC reported that it had 416 U.S. banks on its problem list, equivalent to 5 percent of the nation's banks, up from 305 at the end of March and 117 at the end of June 2008. These problem banks had a combined $299.8 billion of assets at the end of June, compared with $78.3 billion a year before. By this time in 2008, the FDIC had closed 25 banks, compared to 95 in 2009. Then in early October the FDIC seized three small lenders in Michigan, Minnesota, and Colorado, bringing the number of banks that had failed in 2009 to 98.

The FDIC insurance fund guards $6.2 trillion in U.S. deposits. These funds dropped $10.4 billion at the quarter's end, the lowest since mid-1993.

By the end of September 2009, the FDIC was considering asking healthy banks to lend them billions of dollars to rescue its insurance fund, which was quickly running out of money because of a wave of bank failures. Under the law, FDIC does not require permission from the U.S. Treasury to tap into a credit line of up to $100 billion. Borrowing from the banks is allowed under a 1991 law adopted during the savings and loan crisis. The lending institutions would receive bonds from the government at an interest rate that would be set by the Treasury Department and ultimately be paid by the rest of the industry. The bonds would be listed as an asset on the books of the banks.

On September 29, the government announced that the FDIC funds that protect consumer bank deposits had fallen into the red and would remain there into 2012. The FDIC asked the banking industry to prepay $45 billion in fees by the end of the year to give the government more breathing room to handle future failures.

By mid-November 2009, the FDIC had taken over 150 failed banks. In this process the FDIC has seized more than 5,000 homes, subdivisions, buildings, parcels, and other foreclosed assets.

The FDIC plans to add more than 1,600 employees in 2010, with a budget boost of 35 percent to handle bank failures. The agency would spend $2.5 billion to fund its bank failure operations out of its total budget of $4 billion.

See also TROUBLED ASSET RELIEF PROGRAM.

FEDERAL DISCOUNT RATE. The interest rate charged on federal funds. The interest is charged on a discount basis and is a key factor in determining the prime rate charged for commercial loans.

FEDERAL EXPRESS (FEDEX). Coping with slumping volumes, the package delivery company slashed pay for 35,000 employees in December 2008.

In early February 2009, FedEx cut another 900 positions, representing about 2.5 percent of the roughly 35,000 employees working in the freight division of the Memphis, Tennessee company.

In mid-March FedEx reported a 75 percent drop in quarterly profit. By June, FedEx posted a loss of $876 million in the quarter.

On September 17, 2009, FedEx reported a 53 percent fall in quarterly profit. The company reported a profit of $181 million for the first quarter, ending on August 31.

Then on November 10, 2009, the company forecast that it would ship more than 13 million packages on the busiest day of the year, December 14, an increase of 8 percent from the year before.

The company reported on December 9 that its second-quarter 2009 earnings would easily surpass its previous forecast.

FedEx shipped 14.1 million packages on December 13, with sales falling 9.9 percent to $8.6 billion. Profit fell to $345 million.

FEDERAL FINANCING BANK (FFB). Established in 1973 to assist in financing U.S. government agencies; the FFB is authorized to acquire any obligation that is issued, sold, or guaranteed by any federal agency, except those of the Farm Credit System, the Federal Home Loans Banks, the Federal Home Loan Mortgage Corporation, and the Federal National Mortgage Association.

FEDERAL FUNDS. Funds available at a Federal Reserve Bank, including excess reserves of member banks and checks drawn in payment for purchases by the Federal Reserve Bank of government securities.

FEDERAL-FUNDS MARKET. The market in which excess bank reserves are borrowed and lent by federal banks.

FEDERAL FUNDS PAYMENT/TRANSFER. Payment made by check or wire transfer against a bank's account with a Federal Reserve Bank.

FEDERAL FUNDS PURCHASED. Short-term borrowing of reserves from another bank.

FEDERAL FUNDS RATE. The interest rate charged on loans by banks that have excess reserve funds (above the level required by the Federal Reserve) to those banks with deficient reserves. The Fed funds rate is closely watched as an early warning indication of major changes in the national economy.

FEDERAL FUNDS TRANSACTIONS. The reporting bank's lending (federal funds sold) or borrowing (federal funds purchased) of immediately available funds for one business day or under a continuing contract, regardless of the nature of the contract or of the collateral, if any. Due bills and borrowings from the Discount and Credit Department of a Federal Reserve Bank are excluded from federal funds.

FEDERAL GOVERNMENT SECURITIES. All obligations of the U.S. government.

FEDERAL HOME BANK (FEDERAL HOME LOAN BANK). One of twelve regional banks established in 1932 to encourage local thrift and home financing during the Depression. The banks are owned jointly by various savings and loan associations. The Federal Home Loan Bank Board serves as a management body.

On July 2, 2009, the Federal Home Loan Banks' net income dropped 51 percent to $345 million in the first quarter 2009, from $697 million a year earlier. The drop reflected $516 million of write-downs on mortgage securities held by some of the twelve regional banks.

By the end of October, the Federal Home Loan Banks continued to struggle with soured investments in mortgage securities, with a combined third-quarter 2009 loss of $165 million. The loss showed write-downs totaling $1.04 billion in the value of private-label mortgage-backed securities.

FEDERAL HOME LOAN BANK ACT OF 1932. A system that provided a stable source of funds for residential mortgages during the Great Depression. Members may obtain advances on home mortgage collateral and may borrow from home loan banks under certain conditions.

FEDERAL HOME LOAN BANKS. *See* FEDERAL HOME BANK.

FEDERAL HOME LOAN MORTGAGE CORPORATION. *See* FREDDIE MAC.

FEDERAL HOUSING ADMINISTRATION (FHA). Government agency that insures mortgage loans. By September 2009, the FHA's reserves were being pushed below the level required by Congress. At the end of June, 7.8 percent of FHA-backed loans were ninety days late or more, or in foreclosure, up from 5.4 percent a year earlier.

By the end of September 2009, the FHA indicated that its reserves were shrinking rapidly. The agency might require a federal bailout. About 20 percent of FHA loans insured in 2008, and as many as 24 percent of those from 2007, faced serious problems, including foreclosures. The FHA's capital reserves fell far below minimum of 2 percent. On November 12, 2009, the FHA noted that its reserves had been depleted much faster than the agency had anticipated. The capital-reserve fund fell to $3.6 billion as of September 30, down 72 percent from the year before, leaving reserves at just 0.53 percent of the $685 billion in total loans insured by the FHA.

FEDERAL HOUSING ENTERPRISE OVERSIGHT. *See* OFFICE OF FEDERAL HOUSING ENTERPRISE OVERSIGHT.

FEDERAL HOUSING FINANCE AGENCY. *See* FEDERAL HOUSING ADMINISTRATION; HOME PRICES.

FEDERAL INSURANCE RESERVE. A general loss reserve required to be established by a federal association under the rules and regulations of the Federal Savings and Loan Insurance Corporation.

FEDERAL INTERMEDIATE CREDIT BANKS (FICB). Regional banks created by Congress to provide intermediate credit for ranchers and farmers by rediscounting the agricultural paper of financial institutions.

FEDERAL LOAN AGENCY. *See* RECONSTRUCTION FINANCE CORPORATION.

FEDERAL NATIONAL MORTGAGE ASSOCIATION. *See* FANNIE MAE.

FEDERAL OPEN MARKET COMMITTEE (FOMC). The Federal Reserve's most important policy-making group, with responsibility for creating policy for the system's purchase and sale of government and other securities in the open market.

In September 2009, the Federal Open Market Committee held interest rates at a record low. It also extended its $1.25 trillion program of buying mortgage-backed securities into the first quarter of 2010.

See also FEDERAL RESERVE.

FEDERAL REGULATORY POWERS. *See* HOUSE (U.S.) FINANCIAL OVERHAUL PLAN.

FEDERAL RESERVE (FED, THE) (U.S.). The central banking system of the United States as established by the Federal Reserve Act of 1913. The system regulates money supply, determines the legal reserve of member banks, oversees the mint, effects transfers of funds, promotes and facilitates the clearance and collection of checks, examines member banks, and discharges other functions. The Federal Reserve System consists of twelve Federal Reserve Banks, their twenty-four branches, and the national and state banks that are members of the system. All national banks are stockholding members of the Federal Reserve Bank of their district. Membership for state banks or trust companies is optional.

The Fed cut its main interest-rate target by three-quarters of a percentage point to 3.5 percent on January 22, 2008. With global markets in free fall amid recession fears, this reduction temporarily shored up confidence.

Nine days later, on January 31, the Fed lowered interest rates by half a percentage point to 3 percent, seeking to nip an oncoming recession. The 2.25

points in rate cuts since September 2007 approximates the initial pace in early 2001 as the most rapid in two decades.

On October 29, 2008, the Fed cut its benchmark interest rate by 50 basis points, to 1 percent, its lowest level since June 2004.

Together with the U.S. Treasury, the Fed announced $800 billion in new lending programs on November 25, essentially stepping in as a substitute for the crippled American banking system to provide financing for home buyers, consumers, and businesses. They created a $200 billion lending program that bought up loans to consumers and small businesses.

The Fed then announced that it would try to push down home mortgage rates by purchasing $600 billion in debt ties to home loans guaranteed by Fannie Mae, Freddie Mac, and other government-controlled financing firms.

All told, the government took on at least $7 trillion to direct and indirect financial obligations, a staggering sum equal to about half of the annual U.S. GDP.

The U.S. central bank on December 16 lowered interest rates by as much as 75 basis points, to just 0.25 percent. That meant that since the financial crisis escalated in September 2007, the Fed had cut rates from 5.25 percent to the current 1 percent in an effort to pump money into both the banking system and the recessionary economy.

Between September and mid-December, the U.S. government had printed more than $1 trillion in new money, yet failed to slow down the economy's sinking. "Cheap money" would be introduced.

On December 16, the Fed set its benchmark interest rate so low that it would have to reach for new and untested tools in fighting both the recession and downward pressure on consumer prices. The central bank cut its target for the federal funds rate to a range of zero to 0.25 percent. This strategy affected the rate at which banks lend their reserves to one another overnight. This move also reflected the Fed's acknowledgment that the recession was more severe than they had thought in October.

The Fed would turn to "quantitative easing," which involves injecting money into the economy rather than aiming at an interest rate. This strategy was a rather new approach at the Fed, with risks of increased inflation or perhaps even another speculative bubble.

On June 24, 2009, the Fed, believing that the economy was showing signs of a slight improvement, kept interest rates near zero.

On August 25, President Obama reappointed Ben Bernanke to a second four-year term as Federal Reserve chairman.

On September 24, 2009, the Federal Reserve said that it would shorten the maturity on loans it makes to banks under the Term Auction Facility, a program created in December 2007 to provide banks with sufficient cash as the credit crunch worsened. In its place, the Fed would shift the program toward its shorter-term loans of twenty-eight days.

On December 12, 2009, the Federal Reserve imposed rules making it more difficult for banks to hit customers with fees for overdrawing their accounts.

The House of Representatives' Financial Services Committee in a vote of 43–26 approved a measure on November 19, 2009, strongly opposed by the Fed, that would instruct the Government Accountability Office to expand its audits of the Fed to include decisions about interest rates and lending to individual banks. The Fed argues that the provision threatens its ability to make monetary policy without political interference. Some called for Treasury Secretary Geithner to resign.

On December 11, the House of Representatives, in a wave of anti–Wall Street feeling, passed (with a vote of 223 to 202) sweeping legislation aiming to limit the operations of big banks and the powers of the Federal Reserve. Under the stewardship of Congressman Barney Frank, chairman of the House Financial Services Committee, it would, if passed, bring the biggest change to financial regulations since the 1930s. The bill would strip nearly all of the Fed's powers to write consumer-protection laws and permit an arm of Congress to audit the Fed's monetary policy decisions. It would also create a new Consumer Financial Protection Agency under the House Financial Overhaul Plan.

See also AMERICAN INTERNATIONAL GROUP; BAILOUT RESCUE (PLAN) OF 2009 (U.S.); BEAR STEARNS; BEIGE BOOK; BERNANKE, BEN; BOND BUYING; BUSH, GEORGE W.; CENTRAL BANKERS; EMERGENCY ECONOMIC STABILIZATION ACT OF 2008; EXECUTIVE PAY; EXPAND REGULATORY POWERS LEGISLATION; FEDERAL OPEN MARKET COMMITTEE; FINANCIAL REGULATION PLAN (2009); GEITHNER, TIMOTHY F.; GMAC; GOLDMAN SACHS; GREENSPAN, ALAN; HOME MORTGAGES; HOUSE (U.S.) FINANCIAL OVERHAUL PLAN; INDUSTRIAL PRODUCTION; MONEY MARKET MUTUAL FUNDS; MORGAN STANLEY; MORTGAGE LEGISLATION; MORTGAGE RATES; NEW MONEY; PAY; QUANTITATIVE EASING; ROOSEVELT, FRANKLIN DELANO; STRESS TESTS; "TOO BIG TO FAIL"; TOXIC ASSETS; U.S. TREASURY.

FEDERAL RESERVE ACT. Legislation signed by President Wilson on December 23, 1913, establishing the Federal Reserve System to manage the nation's money supply. It is the nation's central bank, which sets monetary policy.

See also FEDERAL RESERVE BANK; FEDERAL RESERVE DISTRICT BANKS.

FEDERAL RESERVE BANK. One of twelve banks created by and operating under the Federal Reserve System. Each Federal Reserve Bank has nine directors.

FEDERAL RESERVE BOARD. The seven-member governing body of the Federal Reserve System; the governors are appointed by the president of the United States, subject to Senate confirmation, for fourteen-year terms. Created in 1913 to regulate all national banks and state-chartered banks that are members of the Federal Reserve System, the board possesses jurisdiction over bank holding companies and also sets national money and credit policy.

FEDERAL RESERVE CURRENCY. Paper money issued by the Federal Reserve Banks that circulates as a legal medium of exchange and is legal tender.

FEDERAL RESERVE DISTRICT BANKS. There are twelve of these central banks, or "banker's banks." They are:

1st District—Boston
2nd District—New York
3rd District—Philadelphia
4th District—Cleveland
5th District—Richmond
6th District—Atlanta
7th District—Chicago
8th District—St. Louis
9th District—Minneapolis
10th District—Kansas City
11th District—Dallas
12th District—San Francisco

FEDERAL RESERVE OVERSIGHT. To tighten their rules for dealing with multinational banks, the U.S. Congress adopted in 1991 a Federal Reserve proposal for policing foreign banks operating in the United States. The law provides that all foreign banks operating in the United States be subject to firm, consolidated supervision in their home country. The legislation gave the Fed new powers to gather financial and ownership information regarding such banks and clarified the Fed's power over these banks in the United States if they superseded state authority.

FEDERAL RESERVE REQUIREMENTS. The amount of money that member banks of the Federal Reserve system must hold in cash or on deposit with a Federal Reserve Bank in order to back up their outstanding loans. The requirement is expressed as a percentage of outstanding loan volume.

FEDERAL RESERVE SYSTEM. *See* FEDERAL RESERVE.

FEDERALS. Items drawn on banks in a large city in which a Federal Reserve Bank is located, although the banks do not belong to the city's clearinghouse association.

FEDERAL SAVINGS AND LOAN ASSOCIATION. One of the associations established by the Home Owners' Loan Act of 1933, and amended in the Home Owners' Loan Act of 1934, which brought existing and newly formed mutual savings banks and building and loan associations under a federal charter.

FEDEX. *See* FEDERAL EXPRESS.

FEINBERG, KENNETH. *See* PAY; PAY CZAR.

FERGUSON, NIALL. *See* CHIMERICA.

FERRE. The Gianfranco Ferre label was placed in bankruptcy administration, a victim of the recession that is impacting luxury-goods firms worldwide. The Italian government placed the firm under the supervision of three government-appointed administrators who will attempt to keep the group operating. The company racked up more than $375 million in net debt to finance expansion.
   See also ITALY; LUXURY GOODS.

FFB. *See* FEDERAL FINANCING BANK.

FHA. *See* FEDERAL HOUSING ADMINISTRATION.

FHLMC. *See* FREDDIE MAC.

FIAT. On December 16, 2008, the Italian automaker announced temporary plant closures resulting from a decline in key markets.
   Chrysler, in January 2009, seeking to bolster its case for long-term survival after its $4 billion government bailout, was trading a 35 percent stake to Italy's Fiat for access to small-car technology and a global sales network.
   Fiat would use this partnership to expand its U.S. foothold, now limited to its luxury brands. Fiat had the option to increase its stake to as much as 55 percent.
   Fiat would provide technology and engineering for Chrysler to make small cars that would meet coming stricter federal fuel-economy standards, saving Chrysler $3 billion or more to develop. Fiat would let Chrysler build small cars using its "platforms"—the automobile industry term for the mechanical underpinnings of a vehicle, including engines—so that Chrysler could broaden its lineup beyond large pickups, SUVs, and minivans.

The alliance had raised questions about whether the U.S. taxpayers were indirectly providing aid to a foreign automaker.

On March 21, Fiat management said that it wouldn't assume any of Chrysler's debt in a potential deal for a 35 percent stake in the company.

By the end of March the Treasury Department pressed Fiat to take an initial 20 percent ownership of Chrysler.

At the end of April, following the United Auto Workers union with Chrysler, Fiat would eventually own 35 percent of Chrysler. Chrysler requires the Fiat merger as well as the cost concession from its debt holders to receive more U.S. aid to avoid bankruptcy. Fiat now agreed to produce at least one small car in a Chrysler plant in the United States and permit Chrysler to use a 3.0 liter diesel engine and a 1.4 liter gasoline engine in its vehicles. Fiat's investment could be worth $8 billion, and hopefully create 4,000 new jobs.

Fiat reported lower third-quarter 2009 earnings on a fall of 16 percent in revenue. Incentive programs raised sales volume by 4.3 percent from a year before. Fiat's third-quarter profit fell $37.5 million.

On June 10, Fiat completed its alliance agreement with Chrysler, largely ending Chrysler's forty-two days of bankruptcy.

See also AUTOMOBILE INDUSTRY; CERBERUS; CHRYSLER; ITALY.

FICB. *See* FEDERAL INTERMEDIATE CREDIT BANKS.

FILENE'S BASEMENT. The retailer filed for Chapter 11 bankruptcy on May 3, 2009.

FINANCIAL ACCOUNTING STANDARDS BOARD (FASB). Voted at the end of March 2009 to change one of its rules and allow banks more leeway to determine for themselves what the mortgage securities they own are worth.

See also MARK-TO-MARKET RULES.

FINANCIAL CRISIS ADVISORY GROUP. This group seeks ways to make the regulatory system less pro-cyclical by allowing banks to postpone recognition of profits in good times so that losses would not be as large as in bad times. In July 2009, the group issued a report dealing with accounting rules, and warned against changing rules in ways that would make it easier for banks to manage earnings.

See also FINANCIAL CRISIS INQUIRY COMMISSION; MARKET CAPITALIZATION.

FINANCIAL CRISIS INQUIRY COMMISSION. Created by both the House of Representatives and the Senate in May 2009. An outgrowth of the Fraud Enforcement and Recovery Act of 2009, the commission was given broad authority to examine the domestic and global causes of the current U.S. financial and economic crisis.

Under the act, the commission will have roughly eighteen months to investigate the circumstances that led to the financial crisis and issue a report to Congress with its findings and recommendations. The commission was given broad investigative authority, including subpoena power and the ability to refer any evidence of criminal activity to the U.S. attorney general and state attorneys general. It must report its findings no later than December 15, 2010.

The commission has ten members, who must be private citizens and may not be employed by any government entity. Its chair is Phil Angelides, a former California Treasurer.

The Commission has been charged to examine topics, such as:

- fraud and abuse in the financial sector;
- capital requirements and regulations on leverage and liquidity;
- lending practices and securitization;
- the availability and terms of credit;
- the quality of diligence undertaken by financial institutions;
- derivatives and unregulated financial products and practices; and
- compensation structures.

Formal public hearings will start in December 2009.

See also FINANCIAL CRISIS ADVISORY GROUP; RECESSION OF 2007–2010.

Cf. PECORA COMMISSION.

FINANCIAL INSTITUTIONS REFORM, RECOVERY AND EN-FORCEMENT ACT OF 1989. Created the Office of Thrift Supervision to regulate federal and most state-chartered thrifts and their holding companies.

FINANCIAL ISOLATIONISM. *See* FINANCIAL PROTECTIONISM.

FINANCIAL OVERHAUL PLAN. *See* HOUSE (U.S.) FINANCIAL OVERHAUL PLAN.

FINANCIAL PROTECTIONISM. A tactic introduced by Gordon Brown, the British prime minister, in January 2009 for the setting of guidelines to prevent countries (primarily of the European Union) from carrying out rescue plans that favor their banks over others.

This form of protectionism involves banks retreating behind national borders by lending more at home and lending less abroad. One result is the loss of credit from foreign banks.

See also PROTECTIONISM.

FINANCIAL REGULATION. *See* EXECUTIVE PAY; FINANCIAL REGULATION PLAN (2009); REGULATION.

FINANCIAL REGULATION PLAN (2009). Proposed by the Obama administration on June 17, 2009, and requiring congressional approval, this sweeping and historic program would overhaul U.S. finance rules including:

a. Creates a Financial Services Oversight Council to guide regulators' activities.
b. Financial firms big enough to be a risk to the financial system would be heavily regulated by the Federal Reserve.
c. Allows the Fed to collect reports from U.S. financial firms that met "certain minimum size thresholds."
d. Treasury would reexamine capital standards for banks and holding firms.
e. Regulators would issue guidelines on executive pay.
f. Creates national bank supervisors and terminating Office of Thrift Supervision.
g. Hedge funds, private-equity funds, and venture-capital funds would register with SEC.
h. Urges SEC to stem runs on money-market mutual funds.
i. Beefs up oversight of insurance by creating office in Treasury to coordinate information and policy.
j. Over-the-counter derivatives, asset-backed securities would be in a regulatory framework.
k. Gives Fed more power over infrastructure that governs these markets, such as pay and settlement systems.
l. Harmonizes powers and authority of SEC and CFTC to avoid conflicting rules.
m. Requires certain loan originators to retain some economic interest in securitized products.
n. Urges SEC to strengthen credit-rating firm regulation.
o. Creates Consumer Financial Protection Agency, with authority over consumer-oriented products.
p. Requires nonbinding shareholder votes on executive pay packages.
q. Requires certain employers to offer an "automatic IRA plan" for retirement.
r. Creates a mechanism that allows the government to take over and unwind large, failing financial institutions.
s. FDIC would act as conservator or receiver, except with broker dealers or securities firms, then SEC takes over.
t. Amends Fed's lending powers to get Treasury secretary's approval.

See also TIER 1 FINANCIAL HOLDING FIRM.

FINANCIAL REGULATORS. *See* REGULATORS; TIER 1 FINANCIAL HOLDING FIRM.

FINANCIAL SERVICES COMMITTEE (HOUSE OF REPRESENTA-TIVES). *See* FEDERAL RESERVE.

FINANCIAL SERVICES OVERSIGHT COUNCIL. *See* FINANCIAL-REGULATION PLAN (2009).

FINANCIAL STABILITY (AND RECOVERY) PLAN. Under the administration of President Obama, the replacement name for the Troubled Asset Relief Program, a bank bailout plan in 2008, from the administration of President George W. Bush. Designed to attack U.S. credit crisis on all fronts.

See also "TOO BIG TO FAIL"; TROUBLED ASSET RELIEF PROGRAM.

Synonymous with BAILOUT RESCUE (PLAN) OF 2009 (U.S.); TARP 2.0.

FINANCIAL STABILITY FORUM (FSF). *See* REGULATORS.

FINANCIALSTABILITY.GOV. The U.S. Treasury's website dedicated to "transparency, oversight, and accountability."

FINANCIAL STABILITY OVERSIGHT BOARD. Regulators from the Federal Reserve and the Treasury Department. This unit was established by the Emergency Economic Stabilization Act of 2008 to help oversee the Troubled Asset Relief Program granted to the Secretary of the Treasury and to help restore liquidity and stability to the U.S. financial system. The board is committed to transparency and accountability in all of its programs and policies, including those established under the Emergency Economic Stabilization Act.

See also TROUBLED ASSET RELIEF PROGRAM.

FINANCIAL TIMES. The British newspaper publisher announced on February 23 that it would reduce staffing costs by offering employees the option of working a shortened week in the summer and extending their annual leave.

FINLAND. *See* FINNAIR; NOKIA CORPORATION.

FINNAIR. In August 2009, the airline posted its fourth consecutive quarterly net loss, with revenue falling 22 percent.

FIONIA BANK. *See* DENMARK.

FIRST LOOK. *See* FANNIE MAE.

FIRST 100 DAYS. *See* OBAMA, BARACK.

FIRST-TIME HOME BUYER CREDIT. Designed for people who close on purchases of their first home after April 8, 2008, and before December 1, 2009, allowing a credit of up to $8,000 with no payback requirement. This credit provides for individuals earning up to $75,000 and couples earning up to $150,000; it was set to expire in November 2009. The credit can be claimed on the following year's tax return.

See AMERICAN RECOVERY AND REINVESTMENT ACT; HOME SALES.

FISCAL RESPONSIBILITY SUMMIT. *See* DEFICIT (BUDGET).

FISHER, IRVING. A long-forgotten economist of the Depression era, he was called by John Maynard Keynes the "great-grandparent" of his own theories. Throughout the Great Depression, he was considered America's foremost economist. In October 1929 he predicted that stocks would reach a "permanently high plateau." His great contribution was an ability to convince decision makers that monetary forces were instrumental in the direction of a real economy. His debt-deflation theory argued that it was critical to defend a nation against deflation, to also concern itself with inside debt and abandoning the gold standard.

In 1911, he wrote *The Purchasing Power of Money* describing with models and flowcharts the quantity theory of money, which holds that the supply of money times its velocity is equal to output multiplied by the price level. He explained how interest rates could deviate from nominal ones. He held that the dollar's value should be maintained relative not to gold but to a basket of commodities. To the end he remained convinced that the depression of the 1930s would be short-lived. In addition, he urged President Hoover to veto the Smoot-Hawley Act, but failed to get the attention of the administration.

See also KEYNES, JOHN MAYNARD; SMOOT-HAWLEY ACT OF 1930.

FLASH ORDERS (TRADING). Permits traders to peek at other investors' orders before they are sent to the wider marketplace. This method gives some traders an edge over everyone else, and the SEC is determined to stamp it out.

On September 17, 2009, the SEC proposed banning these so-called flash orders, which utilize power computers to look at investors' orders. By July 2009, flash orders represented 2.8 percent of the roughly 9 billion shares of stocks traded in the United States. This was known as high-frequency trading. Critics claim that flash orders favor sophisticated, fast-moving traders at the expense of slower market participants. Utilizing lightning-quick technology, these high-frequency traders often issue and then cancel orders almost simultaneously and find out how others trade, creating a two-tiered market.

See also HIGH-FREQUENCY TRADING.

FLEXIBLE MORTGAGE. *See* FLEXIBLE-PAYMENT MORTGAGE; RENEGOTIABLE-RATE MORTGAGE; VARIABLE-RATE MORTGAGE.

FLEXIBLE-PAYMENT MORTGAGE. An interest-only type of loan for the first five years. Two major restrictions apply: each monthly payment must cover at least the interest due, and after five years, payments must be fully amortizing. A rarely used mortgage because it offers the homebuyer only a slight reduction in monthly payments during the early years.

See also RENEGOTIABLE-RATE MORTGAGE; VARIABLE-RATE MORTGAGE.

FLEXICURITY. First used in Denmark, the concept that Europeans will tolerate flexible labor markets (i.e., increased layoffs), as long as they have the security of generous social assistance if things go bad.

FLIPPING HOMES. *See* HOME FLIPPING.

FLOOD PREVENTION. *See* AMERICAN RECOVERY AND REINVESTMENT ACT (OF 2009).

FNMA. *See* FANNIE MAE.

FOMC. *See* FEDERAL OPEN MARKET COMMITTEE.

FOOD AID. The government reported on November 16, 2009, that the number of families struggling to purchase enough food in 2008 climbed 31 percent over the previous year. Seventeen million households indicated some form of food insecurity in 2008, an increase from 13 million families in 2007. In 2008, 6.7 million households had very low food security, up 43 percent from 4.7 million households in 2007.

See also FOOD STAMPS, UNEMPLOYMENT.

FOOD BANKS. Indicating how hard times are in the United States, by December 2008, food banks were trying to feed more people with less food. Signing people up for benefits became more crucial than ever, as more working-class people were finding it difficult to make ends meet and were coming to food banks for assistance.

Demand at food banks increased by 30 percent in 2008.

See also UNEMPLOYMENT.

FOOD PANTRIES. *See* FOOD BANKS.

FOOD SECURITY. *See* FOOD AID.

FOOD SPENDING. In 2008's fourth quarter, consumer spending on food fell at an inflation-adjusted rate of 3.7 percent from the third quarter, the greatest fall in 62 years.

By 2009, the money spent by consumers in food markets and for eating out was lower than the previous year. Generic brands increasingly replaced standard ones as more and more people ate at home. The packaged-food industry was assumed to be recession proof, considering people must eat no matter what.

FOOD STAMPS. Food stamps at one time had a stigma projecting an image of welfare and poverty. Since 2008 the number of people who receive food stamps has increased nearly a third, resulting in a program that feeds more than 36 million citizens. One in eight Americans and one in four children are presently dependent on food stamps, expanding at a pace of approximately 20,000 people a day. There are 239 counties in the country where at least a quarter of the population receive food stamps.

Today nearly 12 percent of Americans receive stamps; 28 percent are African American, 15 percent Latino, and 8 percent whites. Benefits average about $130 a month for each person in the household.

See also UNEMPLOYMENT; WELFARE.

FORD. Ford Motor's U.S. sales plummeted as much as 30 percent in October 2008. Ford, Lincoln, and Mercury car sales were off 27 percent, while light truck sales for the three brands were down more than 30 percent.

When President George W. Bush announced a program to bail out the automobile industry in late December, only General Motors and Chrysler were to be recipients of government monies. Ford claimed that it was not in need of funds to continue operations, thereby relieving them, at least for the time being, from further government controls.

Ford sold 138,458 light vehicles in December, down from 204,787 in the same month in 2007. It was a 32 percent drop in December.

Ford reported on January 2, 2009, that their car and truck sales fell almost 19 percent in 2008. Ford's U.S. market share slipped to about 14 percent for 2008, down from 14.7 percent in 2007. Executives forecast overall 2009 sales to come in at $12.5 million in car sales, while light-vehicles sales could hit $12.2 million.

The year 2008 ended up the worst year for selling cars and trucks since 1992. For example, Ford had projected total industry sales of about 13.5 million, a full 3 million fewer than in 2007. Not since 1974 had the market collapsed that much in a single year.

On January 29, after closing the books on a $14.6 billion loss in 2008, the worst annual result in its 105-year history, Ford Motor Company said that it was drawing the last $10.1 billion from its lines of credit to add to its cash hoard so that it could survive the increasingly bleak vehicle market.

Ford's January sales dropped 40 percent to 93,041.

In mid-March, hourly workers at Ford ratified sweeping cost-cutting changes in their labor contract. Restrictions were made on overtime and unemployment pay, and cutbacks made in work rules and cost-of-living wage increases. Up to half of Ford's cash obligation to its retiree healthcare fund was replaced with company stock.

On April 6, the automaker said its investors agreed to exchange $9.9 billion in debt for cash and stock, a 28 percent reduction in its overall debt.

By the end of April, the Ford Motor Company said it likely wouldn't require a government bailout, reporting a smaller-than-expected loss for the first quarter 2009. Nevertheless, Ford was not out of the woods. On April 24, it announced having lost $1.4 billion, sales fell 43 percent, and it spent $3.7 billion of its cash during the first quarter 2009. It still had $21 billion in the bank, and continued not to request federal bailout funds.

Ford Motor Company returned to profitability in the second quarter 2009 with signs of stabilizing. It reported a profit of $2.3 billion. It is now projected that Ford will break even or perhaps make money in 2011. After four quarterly losses, Ford now had its first quarterly profit.

On August 13, 2009, Ford announced plans to build 495,000 cars and trucks in the third quarter of the year, up 18 percent from a year before. It estimated that its first production goal for the fourth quarter would be 570,000 vehicles, up 33 percent from the 2008 quarter.

Ford posted a 17 percent gain in sales in August, during the Clunker program, while other U.S. automakers saw sales falling.

By October 2009, Ford had weathered the industry's downturn far better than its U.S. competitors, thanks to its ability to minimize its year-over-year sales declines taking advantage of its competitors' weaknesses and securing market share. Ford secured more than five percentage points of U.S. retail market shares in the third quarter 2009 compared with the same period one year earlier, while GM and Chrysler lost ground.

At the beginning of November the company reported a third-quarter 2009 profit of nearly $1 billion.

See also AUTOMOBILE INDUSTRY; JOB BANKS; VOLVO.

Cf. GENERAL MOTORS.

FORECLOSURE (FORECLOSURES). A legal process whereby a mortgagor of a property is deprived of his or her interest therein, usually by means of a court-administered sale of the property. In November 2008, the U.S. Treasury developed a $40 billion program to help delinquent homeowners avoid foreclosure. It was intended to help as many as 3 million beleaguered homeowners by reducing their monthly payments. More than 10 million homeowners were desperate for help.

Experts believed that nearly 5 million families could lose their homes between 2009 and 2011. With this, JPMorgan Chase, Morgan Stanley, and Bank of America said they would halt foreclosures through March 6. It was predicted that as many as 4 million homeowners faced foreclosure proceedings in 2009, up from about 2.2 million in 2008.

On Wednesday, February 18, the administration outlined a proposal to spend at least $50 billion to prevent foreclosures.

Then, on April 14, it was noted that the nation's largest mortgage companies were stepping up foreclosures on delinquent homeowners. Major banks and lending institutions have increased foreclosure activities since March, following a temporary halt to foreclosures in February. The result is a further depression of home prices and increased pressure on bank earnings as troubled loans are written off.

The government, in hoping to expand its $50 billion plan to lower home foreclosures, announced on April 28 a new program to help troubled homeowners modify second mortgages. The Treasury Department will offer cash incentives and subsidies to lenders who agreed to modify the primary or first mortgages of homeowners who had fallen delinquent or were in danger of doing so.

By July, four months into the administration's antiforeclosure effort, the president estimated that "over 50,000" at-risk loans had been modified so that homeowners could afford their payments and keep their homes. By the end of August, the government predicted that the existing program would modify 20,000 bad loans each week. Unfortunately, this effort will not be sufficient. Of the near 4.5 million foreclosures, there will follow distress sales, thereby prolonging the recession.

On August 4, 2009, the Treasury Department indicated that more than 400,000 borrowers have been offered government assistance. Over 235,000 borrowers, or roughly 9 percent of those eligible for the program and at least sixty days past due, have begun trial mortgage modifications, the first step to getting a loan reworked.

By summer's end 2009, one out of eight U.S. households with mortgages was in foreclosure or behind on its mortgage payment during the second quarter.

During this period 6 million loans were either past due or in foreclosure in the second quarter 2009, the highest level ever recorded. Worse, loan defaults were not the only cause of foreclosures, even for homeowners otherwise current on their payments. As cities and counties struggle for income, they have sold their delinquent tax bills to private firms. These firms, which often charge double-digit interest rates and large fees, get to keep what they collect. They also get the right to foreclose on the homes, taking priority over mortgage lenders.

Home prices continued to fall in November 2009. It is expected that another 2.4 million homes will be lost in 2010, while home prices continue to drop another 10 or more percent.

See also BERNANKE, BEN; DEED IN LIEU OF FORECLOSURE; EMERGENCY ECONOMIC STABILIZATION ACT OF 2008; FANNIE MAE; FEDERAL DEPOSIT INSURANCE CORPORATION; FORECLO- SURE LEGISLATION; FORECLOSURE-PREVENTION PLAN; HOME FLIPPING; HOME OWNERSHIP; HOME PRICES; HOUSE (U.S.) FINAN- CIAL OVERHAUL PLAN; HOUSING BAILOUT PLAN; MAKING HOME AFFORDABLE PROGRAM; MODIFYING MORTGAGES; MORTGAGE MODIFICATION; REO (REAL ESTATE OWNED); SHORTCUT FORE- CLOSURE; TROUBLED ASSET RELIEF PROGRAM; UNDERWATER.

FORECLOSURE LEGISLATION. Proposed legislation that would permit bankruptcy judges to lower the payments on home loans to prevent debtors from losing them. By mid-September 2009, the proposal was blocked in Con- gress, after vehement opposition from the banking industry.

FORECLOSURE-PREVENTION PLAN. Announced in mid-March 2009; designed to give several million troubled borrowers another chance to lower their mortgage payments. The government warned that it was also an oppor- tunity for firms to fleece unsuspecting borrowers by charging fees for what they promised would be quick results in negotiating with banks to get easier loan terms. In numerous situations, the firms took the homeowner's money and never delivered the services promised. Some of these companies deliv- ered on their promises but charged fees, often more than $1,000, for services that borrowers can obtain freely.

In July 2008, Congress increased to $360 million the funds it had allocated for foreclosure-prevention counseling free of charge.

See also HOME AFFORDABLE MODIFICATION PROGRAM.

FOREIGN-BORN RESIDENTS. *See* IMMIGRATION.

FOREIGN EXCHANGE RESERVES. *See* CHINA; DEBT.

FORINT. *See* HUNGARY.

FORMOSA. The central bank, in early December 2008, cut its main bench- mark interest rate by three-quarters of a point, to 2.0 percent, the fifth such move in the last two months.

FORTIS BANQUE. A financial service bank, Fortis took on huge debt just after the peak of the credit boom in 2007. In the first nine months of 2008, Fortis posted an $18.36 billion loss. It began to stall in September 2008 following the collapse of Lehman Brothers.

Faced with imminent failure of the bank, the Dutch and Belgian governments initially agreed to a joint salvage operation; in the end, the Dutch went their own way, deciding on October 3 to nationalize the operation in the Netherlands. On October 5, BNP Paribas agreed to acquire Fortis's banking and insurance operations in Belgium and Luxembourg for €14 billion. Fortis's stock was down 95 percent in 2008.

Then on December 18, BNP Paribas suspended its takeover of the Belgian financial services firm following a court ruling that effectively froze the deal.

On April 29, 2009, Fortis shareholders voted to back a takeover by the French bank BNP Paribas, thus ending the run of Fortis as a ward of the Belgian state.

See also BNP PARIBAS.

FOUNDATIONS. Legislation was introduced on March 24, 2009, in the U.S. Senate, intended to encourage foundations to give away more of their funds. If passed, the measure would alter the way foundations are taxed on their investment income, replacing the existing two-tiered system with a single tax rate. Foundations had long argued that the present system effectively penalized them when they gave away more money than usual.

Under present law, private foundations must give their charitable gifts equal to at least 5 percent of the market value of their assets. The proposal urged a single tax rate of 1.32 percent.

401(K) PLANS. *See* RETIREMENT BENEFITS.

FRANCE. French business confidence fell to its lowest level in more than 15 years in October 2008.

On Thursday, November 20, 2008, President Sarkozy introduced a €20 billion ($25 billion) strategic investment fund. He also promised a stimulus package with the aim of investing massively in infrastructure, education, and research.

Then on Friday, November 28, President Sarkozy said he would present a €19 billion program to help the struggling car industry and to further invest in the nation's infrastructure.

On December 5, President Sarkozy vowed to spend some €26 billion over two years in an effort to soften the blow of an economic crisis that had increased jobless lines and risked pushing the economy into recession. His plan, worth about 1.3 percent of the French GDP, was designed to add as much as 0.8 percentage point to growth in 2009.

Among the planned investment projects was €4 billion in state spending on military, research, and infrastructure projects, while €1.8 billion were earmarked for the housing sector.

Sarkozy's plan would widen the French deficit to 3.9 percent of GDP in 2009. The economy was projected to contract by 0.4 percent in 2009, falling into its first recession in more than fifteen years.

French banks increased their lending to consumers and firms in October. The government pledged $13.3 billion in October to recapitalize six banks in exchange for promises to increase lending.

President Sarkozy announced another stimulus package of €26 billion, or $37 billion, as business confidence fell to the lowest in fifteen years and the economic slump continued its downslide. It was projected in mid-December that France would lose 191,000 jobs in the first half of 2009, following a drop of 125,000 in the second half of 2008.

In mid-January 2009, the government considered helping U.S. automakers ride out the credit crunch by covering up to 50 percent of their financing needs. An auto summit was planned. After Germany, Europe's second-largest car market by volume is France. Registrations of new vehicles fell to 74,659 in January, down 7.9 percent from a year earlier and 2.8 percent from December. Renault sales plunged 21 percent in January; Peugeot-Citroen saw an 11 percent slump in registrations. In addition, the market share of French manufacturers fell to 50 percent from 54.1 percent a year earlier.

Unemployment in France soared in December, pushing job losses in the fourth quarter to their highest level in more than two decades. The number of people seeking work rose by 45,000 in December, bringing the number of jobs lost in the fourth quarter to more than 156,000.

Unemployment was expected to rise to 8 percent by mid-2009 from 7.3 percent in last year's third quarter. By February, unemployment rose to 3.5 percent from the previous month to reach 2.38 million, up 19 percent for the year.

On February 2, the prime minister detailed the government's plan for boosting the economy, including 1,000 investment projects and €200 million for payments to low-income families. France's GDP was projected to contract 1.8 percent in 2009.

On February 9, France announced a sweeping $8.5 billion plan to supports its automobile industry. The two largest French carmakers, Peugeot-Citroen and Renault, would each get a five-year loan of €3 billion at an interest rate of 6 percent.

French industrial production dropped 1.8 percent in December 2008. GDP was expected to shrink by 3.3 percent, with unemployment rising to 8.6 percent in February, above the European Union average. For the new school year, 13,500 public-sector teaching jobs had to be cut.

The IMF forecast that France's economy would shrink a little more than 1 percent over 2009 and 2010. Between 2002 and 2007, the economy averaged 1.9 percent growth.

The French economy shrank for the fourth straight quarter, with GDP falling 1.2 percent from the fourth quarter of 2008.

On June 22, 2009, President Sarkozy addressed a joint session of the French Parliament at Versailles. He told lawmakers that he would sharply lower the state's "bad budget deficit," and introduce a government bond issue to finance industrial, education, and cultural projects.

France's economy expanded at an annualized rate of 1.4 percent in the second quarter 2009. By September 2009, the nation's economic outlook appeared brighter. After four consecutive quarters of decline, GDP grew. However, the jobless total reached 2.5 million in July, a jump of 26 percent on the same month a year earlier.

See also BNP PARIBAS; CONSUMER CONFIDENCE; EUROPEAN COMMISSION; ING GROUP; PEUGEOT-CITROEN; SOVEREIGN FUND.

FRANCHISING INDUSTRY. The number of defaults by franchisees increased 52 percent in the fiscal year ending September 30, 2008, from fiscal 2007. Loan losses totaled $93.3 million, a 167 percent jump from $35 million just twelve months earlier.

FRANK, BARNEY (BARNETT). Chairman of the Committee on Financial Services.

See also FEDERAL RESERVE; HOUSE (U.S.) FINANCIAL OVER-HAUL PLAN.

FRAUD. The watchdog and head of the Recovery Act Accountability and Transparency Board, nicknamed the Rat Board, over the $787 stimulus package believed that fraud consumed about 7 percent of all major contracts or over $55 billion.

See also INTERNAL REVENUE SERVICE.

FRAUD ENFORCEMENT AND RECOVERY ACT OF 2009. *See* FINANCIAL CRISIS INQUIRY COMMISSION.

FREDDIE MAC (FEDERAL HOME LOAN MORTGAGE CORPORATION) (FHLMC). Established in 1970, responsible for aiding the secondary residential mortgages sponsored by the Veterans Administration and Federal Housing Administration in addition to nongovernment residential mortgages.

The mortgage finance company, a government-sponsored enterprise (GSE), is now under government control.

On March 20, 2008 federal regulators eased Freddie Mac's capital requirements, a move that allowed the agency to purchase billions of dollars of mortgage securities.

An $821 million loss was announced on August 7, with warnings of further losses. Its shares dropped 19 percent.

Freddie Mac asked the U.S. Treasury on November 14, 2008, for $13.8 billion after a record quarterly loss caused its net worth to fall below zero.

Freddie Mac, which had a net worth of negative $13.7 billion at the end of the third quarter 2008, received the money by November 29. The net loss widened to $25.3 billion after it wrote down tax assets and provided for bad mortgages and securities.

Freddie Mac reported in early March a loss of $23.9 billion for the fourth quarter 2008 and said it required a $30.8 billion injection of capital from the U.S. Treasury. It had a loss of $2.45 billion from the year-earlier quarter. For the entire 2008 period, it had a loss of $50.1 billion compared with a year-before loss of $3.1 billion.

Freddie Mac's losses narrowed to $6.3 billion in the third quarter 2009.

The government owns 79.9 percent of Freddie Mac, and on December 24, 2009, offered a significant new financial support to the housing giant no matter how poorly it performs in the next few years. In addition, it approved a compensation package for its chief executive officer to receive up to $6 million for the coming two years. The pay package includes $900,000 in salary, $3.1 million in deferred payments in 2010 that are not dependent on performance, and an additional $2 million tied to meeting certain objectives.

See also FANNIE MAE; FEDERAL RESERVE; GINNIE MAE; HOUSING BAILOUT PLAN; MORTGAGE-BACKED SECURITY; SECURITIES AND EXCHANGE COMMISSION; U.S. TREASURY.

FREE FALL. *See* INTERNATIONAL MONETARY FUND.

FREIGHT HAULERS. The freight transportation industry remained in a sharp slump by the end of April 2009. U.S. air-cargo volumes dropped 21 percent in February 2009; railroad firms reported declines of 23 percent to 26 percent.

FRUGALITY. In 2009, consumers became increasingly cautious in their spending habits amid fears of a worsening economy over the coming twelve months. Deflation can result from a pattern of hesitation.

See also DEFLATION.

FSF (FINANCIAL STABILITY FORUM). *See* REGULATORS.

FTSE. Stocks in Europe had their worst annual fall in more than twenty years at the end of 2008, its worst performance since records began. FTSE Eurofirst lost 32.4 percent of its value in 2008, substantially larger than its previous biggest annual loss of 24.5 percent.

FUEL TAX. By 2009, there was a call for increasing the current 18.4 cents a gallon federal tax on gasoline and 24.4 cents a gallon tax on diesel. State fuel taxes vary from state to state.

See also AUTOMOBILE INDUSTRY.

FUR INDUSTRY. In 2007, global fur retail sales were a record $15 billion. In this meltdown period, sales in 2008 and 2009 plummeted, as much as 30 percent.

FURLOUGHS. On February 6, 2009, the first of the semimonthly work furloughs across California state agencies would trim $1.3 billion from that state's $143 billion budget, effecting 200,000 employees. For those forced on leave, it meant a 9 percent pay cut to aid the coffers of California. California's unemployment rate at that time was 9.3 percent, among the highest in the country.

By 2009, furloughs that were usually confined to factory workers were hitting the office scene as employers were digging deeper to cut costs. More and more firms were instituting these short-term furloughs as a humane alternative to permanent job cuts.

The arguments for and against unpaid furloughs include:

a. benefits—reduces labor costs quickly, helps keep highly skilled workers, and avoids rehiring and retraining.
b. disadvantages—could drive away top performers, prolongs cost cutting, and drains long-term morale.

Synonymous with TEMPORARY LAYOFFS.

FUTURES TRADING PRACTICES ACT OF 1992. Authorized the Commodity Futures Trading Commission to exempt certain over-the-counter transactions from most of the Commodity Exchange Act. The CFTC would use its new authority to exempt some swap agreements, hybrid instruments, and energy contracts.

G

GAMBLING. Following the meltdown, states struggling to balance their budgets were seeking way to increase their revenues. Gambling had become a growing source of income. The near $100 billion-a-year source of revenue was being considered by states across the country. However, with tourism down from past years, the risks of failure remained high.

GANNETT. The largest newspaper publisher in the nation, it reported in mid-April 2009, a 60 percent decline in first-quarter profits. Gannett publishes dozens of daily papers, and earned $77.4 million in the first three months of the year, compared to $192 million the year before.

Gannet announced at the end of June 2009 that it would cut between 1,000 and 2,000 jobs out of its 41,500 workforce as a result of dramatic drops in advertising income and lower circulation. Net income fell nearly 60 percent from a year before as publishing ad revenue declined more than 34 percent. By the end of the month, the newspaper publisher announced that 1,400 positions would be eliminated from its workforce of 41,500.

On October 19, 2009, Gannett's management reported a 53 percent fall in third-quarter income. Publishing advertising fell 28 percent in the quarter from the year before, an improvement from the 32 percent ad-revenue decline in the second quarter.

GAP. By the end of December 2008, the retailer suffered a 14 percent drop in same-store sales. Fiscal fourth-quarter 2008 net income fell 8.3 percent on a 13 percent sales drop.

Gap's second-quarter profit 2009 fell slightly.

In November 2009, Gap announced that its quarterly profit climbed 25 percent following five straight years of declines. The company reported a profit of $307 million.

See also RETAILING.

GATT. *See* GENERAL AGREEMENT ON TARIFFS AND TRADE.

GDP. *See* GROSS DOMESTIC PRODUCT.

GE. *See* GENERAL ELECTRIC.

GE CAPITAL CORPORATION. *See* GENERAL ELECTRIC.

G-8 (GROUP OF 8). Members of the G-7, plus Russia.
See also G-20.

GEITHNER, TIMOTHY F. President Obama's secretary of the Treasury. He graduated from Dartmouth College, majoring in government and Asian studies. He then completed his master's degree (1985) from Johns Hopkins School of Advanced International Studies and later joined the Treasury Department as an assistant financial attaché at the U.S. Tokyo Embassy. Following a stint at the International Monetary Fund, he was recruited in November 2000 as the president of the New York Fed, the second-most prominent job in the country's central banking system.

A controversial aspect of his career was his role in failing to save Lehman Brothers while at the Fed in New York. It is believed that he was a key decision maker in September 2008 when the government let Lehman Brothers fail and then, two days later, bailed out the insurer American International Group for $85 billion. This was considered an abrupt reversal from the "no new bailout" position taken with Lehman, and initially with AIG.

His much-anticipated speech on February 10, 2009, where he announced the administration's financial rescue plan, was followed by nearly a 5 percent selloff of stocks, the worst drop since President Obama assumed office.

On March 23, Geithner delivered the long-awaited details of his scheme to save the banking system, which dazzled Wall Street. He called for broad regulation of derivative trading, nonbanks, and hedge funds.

TARP has closely been identified with the Treasury secretary. Some people are calling the TARP effort the Hotel Geithner. On November 19, 2009, the Treasury secretary announced his hope to end the bailout fund, TARP, as soon as possible and to use funds from the $700 billion program to reduce debt.

See also BANK RESCUE (PLAN) OF 2009; FEDERAL RESERVE; MAKING HOME AFFORDABLE PROGRAM; TARP; "TOO BIG TO FAIL."

GENDER. *See* WOMEN WORKFORCE.

GENERAL AGREEMENT ON TARIFFS AND TRADE (GATT). On January 1, 1948, a multilateral trade treaty was signed, embodying reciprocal commercial rights and obligations as a means of expanding and liberalizing world trade. It established common regulations and obligations concerning international trading arrangements and the framework for the negotiation of agreements to liberalize world trade. It was accepted by over 80 fully participating nations, with nearly 30 others signing under special arrangements. These nations at that time accounted for almost 80 percent of world trade.

With GATT, following the end of World War II, world trade expanded faster than global output did. With GATT, tariffs worldwide have been cut from an average of 40 percent in 1947 to less than 5 percent today, and consumers have reaped rich rewards in the form of lower prices and better merchandise. GATT, based in Geneva, Switzerland, has been remarkably successful and crucial to a strong world economy.

In 1995, GATT became the World Trade Organization (WTO).

See also PROTECTIONISM; WORLD TRADE ORGANIZATION.

GENERAL DYNAMICS. On March 5, 2009, the firm announced the cut of 1,200 jobs, sending its shares to a six-year low.

The company's third-quarter 2009 earnings fell 9.8 percent. Overall profit for the period was $572 million. Revenue increased 8.1 percent to $7.72 billion.

GENERAL ELECTRIC (GE). Posted fourth-quarter earnings (2008) with shares dropping more than 50 percent. GE expected earnings growth of zero to 5 percent in 2009, from its industrial and media divisions, down from 10 percent in 2008.

In February 2009, GE shrank its dividend by 68 percent, the first such cut since the Great Depression. GE lowered its dividend for the first time in 71 years, to 10 cents a share per quarter from 31 cents,

On March 6, in what was termed a "housekeeping exercise," GE's Capital Corporation unit offered to purchase back $1.46 billion of its bonds as a way to boost its financial flexibility and make it easier to participate in new government financing efforts.

On March 23, GE lost its coveted triple-A credit rating, which it had first won in 1956. By one notch GE's long-term debt was dropped to AA-plus rating by Moody's.

The company's profit fell sharply in the first quarter 2009 from a year earlier, down 36 percent to $2.74 billion. Its revenue for the quarter fell 9 percent, to $38.4 billion.

GE's second-quarter 2009 net income fell 49 percent. Profit at its financial division, GE Capital, declined 80 percent to $590 million.

For its third-quarter 2009 profit there was a 42 percent decline, with a net income of $2.49 billion down from $4.31 billion one year before. Revenue declined 20 percent to $37.8 billion from $47.2 billion. Earnings fell at GE Capital 87 percent to $263 million. The real estate group saw a $538 million loss from a $244 profit one year earlier.

GE projected revenue in 2010 to be roughly $155 billion, similar to 2009, with a profit margin of about 16 percent.

See also MOODY'S.

GENERAL ELECTRIC CAPITAL CORPORATION (GE CAPITAL CORPORATION). *See* GENERAL ELECTRIC.

GENERAL GROWTH PROPERTIES. One of the nation's largest mall operators, it filed for bankruptcy on April 16, 2009, in one of the biggest such collapses in U.S. history. Founded more than fifty years ago, this giant in retailing had 200 malls in forty-four states. The company's shopping centers encompassed 200 million square feet of space and 24,000 tenants. It was unable to refinance the $3.3 billion in debt that had already matured or would be due in 2009.

By November 2009, General Growth Properties revealed to a bankruptcy court that it had reached a deal with lenders and servicers to restructure $8.9 billion of mortgages on seventy-seven malls in anticipation of getting out of bankruptcy protection by the end of December.

GENERAL MILLS. General Mills saw a lower profit for its fiscal third quarter 2008, hurt by high input costs, the strong dollar, and the impact of weak consumer spending on its foodservice business. Its shares dropped 11 percent, with a net income of $288.9 million, down 33 percent a year earlier. Net sales rose 3.9 percent to $3.54 billion.

General Mills reported a 49 percent increase in fiscal second-quarter 2009 earnings. For the quarter ending November 29, 2009, the firm reported a profit of $565 million. Sales climbed 1.7 percent to $4.08 billion on top of 8 percent growth in the prior-year period.

GENERAL MOTORS. Founded in 1908 incorporating Buick Motor Company. On February 13, 2008, GM announced that it ended 2007 $38.7 billion in the red, the largest annual loss ever by an automaker. In July, it indicated plans to sell assets, including its Hummer brand worth $2–4 billion.

GM sales in the United States plummeted 45 percent in October 2008. The company sold nearly 169,000 vehicles in October, down from about 307,000 a year earlier. Car sales dropped 34 percent, while light truck sales declined 51 percent. Rumors spread about a potential merger between GM and Chrysler.

Its revenue in the third quarter fell 13 percent to $37.9 billion from $43.7 billion in November 2007, one year earlier. General Motors, the largest American automaker, had been losing more than $2 billion a month from its cash cushion.

GM shares tumbled on November 11, to 1946 prices; its stock was downgraded on worries that the company would soon run out of cash and shareholders would be wiped out by any federal bailout.

In a bankruptcy, GM's labor contracts with its 479,000 retirees and their spouses would be at risk of termination.

Shareholders had already lost much of the equity that would disappear in a bankruptcy case. Shares had fallen 90.5 percent throughout 2008. GM, with $111 billion in assets, would rank as one of the biggest bankruptcies ever.

In December GM secured $13.4 billion from the U.S. Treasury. GM was unable to meet conditions of the loan. GMAC converted itself into a bank holding company and took $6 billion bailout from the U.S. government.

By late December, President Bush decided to provide funds to both General Motors and Chrysler in order to prevent them from running out of cash.

GM's December decline totaled 31 percent. GM sold 220,030 light vehicles in December compared with 319,837 a year earlier.

January 2009 sales slid 49 percent to 128,198 vehicles. Then on February 10, GM announced that it would cut 10,000 white-collar jobs worldwide in 2009, amounting to 14 percent of its salaried workers globally. GM began offering retirement incentives to 22,000 of its 62,000 union members.

In February, GM presented another plan to Congress asking for up to $16.6 billion. Saab filed for bankruptcy protection and German unit Opel sought state aid.

For the year 2008, GM had a $30.9 billion loss. Revenues fell 17 percent to $149 billion from 2007, as vehicle sales plummeted 11 percent globally. GM consumed $5.2 billion in cash during the fourth quarter on an operating basis, and $19 billion over the year, as the rate of sales decline outpaced the firm's ability to cut costs.

GM lost $9.6 billion in the last three months of 2008, more than $100 million a day, with more than two-thirds of the money borrowed from the government since December 2008.

On February 17, GM offered to drop half of its brands, cut 47,000 jobs out of its 244,000 worldwide workforce, and close five of its North American plants, leaving thirty-three. In exchange for restructuring and deep cuts, GM asked for another $16.6 billion of taxpayers' money (GM had already received $13.4 billion in loans). By March 31, a presidential task force ruled on whether the company had restructured sufficiently to be viable. Failure to receive these funds brought renewed questions of the automaker's survivability, with bankruptcy lying ahead.

By mid-February GM was subsisting on $13.4 billion in government bailout loans. The automaker claimed it had only about $14 billion in cash on hand, and that it was using it at the rate of $2 billion each month. It was asking the president's auto task force for as much as $16.6 billion more, including $4 billion to fund operations in March and April.

On March 12, GM announced that it had sufficient funds to keep operating through the end of March and would not seek the $2 billion government infusion that it had earlier requested.

As part of its restructuring plans, 7,600 factory workers volunteered to leave GM under a buyout program.

Before providing additional government funding for GM, on March 29, Rick Wagoner, GM's Chief Executive, was ousted, assuredly indicating the Treasury Department's deep involvement in the affairs of the nation's largest and oldest car firm.

GM reduced production by idling most of its plants for about two months during the summer 2009. Union members received most of their pay during the shutdown. By the end of March, GM had a 113-day supply of cars and a 123-day supply of trucks sitting unsold on dealer lots.

On April 27, GM outlined its new turnaround plan that would leave the U.S. government controlling the carmaker, creating a potential showdown with its bondholders. Under the program, GM was asking the Treasury Department for another $11.6 billion in loans, on top of the $15.4 billion it had already received. The government would then have at least half ownership of GM, as payment for half of the loans.

At the same time, GM would use stock instead of cash to pay off half the $20.4 billion it owes a United Auto Workers fund to cover retiree health care, leaving the union owning 39 percent of GM.

GM projected a smaller, more-focused car company hoping for profits as early as 2010. By the end of April, management announced a restructuring plan that would nearly wipe out the company's unsecured debt holders and require 42 percent of its dealers to close their doors.

GM had to convince its unsecured bond holder holding $27 billion to accept GM stock instead—stock that might be wiped out in a bankruptcy filing. Unless holders of 90 percent of the debt agreed, the offer would be withdrawn. A May 26 deadline had to be met.

GM also agreed to pay stock instead of $10.2 billion in cash to a trust fund to be managed by the UAW. At the same time, GM would cut 7,000 more union jobs than it had proposed in a February 17 revamping proposal, reducing these ranks to 40,000 from 61,000 by 2010.

It said it would shut down its Pontiac brand and stop making its Saturn by the end of 2009. Its U.S. dealer count would be reduced by 42 percent by the end of 2010, a reduction of 500 more dealers four years sooner than earlier stated.

GM's first-quarter 2009 losses widened significantly to nearly $6 billion. Revenues shrank 47 percent to $22.43 billion from $42.38 billion a year before. The automaker consumed $10.2 billion in cash during the quarter, nearly double the amount it consumed in the fourth quarter 2008.

On May 21, GM received $4 billion in U.S. aid, $1.4 billion more than it had originally requested.

On May 29, Magna was chosen as preferred bidder for GM Europe after Fiat pulled out.

GM, which hadn't made a profit since 2004, filed for bankruptcy protection on June 1, becoming the second-largest industrial bankruptcy in history (the largest bankruptcy was WorldCom's filing in 2002). The company announced that owners of 1,100 U.S. dealerships would be dropped from its retail network. GM had been hemorrhaging for decades. For the past thirty years, it had been losing nearly one percentage point of market share each year. It sold 45 percent of new vehicles in the United States in 1980, 35 percent in 1990, 28 percent in 2000, and 19 percent by June 2009.

GM planned to close seventeen factories and parts centers and lop off 20,000 more jobs by the end of 2011.

GM and the UAW agreed to a new restructuring plan, and left the U.S. government owning as much as 70 percent of the carmaker. Ten percent of the new GM would be owned by existing bondholders, while a UAW union health care fund would own 17.5 percent. The Canadian government would own the remaining 12.5 percent. GM ceased being part of the Dow Jones Industrial Average (after eighty-four years) one week later.

After finding purchasers for its Hummer and Saturn brands, GM negotiated an agreement to sell its Saab unit to Koenigsegg, a Swedish maker of high-performance cars. The arrangement is tied to a $600 million loan backed by the Swedish government.

GM cut 4,000 U.S. white-collar jobs by October 1, 600 more than it earlier declared. This totaled more than 6,000 salaried jobs in total in 2009. Executive ranks were reduced by 34 percent.

On July 10, GM emerged from bankruptcy, and then announced plans to ask more than 400 of its 1,300 executives to resign or retire. The bankruptcy journey, which began on June 1, had in its forty days of bankruptcy protection reduced its debt by more than $40 billion, with the loss of factories, workers, brands, and scores of dealerships across the United States. The best of GM's assets, including Chevrolet and Cadillac brands, were formally transferred to the "new" GM in court on July 10.

On July 22, GM posted its sixth consecutive quarterly decline in global sales. These sales declined 15 percent worldwide to 1.93 million cars, from the same period one year earlier. U.S. sales fell 32 percent in the same period.

On August 1, 2009, GM returned to the auto-leasing market. Leasing represents about 20 percent of GM's new-car business.

On August 3, GM announced that the expected layoffs of factory workers who volunteered through a buyout and early retirement totaled about 6,000. The company was still about 48,000 hourly workers short, which is 7,500 employees more than its year-end goal of 40,500. Workers who resigned received cash payments of $20,000 to $115,000, with the largest amount going to those who gave up retirement benefits other than their pensions. Departing workers also received a voucher worth $25,000 toward a new-vehicle purchase.

Even during the Clunker program in August 2009, GM sales dropped 20 percent.

GM announced on September 2 that its sales growth in China, its fastest growing market, was expected to increase 40 percent in 2009. Sales from its Chinese passenger-vehicle joint venture more than doubled in August 2009 from a year before to 21,127. GM's sales doubled in China in the third quarter 2009 from the year before. The company's 478,000 vehicles sales in China help make GM a successful world player, with China presently accounting for at least 25 percent of GM's global sales, compared with 10 percent one year earlier.

In order to persuade people that its cars are as good as its competitors', GM launched in mid-September 2009 a campaign featuring a 60-day money-back guarantee, running until November 30. Customers will be able to return cars between thirty-one and sixty days after purchase and with less than 4,000 miles.

On September 10, 2009, GM agreed to sell a 55 percent stake in its Opel unit to Magna, making Magna one of the world's largest car parts makers. However, on November 1, GM reversed its decision.

In mid-November 2009, GM announced its plans to pay back a $6.7 billion loan to the U.S. government, beginning toward the end of the year. The company hoped to repay its obligation by the middle of 2011 by returning $1 billion per quarter. It also expects to repay the Canadian government $200 million each quarter.

On November 16, 2009, GM reported a $1.15 billion third-quarter loss. Its revenue fell 26 percent to $28 billion from the 2008 period.

See also AUTOMOBILE INDUSTRY; AUTO TASK FORCE; CHRYSLER; CONTROLLED BANKRUPTCY; DELPHI; GMAC; HUMMER; MAGNA; OPEL; PRESIDENTIAL TASK FORCE ON AUTOS; SAAB; SUBSIDIES; U.S. TREASURY; WAGONER, RICK.

Cf. FORD.

GENERIC FOOD. *See* FOOD SPENDING.

GEORGIAN BANK. *See* BANK FAILURES.

GERMANY. An index of business confidence fell to a five-year low at the end of October 2008, the lowest level since 2003. On November 5, 2008, Chancellor Merkel's cabinet approved a near $30 billion stimulus package in a bid to unlock more than twice that amount in investments and help Germany, the world's biggest exporter, to weather a sharp global slowdown.

Officially, Germany, with the largest economy in Europe and fourth-largest in the world, entered a recession on November 13. Germany's GDP contracted 0.5 percent in the third quarter—more than the 0.2 percent decline that had been anticipated. That followed a decline in the second quarter of 0.4 percent.

German unemployment fell to 7.1 percent in November as the number of people out of work hit a sixteen-year low. There were increasing signs that the economic crisis would soon hit the job market.

On December 4, the government announced a €500 voucher plan to be given to every adult, on the condition that he or she purchase something. It would be an expensive program, costing about $51 billion. This complicated program required that Germans pay €200 to receive the €500 voucher.

The central bank predicted in early December that its economy would shrink 0.8 percent in 2009. By contrast, a private research firm believed the German economy would shrink 2 percent in 2009.

The government ended its economic summit on December 15, saying that their employers would sustain a "voluntary no-firing" policy as part of efforts to pull the country out of recession. Chancellor Merkel called the session to develop an approach to deal with the economic crisis. Evidence around the country indicated that many large firms had set policy to at least temporarily close factories, create shorter work weeks, and in some cases dismiss employees for the time period. Merkel's strategy appeared to run contradictory to most other EU governments.

Pressure was put on the government to increase its stimulus package by a further €25 billion, or about 1 percent of GDP.

On the last day of the year 2008, Germany received European Commission approval for two programs: a $21.2 billion loan effort for companies affected by the credit crunch and a measure permitting the government to provide aid of as much as €500,000 per firm.

Germany's chancellor agreed on January 5, 2009, to give Europe's biggest economy an extra stimulus of up to $70 billion in an effort to cushion it against a deepening recession. This added to an existing $31.35 billion package given earlier.

On the day that China passed Germany as the third-largest economy in the world, it was announced that the German economy had contracted by as much as 2 percent in the final quarter of 2008. German GDP increased 1.3 percent for all of 2008, a modest growth rate that masked a steep decline late in the year and was significantly slower than the 2.5 percent rate for 2007.

Although the German government forecast in March that the GDP for 2009 would fall only 2.25 percent, the Commerzbank forecast projected a 6 percent to 7 percent drop. Germany, the largest European economy, led the way down with a 3.8 percent decline in the first quarter.

Germany's GDP, the value of all its goods and services, fell by nearly 7 percent in the year ending June 2009, driven largely by foreigners purchasing fewer German goods. Germany's exports make up 47 percent of its GDP, but exports had been dropping 17 percent over the year.

In mid-July, the government stated that its GDP shrank 2.2 percent in the fourth quarter of 2008 from the previous three months and then contracted a further 3.8 percent in the first quarter of 2009. Germany exported 23.5 percent less in the first six months of 2009 than it did in 2008.

Chancellor Angela Merkel and her party Christian Democrats won re-election at the end of September 2009. The government projected that the economy would contract by 5 percent in 2009 and was expected to grow by 1.2 percent in 2010.

On November 1, 2009 GM announced that it would reverse its earlier decision and backed out of a deal to sell both Vauxhall and Opel to Magna International, the Canadian auto parts maker. Instead the board reflected GM's increasing self-confidence in its future ability to expand the markets for these two car companies.

Germany's industrial production rose 2.7 percent in September 2009, with a 5.9 percent increase in capital goods production.

See also ARCANDOR; AUTOMOBILE INDUSTRY; BASF; DAIMLER; DEUTSCHE BANK; JOB BANKS; METRO; TOYOTA; VOLKSWAGEN.

G-5 (GROUP OF 5). Composed of the United States, Great Britain, France, Germany, and Japan.

GILT EDGE. *See* MOODY'S.

GINNIE MAE (GOVERNMENT NATIONAL MORTGAGE ASSOCI-ATION). An agency formed in the Department of Housing and Urban Development. Its primary function is in the area of government-approved special housing programs, offering permanent financing for low-rent housing.

See also FANNIE MAE; FREDDIE MAC; GINNIE MAE PASS-THROUGH SECURITIES; GINNIE MAE TRUSTS; GINNIE MAE II; MORTGAGE-BACKED SECURITY.

GINNIE MAE PASS-THROUGH SECURITIES. Under this program, principal and interest payments collected on mortgages in specified pools are "passed through" to holders of GNMA-guaranteed certificates after deduction of servicing and guaranty fees. Actual maturity of these certificates is forty years, but the average life is approximately twelve years because of prepayments. The minimum denomination of certificates is $25,000 and issuance is in registered form only.

GINNIE MAE TRUSTS. Closed-end unit investment trusts made up of Ginnie Mae certificates. The cost is $1,000 per unit with a sales charge of around 4 percent. The monthly payments cover earned interest and amortization—the same as having direct participation in Ginnie Mae certificates, which are available only in the larger denominations.

GINNIE MAE II. Started in July 1983, similar to the original Ginnie Mae with other advantages. Allows originators to join together to issue jumbo pools, which combine mortgages from different issuers into a single package, as well as continue to be sole issuers. Holders of Ginnie Mae II are paid on the twenty-fifth day of the month, in contrast to the fifteenth day of the month for the original Ginnie Mae; thereby the ten-day delay lowers the yield on the securities by about five points.

GLASS-STEAGALL ACT OF 1933. A federal legislative safeguard designed to prevent commercial banks from engaging in investment banking activities; it also authorized deposit insurance. No longer active. This legislation was an immediate outgrowth of the Pecora Commission investigation.

See also BANKING ACT OF 1933; GRAMM-LEACH-BILLEY ACT OF 1999; PECORA COMMISSION.

GLITNIR. *See* ICELAND.

GLOBAL ECONOMIC OUTPUT. The Asian Development Bank warned on March 9, 2009, that the value of financial assets worldwide reached more than $50 trillion, the equivalent to a year's global economic output, including $9.6 trillion of losses in developing areas of Asia alone. The bank took into account falling stock market valuations and losses in the value of bonds supported by mortgages and other assets. About a fifth of the losses in dollar terms arose from the depreciation of many currencies against the U.S. dollar.

GLOBAL MERCHANDISE TRADE. Shrank by 9 percent in 2009, the first decline since 1982.

GLOBAL MERGERS. Activity in 2008 fell 29 percent.
See also MERGERS AND ACQUISITIONS.

GLOBAL SLUMP. *See* G-20.

GLOBAL TRADE. Tariff barriers may be the protectionist's primary wall to protect national industries, along with subsidies and currency levers.

Tariffs on goods had fallen from a worldwide average in 1986 of 26 percent to 8.8 percent in 2007.

The dollar value of exports in 2009 in nearly fifty countries was about one-third lower than in May 2008. The average value of exports, accounting for three-quarters of world trade, fell by 15.4 percent in November 2008, and dropped by 12.2 percent in January 2009.

Global trade flows fell in August 2009 after climbing for the two previous months. Trade volumes fell 2 percent from July. The IMF said that world trade fell 11.9 percent overall in the year, the biggest since the Great Depression. A modest 2.5 percent increase was projected by the IMF for 2010.

See also PROTECTIONISM; SMOOT-HAWLEY ACT OF 1930; TRADE; WORLD TRADE ORGANIZATION.

GLOBAL TRADE FLOWS. *See* GLOBAL TRADE.

GLOBAL UNEMPLOYMENT. In February 2009, Dennis C. Blair, director of U.S. national intelligence, told Congress that instability caused by the global economic crisis had become the biggest security threat facing the United States, outpacing terrorism.

Protectionism fears also abounded as countries throughout the world were seeking ways of cushioning their local economies and businesses.

See also PROTECTIONISM; UNEMPLOYMENT.

GMAC (FINANCIAL SERVICES). Provides financing for GM dealers and its customers as well as home mortgage loans through one of its divisions. The company is 51 percent owned by Cerberus Capital Management, the investment fund that also owns Chrysler. GM owns the remaining 49 percent of the firm.

Investors holding about $10.5 billion in bonds agreed to revise terms of a debt swap, bringing the company closer to getting rescue funds from U.S. banking programs.

On December 24, 2008, the Federal Reserve approved the eighty-nine-year-old GMAC Financial Services' request to become a bank holding company. That designation made GMAC eligible to receive a portion of the $700 billion bailout fund and get emergency loans directly from the Fed. This decision bolstered General Motors' ability to survive.

On December 30, GMAC resumed financing to a wider range of car buyers, a day after the U.S. Treasury injected billions of dollars into the lender. Under the financing deal, the Treasury injected $5 billion into GMAC as part of a deal that let the lender convert itself into a bank holding company and enabled it to borrow money at low rates from the Federal Reserve.

The lender awaited FDIC approval to issue FDIC-insured debt. On May 5, GMAC reported a loss for the first quarter 2009 of $675 million, widening from a loss of $589 billion a year before. The results were aided by a $631 million after-tax gain from retiring debt. Without this gain, GMAC's loss had totaled about $1.3 billion.

On August 4, 2009, GMAC posted a wider second-quarter loss of $3.9 billion, compared to a loss of $280 million a year before. Revenue dropped during the quarter by 28 percent, to $1.27 billion, from $1.76 billion one year earlier.

While other financial institutions were doing well, by October 2009 GMAC negotiated with the Treasury Department for its third helping of taxpayer funds.

On December 30, 2009, the government said that it would provide GMAC Financial Services an additional $3.8 billion in capital and assume a majority stake in the firm. This would be in addition to the $12.5 billion already received since December 2008.

See also CHRYSLER; FEDERAL RESERVE; GENERAL MOTORS.

G-NEXT. An inclusion of new members such as China, India, and Brazil in the G-20.

See also G-20.

GOLD. Gold climbed $22.10 to $857 a troy ounce on January 3, 2008, the highest ever. Gold closed at $857.20 at the end of the year, an advance of 5.8 percent.

In another sign of flagging investor confidence, gold topped $1,000 an ounce on February 20. The previous high and record was on March 8, 2008, when gold hit $1,003.20. Then, on February 21, gold delivery rose $25.70, or 2.6 percent, to $1,001.80. It then dropped.

By mid-September 2009 gold traded at about $1,000, the highest level since February. Gold had risen 9.7 percent since mid-July 2009.

By December 2, gold surged to a record high of $1,200 a troy ounce, only to retreat by December 10 to $1,120.40 a troy ounce.

GOLDEN PARACHUTE. Employment contract for top management, usually long term, providing for continued compensation in the event control of a company changes hands.

In February 2009, President Obama restricted severance packages for dismissed executives receiving government bailout funds.

See also AUTOMOBILE INDUSTRY; CLAWBACKS; HOUSE (U.S.) FINANCIAL OVERHAUL PLAN.

GOLDMAN SACHS. Goldman Sachs transformed itself in September 2008 into a deposit-taking bank holding company with direct access to borrowing from the Federal Reserve. The firm was now legally bound to take fewer risks.

Goldman Sachs, the envy of Wall Street, had not reported a loss since the U.S. stock market crash of 1929. But the panic of 2008 ended its profitable run. On December 16, 2008, Goldman announced a quarterly loss of $2.16 billion, or $4.97 a share, resulting from its investments plunging in value. Goldman shares were at $65.89 on December 15, down about 70 percent in 2008.

At the end of the third quarter 32,569 people were employed by Goldman, down by 8 percent.

Revenue in Goldman's big trading and principal investment business was a negative $4.36 billion, in contrast to a positive $6.93 billion in the fourth quarter of 2007.

By February 2009, Goldman Sachs was determined to repay the $10 billion it got from the federal government as soon as possible, in order to end the toughened scrutiny that came with the money. Returning these funds would put pressure on other financial institutions to do the same and would, in the long run, add to the prestige of Goldman.

Goldman announced on April 13 its intentions to get out from under government control. It purported to raise $5 billion by selling new common shares to investors. It would be used to help repay the $10 billion government bailout money received in 2008. GS also paid a $1.1 billion interest charge to the government. By returning funds to the government, Goldman Sachs hoped that the restrictions on pay would be lifted, which would allow it to better compete with firms such as foreign banks that don't have these restrictions.

At the same time, Goldman Sachs announced profits of $1.66 billion in the quarter, or $3.39 a share, marking a strong comeback from a loss in late 2008. The day before, the investment bank sold $5 billion worth of shares in an effort to raise money to repay the U.S. government for its bailout funds. Then on April 14, Goldman stocks fell $15.04, or 12 percent, to $115.11.

Goldman Sachs announced on July 14 that its net income in the second quarter 2009 was $3.44 billion, or $4.93 a share, more than the company earned in all of 2008. Net revenue was up 46 percent to $13.76 billion. The firm set aside $11.36 billion for compensation and benefits during the year's first six months, enough to pay each employee $386,429 for the period.

Goldman posted its richest quarterly profit in its 140-year history. Employees could, on average, earn roughly $770,000 in 2009. The firm earmarked $16.71 billion for employee compensation in 2009.

On October 15, 2009, Goldman Sachs reported an impressive quarter with a profit of $3.19 billion for the three months ended September 25, up from $845 million from a year prior.

On November 17, GS announced that it would launch a $500 million small-business assistance program, along with Warren Buffet. This would be the firm's largest charitable gift in its history. There would be $250 million set aside for charities, $200 million for investor education, and $50 million for community-development grants. GS would fund firms employing at least four full-time workers and having revenues from $150,000 to $4 million in the most recent fiscal year. Firms had to be operating for at least two years and work "predominantly in underserved markets."

To defuse public outrage over its year-end bonuses to its top thirty executives on December 10, 2009, the firm announced that these senior managers would not be receiving cash bonuses. Only stock would be offered that cannot be sold for five years. This situation is only for 2009 and did not impact the more than 31,000 other employees, consultants, and temporary workers.

See also BLANKFEIN, LLOYD; BUFFETT, WARREN E.; FEDERAL RESERVE; HIGH-FREQUENCY TRADING; INVESTMENT BANKING; "TOO BIG TO FAIL"; TROUBLED ASSET RELIEF PROGRAM.

Cf. JP MORGAN CHASE; MORGAN STANLEY.

"GOOD BANKS." *See* "BAD BANKS"; "NEW BANKS."

GOODYEAR TIRE AND RUBBER COMPANY. America's largest tire manufacturer, it posted a fourth-quarter 2008 loss with plans, announced February 18, 2009, to cut another 5,000 jobs.

The company broke a pattern of three quarterly losses, with earnings falling by as much as $125 million. For the third quarter 2009, earnings more than doubled to $72 million, from $31 million a year before. Sales fell 15 percent to $4.39 billion.

See also AUTOMOBILE INDUSTRY.

GOODY'S FAMILY CLOTHING. Filed for Chapter 11 bankruptcy protection in January 2009.

GOOGLE. Google's growth remained slow in the second quarter 2009. The firm inched up 2.9 percent from a year earlier to $5.52 billion, down from a 6 percent growth in the first quarter, and far below the 39 percent growth Google witnessed in the second quarter one year earlier.

In the third quarter 2009, Google's revenue increased 7 percent from the year before to $5.94 billion. Net income rose 27 percent to $1.64 billion from a year before.

See also COMPUTERS.

GOVERNMENT NATIONAL MORTGAGE ASSOCIATION. *See* GIN-NIE MAE.

GOVERNMENT SPENDING. *See* FISHER, IRVING; KEYNES, JOHN MAYNARD.

GOVERNMENT-SPONSORED ENTERPRISE (GSE). GSE debt is held by financial institutions around the world.
   See also FANNIE MAE; FREDDIE MAC.

GOVERNMENT TRANSFERS. *See* AMERICAN RECOVERY AND RE-INVESTMENT ACT (OF 2009).

GRADUATED-PAYMENT ADJUSTABLE MORTGAGE. A mortgage with an adjustable rate; the borrower and lender share interest-rate risk.
   See also GRADUATED-PAYMENT ADJUSTABLE MORTGAGE LOAN.

GRADUATED-PAYMENT ADJUSTABLE MORTGAGE LOAN. A mortgage instrument that combines features of the graduated payment mortgage and the adjustable mortgage loan; authorized by the Federal Home Loan Bank Board in July 1981. Lenders are able to offer mortgage loans where the interest rate may change to reflect changes in the market place and where the monthly payments for the first ten years may be set at a lower amount than required to fully amortize the loan.

GRADUATED-PAYMENT MORTGAGE. First insured by the Federal Housing Administration in 1977, where payments are much lower at first than for traditional level-payment mortgages. Prices then rise gradually and level off after a few years. The idea is to put home ownership within reach of young people who might otherwise be forced by spiraling housing prices and high interest rates to remain renters.
   See also PLEDGED-ACCOUNT MORTGAGE.

GRAMM-LEACH-BILLEY ACT OF 1999. Repealed the Glass-Steagall Act's wall between banks and securities firms, allowing some institutions to engage in commercial banking, securities underwriting and dealing, and insurance underwriting.
   See also GLASS-STEAGALL ACT OF 1933.

GREAT DEPRESSION (OF THE 1930S). In the 1930s, total government spending as a share of the economy was less than 20 percent and the unemployment rate averaged more than 17 percent. By 1933, the U.S. economy had shrunk by one-third in real terms since 1929. Industrial production had fallen by 40 percent. Job losses in 1930 shed 4.8 percent of the labor force. In

1931, it was 6.5 percent; in 1932, another 7.1 percent. Unemployment eventually soared to 25 percent, from 3 percent in 1929.

Due particularly to the entry of the United States in World War II, total government spending as a share of the economy rose to 52 percent and peaked at nearly 70 percent in 1944, when unemployment fell to 1 percent.

Economists define "depression" differently. For example, some see it as a period of 10 percent unemployment plus two consecutive quarters of economic contraction. There are two major criteria—a decline in real GDP that exceeds 10 percent, or a recession that lasts more than three years.

Unlike the depression of the 1930s, real gross domestic product rose in 2008, despite a bad fourth quarter. GDP declined 2 percent in 2009. The 1929 stock market crash didn't topple major banks or corporations; it merely wiped out a generation of speculators.

See also EX-IM BANK; KEYNES, JOHN MAYNARD; PECORA COMISSION; RECESSION OF 2007–2010; ROOSEVELT, FRANKLIN DELANO; STANDARD & POOR'S.

Cf. RECESSION.

GREAT MODERATION. A period of low inflation and shallow recession; in the United States lasting twenty-six years, from 1982 until 2008.

GREAT RECESSION. *Synonymous with* RECESSION OF 2007–2010.

GREECE. By the end of summer 2009, recession was present and the nation's economy was projected to fall for the remaining months of the year. Tourist receipts were down by 15–20 percent. Greece's budget deficit hit 6–7 percent of GDP for the year. On November 13, 2009, data indicated that the nation's economy contracted by 0.3 percent; GDP in the January–March period declined 0.5 percent.

The country's 2009 budget deficit was 12.7 percent of GDP and its debt was estimated to be about $440 billion, more than 110 percent of the country's GDP. The president declared on December 14 that it would reduce its budget deficit radically over the coming four years, from nearly 13 percent of GDP to 3 percent in 2013. Greece suffered another blow to its economy when its debt rating was downgraded a second time.

GREENBERG, MAURICE RAYMOND "HANK." Joined what is today AIG in 1960 and became president in 1968. AIG conducted business in 130 countries. In 2005 he was forced to resign as the result of a major accounting scandal. The New York attorney general threatened to bring criminal charges again Greenberg.

See also AMERICAN INTERNATIONAL GROUP.

GREEN ENVIRONMENT. With the global economic downturn in 2008, the ensuing cheap prices for oil and coal threatened to upend future environmental regulations and programs. Almost all green energy projects rely on heavy public spending, subsidies, and loans for their success. Cheap fossil fuels undercut their appeal.

GREEN JOBS PROGRAM. As part of President Obama's plan in 2009 to revive the U.S. economy, he proposed pouring billions of dollars into a green jobs program, both to advance the economy and to lay the groundwork for a more energy-efficient nation. It would include weatherizing hundreds of thousands of homes, installation of smart meters to monitor and reduce home energy use, and billions of dollars in grants to state and local governments for mass transit and infrastructure projects.

In 2009, he planned to devote $150 billion over ten years to energy efficiency and alternative energy projects to wean the nation from the fuels that were the main causes of the heating in the atmosphere.

GREENSPAN, ALAN. A lifelong libertarian and supporter of free markets, he was chairman of the Federal Reserve for the better part of two decades.

See also FEDERAL RESERVE; LONG-TERM CAPITAL MANAGEMENT.

GROSS DOMESTIC PRODUCT (GDP) (U.S.). The total goods and services produced in a nation over a given time period, usually one year. The market value of a country's output attributable to factors of production located in the country's territory.

U.S. Commerce Department announced on December 23, 2008, that the GDP, the broadest measure of economic activity, declined at an annual rate of 0.5 percent in the July–September quarter. Corporate profits fell 1.2 percent in that quarter. The decline in corporate profits was slightly larger than the 0.9 percent fall estimated a month earlier.

The Commerce Department stated on March 26 that the nation's economy dropped by 6.3 percent at the end of 2008, the worst showing in a quarter of a century.

The U.S. economy shrank significantly in the first quarter 2009 with its worst six-month performance in fifty-one years. The GDP declined at an inflation-adjusted 6.1 percent annual rate, nearly matching the 6.3 percent drop in the fourth quarter 2008. Business investment plunged, as did exports. This recession marked the first time since 1975 that the U.S. economy had contracted for three quarters in a row.

The government was becoming more hopeful when they announced on April 29 that there was a large drop in inventories and an upsurge in consumer spending, both suggesting that the economy might be closer to a turnaround.

On June 25, 2009, it was reported that the U.S. GDP fell at a revised 5.5 annual rate from January to March. This was a revision from an earlier statement. Overall, the 5.5 percent drop marked a modest but important improvement from the fourth-quarter fall of 6.3 percent, which appears to be the low point of the recession 2008–2009.

GROUP OF EIGHT. *See* G-8.

GROUP OF FIVE. *See* G-5.

GROUP OF SEVEN. *See* G-7.

GROUP OF TWENTY. *See* G-20.

GROUP OF TWO. *See* G-2.

GSE. *See* GOVERNMENT-SPONSORED ENTERPRISE.

G-7 (GROUP OF 7). A group of industrialized nations, including the United States, Japan, Germany, France, and Great Britain, plus Canada and Italy.
   See also G-8; G-20.

G-77. Developing nations and others.

G-20 (GROUP OF 20). Leaders of the Group of 20 met in Washington, D.C., on November 14–15, 2008, to revive their economies and to overhaul financial regulations. The group planned its next meeting for the end of March 2009. These rich and emerging nations represent almost 90 percent of global GDP, comprising nineteen industrialized and emerging countries and the European Union.

Stimulus spending estimates for the G-20 countries as a percentage of their GDP in 2009 are:

Saudi Arabia—3.3 percent
Spain—2.3 percent
Australia—2.1 percent
United States—2.0 percent
China—2.0 percent
South Africa—1.8 percent
Russia—1.7 percent
South Korea—1.5 percent
Mexico—1.5 percent
Germany—1.5 percent
Canada—1.5 percent
Japan—1.4 percent
United Kingdom—1.4 percent

Indonesia—1.3 percent
Argentina—1.3 percent
France—0.7 percent
India—0.5 percent
Brazil—0.4 percent
Italy—0.2 percent
Turkey—0.0 percent

A global slump existed on the eve of the summit of the G-20. Gordon Brown, the architect and organizer of the summit, called for a "New Deal" to tackle the economic crisis. The day before the summit opened, President Obama conceded U.S. culpability in starting the global financial crisis, but then called on those in attendance to do more to end it.

The one-day meeting was held on April 2, 2009, in London; new evidence was used as background for the meeting. The eurozone showed inflation at 0.6 percent through March, the lowest level since official records began in 1996. And together, the world economy shrank by 2.75 percent in 2009, according to the OECD.

Leaders at this summit agreed to quadruple the financial capacity of the IMF with a $1.1 trillion commitment in order to revive trade, which was expected to contract in 2009 for the first time in thirty years. It also promised to clamp down on tax havens and to tighten financial regulations, making large hedge funds comply with domestic regulators and disclose how much they have borrowed, and making certain that there is effective oversight, even if the funds are operating across national borders.

The scorecard for the G-20 April 2 meeting, with a commitment of $1.1 trillion, was:

Pledged Resources
- increased resources for the IMF—$500 billion
- new special drawing rights allocation—$250 billion
- increased lending by multilateral development banks—$100 billion
- increased support for trade finance—$250 billion
- additional lending to poorest countries, financed by IMF gold sales—$6 billion

Other Commitments
- Establish a Financial Stability Board, whose purpose would be to assess weaknesses in the global financial system and to oversee action to correct these weaknesses.
- Ensure regulators have necessary access to financial information.

- Require that hedge funds are registered and regularly disclose their financial information, including leverage, to regulators.
- Develop means to control the use of illegal tax havens, in part by increasing disclosure requirements for taxpayers.
- Support greater transparency in the reporting of financial executives' compensation, and ensure that boards of directors play a greater role in the setting of executives' pay.

The $1.1 trillion pledge was deceiving. About $500 billion represented increased direct financing for the IMF. Less than half of that amount had been committed by Japan, the EU, Canada, and Norway. China would provide $40 billion, and the United States $100 billion (which must be authorized by Congress). A shortfall of $145 billion of the $500 billion was expected.

On September 24–25, 2009, the Group of 20 met in Pittsburgh, Pennsylvania. Members agreed that the G-20 would henceforth be the permanent council for international economic cooperation, eclipsing the Group of 7 and Group of 8. Support was given to an agreement that would require members to subject their economic policies to a type of peer review. Another recommendation was that bonuses be reduced, or "clawed back" after being awarded, if a bank's performance suffers. Throughout the meeting of the world's industrial nations, the police were out in force attempting to control protestors (estimated to be 3,000 to 4,000), some of whom were arrested.

At the Pittsburgh meeting, China and Japan announced that they would rely less on exports and more on domestic consumption; the United States would work to cut its budget deficit; member nations would require higher levels of capital in banks and other financial institutions; and Europe would make tough structural reforms to prod business investment. In addition, it was agreed upon that there was to be a major shift in ownership of the International Monetary Fund.

See also AUSTRALIA; BUSINESS 20; EUROZONE; G-NEXT; G-7; HEDGE FUNDS; INTERNATIONAL MONETARY FUND; OBAMA, BARACK; ORGANIZATION FOR ECONOMIC COOPERATION AND DEVELOPMENT; REGULATORS; SUMMIT OF NOVEMBER 4, 2008; TAX HAVENS; WORLD BANK.

G-2 (GROUP OF 2). Unofficially, by 2009, the two power nations of the world—China and the United States.

GUINNESS. The Irish beer maker announced in mid-January 2009 that it would alter or abandon plans to reform production in Ireland and open a new state-of-the-art brewery because of the struggling global economy.

GULF ARAB STATES. *See* MIDDLE EAST.

GULF CO-OPERATION COUNCIL. Composed of Bahrain, Kuwait, Oman, Qatar, Saudi Arabia, and the United Arab Emirates, it had economies that tripled between 2003 and 2008, to an overall GDP of close to $1 trillion.

Unemployment, since 2008, was expected to rise as thousands more young people, many of them graduates with high expectations, entered the job market. Social unrest could occur.

A proposed Gulf Cooperation Council monetary union has been in the making for thirty years, with a central bank and other financial institutions. In mid-May, the United Arab Emirates withdrew from negotiations, a blow to integration of the region.

See also DUBAI; MIDDLE EAST; UNITED ARAB EMIRATES.

H

HACKING. The economic fall made firms more vulnerable to computer attacks as they reduced spending on security software. Businesses need to regularly upgrade computer security systems because criminals are constantly exploiting new vulnerabilities and developing new methods to avoid detection.

HALLIBURTON. The oil field provider reported on April 20 that its 2009 first-quarter profit fell 35 percent following a drop in crude oil prices and lower exploration and spending by its customers. Its revenue declined 3 percent to $3.91 billion, from $4.03 billion a year earlier.

In October 2009 Halliburton reported its first significant quarterly revenue increase for the year. The company showed a third-quarter profit of $262 million, down 61 percent from $672 million a year before. Revenue, however, fell 26 percent to $3.59 billion. Halliburton's revenue climbed 3 percent sequentially.

HAMILTON SUNDSTRAND. *See* UNITED TECHNOLOGIES.

H&M (HENNES & MAURITZ). With over 1,700 stores worldwide, the company reported poor sales in October 2009. Sales fell 3 percent, the firm's sixth straight month of declining sales.

HAMP. *See* HOME AFFORDABLE MODIFICATION PROGRAM.

HAMPTONS, THE. *See* WEALTH.

HARLEY-DAVIDSON. In January 2009, the motorcycle manufacturer announced that it would cut 1,100 jobs over two years, close some facilities, and consolidate others as it grapples with the meltdown and slowdown in motorcycle sales. Its fourth-quarter profit for 2008 fell nearly 60 percent.

On July 16, the management of Harley-Davidson announced plans to eliminate 700 hourly jobs and 300 nonproduction, mostly salaried workers, in addition to the 1,400 previous reductions.

The firm's second-quarter 2009 profit fell 91 percent. Revenue dropped 27 percent to $1.15 billion as retail motorcycling sales fell 30 percent.

Retail sales declined 35 percent in the United States and eighteen countries overseas.

Harley-Davidson reported on October 15, 2009, an 84 percent fall in third-quarter profit. Operating losses for the financing arm of the business totaled $110.8 million for the first nine months of the year.

HARVARD UNIVERSITY. The wealthiest university in the world announced that it would freeze salaries for some professors and nonunion employees in the 2010 fiscal year as the university braced for a drop of its endowment. On September 10, 2009, Harvard announced that its endowment shrank to $26 billion, a 27 percent decline.

See also ENDOWMENTS.

Cf. COLUMBIA UNIVERSITY; YALE UNIVERSITY.

HEAD START. *See* EDUCATION.

HEALTH CARE. Under the Economic Stimulus Plan of 2009, researchers would receive $1.1 billion to study the effectiveness of doctors' treatments.

See also AMERICAN RECOVERY AND REINVESTMENT ACT (OF 2009); AUTOMOBILE INDUSTRY; COBRA; JOHNSON & JOHNSON; MEDICAID; STATES (U.S.); UNEMPLOYMENT.

HEALTH-INFORMATION TECHNOLOGY. *See* AMERICAN RECOVERY AND REINVESTMENT ACT (OF 2009); ELECTRONIC HEALTH RECORDS.

HEALTH INSURERS. The nation's largest health insurers reported their first-quarter 2009 earnings and most showed that they lost subscribers due to unemployment, increasing the number of uninsured citizens. The country's largest insurer, WellPoint, with nearly 35 million medical-plan members, reported a 1.3 percent drop in first-quarter net members. It lost 500,000 net members since the end of December 2008.

See also WELLPOINT.

HEARST CORPORATION. Announced on February 24, 2009, that it might close its *San Francisco Chronicle* newspaper unless it could quickly slash costs. The loss of the *Chronicle* would shutter the twelfth-largest U.S. paper and Northern California's largest daily. Hearst purchased the paper in 2000 for $660 million, sinking more than $1 billion into it, including the purchase price and its operating losses over the past ten years. Since 2001 it has lost about one-third of its readers, with a weekday circulation currently averaging about 340,000 copies.

HEDGE. A trade that reduces the risk of the individual or firm's current position. A person attempts to "hedge" against inflation by the purchase of securities whose values should increase proportionally in response to inflationary developments. Similarly, someone that holds a large amount of debt issued by one company might seek to short that company's stock, under the belief that if their debt lost value, the company stock price would also fall, and the short stock position would compensate the investment losses suffered by the debt.

Hedges are rarely perfectly aligned. Many of the massive losses experienced by the financial industry in 2008 and 2009 were hedged, but past a certain point of losses, or due to a lack of direct correlation between the hedging investments and the products that experienced the losses, the hedges became ineffective.

Stock prices and bond values do not move in an exact inverse lockstep, so shorting stock while holding bonds or vice versa does not provide a true and complete hedge against price moves. Credit-default swaps were designed to overcome this problem, conceived as a tool to hedge the counter-party risk of holding a company's debt, though in turn they spawned further problems of their own.

See also CREDIT-DEFAULT SWAP.

HEDGE FUNDS. Coined by Alfred Winslow Jones in 1949, the term described an investment vehicle that simultaneously bought and sold short-shares, thereby lowering sensitivity to overall movements in the market. It is an aggressively managed portfolio of investments that uses advanced investment techniques, such as leveraged, long, short, and derivative positions in both domestic and international markets, with the goal of generating high returns (either in an absolute sense or over a specified benchmark). Legally, hedge funds are most often set up as private investment partnerships with a limited number of investors and require a very large initial minimum investment.

In December 2008, investors pulled a net $32 billion from hedge funds, making 2008 the first year the funds had significant outflows and ending the industry's eighteen years of asset growth.

Hedge funds had a major shakeout in 2008, with the average fund losing almost 20 percent of its value. The year 2009 started with little more than half the nearly $2 trillion in investors' money that was held in 2008.

Hedge funds globally lost about 18 percent of their value in 2008. The unregulated industry dropped last year by about a fifth to $1.55 trillion in November 2008.

Hedge funds were expected to eliminate 20,000 positions worldwide in 2009; a record 14 percent of the industry's workforce, as investment losses and client withdrawals eroded fees. This number was on top of the 10,000 jobs lost in 2008.

Hedge fund assets rose by $100 billion in the second quarter 2009, the first quarterly increase in a year.

See also CONVERTIBLE-ARBITRAGE FUNDS; EXECUTIVE PAY; FINANCIAL REGULATION PLAN (2009); G-20; HEDGE; HOUSE (U.S.) FINANCIAL OVERHAUL PLAN; LONG-TERM CAPITAL MANAGEMENT; "SHADOW BANKS."
Cf. EXCHANGE-TRADED FUND.

HENNES & MAURITZ. *See* H&M.

HERMES. The luxury goods manufacturer reported in August 2009 modestly higher first-half revenue.
See also LUXURY GOODS.
Cf. TIFFANY.

HERTZ. The second-largest U.S. rental-car company cut in January 2009 more than 4,000 jobs to reduce costs as business and consumer travel slowed because of the global recession. Twelve percent of its workforce would be lost, resulting in a savings of $150–$170 million in 2009.

In February, Hertz reported a net loss of $1.21 billion, compared with a year-earlier profit of $80.7 million. Revenue fell 16 percent to $1.78 billion from $2.14 billion.

Hertz reported at the end of July that its profit fell 92 percent.
Cf. AVIS; ENTERPRISE.

HEWLETT-PACKARD COMPANY (HP). On February 18, 2009, the technology giant posted a 13 percent drop in quarterly profit as sales in its computer and printing divisions plunged 19 percent from a year earlier. On February 22, HP, which had already cut 24,000 jobs earlier, announced that it could cut salaries by 2.5–20 percent and reduce contributions to employee 401(k) plans.

HP had a 17 percent profit drop and announced in May that it would cut an additional 2 percent of its workforce, or more than 6,000 jobs. In August 2009, it posted a 19 percent drop in quarterly profit as sales fell sharply. HP's overall revenue fell 2 percent to $27.45 billion.

HP's results for the second quarter 2009, ending in July, were mixed. PC shipments rose 2 percent from the year before, but revenue fell 18 percent.

On November 23 HP posted a 14 percent increase in quarterly 2009 profit despite an 8 percent fall in revenue. Sales of PC units climbed 8 percent.
Cf. DELL INC; INTEL.

HIGHBALLING. Considered a fraudulent swap method. The customer's holdings can be purchased by a dealer above the current market value in order that the dealer does not have a loss. The customer swaps for a new holding above its market value and the dealer accepts the loss on the purchase so as to build in a present gain on the sale.

HIGHER-MILEAGE CARS. *See* ENERGY EFFICIENCY.

HIGH-FREQUENCY TRADING. Using supercomputers, companies make trades in a matter of microseconds, or one-millionth of a second. Goals vary. Some trading firms try to catch fleeting moves in everything from stocks to currencies to commodities. They search for signals, such as the movement of interest rates, indicating which way parts of the market can shift in short periods. Some try to find ways to take advantage of subtle quirks in the infrastructure of trading. Other companies are market makers, providing securities on each side of a buy and sell order. Some firms trade on signals and make markets.

See also FLASH ORDERS (TRADING).

HIGH-GRADE BONDS. *See* MOODY'S.

HIGH-NET-WORTH INDIVIDUALS. *See* WEALTH.

HIGH-SPEED TRADING. *See* NAKED SHORT SELLING.

HIGHWAY CONSTRUCTION. *See* OBAMA, BARACK; ROOSEVELT, FRANKLIN DELANO.

HIRING. *See* HIRING RATE.

HIRING RATE. Although the hiring rate continued to fall, by May 2009, indications were that the bottom might soon arrive. Firms continued to be skittish about hiring and employees were less willing to quit.

By the end of October, when the unofficial close of the recession was announced, most employers had not resumed hiring. The United States had shed 7.2 million jobs since December 2007 when the recession began. Were the job market to evolve jobs as fast as it did during the 1990s boom, adding 2.15 million private-sector jobs each year, the United States wouldn't return to a 5 percent unemployment rate until late 2017.

HISPANICS. By October 2009, the unemployment rate for Hispanics was 13.1 percent.

See also IMMIGRATION; LIVING STANDARDS; MEXICO; REMITTANCES; UNEMPLOYMENT.

Cf. AFRICAN AMERICANS.

HITACHI. In January 2009, announced that it would post a full-year net loss of $7.8 billion. It would eliminate 7,000 jobs and freeze capital spending.

H. J. HEINZ COMPANY. Earnings slid 9.8 percent for its fiscal fourth quarter of 2008. For the quarter ended April 29, 2009, profit fell to $175.1 million and revenue dropped 5.6 percent to $2.54 billion.

HNWIS (HIGH-NET-WORTH INDIVIDUALS). *See* WEALTH.

HOARDING. *See* HOOVER, HERBERT.

HOCKEY STICK RECESSION. *See* RECESSION.

HOLDING COMPANY. A corporation that owns the securities of another, in most cases with voting control.

HOLDING COMPANY (MULTIPLE-BANK). A bank holding company, however defined, that owns or controls two or more banks.

HOME AFFORDABLE MODIFICATION PROGRAM (HAMP). Provides homeowners with loans owned or guaranteed by Fannie Mae or Freddie Mac an opportunity to refinance into more affordable monthly payments. The program commits $75 billion to keep 3 to 4 million Americans in their homes by preventing avoidable foreclosures.

HAMP works well when two things occur: First, if a large proportion of mortgages in trial relief qualify for permanent modification. And then, if re-default rates on modified loans stay low. HAMP's major shortcoming is that it failed to meet its aim to reduce home-owner payments while not creating further big losses for the banks or hitting the taxpayer for even greater cash.

See also AMERICAN RECOVERY AND REINVESTMENT ACT (OF 2009); FORECLOSURE.

HOME APPRAISALS. *See* APPRAISALS.

HOME BUYER TAX CREDIT. *See* HOME SALES; UNEMPLOYMENT BENEFITS.

HOME CONSTRUCTION. New home construction fell to record lows in 2008. It declined 15.5 percent from November to December to an annual pace of 550,000 homes, the slowest pace since the Commerce Department started compiling the data in 1959.

The pace of new home construction in December was 45 percent below its levels from a year earlier. In 2008 904,300 housing units were started, a drop of 33 percent from 2007. Thus, 2008 became the worst year for housing starts on record.

Home construction surged in June 2009. New homes rose in June by 3.6 percent from the month before to a seasonally adjusted annual rate of 582,000. It was the third consecutive monthly gain, although significantly below the pace of 1.1 million of June 2008. Overall, the gain was led by a 14.4 percent increase in construction of single-family homes—the largest monthly increase in four years and the fourth consecutive improvement in 2009. However, reversals would follow.

On November 18, 2009, the government reported that home construction again slowed unexpectedly in October 2009 to the lowest level in six years, since April. The rate of single- and multiple-family home building indicated an overall decrease of 10.6 percent in housing starts from September, to only 529,000 units.

See also APPRAISALS; D.R. HORTON; FIRST-TIME HOME BUYER CREDIT; HOME SALES; PULTE; TOLL BROTHERS.

HOME DEPOT. The home-supply chain said in early 2009 that it would cut 7,000 jobs, or 2 percent of its workers, and close more than thirty-four of its stores.

On February 24, the company announced a fourth-quarter loss. It had a 9.2 percent drop in same-store sales, which was less than rival Lowe's posting of a 9.9 percent loss; gross profit margin declined 0.2 percent in the quarter, compared to a drop of 1.15 percent for Lowe's.

Home Depot forecast in June that it expected its fiscal-year earnings per share, to fall 20 percent to 26 percent from a year earlier.

On August 18, Home Depot posted a 7 percent fall in quarterly profit on a 9 percent decline in sales. About one-fourth of the fall came from declines in big-ticket items such as kitchen models.

Home Depot's fiscal third-quarter 2009 profit fell also. Earnings were $689 million down from $756 million the year before. Revenue declined 8 percent to $16.36 billion as same-store sales fell 6.9 percent.

Cf. LOWE'S COMPANIES.

HOME FLIPPING. Investors seeking bargains at foreclosure auctions in order to quickly resell for a profit. Often there is no opportunity to inspect the property or even determine if tenants are still residing in the home. The bank, upon the sale, gets money for the property right away, even if it isn't sufficient to cover the loan balance due.

HOME MORTGAGES. The president's 2010 proposed budget sought to raise $318 billion over ten years by lowering the value of itemized tax deductions for the wealthy—including interest paid on home mortgages. Households that paid income taxes at the 33 percent and 35 percent rates would only be able to claim deductions at the 28 percent rate; meaning that for every $1,000 in deductions, a household in the top tax bracket would realize a tax savings of $280, down from the current $350. The proposal wouldn't take effect until 2011.

By March 2009, more than a tenth of American households with home mortgages were overdue on payments or in foreclosure. Eleven percent of mortgages on one- to four-family homes were at least one month overdue at the end of 2008.

On September 23, the Federal Reserve, in order to keep interest rates low for home purchasers through early 2010, extended and decided to gradually phase out its purchase of mortgage-backed securities.

About 3.4 percent of households, or about 1.9 million homeowners, were by November 2009 120 days or more overdue on their payments.

See also APPRAISALS; BUDGET (U.S.) (FISCAL YEAR 2010); CITI-GROUP.

HOME OWNERSHIP. Fell in the first quarter 2009 to its lowest level since 2000, with the largest decline among younger buyers, who at one time benefited from easier credit that helped fuel the housing boom.

See also FORECLOSURE; HOME MORTGAGES; HOME PRICES; HOUSING; SPAIN; UNITED KINGDOM.

HOME PRICES. Prices in twenty of America's biggest metropolitan areas fell lower in November 2008, dropping 18.2 percent from a year earlier. Prices in eleven of those twenty areas fell at record rates, and fourteen areas reported double-digit declines from November 2007.

U.S. home prices declined 3.4 percent on a seasonally adjusted basis during the fourth quarter of 2008. The drop surpassed the 2 percent decline reported for the third quarter and was the largest decrease in the index's eighteen-year history of the Federal Housing Finance Agency.

Sales of previously owned homes fell 5.3 percent in January 2009 from December 2008. Existing sales fell to an annual rate of 4.49 million in January, the slowest rate in more than a decade. Sales were down 8.6 percent from January 2008.

The median home price fell to $170,300, its lowest point since March 2003. The median price in January was down 26 percent from its peak of $230,000 in July 2006.

New home sales fell 10.2 percent in January to a seasonally adjusted annual rate of 309,000. That was the lowest since at least 1963, when the data was first tracked.

The federal government's gauge of home prices climbed in January for the first time in ten months.

In February, home prices declined sharply, by 18.6 percent, but for the first time in sixteen months the annual pace of decline slowed.

The Federal Housing Finance Agency reported on March 24 that home prices increased 1.7 percent from December 2008, though they were still down from about 10 percent from their April 2007 peak.

By May, the downturn in home prices had left nearly 30 percent of U.S. homeowners owing more on a mortgage than their homes were worth. The increase in the number of such underwater borrowers was staggering, making it more difficult for owners who get into financial trouble to refinance or sell their homes.

On July 28, 2009, it was announced that home prices in major U.S. cities registered the first monthly gain in nearly three years. Prices in twenty cities rose 0.5 percent for the three-month period ending in May, compared with the three months ending in April. Nevertheless, home prices remained down about 17 percent from a year earlier.

Home prices increased for the fourth consecutive month in October 2009. However, some analysts warn that these increases are being propped up by the government and that they could resume falling in the coming months as that support disappears.

By November 2009, home prices continued to fall as sales of heavily discounted foreclosed properties dragged the market down. Median prices of existing homes fell in 123 of 153 metropolitan areas during the third quarter compared to a year before. The national median price was $177,900, down 11.2 percent from the third quarter 2008. It is expected, as the surge in foreclosures continues, that home prices will continue to fall in 2010.

See also FORECLOSURE; HOME MORTGAGES; HOME SALES; UNDERWATER.

HOME REPOSSESSIONS. *See* FORECLOSURE; HOME MORTGAGES; HOUSING; UNITED KINGDOM.

HOME SALES. In March 2009, throughout the country, 19 million houses and apartments, nearly one out of every seven, were vacant, the highest percentage since the 1960s. However, only about 6 million of those homes were for sale or rent.

Before March, new home sales began to rise by 4.7 percent, for the first time in seven months, attributed to low mortgage rates and the significant drop in prices. The median sales price for a new home was $200,900, compared to $251,000 in February 2008.

As the figures arrived, March home sales continued their slide, falling 3 percent, to a seasonally adjusted annual rate of 4.57 million units. Both high inventories and distressed sales pushed down prices. The median existing home price was $175,200, down 12.4 percent from a year earlier.

Existing home sales rose 2.9 percent in April compared to March, to a 4.68 million annual rate. The increase nearly reversed March's decline, though the sales were 3.5 percent below the level in April 2008. Sales of distressed properties, such as homes in foreclosure, accounted for 45 percent of the April total.

Existing home sales rose in May, climbing to the highest level in seven months. Sales of previously owned homes increased 2.4 percent, compared with April, to a seasonally adjusted 4.77 million annual rate. Sales were now two-thirds of the peak levels they reached in 2005. At this current rate, it would take nearly ten months to clear the 3.8 million homes on the market. The median price for a house was $173,000 in May, up 3.8 percent from April, but down 16.8 percent from a year earlier.

Sales of new homes in the United States posted their largest monthly gain in nearly eight years in June 2009. On July 27, the government reported that sales of new single-family homes rose 11 percent; adjusted to a rate of 384,000 a year, the highest level since November 2008. Sales of existing homes in July jumped at the fastest rate in ten years. For single-family houses, sales increased 7.2 percent for the month to a seasonally adjusted annual rate of 5.24 million.

Then in August, existing home sales fell 2.7 percent to a seasonally adjusted annual rate of 5.10 million units, following four straight months of increases. This was a reversal from July, when sales rose at the fastest rate in ten years to a pace of 5.24 million.

Sales of new homes rose 0.7 percent in August 2009 from the previous month, to a seasonally adjusted annual rate of 429,000. The supply of unsold houses eased also, dropping to 7.3 months in August from 7.6 months in July. The median price for new homes was $195,000 in August, down 11.7 percent from a year before.

In September, with the $8,000 first-time home buyer tax credit scheduled to end November 30, 2009, and prices for homes still low, sales of existing homes rose 9.4 percent from August's level. Then in early November the president signed a law extending through spring 2010 a temporary tax credit of up to $8,000 for some first-time home buyers. The law also added a new tax credit of up to $6,500 for certain repeat home buyers. The government estimated that this new law would cost a total of $11 billion.

Existing home sales for October 2009 rose to the highest level in more than two years. Sales increased 10.1 percent to an annual rate of 6.1 million. That level was last achieved in February 2007, prior to the collapse of the housing sector. A significant contributor to this increase was the $8,000 first-time home buyer tax credit.

Sales of existing homes rose 7.4 percent in November from the previous month to a seasonally adjusted annual rate of 6.54 million units—the highest rate since February 2007. Sales were 44 percent higher than a year before, with the median sales price for the month at $172,600, up from $172,200 in October, the first monthly rise since June.

Sales of newly built homes fell 11.3 percent in November to a seventeen-month low.

See also APPRAISALS; FORECLOSURE; HOME PRICES.

HONDA. Cut its full-year forecast for net profit by 62 percent. For the fiscal year ending March 31, 2008, Honda lowered its net profit forecast to $2.08 billion, a continuing sign of the drop in demand that has hammered the global car industry.

It was the carmaker's third profit warning of the year, highlighting how tough the market had become. Honda's U.S. sales dropped 31.6 percent in 2008, following a decline of 35 percent in December.

Honda said in January 2009 that it would reduce its domestic output by an additional 56,000 units and expected its Japanese production to total 1.17 million units in its business year, against its original target of 1.31 million.

On January 30, Honda announced a 90 percent drop in net profit for the December quarter.

Honda Motor, the second-largest automaker in Japan, made 77,224 vehicles in January, 23 percent fewer than at the same time the year before.

In April, Honda had a net loss of $1.92 billion in the quarter ending in March. Sales declined 42 percent. It was Honda's first net loss on a quarterly basis in more than fifteen years. The company announced in July 2009 that its net profit for the first fiscal quarter ending June 30 tumbled 96 percent from a year before.

Honda Motor Company reported that its fiscal second-quarter 2009 profit fell 56 percent. Profit for the period ending September 30 was $586.1 million. Sales tumbled 27 percent.

See also AUTOMOBILE INDUSTRY; JAPAN.

HONEYWELL. Reported a 38 percent decline in first-quarter profit 2009. Its net income fell to $399 million, from $647 million the previous year.

On July 27, Honeywell reported that its second-quarter earnings fell 38 percent. Revenue dropped 22 percent to $7.56 billion from $9.67 billion one year earlier.

Honeywell's third-quarter 2009 earnings fell 15 percent. The company posted a third-quarter profit of $608 million, down from $719 million a year before. Net sales fell 17 percent to $7.7 billion.

HONG KONG. Hong Kong climbed out of the recession in the second quarter 2009, with a 3.3 percent growth in the second quarter from the first quarter.

To prevent a real estate bubble, bankers increased the down payment on luxury homes to 40 percent from the current 30 percent.

See also TAX HAVENS.

HOOVER, HERBERT. President Hoover was far more active than he gets credit for in the post 1929 crash. His primary method of combating the crisis was by having the government make large loans to big banks, in the hope that they would restore confidence. It didn't work. He also established the Reconstruction Finance Corporation to make loans to tax-starved state governments, among other entities. Hoarding was a problem in the 1930s because dollar bills (or in many cases, gold) stuffed under a mattress didn't help the banking system.

See also PECORA COMMISSION; RECONSTRUCTION FINANCE CORPORATION; ROOSEVELT, FRANKLIN DELANO.

HOTEL GEITHNER. *Synonymous with* TROUBLED ASSET RELIEF PROGRAM.

HOTELS. Hotel occupancy indicated that revenue was down 16.1 percent in 2009. The forecast for all of 2009 was a decline of 17.1 percent, and in 2010 another 4 percent.

Hotel per-room revenue continued to decline in December 2009. The average for revenue per available hotel room was $54.58 in October, down 16.8 percent from the same month a year before.

See also ACCOR; MARRIOTT; STARWOOD.

HOTEL WORK. *See* STARWOOD; UNEMPLOYMENT.

HOUSE (U.S.) FINANCIAL OVERHAUL PLAN. On December 11, 2009, the U.S. House of Representatives passed a sweeping measure putting new brakes on financial institutions. Provisions include:

a. Consumer Protection
   • Consolidate authority for protecting consumers into one agency. The agency would set and enforce rules on a variety of financial items, including credit cards, mortgages, and loans. Retailers and auto dealers are among the few who would be exempt from the agency's oversight.
   • Preserve the federal government's ability to preempt tougher state consumer protection laws under certain conditions.
   • Allow consumers to sue credit-rating agencies for flawed evaluations of financial products.
b. Executive Compensation
   • Give shareholders the right to vote on compensation and "golden parachute" severance packages and require that independent directors sit on compensation committees.
   • Allow regulators to ban "inappropriate or imprudently risky" compensation practices for banks and other financial institutions.
c. Federal Regulatory Powers
   • Establish a council of federal regulators to monitor the market.
   • Impose stricter standards and regulations on firms that are large enough or interconnected enough to put the entire economy at risk. The gov-

ernment would set up a $150 billion fund—financed by assessments on large financial firms—to dissolve any "large and highly complex" financial companies that it deemed too risky.
- Merge the Office of the Comptroller, which supervised federally chartered banks, with the Office of Thrift Supervision, which supervised savings and loans.
d. Regulation of Derivatives
- Impose tighter restrictions on the largely unregulated derivatives market and require many derivatives to be traded through clearinghouses where they could be monitored by the Securities and Exchange Commission and the Commodity Futures Trade Commission.
e. Other
- Require hedge funds and private-equity companies with more than $150 million in assets to be registered with the SEC and to disclose financial information. Venture capital companies and Small Business Investment Companies would be exempt.
- Redirect $4 billion from the bank bailout fund to provide low-interest loans to the unemployed and homeowners struggling to keep their residences and to purchase and repair abandoned and foreclosed homes.

See also FEDERAL RESERVE.

HOUSEHOLDS. *See* HOUSING.

HOUSING. Housing starts, which were still soaring as recently as 2005, hit a new twenty-year low in 2008. Meanwhile residential-property prices were falling in twenty-three of forty-five nations.

Housing sales dropped sharply in November. Sales of existing homes declined to a seasonally adjusted rate of 4.49 million in November, down 8.6 percent from October and 10.6 percent from November 2007. The median price of a home was $181,300 in November, down 13 percent from 2007, and the lowest level since February 2004.

Housing values had plummeted since the peak of the market in July 2006, when the median home price in the United States was $230,200. In November, the median price of a new home was $220,400, down 11.5 percent from a year earlier. It was the biggest year-over-year price decline since a 12.7 percent drop in March.

Housing starts in December fell by a steep 18.9 percent from the previous month, to a seasonally adjusted 625,000.

In Britain, house prices were projected to fall 10 percent for 2009.

The median price for a single-family house fell 14 percent to $169,000 in the first quarter from a year earlier. That median price is down 26 percent from a peak of $227,000 in the third quarter of 2005.

The net worth of U.S. households rose 5 percent in the third quarter 2009 with a gain to $53.4 trillion, marking the second straight quarterly increase.

The good news is that year-over-year declines eased steadily and dramatically in 2009. The average drop in home prices for twenty major cities in October versus a year before was 7.3 percent, down from 9.4 percent in September and 19 percent in January.

See also APARTMENT VACANCIES; BERNANKE, BEN; CHINA; DISTRESSED SALES; FORECLOSURE; FREDDIE MAC; HOUSING BAILOUT PLAN; MORTGAGE RATES; MORTGAGE-REPLACEMENT LOANS; UNITED KINGDOM.

HOUSING AGENCIES. *See* HOUSING FINANCE AGENCIES.

HOUSING BAILOUT PLAN. To reduce foreclosures, a program was announced by President Obama on February 18, 2009, in Phoenix, Arizona. Two groups were primarily affected by the president's plan. People who couldn't afford their mortgages and had fallen behind on their monthly payments, which included about 3 million households, made up the first group. The second group consisted of more than 10 million households that could afford their monthly payments but whose houses were worth less than what was owed on their mortgages.

For the first group, $50 billion would be spent to entice banks to lower the monthly payments of people who otherwise couldn't afford to stay in their homes. The money came from the funds already allocated from the financial system bailout.

By early March, details of this mortgage bailout plan to aid one in nine U.S. homeowners was presented. It called for reduction payments for distressed borrowers through modifications of loan terms.

The plan also involved refinancing mortgages for some people who were current on their payments but had little or no equity in their homes. Loan mods are modifications of loan terms. This modification plan terminates December 31, 2012.

On July 1, 2009, the government expanded the number of borrowers who could refinance home loans. Borrowers with mortgages worth up to 125 percent of their home's value can now be eligible to refinance under the program, up from a 105 percent limit. The problem continued to pull down the housing market, as nearly 30 percent of homeowners with mortgages owe more than their homes are worth.

See also FORECLOSURE; HOUSING; MORTGAGE BAILOUT; UNDERWATER.

HOUSING FINANCE AGENCIES. Those agencies operated by state government, catering to first-time homeowners, they either originate mortgage loans to state residents or guarantee loans made by lenders. In 2007, state housing agencies issued $17 billion in bonds that funded 126,611 mortgages. By September 2008, these credit markets were frozen.

HOUSING INVENTORIES. The number of homes listed for sale. In twenty-seven major cities at the end of November 2009 inventory was down 2.4 percent compared with a month before. The inventory for that month was down 28 percent.

HOUSING PLAN. *See* FANNIE MAE; FREDDIE MAC; GINNIE MAE; HOUSING BAILOUT PLAN; MODIFYING MORTGAGES.

HOUSING STARTS. Plunged to new lows in January 2009 as a large number of vacant homes, tight mortgage financing, and a deepening recession created the worst housing market in a half century. Starts fell 16.8 percent in January from a month earlier.

In March, housing starts tumbled 10.8 percent to an annual rate of 510,000 units. Starts of single-family homes remained flat from February at 358,000, marking the third straight month around that low level.

Housing construction climbed in August 2009 to the highest level in nine months, rising 1.5 percent to an annual rate of 598,000 units. The increase pushed building activity to the highest level since November 2008 and left home construction 24.8 percent above the record low hit in April.

Housing starts increased 0.5 percent in September to a 590,000 seasonally adjusted annual rate.

See also HOME CONSTRUCTION; HOUSING; MORTGAGE RATES; WEYERHAEUSER.

HRYVNIA. *See* UKRAINE.

HSBC. Based in London, the largest bank in Europe, by December 2008, faced a sharp slowdown in emerging markets, where it earned the bulk of its profits previously. HSBC shares dropped 17 percent.

HSBC announced on March 2, 2009, a plan to draw a line under its troubled subprime mortgage lender and asked investors for $18 billion of new capital to prepare for a further drop in the global economy. HSBC would close most of its finance branches and cut 6,100 jobs.

HUMMER. On October 9, 2009, General Motors completed an arrangement to sell its Hummer brand to Sichuan Tengzhong Heavy Industrial Machinery Company, marking China's first major entry into the U.S. auto market. It was sold for $150 million, with GM manufacturing the vehicles until not later than 2012. Hummer sales were down 64 percent by October 2009 from a year before. In September 2009, GM had sold just 426 of the trucks in the United States.

Cf. TATA MOTORS.

HUNGARY. Hungary's public debt in November 2008 was more than 60 percent of GDP. Hungary's current-account deficit in 2008 amounted to 5.5 percent of GDP. The weak forint meant higher interest payments. Should that trend increase, Hungary risked bankruptcy.

Hungary received $15.7 billion from the IMF in October. Its central bank cut its interest rates by half a point from the 11.5 rate that it set in October, as part of a $25 billion international bailout.

The national bank reduced its key interest rate to 9.5 percent from 10 percent in mid-January 2009 and forecasted a lower-than-expected point cut in less than 2 months, as it sought to shore up its ailing economy.

Hungary's currency, the forint, plunged to a new low against the euro on March 4, declining more than 20 percent against the euro since the beginning of 2009. Then, on March 6, its currency slipping further, Hungary attempted to assure depositors that their funds were safe to avoid a run on the banks, but the effort failed to stabilize the currency.

The central bank's plan was to intervene in foreign-exchange markets, using funds it gets from the EU to do so.

By mid-September 2009, the government cut public spending by 3.8 percent of GDP and reduced the budget deficit from 9.2 percent of GDP in 2006 to just 3.4 percent in 2008.

Hungary's central bank slashed its key interest rate to a three-year low of 7 percent from 7.5 percent. In September 2009, annual consumer-price inflation was 4.9 percent.

See also EASTERN EUROPE.

HUNTSMAN. In mid-January 2009, the chemical manufacturer would begin cutting more than 9 percent of its workforce and close a titanium dioxide plant as it continued to scale back operations.

HYPO GROUP ALPE ADRIA. *See* AUSTRIA.

HYUNDAI MOTOR COMPANY. South Korea's largest carmaker by sales announced that its fourth-quarter net profits in 2008 declined 28 percent as the weaker Korean won failed to cushion the impact of the global economic downturn.

The firm postponed a $600 million investment to start production in Brazil at a plant in the first half of 2011. Additionally, it adjusted plans to build a $394.2 million plant in Russia by January 2011.

First-quarter 2009 net profit fell 43 percent.

Hyundai's second-quarter net profit jumped 48 percent to a record. Through November 2009, the automaker sold 401,267 cars and light trucks in the United States, up 6.2 percent from 2008, while the overall market fell 24 percent. Its sales represented 4.3 percent of the U.S. market, up 1.2 points from the year before.

See also AUTOMOBILE INDUSTRY.

I

IBERIA (IBERIA LINEAS AEREAS DE ESPANA). Spain's largest airlines by sales, in March 2009 it posted a net loss of $24 million, or €19 million, for the three months that ended December 31, 2008, compared with a net profit of €105 million one year before. The airline saw its 2008 net profit plunge 90 percent.

Higher fuel costs and plummeting demand during the meltdown period indicated greater bumps ahead.

On November 12, 2009, the airline agreed to merge with British Airways. *See also* BRITISH AIRWAYS.

IBM. *See* INTERNATIONAL BUSINESS MACHINES CORPORATION.

ICELAND. In 2003, Iceland's three biggest banks had assets of only a few billion dollars, about 100 percent of its GDP. Over the next three and one-half years they grew to over $140 billion and their holdings were much greater than the nation's GDP. As the banks were lending Icelanders money to purchase stocks and real estate, the value of the country's stock and real estate went through the roof. From 2003 to 2007, while the U.S. stock market was doubling, the Icelandic stock market multiplied by nine times. Reykjavik real estate prices tripled. By 2006, the average Icelandic family was three times as wealthy as it had been in 2003. By 2007, Icelanders owned roughly fifty times more foreign assets than they had in 2002.

Until spring 2008, the Icelandic economy was strong; its GDP per capita was about $40,000. Unemployment hovered between 0 and 1 percent.

Iceland's financial problems erupted in the spring when the country's banks, bloated with deposits and debts, began to falter. As the financial crisis picked up momentum around the world, Iceland's banking system began to crash.

Iceland effectively went bust after October 6.

On October 28, the central bank of Iceland raised interest rates by a huge 6 percentage points, to 18 percent, an increase that aimed to satisfy the International Monetary Fund and hopefully to restore trust in the country's shattered currency.

By November 1, it was nearly impossible to get foreign currency in or out of the country. Many banks refused even to transfer money to Iceland. Importers were having difficulty paying their foreign bills, and exporters were having trouble getting paid by their foreign customers.

The key interest rate in November stood at 18 percent. The krona, Iceland's currency, had declined 44 percent in 2008. Salaries were frozen, food prices increased rapidly, and unemployment climbed.

Overnight, people lost their entire life savings. The three major Icelandic banks—Glitnir, Landsbanki, and Kaupthing, combining up to 90 percent of Iceland's financial system—failed and were nationalized. These three banks made loans equivalent to about nine times the size of the nation's booming economy, up from about 200 percent of GDP after privatization in 2003.

Prices soared. Banks rationed foreign currency, and companies were finding it difficult to do business overseas. The local krona was at 65 to the dollar in 2007; in 2008 it was at 130. Iceland's banking collapse was the biggest, relative to the size of the economy, that any country has ever suffered.

Iceland received $2.1 billion from the IMF in October, and needed an additional $4 billion in loans. The IMF projected a 9.6 percent decline in Iceland's economy in 2009, and the failure of the banks would cost its taxpayers more than 80 percent of GDP.

Unexpectedly, on November 12, the IMF $6 billion bailout of Iceland was put on hold amid haggling over how the country would compensate overseas customers who lost deposits in failed Icelandic banks.

On November 16, the government announced that it would cover European depositors at failed banks, breaking an impasse that had held up the dispersal of billions of dollars in international aid.

Happily, on Thursday, November 20, Iceland finally got international backing for its bailout plan. Nordic countries followed up on the $2.1 billion loan to Iceland approved by the IMF with additional funding of $2.5 billion. Norway, Sweden, Finland, and Denmark contributed.

Additional funds from Russia, Poland, and the Faroe Islands brought the value of the package to about $5.2 billion. At the same time, the IMF's board approved a deal for Iceland, making $827 million immediately available to the country. The remainder of the loan was to be paid out in eight equal installments, subject to quarterly reviews. All told, Iceland borrowed at least $10 billion or about $33,000 for each of its 300,000 residents.

As expected, thousands of Icelanders demonstrated on November 22, demanding the resignation of the country's prime minister and central bank governor for failing to stop the financial meltdown. The economy was expected to contract 10 percent in 2009, with soaring unemployment and plummeting consumer confidence. The government's top priority was to stabilize the currency, whose fall has increased inflation, forced up domestic interest rates, and raised the costs of foreign funding.

Iceland's central bank vowed at the end of November to restrict banks' access to credit until foreign exchange stability was achieved and said it would not rule out interest rate increases or intervention to help its currency.

By December 1, the government of Iceland was considering a variety of options to solve its currency problems, including the possibility of adopting the euro without joining the European Union.

As inflation surged to an eighteen-year high of 17.1 percent in November, and unemployment was forecast to rise to 7 percent by the end of January 2009 from a previous three-year high of 1.9 percent, about half of Icelanders aged eighteen to twenty-four were considering leaving the country.

Indicating the severity of Iceland's economy, unemployment rose to 3.3 percent in November, from 1.9 percent in October, making it the highest level since May 2004.

Its economic contraction in 2009 pushed the budget into its biggest deficit—projected to be $1.43 billion, thereby depleting emergency loans.

On Monday, January 26, 2009, Iceland's coalition government collapsed, the latest casualty from the global financial crisis.

On Sunday, February 1, Johanna Sigurdardottir became Iceland's interim new prime minister, and Iceland became the first country to change its government as a direct result of the global financial crisis.

The last of Iceland's major banks, Straumur-Burdaras Investment Bank, was taken over by the nation's Financial Supervisory Authority and shut down. The bank was the fourth-largest financial services firm in Iceland, and stayed afloat until March 9.

A new left-wing government, the first in two decades, was voted into office on April 25.

By May, Iceland's new government said it would ask Parliament to vote on whether the nation should start membership talks with the European Union.

Over the years, the nation's market capitalization rose to more than 250 percent of GDP, making it the most highly valued in the world. By mid-year 2009, it was around 16 percent. Iceland had debt equal to 120 percent of its €14 billion of GDP, and a budget deficit of about 13 percent of output in 2009.

After six days of debate, Iceland's parliament voted narrowly (33 to 28) on July 16 to apply to join the European Union. Membership in the EU would lead to Iceland holding euros rather than kronas and would have a significant effect on the value of their currency, which had lost 85 percent of its value against the euro since the crisis began.

On July 20, the government announced that it would recapitalize its stricken banks with a $2.1 billion government bond issue, setting the basis for a future agreement with creditors to settle outstanding debt and restart the nation's financial system. Following recapitalization, planned for August 14, the state would only own a 13 percent stake in the country's largest bank.

Then on August 28, 2009, Iceland's Parliament passed legislation enabling the government to repay the Netherlands and Britain about $6 billion that they had given depositors who lost money in Icelandic savings accounts during the financial meltdown.

By October 2009 Iceland agreed to loan terms from the UK and the Netherlands to repay the losses by foreign depositors.

By December 2, Iceland had privatized its second bank in less than two months, leaving just one of its three large lenders in government hands. Foreign creditors of the former Kaupthing Bank will take an 87 percent stake in Arion Bank, the renamed lender created from Kaupthing's remains.

See also INTERNATIONAL MONETARY FUND; MEXICO; STANDARD & POOR'S; UNEMPLOYMENT.

Cf. LATVIA.

IDENTITY THEFT. By 2009, identity thieves, responding to stories of bank failures and other events related to the current global meltdown, came up with new scams designed to exploit consumers' fears. For example, there were incidents of "phishing" e-mails that appeared to come from the receiver's bank, falsely informing the person that his or her account information needed updating because of a recent merger.

ILLEGAL IMMIGRATION. *See* IMMIGRATION.

IMF. *See* INTERNATIONAL MONETARY FUND.

IMMETT, JEFF. CEO of General Electric Corporation.
See also RESET ECONOMY.

IMMIGRANTS. *See* IMMIGRATION; LATIN AMERICA; REMITTANCES; SPAIN; UNEMPLOYMENT.

IMMIGRATION. From January 2008 to September 2008, 724,000 fewer people attempted to enter the United States from Mexico, the lowest annual figure since the 1970s, partly resulting from the economic slowdown. At the same time, unemployment among Hispanic Americans in particular has climbed from 5.7 percent to 8.6 percent, higher than for white or African Americans.

Immigrants coming to the United States on work or trainee visas ultimately outperform American-born workers and add to the nation's productivity. In general, the most successful immigrants were those with temporary work visas linked to their skills, or student/trainee visas. Those who were legal permanent residents performed as well as those born in the United States, and dependent immigrants with temporary visas were less productive than native-born Americans. The controversy continues.

By spring of 2009, a new government strategy gradually evolved for dealing with the illegal immigration problem in the United States. Increasingly, federal immigration authorities sent employers of illegal immigrant workers written notices that they faced civil fines and that they would have to discharge any workers confirmed to be unauthorized.

The number of foreign-born residents of the United States declined for the first time since at least 1970. Nearly 38 million foreign-born people lived in the United States in 2008 or 100,000 less than the year earlier.

On November 19, 2009, immigration authorities reported that it would audit about 1,000 U.S. employers to slow down the hiring of illegal immigrants. Found violators would be fined and pressed with civil or criminal charges.

Foreign-born residents, making up 12.5 percent of the U.S. population in 2008, yield nearly 40 percent of technology firms' founders and 52 percent of founders of companies in the Silicon Valley.

Clearly, the meltdown altered the image of U.S. opportunity. In the year ending July 2009, the country attracted about 855,000 more new immigrants from overseas than it sent to other countries. That was 14 percent lower than the nine-year annual average.

See also MIGRANT WORKERS; REMITTANCES; UNEMPLOY-MENT.

IMPERIAL COUNTY, CALIFORNIA. *See* UNEMPLOYMENT.

IMPORT DUTIES. *See* BUY AMERICAN, PROTECTIONISM, SMOOT-HAWLEY ACT OF 1930.

IMPORTS (U.S.). Imports, as reported on April 9, 2009, fell by 5 percent in February, as businesses reduced spending on foreign-made goods, and consumer demand for imported items remained low. The U.S. imported $8.2 billion less in goods and services in February 2008, and fell to $152.7 billion, while exports climbed to $126.8 billion.

By the end of the first quarter, U.S. imports declined 34 percent from the previous three months. Imports into countries using the euro from outside the area were down 21 percent compared with the first quarter of 2008.

As the U.S. trade deficit eased in May to its lowest level in nearly a decade, exports increased 1.6 percent while import sales slowed. On July 10, the government announced that difference in U.S. trade flows unexpectedly narrowed by 9.8 percent to approximately $25 billion, becoming the smallest deficit since November 1999. Imports were down 0.6 percent from April 2009.

Cf. EXPORTS (U.S.); TRADE DEFICIT.

INDEX OF INDUSTRIAL PRODUCTION. *See* INDUSTRIAL PRODUCTION.

INDIA. India is Asia's third-largest economy. After growing into a $1 trillion economy, India felt the effect of the global turmoil in its lending and property markets. Industries, particularly carmakers, were being pinched by a slowdown in demand. Policy makers in India ratcheted down their expectations for growth, which was expected to drop in the fiscal year ending March 2009 from 9 percent to 7 percent.

Exports in October 2008 fell by 12 percent compared with the same month in 2007; hundreds of small textile companies went out of business; some of the primary manufacturing giants, automobiles as an example, suspended production. The central bank revised its estimate of economic growth, perhaps still overly optimistic, down to 7.5–8 percent. It was anticipated that the rate could fall to 5.5 percent or less, the lowest since 2002.

India's exports fell for a second consecutive month. Overseas shipments dropped 9.9 percent, to $11.5 billion, from a year earlier after contracting 12.1 percent in October, the first decline in seven years.

On December 7, the government of India announced that it would seek approval for extra spending to buttress its economy in the face of the global slowdown. The spending, worth 200 billion rupees, or $4 billion, was one of a series of measures, including lowering taxes on several products, promoting growth in home loans, and allowing a state-run organization to issue tax-free bonds worth 100 billion rupees to finance infrastructure projects.

India's federal and state fiscal deficit topped 7 percent of GDP in 2008, one of the highest levels in the world. The federal deficit alone exceeded its 2.5 percent target.

In January 2009, India announced its second monetary and fiscal stimulus package within a month.

India's remarkable growth of the past five years was powered in large part by huge amounts of cash and investment. Investment accounted for about 39 percent of the nation's GDP in fiscal 2008, up 25 percent from five years before. However, beginning in 2009, foreign loans and direct investment declined by nearly a third, and in the last quarter of 2008, the economy's growth rate plummeted to about 5.3 percent.

The 2008–2009 meltdown also dried up funding in India's legendary Bollywood industry, and moviemakers are dropping projects and slashing budgets. Thirty percent fewer films were made in India in 2009, bringing the total to about 700. The production volume continued to decline as investors were reluctant to reenter the film market.

In early July the Indian government unveiled a $210 billion budget that increased welfare and rural spending in an effort to stimulate economic growth, but it also will widen the fiscal deficit to its largest gap in 18 years.

By December 2009, India's economy was expanding at its fastest rate in more than one year. GDP grew 7.9 percent from the previous period of July–September. That translates into a 13.9 percent annualized pace from the earlier quarter.

See also EMERGING MARKETS.

Cf. CHINA.

INDONESIA. On December 4, 2008, the central bank of Indonesia cut its main lending rate by a quarter-point, to 9.25 percent. Then, in early February 2009 its central bank lowered its interest rate from 8.75 percent to 8.25 percent.

See also SOUTHEAST ASIA.

INDUSTRIAL & COMMERCIAL BANK OF CHINA. The Hong Kong unit of China's biggest bank announced in March 2009 that its 2008 net profit fell 40 percent.

See also CHINA.

INDUSTRIAL BANKS. Banks that primarily make loans to businesses. Often these less controlled banks engage in risky practices away from the routine oversight by the Federal Reserve. These banks hold $130 billion, only about 1 percent of federally insured bank deposits. They cannot have checking accounts, and thus they have no retail branches. Some of these banks, mostly based in Utah, have over the past year converted to commercial banks to quality for federal bailout funds, which led to a significant fall in overall assets. President Obama wants to place these industrial banks under greater government scrutiny.

INDUSTRIAL OUTPUT. By July 2009, U.S. industrial output climbed for the first time in nine months, led by auto manufacturers. Output climbed 0.5 percent in July, as reported by the Federal Reserve on August 14, 2009. Manufacturing output rose 1 percent in July, the largest gain since December 2006.

See also INDUSTRIAL PRODUCTION.

INDUSTRIAL PRODUCTION. The Federal Reserve's index of industrial production rose 0.8 percent in August 2009 from July, when it increased 1 percent. That marked the first time that the index climbed for two consecutive months since the beginning of the recession.

Industrial production rose by 0.7 percent in September 2009 for the third consecutive month

See also INDUSTRIAL OUTPUT.

INDUSTRIAL SUPPLY SALES. *See* EXPORTS.

INDYMAC BANK (BANCORP). IndyMac played a pivotal role in the financial crisis. The firm's collapse under the weight of bad mortgage debt sparked bank runs across the country. It had thirty-three bank branches in Southern California with about $6.5 billion in deposits, about half the firm's worth, when it failed in July 2008.

On January 2, 2009, a seven-member group of investors formed to purchase the remnants of IndyMac Bank for $13.9 billion. IMB Management Holdings would invest $1.3 billion in deposits, a $16 billion loan portfolio, and a loan servicing business overseeing $158 billion in mortgages.

The name IndyMac did not survive. The government had run IndyMac since the Pasadena thrift collapsed.

Cf. COLONIAL BANCGROUP.

INFLATION. An increase in the price level creating a decrease in the purchasing power of the monetary unit.

Increasing prior to the economic crisis in the fall 2008, inflation fell to near zero. By December, inflation was no longer considered a major issue in the U.S. economy, as gasoline prices fell. Deflation was to be a primary concern.

See also EUROZONE; FEDERAL RESERVE; VENEZUELA.

Synonymous with "SILENT KILLER."

Cf. DEFLATION; REFLATION; STAGFLATION.

INFRASTRUCTURE. *See* OBAMA, BARACK; PUBLIC WORKS.

ING GROUP. On January 26, 2009, the Dutch financial services firm announced that it would cut 7,000 jobs. ING received €10 billion (about $13 billion) from the Dutch government in October 2008 to bolster its capital when it posted a net loss for the full year of 2008 of approximately €1 billion.

INITIAL PUBLIC OFFERINGS (IPO). By November 2008, there was a growing slowdown in all sectors of companies newly offering stock to the public. The credit crisis had turned the shares of many blue-chip financial firms into penny stocks, and almost all recent financial IPOs had failed.

In 2008, 662 firms went "public," raising a combined $77 billion, down from the 1,711 offering that raised $278.8 billion in 2007. In the United States, 33 stock market listings raised $26.4 billion in 2008. That was down from the 186 offerings that raised $41.3 billion in 2007.

Every region throughout the globe posted declines of more than 80 percent in the number of deals executed. For the last quarter of 2008, the number of IPOs in Europe dropped 95 percent to just 7, from 140 a year earlier, while in North America, the number dropped 92 percent to 9 from 112. Latin America showed a decline of 96 percent to 1 deal, down from 25 deals. The number of Asia-Pacific deals dramatically fell 84 percent to 37 from 230 a year before.

Throughout the meltdown, IPOs all but dried up. Then in the summer 2009, a healthy comeback was evident, indicating the public's increasing taste for risk taking. The demand for IPOs in part reflected a scramble among money managers who during the recession stayed on the sidelines. In September the largest IPO money-raising took place since the week of April 20, 2008.

INSTITUTE FOR SUPPLY MANAGEMENT. Their index of nonmanufacturing activity showed that economic activity in service and other non-manufacturing sectors was at 42.9 in January 2009, up 2.8 percentage points from December 2008. A number below 50 represents contraction; above 50 is expansion. It was the fourth straight month of contraction.

See also MANUFACTURING.

INSTITUTE OF INTERNATIONAL FINANCE. A bankers' group, it projected a 30 percent decline in net flows of private capital for 2008 compared to 2007.

INSURANCE. *See* AMERICAN INTERNATIONAL GROUP; METLIFE; TRAVELERS.

INSURANCE REGULATIONS. *See* MCCARRAN-FERGUSON ACT OF 1945.

INSURERS. By March 2009, mounting losses weakened these firms' capital bases and eroded investor confidence. A dozen life insurers applied for aid from the government's $700 billion TARP.

See also LIFE INSURERS.

INTEL. Announced in January 2009 that it would close several older factories, displacing 5,000 to 6,000 workers, as the firm reacted to a sharp drop in demand for its computer chips. Had a 90 percent drop in fourth-quarter 2008 earnings. About 6 to 7 percent of its workforce of 84,000 would lose their positions.

Revenue of $8.2 billion was reported on January 21, off 19 percent from the quarter that ended in September 2008, and off 23 percent from the year earlier.

On August 28, 2009, Intel boosted its third-quarter revenue forecast by 6 percent.

Cf. DELL INC.

INTERBANK RATE. *See* LIBOR.

INTEREST RATE DERIVATIVES. *See* DERIVATIVE(S); LONG-TERM CAPITAL MANAGEMENT.

INTEREST RATES. By mid-June 2009, interest rates continued to rise, threatening to dim prospects for a housing recovery and dim the government's economic stimulus efforts. For example, on June 10, rates on thirty-year fixed-rate mortgages climbed to 5.79 percent, up from 5 percent two weeks before.

See also FEDERAL RESERVE.

INTERMEDIARIES. Financial organizations (e.g., commercial banks, savings and loan associations) that accept deposits on which they pay interest and then reinvest those funds in securities with a higher yield.

INTERNAL REVENUE SERVICE (IRS). The federal agency empowered by Congress to administer the rules and regulations of the Department of the Treasury, which includes the collection of federal income and other taxes. It is divided into nine regions with sixty-four districts and is also responsible for the investigation of tax frauds.

See also TAXPAYERS.

INTERNATIONAL BANK FOR RECONSTRUCTION AND DEVELOPMENT. *Synonymous with* WORLD BANK.

INTERNATIONAL BUSINESS MACHINES CORPORATION (IBM). Following an announcement on January 20, 2009, that it had record earnings, on a slight sales decline 10,000 to 16,000 of its workers were cut.

By mid-March about 5,000 out of a total work force of 400,000 North American employees were told that they would be let go. Many of these positions were then transferred to India. Foreign workers accounted for 71 percent of IBM's employees.

On April 20, IBM posted a 1 percent decline in quarterly profit and an 11 percent drop in sales. IBM had a net income of $2.30 billion for the quarter, down from $2.32 billion a year before.

IBM's second-quarter profit rose 12 percent, but sales dropped.

IBM's third-quarter 2009 profit was 14 percent higher, climbing to $3.21 billion.

INTERNATIONAL COUNCIL OF SHOPPING CENTERS. *See* RETAILING.

INTERNATIONAL ENERGY AGENCY. Projected that worldwide demand for oil would actually decline in 2008, for the first time since 1983.

See also OIL EXPLORATION.

INTERNATIONAL INVESTMENTS. *See* CROSS-BORDER INVESTMENT FLOWS.

INTERNATIONAL LABOR ORGANIZATION. *See* GLOBAL UNEMPLOYMENT.

INTERNATIONAL LEASE FINANCE CORPORATION. *See* AMERICAN INTERNATIONAL GROUP.

INTERNATIONAL MONETARY FUND (IMF). A fund founded in 1944 when the world monetary system operated on a gold standard. The fund's mission was to act as a lender of last resort when nations encountered balance-of-payments shortfalls. It is an independent international organization of the United Nations. It is authorized to supplement its resources by borrowing; its purposes include promoting international monetary cooperation; expanding international trade and exchange stability; assisting in the removal of exchange restrictions and the establishment of a multilateral system of payments; and alleviating any serious disequilibrium in members' international balance of payments by making the resources of the fund available to them under adequate safeguards.

On November 7, 2008, EU countries urged that the United States sign onto a 100-day deadline for action on strengthening the IMF, reshaping the structure of global financial governance, and imposing greater regulation on the sector.

Also, in November, the IMF detailed a $2 billion package for Iceland; Pakistan would get $10 billion, Hungary $25 billion, and Ukraine $16.5 billion. Other nations hoping to receive IMF funding included Belarus, Bulgaria, Latvia, Romania, and Serbia.

The IMF had $255 billion in uncommitted usable resources and the ability to elicit funds from countries that were reluctant to act on their own.

The IMF also announced that it would lend as much as $100 billion to economically healthy countries, such as Brazil, Mexico, Singapore, and South Korea, all having trouble borrowing as a result of the turmoil in the global markets.

The United States has 16.77 percent of the total voting weight at the IMF. Germany has 5.88 percent, and Britain and France both have 4.86 percent. China has 3.66 percent.

By mid-November, the IMF had less than $250 billion at its disposal, while it needed three times that much to avert a meltdown in emerging economies like South Korea or Brazil.

On November 16, the IMF reached an agreement in principle with Pakistan to provide a $7.6 billion stand-by loan, subject to the approval of the IMF executive board.

The IMF needed another $150 billion to help counter the hit to emerging markets and poorer countries from the worsening global economic downturn.

The fund would make a significant increase in its $1.4 trillion projection of global financial losses and write-downs.

In February 2009, the IMF finalized a $100 billion loan from Japan and considered issuing bonds for the first time in its history as part of an effort to double the financial resources it has to fight the deepening global recession.

On February 22, leaders of France, Germany, the United Kingdom, and other European nations, fearful of a further meltdown, especially in Eastern Europe, called for the IMF to double its resources to $500 billion to head off problems in countries already hit hard by the global economic and financial crisis. The IMF also wanted to double its lending ability to bolster confidence that it could handle other borrowers amid the crisis.

On April 2, at the G-20 meeting in London, world leaders agreed to pump up the IMF's financial capacity fourfold, to $1 trillion, to help handle crises in developing countries, and they assigned the IMF responsibility for monitoring whether G-20 nations were adequately stimulating their economies and transforming their regulatory systems. In addition, the IMF was charged with providing early warnings of deepening financial problems.

The managing director of the IMF declared in mid-April 2009 that the global economy may be nearing a bottom and that the "free fall" was soon to end. In a study of 122 recessions across twenty-one advanced economies since 1960, the IMF found that global finance-based crises tend to last twice as long as an average recession, at more than seven quarters. They tended to be more severe, with real GDP contracting 4.8 percent versus an average of 2.7 percent.

Resulting from the G-20 meeting in early April 2009, it was concluded that the IMF should both have more resources and play a broader role in the world economy than in the past decades. Leaders determined that the IMF should have an increase in resources by $500 billion to $750 billion, and that it would be allowed to issue $250 billion worth of its own currency, the Special Drawing Right (SDR), to ease liquidity in emerging and developing nations.

SDRs are often called the IMF's currency, but are truly a unit of account. It is defined as the value of a fixed amount of yen, dollars, pounds, and euros, expressed in dollars at the current exchange rate.

At their late-April meeting in Washington, D.C., finance ministers focused on the $4.1 trillion—which the fund projected to lose from the global economic meltdown—and the $1.1 trillion needed to repair it. The IMF estimated that banks and other financial organizations had total losses of $4.05 trillion in the value of their holdings. Of that amount, $2.7 trillion was from loans and assets originating in the United States. The estimate had risen from $2.2 trillion in the fund's interim report in January, and $1.4 trillion in October 2008.

The IMF reported that the world economy would contract 1.3 percent in 2009, with the United States contracting 2.8 percent in 2009 and no growth in 2010.

By mid-September 2009, the IMF moved to increase its influence by stepping up its lending capacity to developing nations, thanks to a commitment by the Group of 20 in London in April. The IMF was charged with working with the Financial Services Board, a panel of central bankers and regulators, to signal early warnings of economic and financial risks, and to assess how much fiscal stimulus G-20 countries are making available. The IMF calculates that the global financial crisis will yield $3.4 trillion in losses for financial institutions between 2007 and 2010, projecting total losses alone in the banking sector to reach $2.8 trillion.

See also BANK RESCUE (PLAN) OF 2009; BELARUS; BRETTON WOODS; CHINA; EUROPEAN UNION; EUROZONE; GEITHNER, TIMOTHY F.; GLOBAL TRADE; GLOBAL UNEMPLOYMENT; G-20; HUNGARY; ICELAND; LATVIA; PAKISTAN; RECESSION; RECOVERY; ROMANIA; TURKEY; UKRAINE; UN ECONOMIC COUNCIL.

INTERNET. In December 2007, the number of Internet searches on the word "unemployment" was 2.69 million. One year later, the figure rose to 8.21 million.

INTERNET ADVERTISING. Expected to be minimally impacted by the 2008–2009 economic meltdown.
See also ADVERTISING.

INTERNET MONEY. *See* TECHNOLOGY INVESTMENT.

INVENTORIES. Businesses cut their inventories by 0.7 percent in November 2008, the largest decline in seven years and the third straight month that stockpiles were reduced as firms scrambled to cope with huge declines in sales.

By April 2009, inventories were shrinking significantly as stockpiles of goods declined. In major manufacturing companies, inventories were now about 15 percent lower than a year earlier. Inventories are important for estimating economic growth because they deal with future levels of output. GDP includes goods and services, both sold and unsold and retained as inventory. Quarterly GDP reflects the change in inventories. An increase in inventories occurs when production exceeds sales, which then adds to the reported growth rate, while a decrease in inventories subtracts from it.
See also RETAILING.

INVESTING. *See* CARRY TRADE; CROSS-BORDER INVESTMENT FLOWS; U.S. GOVERNMENT DEBT; ZERO-RATE.

INVESTMENT ADVISERS ACT OF 1940. This act imposed registration and other requirements on investment advisers and firms that provide investment advice for compensation and requires that advisers maintain certain books and records.

INVESTMENT BANKING. In 2009 the volume of initial public offerings had fallen by more than half since 2007. Finance, which accounted for a staggering 40 percent of corporate profits until recently, faces years of decline.

INVESTMENT COMPANY ACT OF 1940. For mutual fund firms and some other investment companies, the act established requirements for disclosure of investment practices, capital structure, and financial condition. It requires SEC registration and also created exemptions.

IPO. *See* INITIAL PUBLIC OFFERINGS.

IRAQ. The government announced in February 2009 that it was considering budget cuts of about $4.2 billion, or 7 percent of the year's spending plan, as it scrambled to cope with low oil prices. For the non-oil sectors, the government had frozen hiring.

See also WARS IN AFGHANISTAN AND IRAQ.

IRELAND. On December 15, 2008, the government announced that in January 2009 it would bolster bank capital by tapping funds set aside during the economic boom to cover future state pension obligations. A total of $13.6 billion was promised.

On December 22, the Irish government announced that it would inject 5.5 billion pounds into Ireland's three largest lenders, Bank of Ireland, Allied Irish Banks, and Anglo Irish.

Dublin's nationalization of Anglo Irish Bank capped the swift demise of the lender as its shares were suspended on January 16, 2009. Government legislation would provide "fair compensation" for the bank's shareholders.

The government announced on April 8 that it would take commercial-property assets off the books of six of its largest lenders and house them in a new state agency, in order to restore confidence in the nation's financial system. If needed, the state would take majority stakes in Ireland's two primary banks. This move made Ireland the first nation in the eurozone to use an industry-wide, government-sponsored "bad bank" to remove toxic assets from the banking system.

By April, roughly 180,000 Poles, Czechs, and other Eastern Europeans that had come to Ireland before 2004 were now returning to their homeland as unemployment reached 10.4 percent. Ireland's population, now 4.1 million, had previously seen a foreign-born population rising to 11 percent in 2006, from 7 percent in 2002.

Ireland faced the worst recession in the developed world. Retail sales plummeted 16.4 percent in the first quarter of 2009, falling 17.9 percent in March from a year earlier. Its consumer price index fell 4.7 percent in May, the worst drop since 1933.

Ireland's GDP fell by 1.5 percent in the first quarter 2009, leaving it 8.5 percent lower than in the same period one year earlier.

Unemployment reached a fourteen-year high of 12.2 percent in July 2009. Economists believe Ireland could see outflows of up to 40,000 people a year, the equivalent of nearly 2 percent of the country's labor force.

Although Ireland pulled out of the recession in the third quarter 2009, experts warned that major hurdles for the government remained, such as Irish GDP being down 7.5 percent in 2009 and expected to be down another 1.3 percent in 2010, as the nation's unemployment rate of 12 percent stabilizes.

IRS. *See* INTERNAL REVENUE SERVICE.

ISRAEL. As a nation increasingly dependent on exporting high-tech equipment, Israel's economy has suffered since the meltdown began.

On August 24, 2009, Israel's central bank raised its key interest rate to 0.75 percent from 0.5 percent. The Bank of Israel became the first central bank to raise its key interest rate, showing that the global economy is emerging from the Great Recession.

In mid-November 2009 Israel's central bank raised its key interest rate to 1 percent after the bank pegged the nation's inflation in October at 2.9 percent. The government reported that the economy grew for the second consecutive quarter, with third-quarter growth at 2.2 percent.

Israel's economy has grown at least 4 percent a year from 2004 to 2008 with only a 7.8 percent unemployment rate.

ISSUES OF STOCKS AND BONDS. In 2008, tumbled 38 percent to $4.71 trillion.

ITALY. At the end of November 2008, Italy presented an economic stimulus package totaling €80 billion, or $103 billion. The government would also make a one-time cash payment to Italy's poorest families, freeze tolls on highways, and require banks to limit mortgage rates as part of its plan.

Italian industrial production fell in the final month of 2008, dropping 2.5 percent from November, adjusted for the season and for the number of working days, as output of intermediate and investment goods plunged.

Italy's economy contracted 2.4 percent in the first quarter of 2009 from the previous quarter, the largest decline since data was collected in 1980.

See also FERRE; FIAT.

J

JAGUAR. *See* TATA MOTORS.

JAL. *See* JAPAN AIRLINES.

JAPAN. On August 31, 2008, Japan unveiled a $106 billion economic stimulus package that included tax cuts and loan guarantees.

On October 27, the Nikkei—Japan's stock market—plunged to its lowest level in twenty-six years and overall fell by half in 2008.

In early November, the Japanese central bank cut its benchmark interest rate for the first time in seven years. The overnight lending rate between banks was lowered from 0.5 to 0.3 percent, reducing borrowing costs in order to rekindle growth in the country. It was also aimed at easing a growing credit crunch in Japan.

The world's second-largest economy officially slipped into recession on November 17, hurt by weak export growth and steep cuts in corporate spending during the deepening global slowdown. Japan's GDP shrank at an annual rate of 0.4 percent from July to September after declining a revised 3.7 percent in the previous quarter.

Exports fell in October for the first time in nearly seven years, dashing hopes that Japan and the Southeast Asian region would be able to help the global economy during the credit crisis. Exports declined 7.7 percent in October, with exports to China alone falling 4 percent, the first decline since 2002.

The Bank of Japan announced on December 2 that it took emergency measures to ease an acute squeeze in corporate financing that threatened to push the largest Asian economy deeper into recession. Steps included a program that allowed commercial banks to borrow unlimited funds at low interest rates from the central bank, provided that they had sufficient collateral to guarantee the loans.

China's slowdown was also having considerable impact on Japan's economy, as Japan's economy shrank at the annualized rate of 1.8 percent in the three months to September, far worse than expected.

On December 11, Japan's prime minister announced an emergency stimulus package to jolt the economy by spending trillions of yen to create jobs, increase business loans, and help laid-off workers. The value of the package was approximately $250 billion, which included tax cuts for homeowners and companies that build or purchase new factories and equipment, as well as grants to local governments to support job creation.

Manufacturing in Japan continued to decline as the country suffered its sharpest fall in decades, and total manufacturing output was at its lowest level in seven years.

Industrial output plunged 8.1 percent in November, the nation's largest decline on record. Manufacturing output, as reported on December 25, indicated an expected drop of 11.1 percent. Exports in November had dropped 26.7 percent from a year earlier, indicating the worsening condition of Japan's battered economy.

Exports tumbled by a record 35 percent for December 2008. Japan posted a trade deficit of $3.56 billion in December, wider than the 225-billion-yen deficit of the previous month.

Overall exports totaled 4.83 trillion yen in December, down from 7.43 trillion yen in 2007. For all of 2008, Japan's trade surplus shrank 80 percent to 2.16 trillion yen, as exports fell 3.4 percent and imports grew 7.9 percent.

In this downturn, Japan's unemployment was rapidly rising. Projections were for 1.5 million job losses by the end of 2010, lifting the unemployment rate from 4 percent in 2008 to over 6 percent projected for 2009.

The world's second-largest economy deteriorated at its worst pace since the oil crisis of the 1970s, damaged by declining exports and anemic home spending. The nation's real GDP shrank at an annual rate of 12.7 percent from October to December of 2008, after contracting for the two final quarters of the year. When compared with the third quarter of 2008, the economy plummeted 3.3 percent. The fourth-quarter results were Japan's worst quarterly drop since its economy contracted at an annual pace of 13.1 percent in the first three months of 1974.

By February, Japan, the largest holder of U.S. Treasury bonds, was in the midst of its worst recession in fifty years. Exports dropped, industrial production was plummeting 30 percent from a year before, and its GDP was falling 12 percent in 2009.

Industrial output plunged by a record 10 percent in January, further evidence that the country's worst recession in decades was intensifying.

On March 13, the government called for another round of public spending to aid its ailing economy, putting the government in conflict with Europe, which was resisting additional deficit spending programs to help pull the global economy out of its meltdown.

Japan's exports fell at a record rate in February 2009. Demand for Japanese goods continued to shrink in overseas markets, including the United States and China, with overall exports falling a record 49 percent, the fifth straight month of decline. That, along with a 43 percent drop in imports, gave Japan a trade surplus for the first time in five months.

At the end of March, Japan's parliament enacted a record $897.16 billion budget for its next fiscal year, paving the way for the government to carry out its third stimulus package and accelerate work on its next steps to revive growth.

On March 30, the government announced that it was prepared to implement new stimulus steps that would exceed 2 percent of its GDP. Greater concern existed that without further efforts of economic input from the government, Japan's GDP would shrink by 5.8 percent in 2009, far worse than contractions of 2.6 percent in the United States and 3.2 percent for the eurozone.

A new stimulus package was introduced by the government on April 10, with spending of at least $100 billion as the nation grappled with the worst recession since World War II. The package would work in five areas: creating a safety net for workers who do not have the status of "permanent" staff, aiding corporate financing, increasing spending on solar-power systems, lowering public anxiety over medical and nursing care services, and revitalizing regional economics. By early April, Japan's prime minister ordered the nation's largest supplemental budget, containing more than $100 billion of fresh spending, to boost the world's second-largest economy. It would exceed 2 percent of its GDP.

On April 27, the government said that the economy was expected to contract by a record 3.3 percent in the current fiscal year. The new projection was much more negative than the 1.5 percent decline reported a month earlier, which at the time was the worst performance since the government began measuring growth in 1955.

Japan is expected to face declining prices for the next two fiscal years and will face a protracted stretch of deflation.

After shrinking 9.4 percent in February, Japan's industrial production increased 1.6 percent in March. On May 19, the government announced that its GDP shrank 4 percent in the first quarter from the previous one. The latest reading translates into an annualized contraction of 15.2 percent, the worst performance since 1955.

At the end of May, Japan enacted a record $143.73 billion extra budget, enabling the government to execute new stimulus steps to support an economy that improved mildly after six months of shrinking at a double-digit pace. The package contained spending and tax cuts valued at 3 percent of Japan's annual economic output.

Unemployment in Japan rose to 5.2 percent in May from 5 percent in April.

Japan's economy grew for the first time in five quarters, pulling the economy out of its longest recession since World War II. The nation's real GDP grew 0.9 percent in the second quarter from the first quarter, an annual pace of expansion of 3.7 percent.

Despite a 1.9 percent increase of industrial output in July 2009, deflation and job losses had become a twin blow for Japan. Deflation worsened while the jobless rate rose to a record 5.7 percent that month, a 0.3 percent increase from the previous month. As prices dropped, companies laid off workers, up 830,000 workers from the year before. On August 31, 2009, Japan's opposition party won an overwhelming victory and promised to do away with American-style, pro-market reforms in order to lead the nation out of its long slump. Japan was determined to avoid using market forces to raise productivity.

On September 11, the government announced that its economy grew a revised 0.6 percent in the second quarter 2009.

Gross public debt mushroomed in Japan during years of stimulus spending, and in 2009 it passed 187 percent of the Japanese economy. That debt could soon reach twice the size of the $5 trillion economy, the largest, in real terms, the world has ever seen. (Japan's outstanding debt is as big as the economies of Britain, France, and Germany combined.)

Deflation continues to worry the government. Consumer prices continued to fall for three consecutive years. The country's central bank projects a decline of 1.5 percent for the current fiscal year and 1 percent for 2010. The country's central bank predicted the economy would remain in deflation over the next two fiscal years. On October 30, 2009 the government indicated that its core consumer price index fell 2.3 percent on year in September, the seventh straight fall. It predicted real GDP to climb by 1.2 percent in fiscal year 2010 and grow by 2.1 percent in 2011.

Japan's economy rebounded in the third quarter 2009. The government reported that its GDP growth was 1.2 percent over the previous quarter, a 4.8 percent annualized pace. It was the country's second consecutive quarter of expansion, the fastest growth since early 2007. The official end to the recession in Japan was declared.

During the third quarter 2009 the domestic demand deflator—a measure of changes in prices of goods and services except for exports and imports—fell 2.6 percent, its fastest pace since 1958. It is expected that Japan's national debt will rise to more than 200 percent of its GNP in 2011 from 170 percent in 2007, the highest among rich nations.

On December 1, Japan's central bank announced that it would inject as much as $115.68 billion into its economy already facing deflation and a soaring currency. The following day, the government planned to raise a stimulus effort that could total more than $80 billion. The program would finance measures such as loan guarantees for small firms and incentives for consumers to purchase more energy-efficient electronics.

Not willing to tolerate zero inflation or falling prices, on December 18, 2009, the Bank of Japan left its interest rate near zero.

On December 30 the government released a draft economic strategy that targets an average annual growth rate of more than 2 percent over the coming ten years.

See also CANON; CHINA; HONDA; INTERNATIONAL MONETARY FUND; JAPAN AIRLINES; MANUFACTURING; MERGERS AND ACQUISITIONS; MITSUBISHI; NIKKEI; TOSHIBA; TOYOTA; WORLD TRADE; YEN; ZOMBIES.

JAPAN AIRLINES (JAL). On September 15, 2009, Japan Airlines announced that it would slash its workforce by 14 percent by the end of 2011. The company is planning to reduce its 48,000-strong workforce (at one time it had 54,000 workers) by 6,800 employees. The airline needs as much as $1.65 billion in new funds. In its fiscal first quarter ended in June 2009, the airline lost more than $1 billion. Management predicted a net loss of $691 million for the full business year.

On October 29 the government set the stage for a large bailout of the airline, urging the company to seek state support. The airline posted a loss of $357 million in the quarter. This compares to a $448 million profit in 2008. In the quarter reported in November 2009, sales declined by 26 percent to $4.8 billion.

At the end of November 2009, Japan Airlines had obtained government approval to receive up to $1.1 billion in emergency loans aimed at preventing the firm from grounding flights.

By year's end 2009, JAL was still considering an out-of-court restructuring with a bankruptcy protection filing on the horizon should it fail to persuade more than two-thirds of about 8,800 retirees to accept a benefits-reduction plan.

See also AMERICAN AIRLINES.

JAPANESE YEN. *See* YEN.

J.C. PENNEY. By January 2009, same-store sales within its department store division had fallen 8.1 percent from the previous year.

On February 20, the company reported a 51 percent drop in fourth-quarter profits as customers reduced spending on clothing and other discretionary items. Sales fell almost 10 percent, to $5.76 billion from $6.39 billion, with sales at stores open at least a year falling 10.8 percent.

J.C. Penney had a flat, no-growth fiscal second quarter 2009 and posted a loss of $1 million. The retailer reduced inventories by 12 percent in the second quarter.

On November 13, 2009, the company reported a 78 percent drop in fiscal third-quarter profit, posting a profit of $27 million, compared with $124 million the year before. Sales declined 3.2 percent to $4.12 billion.

See also RETAILING.

JEWELRY. The recession, as reported in February 2009, pummeled jewelers. The 2008 Christmas sales season usually accounted for an average of 30 percent of their annual revenue. Sales of luxury items, including jewelry, fell 34 percent during this period compared to a year earlier.

About 1,500 mostly small jewelry stores closed in 2008, with larger stores also shutting hundred of branches.

See also BULGARI; LUXURY GOODS; RETAILING; SWATCH GROUP; TIFFANY; ZALES.

JIABAO, WEN. *See* CHINA.

JOB BANKS. The era when factory workers from General Motors and Chrysler could collect nearly their full salary after they lost their jobs ended in February 2009. Both automakers announced the end of their job bank program. Ford Motor Company, which had not borrowed money from the government, did not announce changes to its job bank.

JOB CREATION. On December 8, 2009, President Obama pressed for a job creation program to place an additional $50 billion toward infrastructure spending, utilizing unspent TARP funds.

On December 14, 2009, U.S. House of Representatives leaders unveiled a $75 billion job creation package.

See also U.S. CENSUS.

JOBLESS (BENEFITS) CLAIMS. On September 22, 2009, the House of Representatives voted to extend unemployment insurance benefits for jobless citizens in two dozen states by thirteen weeks.

On October 8 the government noted that first-time claims for unemployment insurance fell to a seasonally adjusted 521,000 from the previous week's upwardly revised total of 554,000.

For the week ended December 12, 2009, jobless benefit claims rose 7,000 to a seasonally adjusted 480,000. The four-week average of new claims, which purports to smooth volatility in the data, dropped 5,250 to 467,000— its fifteenth consecutive fall.

See also OVERTIME; TROUBLED ASSET RELIEF PROGRAM; UNEMPLOYMENT.

JOBLESSNESS. *See* UNEMPLOYMENT.

JOBLESS RATE. *See* UNEMPLOYMENT.

JOB LOSS. *See* UNEMPLOYMENT.

JOB OPENINGS. In August 2008, there were 4.65 million job openings in the country. The number of U.S. job openings sank below 3 million in January 2009, the lowest level since its series began in late 2000, and a key reason why the unemployment rate had risen sharply to 8.1 percent. By comparison, new job openings averaged more than 4 million per month from 2005 through 2007.

By November 2009 the government found that the number of job openings in the country increased slightly in August and September, the first two-month increase since early 2007.

The number of U.S. job openings shrank to a seasonally adjusted 2.5 million in October 2009 from about 2.6 million the prior month, while the number of hires fell to 3.9 million, falling below the 4 million mark for the first time since June 2009.

See also TAX CREDITS.

JOB PRESERVATION. *See* SOUTH KOREA.

JOBS DOWNTURN. *See* UNEMPLOYMENT.

JOBS PROGRAM. *See* TROUBLED ASSET RELIEF PROGRAM.

JOB STARTS. *See* JOB CREATION.

JOHNSON & JOHNSON. The weak economy continued to hurt the health care company's results in 2009. First-quarter 2009 profit declined 2.5 percent and net income was $3.5 billion, or $1.26 a share, compared with $3.6 billion, or $1.26 a share, a year earlier. Sales had dropped 7.2 percent to $15.02 billion from $16.19 billion the year before.

J&J's second-quarter 2009 profit fell 3.6 percent, with sales harmed by unfavorable currency rates, competition from generic drugs, and tighter consumer spending. Sales fell 7.4 percent to $15.24 billion from $16.45 billion. Net income of $3.21 billion fell from $3.33 billion one year earlier.

On November 1, 2009, Johnson & Johnson announced that it would eliminate as many as 8,200 jobs, or 7 percent of its workforce.

JONES, ALFRED WINSLOW. *See* HEDGE FUNDS.

JONES APPAREL GROUP. Announced a detailed cost-cutting plan to deal with slumping retail sales. Had a fourth-quarter 2008 loss and an $840 million goodwill write-down. Cut its quarterly dividend 64 percent, to five cents a share, while also reducing a capital spending program from $70 million in 2008 to $45 million for 2009.

See also RETAILING.

JORDAN. *See* MIDDLE EAST.

JOURNAL REGISTER CO. The owner of the *New Haven Register* and nineteen other daily newspapers filed for Chapter 11 protection on February 22, 2009.

JP MORGAN CHASE (JP MORGAN). A giant in the wholesale financial services area. Clients include corporations, institutional investors, hedge funds, governments, and affluent individuals in more than 100 countries. JP Morgan is part of JPMorgan Chase & Co., a leading global financial services firm with assets of nearly $2 trillion.

JP Morgan survived the meltdown and proceeded to purchase other banks, including Washington Mutual and Bear Stearns.

After repaying $25 billion in federal money, it reported on July 16 strong quarterly earnings of $2.7 billion. JP Morgan Chase's profits were up 36 percent from $2 billion a year earlier. Revenue climbed 39 percent from the year before to a record $27.7 billion.

Third-quarter 2009 earnings rose sevenfold to $3.59 billion for JP Morgan Chase. Profits jumped to $3.59 billion.

See also BEAR STEARNS; INVESTMENT BANKING; "TOO BIG TO FAIL"; WASHINGTON MUTUAL.

Cf. GOLDMAN SACHS.

JPMORGAN CHASE & CO. The parent entity of JP Morgan Chase.
See also JP MORGAN CHASE.

JUNK. *See* MOODY'S; STANDARD & POOR'S.

JUNK RATINGS. *See* FALLEN ANGELS.

K

KAUPTHING BANK. *See* ICELAND.

KAZAKHSTAN. In November 2008, with oil prices falling and investors fleeing high-risk markets, Kazakhstan's economy fell by 50 percent, to 5 percent from an average of 10 percent since 2000. Average wages dropped 1.1 percent.

On February 2, the government declared that it would take controlling stakes in two private banks as a condition of keeping them from a possible bankruptcy filing.

Two days later, the central bank allowed a 25 percent devaluation of its national currency to protect its foreign-exchange and gold reserves and boost the country's manufacturing competitiveness.

On April 24, Kazakhstan's largest bank stated that it would no longer repay $11 billion in foreign debt, but would pay only interest to foreign creditors.

Some of the world's largest banks funneled more than $10 billion in loans into Kazakhstan's largest bank—Bank Turalem (BTA). By fall 2009, the bank loaned billions of dollars to finance mostly real estate programs in Russia and Ukraine. Now most of the loans have gone bad rapidly.

See also CENTRAL ASIA.

KBC. A Belgian banking and insurance group, received in January 2009 a €2 billion, or $2.59 billion, cash injection from the Flemish government.

KELLOGG COMPANY. The nation's largest cereal maker saw third-quarter 2009 profit increase 5.6 percent by cutting costs and having lower commodities prices. The company posted a profit of $361 million, and its gross margin improved to 43.9 percent from 42.7 percent. Revenue fell 0.3 percent to $3.28 billion.

Cf. PROCTER & GAMBLE.

KEYNES, JOHN MAYNARD. An influential British economist whose analysis of the Great Depression redefined economics in the 1930s, asserting that increased government spending during a downturn could revive the economy. His 1936 book *The General Theory of Employment, Interest and Money* expected that general employment was always positively correlated with the aggregate demand for consumer goods. Keynes argued that government should intervene in the economy to maintain aggregate demand and full employment, with the goal of smoothing out business cycles. During recessions, he believed, government should borrow money and spend it. To this day, his departure from classical economics is debated. Critics argue that government action to stimulate aggregate demand is wrong. They in turn argued that the boom and bust of the business cycle is primarily a monetary phenomenon created by governments' artificial inflation of money and credit.

The theory beneath the American Recovery and Reinvestment Act of 2009 is called the *Keynesian multiplier*, which was first posited around 1931.

See also AMERICAN RECOVERY AND REINVESTMENT ACT (OF 2009); FISHER, IRVING; GREAT DEPRESSION (OF THE 1930S); SMOOT-HAWLEY ACT OF 1930.

KEYNESIAN MULTIPLIER. *See* KEYNES, JOHN MAYNARD.

KODAK. *See* EASTMAN KODAK.

KOENIGSEGG. Swedish sports-car maker received about $600 million from the European Investment Bank in October 2009 to help finance the acquisition of GM's Saab unit. By November the GM acquisition collapsed.

See also GENERAL MOTORS; SAAB.

KOREA. In December 2008, the Bank of Korea cut its benchmark interest rate by a full percentage point, its biggest cut ever, to 3 percent.

By the beginning of 2009, the Bank of Korea cut its benchmark interest rate to 2 percent, a record low, to aid the plunging South Korean economy.

KPS. *See* WATERFORD WEDGWOOD.

KRONA. *See* ICELAND.

KRUGMAN, PAUL. An East Coast liberal establishment member, an economics columnist for the *New York Times*, an economics professor at Princeton University, and a Nobel Prize winner in economics. He is considered President Obama's toughest liberal critic.

On March 23, 2009, he said "Tim Geithner the Treasury secretary has persuaded President Obama to recycle Bush administration policy—specifically, the 'cash for trash' plan proposed, then abandoned, six months ago by then-Treasury secretary Henry Paulson. This is more than disappointing. In fact, it fills me with a sense of despair."

On March 9, he said, "So here's the picture that scares me. It's September 2009, the unemployment rate has passed 9 percent, and despite the early round of stimulus spending it's still headed up. Mr. Obama finally concedes that a bigger stimulus is needed. But he can't get his new plan through Congress because approval for his economic policies has plummeted, partly because his policies are seen to have failed, partly because job-creation policies are conflated in the public mind with deeply unpopular bank bailouts. And as a result, the recession rages on, unchecked."

On February 6, he said "Somehow, Washington has lost any sense of what's at stake—of the reality that we may well be falling into an economic abyss, and that if we do, it will be very hard to get out again."

KUWAIT. In October 2008, Kuwait's Gulf Bank disclosed a $1 billion loss stemming from bad foreign-exchange bets. In January 2009, the government took a 16 percent stake in the bank to keep it from collapsing.

In February, with falling oil prices, plummeting stocks, and a softening real estate market, Kuwait faced a banking crisis. In response, the government announced a $5.4 billion package to prop up banks—the only bailout plan thus far among all Persian Gulf states.

In mid-April, Kuwait's central bank cut its discount rate by a quarter of a percentage point to 3.5 percent, as the oil-rich nation sought to stimulate bank lending.

Cf. DUBAI.

L

LAFARGE. The French basic-materials firm had a net debt of $23 billion and a market capitalization of $12 billion. Lafarge had sufficient liquidity to cover maturing debt until mid-summer 2010.

LAGOS. *See* AFRICA.

LAND ROVER. *See* TATA MOTORS.

LANDSBANKI. *See* ICELAND.

LATIN AMERICA. From 2004 to the fall of 2008 Latin America's economy grew at an annual average rate of over 5 percent, inflation remained low, credit was expanded, and exports boomed. The proportion of people living in poverty fell from 44 percent in 2002 to 33 percent in 2008.

Since September 2008, Latin America had seen many of its stock markets crash, currencies shaken, and credit drying up.

In 2009, it was projected that the current meltdown in the United States would not be felt severely in Latin America. It was predicted that there would be a 2.5 percent growth in Latin America in 2009, down from earlier predictions of 3.2 percent

See also ARGENTINA; AUTOMOBILE INDUSTRY; BRAZIL; MEXICO; PUERTO RICO; WORLD TRADE.

LATVIA. In October 2008, the jobless rate was 5.6 percent. Unemployment in 2009 was projected by the government to reach 10 percent and then 10.8 percent in 2010, before falling to 8.4 percent in 2011.

The IMF bailed out Latvia with more than €7 billion in mid-December. The arrangement did not require Latvia to devalue its currency. Now, the country faced a 5 percent or larger contraction of its GDP in 2009. Tax rises and spending cuts were worth a full 7 percent of GDP, and public-sector salaries declined by 15 percent.

As foreign capital dried up, GDP fell by 4.6 percent.

Latvia's center-right coalition government collapsed on February 20, a victim of the country's growing economic and political turmoil. (It was the second government to fall, following Iceland's collapse during the financial crisis.) Latvia's GDP shrank at an annual rate of 10.5 percent in January, and by the end of 2009, the economy was projected to shrink by 12 percent or more.

Less than 3 months after securing $10.5 billion in emergency funding, Latvia, considered the weakest country of among the East European economies, backtracked on a deal that the IMF hoped would lower the risk of a regional meltdown.

On July 2, the European Commission announced that it would release $1.7 billion to Latvia to help the nation head off a collapse of its economy and to maintain its currency link to the euro.

On July 28 the IMF and the European Union agreed to give Latvia a $2 billion loan to help its economy during the recession. Latvia's economy fell during the year and is less than $25 billion GDP. The IMF approved on August 27 the disbursement of $278.5 million to Latvia. These funds are critical, as the nation's economy shrank 20 percent in the second quarter 2009. The nation's second-quarter current account displayed a surplus of 14.2 percent of GDP, compared to 15.1 percent the previous year. The economy decreased 18.7 percent year-on-year.

The government is attempting to keep its 2010 budget down to 8.5 percent, a condition for the continuation of an $11 billion IMF bailout package.

See also EASTERN EUROPE.

Cf. BALTICS; ESTONIA; ICELAND.

LAW FIRMS. The economic slowdown triggered layoffs in law firms across the nation. In 2008, profits on average were down 8 percent to 12 percent, after fifteen years of growth.

By 2009, the largest U.S. law firms were firing attorneys and delaying new hires. More than 3,000 lawyers lost their jobs in the first three months of 2009. Partner profits were down an average of 4 percent in 2008 at the highest-grossing firms.

According to government figures, the number of unemployed lawyers jumped 66 percent in 2008, to a ten-year high of 20,000.

One of the changes resulting from the recession is how companies are pushing law firms for flat-fee contracts instead of hourly billings. Critics of the hourly schedule argued that this billing practice encourages the incentive to rack up larger bills. In 2009, 50 percent of corporate legal matters are now billed on a contract basis. Some companies claim that flat-fee billing can lower legal costs from 15 percent to 20 percent. Funds spent on alternative billing arrangements totaled $13.1 billion in 2009, versus $8.6 billion in the same time frame in 2008.

LAWYERS. *See* LAW FIRMS.

LAYOFFS. *See* UNEMPLOYMENT.

LAZARD. Had a first-quarter 2009 loss accompanied by its shares falling 9.8 percent, or $53.5 million, compared with a net income of $7.8 million in the year earlier. Revenue fell 19 percent to $4.25 billion.

Lazard's third-quarter 2009 profit was $37.4 million, with revenue rising to a record $119.1 million in the quarter. Revenue rose 1.5 percent to $411.7 million.

LEASING. *See* GENERAL MOTORS.

LEGACY ASSETS. Often used interchangeably with toxic assets.
See also PUBLIC-PRIVATE INVESTMENT FUND.

LEGACY LOANS PROGRAM. *See* PUBLIC-PRIVATE INVESTMENT FUND.

LEGACY SECURITIES PROGRAM. *See* PUBLIC-PRIVATE INVESTMENT FUND; TOXIC ASSETS.

LEHMAN BROTHERS. Lehman Brothers announced on June 17, 2008, that it would post a $2.8 billion quarterly loss. Then on July 1, Lehman's shares tumbled to their lowest level since 2000, with expectations that the firm might have to sell itself.

On September 15, Lehman Brothers filed for bankruptcy, the largest casualty to date of the global credit crisis. It was the biggest investment bank to collapse since 1990. In the days before it was allowed to fail, U.S. Treasury officials made it clear that they did not think the bank's collapse would have a major impact on the nation's economy. How wrong they were.

Lehman's fall was intimately tied to myriad derivatives and complex mortgage securities, which held billions of dollars in securities backed by home loans and other assets of uncertain worth.

The result of Lehman's subsequent failure was for banks across the globe, fearing for their own solvency, to stop lending. In addition, issuance of corporate bonds, commercial paper, and a wide variety of other financial products largely ceased. Credit-financed economic activity was brought to a virtual standstill.

Under Chapter 11 of the federal bankruptcy code, firms receiving protection from creditors have a chance to reorganize. Although Lehman filed for Chapter 11 protection, the company was not expected to emerge from proceedings. But there were advantages to Lehman if its bankruptcy was well managed. It could find buyers for Lehman's businesses so long as they were willing to continue employing its workers.

In one twenty-four-hour period, Lehman lost $1.6 billion when the Chicago Mercantile Exchange closed out all of Lehman's positions.

U.S. Treasury experts argued that bailing Lehman out would have wrongly rewarded it for bad behavior and excessive risk taking, and thereby would have given the U.S. financial sector a green light for future bad behavior.

Lehman had assets of $639 billion at the end of May. It owed about $110.5 billion on account of senior unsecured notes, $12.6 billion on account of subordinated unsecured notes, and $5 billion on account of junior subordinated notes. By the end of August, Lehman had $600 billion of assets financed with just $30 billion of equity.

Lehman's real estate holdings were part of its huge problems for survival. As of September 12, 2007, Lehman's valuation of its commercial and residential real estate holdings was $22.9 billion. As of December 31, 2008, it had fallen to $15.9 billion valued by the firm overseeing the bankruptcy. The number of properties on which Lehman's loans were restructured was 900.

The filing represented the end of a 158-year-old company that employed nearly 26,000 people. Possessing so little capital meant that a 5 percent decline in assets would have wiped out the value of the firm.

The bankruptcy filing of what was once the fourth-largest investment bank in the United States came after a weekend of heated negotiations among regulators and Wall Street firms about Lehman's fate. The U.S. government refused to backstop Lehman's worst assets the way it backstopped Bear Stearns's earlier sales to JP Morgan.

Prospective bidders refused to buy Lehman without government support. In the end, Lehman was allowed to fail.

Part of the controversy was whether the federal government should have stepped in to save Lehman, or whether allowing it to fail was in the best interests of the national economy.

In the end, Barclay's Bank of Britain negotiated a deal to buy most of Lehman's businesses out of bankruptcy. Barclay's agreed to take over the Fed's lending role and the transfer was made. Barclay's acquired the majority Lehman's North American and European business lines.

Lehman's demise has been rationalized by those responsible for its failure: "Lehman Brothers had to die for the rest of Wall Street to live."

In mid-September 2009, the bankruptcy estate of Lehman Brothers Holdings accused some former executives of working with Barclays PLC of the UK to provide a "windfall" of at least $8.2 billion when it purchased Lehman's broker-dealer business in the fall 2008. This happened when Barclays gave $45 billion to Lehman in exchange for $50 billion in securities. Instead of permitting Lehman to later purchase back the securities for $45 billion, executives of both firms decided to leave the securities with the UK bank, resulting in the "windfall."

One year after Lehman's demise and bankruptcy—the largest Chapter 11 case in American history—the firm continues to be involved in the future of its clients. As of September 11, 2009, 9,763 claims had been filed in federal bankruptcy court in Manhattan. For example, Lehman by September 2009 had 1.2 million derivatives transactions outstanding with 6,500 trading partners. The cash that is recovered from Lehman's U.S. derivatives business will be a major source of funds for the bankruptcy estate, to be used for paying out on credit claims. It will take years to sort everything out.

See also BEAR STEARNS; CREDIT-DEFAULT SWAPS; EXPORTS; FORTIS BANQUE; GEITHNER, TIMOTHY F.; MONEY MARKET MUTUAL FUNDS; SECURITIES AND EXCHANGE COMMISSION; "TOO BIG TO FAIL."

Cf. CIT GROUP.

LEHMAN BROTHERS HOLDINGS INCORPORATED. *See* LEHMAN BROTHERS.

LEMON SOCIALISM. Where taxpayers bear the cost if things go wrong, but stockholders and executives get the benefits if things go right.

See also STRESS TESTS; ZOMBIES.

LENDING. Top beneficiaries of federal cash from TARP saw outstanding loans decline 1.4 percent in the fourth quarter 2008. Ten of the thirteen big beneficiaries of TARP saw their outstanding loan balances decline by a total of $46 billion.

Those thirteen banks had collected the majority of the roughly $200 billion the government had given out.

By mid-April 2009, bank lending had fallen at a sharper rate than earlier realized, despite government efforts to pump billions of dollars into the financial sector, specifically to spur lending. The total dollar amount of new loans declined in three of the four months the government had reported this data. All but three of the nineteen largest TARP recipients originated fewer loans in February than they did at the time they received federal infusions.

The Treasury measured the monthly lending change at the top twenty-one TARP recipient banks by calculating the median change, which some experts say understated the decline. Between January and February, the median fell 2.2 percent, but total lending declined 4.7 percent.

Lending by banks continued to slow into mid-2009 as bankers and borrowers were cautious about taking risks. The total amount of loans held by fifteen large U.S. banks shrank by 2.8 percent in the second quarter 2009, and more than half of the loan volume in April and May came from refinancing mortgages and renewing credit to businesses, not new loans. Financial institutions are clamping down on lending to conserve capital as a cushion against mounting loan losses. And loan demand fell as firms sidelined expansion plans and consumers were spending less.

See also "TOO BIG TO FAIL"; TROUBLED ASSETS RELIEF PROGRAM.

LENOVO. China's biggest personal-computer maker cut about 2,500 jobs or 11 percent of its work force in early 2009.

See also CHINA.

LEVERAGED BUYOUT FIRMS. In 2008, the leveraged buyout business nearly stopped. Deal volume fell around 70 percent from 2007 as buyout firms sold companies worth only around $6 billion in the last quarter, a small fraction of the $110 billion of sales in the second quarter of 2007. Things did not look any better for 2009.

See also EQUITY BUYOUT.

LEVI STRAUSS. On April 13, 2009, the denim manufacturer announced a 50 percent decline in fiscal first-quarter net income and a 12 percent slide in revenue. Profits fell to $48 million in the quarter ending March 1, from $97 million in the same period one year before. Sales slipped to $951 million, from $1.1 billion a year earlier.

Sales dropped 3 percent in its fiscal second quarter 2009, but Levi Strauss continued to add stores.

LEWIS, KENNETH D. *See* BANK OF AMERICA.

LG. A Korean maker of flat-screen televisions, it posted a record loss in the fourth quarter 2008, its first loss in seven quarters. LG reported a net loss of 684 billion won, or $506 million for the quarter. A year earlier, it had a net profit of 760 billion won, and it posted a profit of 295 billion won in the third quarter of 2008.

LG Electronics, South Korea's second-largest electronics maker by revenue, cut its expenses by $2.19 billion in early February 2009, by reducing manufacturing costs and unnecessary expenses. The firm hoped to avoid cutting jobs or capital investment.

LG Display's management stated that its second-quarter profit 2009 fell 60 percent from a year earlier.

LIBOR (LONDON INTERBANK OFFERED RATE). A measure of what major international banks charge each other for large-volume loans of eurodollars, or dollars on deposit outside the United States.

The common benchmark interest rate has crept up, from 1.1 percent in mid-January 2009 to 1.3 percent in early March 2009.

LIECHTENSTEIN. *See* TAX HAVENS.

LIFE INSURANCE COMPANIES. *See* LIFE INSURERS; METLIFE.

LIFE INSURERS. The U.S. Treasury decided in early April 2009 to extend bailout funds to a number of struggling life insurance firms. The Troubled Asset Relief Program would be used to provide assistance. Shares of life insurers had already fallen more than 40 percent in 2009, and had trouble raising funds.

Only insurers that owned federally chartered banks would qualify for the extended program, and they would have access to the Treasury's Capital Purchase Program, which injects funds into banks. Any life insurer receiving TARP funds would have to comply with strict executive compensation rules set by Congress.

See also METLIFE.

LILLIAN VERNON. Filed for Chapter 11 bankruptcy on February 21, 2008.

LIMITED BRANDS. Posted a fiscal second-quarter 2009 loss of 27 percent. Earnings were $74.3 million, down from $102 million a year earlier.

LINENS 'N THINGS. On May 3, 2008, filed for Chapter 11 protection from creditors, with plans to shut 120 stores.

LITHUANIA. Lithuania's GDP fell at a double-digit rate in the first quarter 2009. GDP declined 12.6 percent from the year earlier. A slump of 10 percent was predicted.

See also BALTICS.

LIVING STANDARDS. On September 10, 2009, the government announced that the Great Recession of 2007–2010 slashed families' earnings, increased poverty, and left more people without health insurance. Median household income, adjusted for inflation, fell 3.6 percent in 2008 to $50,303, the sharpest year-over-year fall in forty years. The poverty rate, at 13.2 percent, was the highest since 1997, and about 700,000 more people didn't have health insurance in 2008 than the year earlier.

The fall in medium income affected all races. The largest decline, 5.6 percent, was among Hispanics. The median income for Asians fell 4.4 percent, while black incomes fell 2.8 percent and non-Hispanic white fell 2.6 percent.

About 54 million people were living below the poverty line, about 3 million more than in 2007.

See also UNEMPLOYMENT.

LIZ CLAIBORNE. The apparel company said on February 3, 2009, that it would cut 725 jobs, or 8 percent of its workforce, as it tried to endure a consumer spending slowdown that had been particularly brutal for apparel retailers.

On August 12, 2009, the company reported a loss of $82.1 million with its seventh consecutive quarterly loss. Sales fell 29 percent to $683.8 million.

LLOYDS. Lloyds Banking Group and the government of the UK struck a deal in early March 2009 in which the government would insure more than $353.2 billion in Lloyds' assets and increased its stake in the bank to as much as 75 percent.

On June 30, 2009, Lloyds said it would cut an additional 2,100 jobs as part of its reorganization.

Cf. ROYAL BANK OF SCOTLAND.

LOAN MODIFICATIONS. On October 8, 2009, the government announced that it had met its goal of beginning trial loan modifications for a half million financially troubled homeowners. The $8,000 tax credit for first-time home buyers was recommended to be extended, indicating that the housing market still required assistance from the federal government.

See also MAKING HOME AFFORDABLE PROGRAM.

LOAN MODS. *See* HOUSING BAILOUT PLAN; LOAN MODIFICATIONS; MAKING HOME AFFORDABLE PROGRAM.

LOBBYISTS. The number of active lobbyists declined 2 percent in 2008 to 15,900, recording its first yearly drop in seven years.

LOCAL TAXES. *See* STATES (U.S.).

LOCKE, GARY. President Obama's Commerce secretary. He was formerly a two-term governor of the state of Washington.

LOCKHEED MARTIN CORPORATION. Second-quarter 2009 profit fell 17 percent, with sales slightly up.

In August 2009, Lockheed Martin announced that it would cut nearly 5 percent of its space-operations workforce, or 800 jobs.

Lockheed Martin management reported a 1.9 percent increase in third-quarter 2009 profit.

LONDON INTERBANK OFFERED RATE. *See* LIBOR.

LONG-TERM CAPITAL MANAGEMENT. Not allowing Long-Term Capital Management to collapse in 1998 laid the foundation for the current crisis. Had regulators been less concerned with protecting the hedge fund's creditors, things might have been better today.

Advised by "quants" (quantitative analysts), unsound, unfounded bets were made including investments in interest-rate derivatives.

With their bailout as a precedent, creditors came to believe that their loans to unsound financial institutions would be made good by the Fed.

Under Alan Greenspan's watch, the Fed organized a consortium of firms to purchase out Long-Term Capital Management and to cover their debts.

LONG-TERM DEBT. *See* MORTGAGE CREDIT.

LOOTING. The concept of investors borrowing huge amounts of money, making considerable profits when times were good, and then leaving the government holding the bag for their eventual (and predictable) losses. Because the government was unwilling to let big, interconnected financial firms fail, and because people at those companies knew it, they engaged in excessive risk taking.

LOS ANGELES TIMES. See NEWSPAPERS.

LOSS SHARES. *See* LOSS SHARING.

LOSS SHARING. Provides healthy banks with an incentive to take on troubled assets of a failed institution, with the government agreeing to assume the majority of future losses. The buyer usually takes the failed bank's deposits, leaving most of the assets to be managed and sold by the Federal Deposit Insurance Corporation.

The practice is largely a response to the number of bank failures of the past two years, stretching the FDIC's financial resources. The FDIC had just $10.4 billion in its deposit-insurance fund at the end of June 2009, down from more than $50 billion one year earlier. The FDIC agreed to absorb these losses.

See also FEDERAL DEPOSIT INSURANCE CORPORATION; "TOO BIG TO FAIL."

"LOST YEAR." *See* EUROPEAN COMMISSION.

LOUISIANA-PACIFIC CORPORATION. A major provider of lumber for homes and a housing developer itself, sales fell 38 percent to $1.28 billion from $2.04 billion, a year earlier.

Cf. WEYERHAEUSER.

LOWE'S COMPANIES. The second-largest home improvement retailer in the United States announced on February 20, 2009, that its fourth-quarter profit fell 60 percent, with forecasts for 2009 also downward. Revenues fell 4 percent, to $9.98 billion from $10.4 billion a year earlier. Lowe's posted a 9.9 percent decline in same-store sales. Gross profit margin declined 1.15 percent points.

On August 17, 2009, Lowe's reported a 19 percent fall in quarterly earnings. Sales fell 9.5 percent from a year before. It was the firm's 12th consecutive quarter of same-store sales declines.

See also RETAILING.

Cf. HOME DEPOT.

L-SHAPED RECESSION. *See* RECESSION.

LUFTHANSA. The airline posted on April 29, 2009, that it had a net loss of €256 million, compared with a profit of €44 million one year earlier.

On September 3, 2009, Lufthansa took over Austrian Airlines. Prior to this takeover, Austrian Airlines was 42 percent owned by the government.

LUXEMBOURG. *See* TAX HAVENS.

LUXURY AUTOMOBILES. *See* AUTOMOBILE INDUSTRY.

LUXURY GOODS. Luxury goods sales soared until 2008. By year's end luxury brands were suffering. In October 2008, sales in such items dropped 20.1 percent. Advertising pages at the top U.S. luxury magazines fell 22 percent from a year earlier. Demand for luxury goods was expected to drop from 3 to 7 percent in 2009.

For example, Bulgari, an upscale jeweler based in Rome, saw profits in 2008 plunge 44 percent in the third quarter of 2008. Shares closed in December at €4.76, less than half of what they had closed at a year earlier.

Luxury goods had a decline over the 2008 Christmas season of 21.2 percent, compared with a rise of 7.5 percent in 2007. For 2009 it was projected that the sales of luxury goods including clothing, jewelry, and fashion accessories would be down 8 percent to about $227 billion.

See also AUTOMOBILE INDUSTRY; BULGARI; COACH; ESCADA; FERRE; JEWELRY; LVMH; MORGAN; NEIMAN MARCUS; NORDSTROM; RETAILING; SWATCH GROUP; TIFFANY; WINE MARKET.

LVMH (LVMH MOET HENNESSY LOUIS VUITTON SA). The world's largest luxury-goods group by revenue, posted on July 27, 2009, a 23 percent drop in first-half profit resulting from the global recession.

See also LUXURY GOODS.

M

MACRO-PRUDENTIAL PHILOSOPHY. A regulation that seeks to take account of the whole system's vulnerabilities, as well as the health of individual banks by, for example, adjusting capital charges over the economic cycle.

Cf. MICRO-PRUDENTIAL PHILOSOPHY.

MACY'S. In January 2009, the retailer announced that it would close 11 underperforming stores in nine states, affecting 960 employees.

On February 2, it estimated that 7,000 jobs, or 4 percent of its workforce, would be eliminated and announced that it was taking other steps to cut costs.

The Cincinnati-based operator of 840 department stores also cut its dividend by 62 percent, ended merit pay increases for executives, and slashed its 2009 capital-spending budget by another $100 to $150 million, down to around $450 million. The original budget was $1 billion.

On February 24, Macy's reported that its profits declined 59 percent. It earned 73 cents a share in the fiscal fourth quarter ending January 31, compared with $1.73 a share a year earlier.

On August 12 Macy's reported that its sales continued to decline, with earnings falling 90 percent to $7 million in its second quarter 2009, compared with $73 million the year before. Sales in the quarter dropped 9.7 percent to $5.16 billion.

Macy's third-quarter 2009 loss was $35 million on a 3.9 percent sales decline. Sales fell to $5.3 billion; sales at stores open for at least one year declined 3.9 percent, with online sales increasing 21 percent. The store's stock by mid-November 2009 was down 16 percent from the October high, trading at less than twelve times consensus earnings for the year ending January 2011.

See also RETAILING.

MAERSK. *See* MOLLER-MAERSK.

MAGAZINES. Newsstand sales of magazines fell at their fastest rate in decades during the second half of 2008. The downward trend accelerated from a 6.3 percent drop-off in the first half of 2008.

By the end of the first quarter 2009, magazine advertising pages dropped nearly 26 percent. Only fifteen magazines had more ad pages in this quarter than they did one year earlier.

MAGNA. The huge Canadian auto supplier won a bid to buy GM Europe from General Motors.

By the end of August 2009, Germany pressed GM to complete the sale, which includes Opel and Vauxhall.

On September 10, GM agreed to sell a majority stake in its European operations to Magna International. GM would not be paid anything for the stake in its money-losing Opel and Vauxhall business, while Magna agreed to invest in the operations and the government of Germany pledged to finance the plan and help fund Opel with about $6 billion in loans. GM's 55 percent sale of its Opel unit would make Magna one of the world's biggest car parts makers with $23.7 billion in revenue and 71,000 employees worldwide.

Then, on November 1, 2009, GM backed out of the deal to sell both Opel and Vauxhall to Magna International.

See also GENERAL MOTORS.

MAKING HOME AFFORDABLE PROGRAM. The government program, initiated in the spring of 2009, uses a series of incentives, one of which is $1,000 to the servicers for every mortgage they modify, to help keep people in their homes and prevent foreclosures. And yet, by summer 2009, the rising tide of foreclosures remained the single largest threat to economic recovery. Congress passed a law immunizing the servicers from lawsuits that could arise for modifying mortgages.

See also FORECLOSURE; HOME MORTGAGES; MORTGAGE MODI-FICATION; MORTGAGE SERVICERS.

MAKING WORK PAY. A credit concept of President Obama's economic platform, making available a tax credit of $500 for individuals and up to $1,000 for families to be received through a temporary reduction in payroll tax withholdings to households with annual incomes as high as $200,000.

The economic stimulus package originally gave Making Work Pay tax credit for two years. In its final version, it was scaled back. The package set the value of the benefit at $400 for individual workers, down from $500 and at $800 for couples, down from $1,000. The benefit phased out funds for workers making $75,000 a year and for couples earning $140,000.

See also AMERICAN RECOVERY AND REINVESTMENT ACT (OF 2009).

MALAYSIA. *See* SOUTHEAST ASIA.

MALL PROPERTIES. Vacancy rates at malls in the largest 76 U.S. markets rose to 8.6 percent in third quarter 2009, a rise from 8.4 percent.

See also GENERAL GROWTH PROPERTIES.

MANUFACTURING. Converting raw materials into a completed product by a mechanical, electrical, or chemical (i.e., not manual) process.

February 2008 figures showed that manufacturing activity was at a five-year low amid slowing demand and rising prices. By December 2008, global manufacturing was shrinking rapidly. In the United States, the Institute for Supply Management's index plunged from 38.9 percent to 36.2, the lowest level since 1982. A reading below 50 indicated activity was dropping.

The manufacturing index in the eurozone fell to 35.6, a low for the eleven-year survey. Britain's index dropped to 34.4 and in Japan it fell to 36.7.

The Institute for Supply Management reported that their manufacturing index for the United States was 32.4 in December, down from 36.2 in November. In Europe, the index dropped to 33.9 from 35.6.

By 2009, it was evident that manufacturing had slumped around the world, with a 17 percent annualized global contraction. Output declined 4 percent in the last three months of 2008, compared to the previous quarter, reflecting lower spending and a lack of available financing for autos, housing, and capital equipment.

After eighteen months of layoffs, the manufacturing sector grew in August 2009 as new evidence emerged that the economy was pulling out of recession.

On November 17, 2009, the government reported a sharp slowdown in manufacturing activity in October. Although production climbed 0.1 percent for the month, growth is weak. Capacity utilization was flat across the manufacturing areas at a combined level of 67.6 percent.

Ultimately, more than 2 million U.S. manufacturing jobs were lost in the Great Recession.

See also INSTITUTE FOR SUPPLY MANAGEMENT.

MARCHIONNE, SERGIO. The chief executive of Italy's Fiat. Since Chrysler was placed in bankruptcy at the end of April 2009, Fiat will provide the U.S. firm with technology for small, fuel-efficient models and access to its dealerships in Europe and Latin America.

See also CHRYSLER.

MARKET CAPITALIZATION. At the stock market's peak, the market capitalization of twenty-nine of the largest financial firms on October 9, 2007, was $1.86 trillion. The breakdown in billions of U.S. dollars was:

Citigroup—$236.7
Bank of America—$236.5

American International Group—$179.8 (To prevent a global financial panic, the government took over the company and provided more than $180 billion in financing. It may take years to unwind AIG's bad investments.)

JP Morgan Chase—$161.0

Wells Fargo—$124.1

Wachovia—$98.3 (Bank failed and was bought by Wells Fargo in January 2009.)

Goldman Sachs—$97.7

American Express—$74.8 (Has repaid its TARP investment and bought the warrants held by the government. But its revenue and profits have fallen, a victim of the weak economy.)

Morgan Stanley—$73.1

Fannie Mae—$64.8 (Failed along with Freddie Mac in August 2008; both were taken over by the government. Their futures are bleak as they continue to lose money.)

Merrill Lynch—$63.9 (Acquired by Bank of America in September 2008.)

U.S. Bankcorp—$57.8

Bank of New York Mellon—$51.8

Freddie Mac—$41.5

Lehman Brothers—$34.4 (Failed and liquidated in September 2008.)

Washington Mutual—$31.1 (Bought by JP Morgan Chase in 2008.)

Capital One Financial—$29.9

State Street—$27.5

SunTrust Banks—$27.0

BB&T—$23.2

Fifth Third Bancorp—$18.8

National City Corp.—$16.4

Northern Trust—$15.8

Bear Stearns—$14.8

Keycorp—$13.2

Marshall & Ilsley—$11.6

Legg Mason—$11.4

Countrywide Financial—$11.1

Comerica—$8.3

One year after Lehman declared bankruptcy, seven financial giants disappeared—Lehman Brothers, Bear Stearns, Merrill Lynch, Wachovia, National City, Washington Mutual, and Countrywide. The remaining twenty-two firms that still publicly traded on September 11, 2009, were now $947 billion. Their market capitalization was:

JP Morgan Chase—$167.1

Bank of America—$146.8 (It has been hurt by its acquisition of Merrill Lynch and massive layoffs in its consumer banking businesses.)

Wells Fargo—$128.1 (Government stress tests found that the bank needed almost $14 billion, but it was able to raise the money quickly from private investors. It continues to have a large portfolio of troubled loans.)

Citigroup—$105.5 (The hardest hit of the large institutions, it still had huge amounts of bad loans. However, a plan to split up the bank appeared by mid-September.)

Goldman Sachs—$91.8 (Converted from an investment bank to a commercial bank in order to qualify for FDIC insurance. Recently had its most profitable quarter ever.)

U.S. Bancorp—$41.8

American Express—$40.6

Morgan Stanley—$39.2 (Converted from an investment bank to a commercial bank.)

Bank of New York Mellon—$34.5

American International Group—$26.2

State Street—$26.1

BB&T—$18.4

Capital One Financial—$17.3

Northern Trust—$14.1

SunTrust Banks—$10.9

Fannie Mae—$9.1

Fifth Third Bancorp—$7.8

Freddie Mac—$6.1

Keycorp—$5.2

The financial sector's share of the stock market shrank for these institutions, as well as their share of the overall stock market. At their peak on October 9, 2007, the total market value was $19.1 trillion, with the financial sector representing 20.4 percent. One year following the collapse of Lehman Brothers, it was down to $12.4 trillion, representing 16.6 percent of the financial sector.

MARKET REFORM. *See* JAPAN.

MARKS & SPENCER. In January 2009 announced 1,230 job cuts and the closing of twenty-seven of its stores. It suffered its worst quarterly revenue drop in a decade, with sales falling by 7.1 percent in the quarter ending December 27, 2008.

The retailer eliminated 450 jobs at its head office in London and from closing the stores. Sales fell 7.1 percent in the third quarter 2008; clothing and furniture sales fell 8.9 percent and food fell 5.2 percent.

For its fiscal first quarter of 2009, Marks & Spencer posted a 1.4 percent sales drop.

Second-quarter 2009 group sales rose 2.7 percent, due in great part to a 9.6 percent rise in international sales and a 30 percent increase in online sales. Marks & Spencer reduced its staff by 1,230 workers and closed some of its stores.

See also RETAILING.

MARK-TO-MARKET RULES. The Financial Accounting Standards Board announced on April 2, 2009, that they were making it easier for banks to limit losses by pushing for steps to aid banks weighed down by troubled assets. The proposed changes would lessen the need for banks to take an earnings hit when assets ran into trouble. Banks had argued that mark-to-market rules required them to value their securities at current market prices, which restricted their capital unfairly by forcing them to report huge paper loses on securities that they said would regain value when the financial crisis eased. Opponents argued that substituting wishful thinking for real-world prices would just make investors distrust banks even more than they do already.

See also "TOO BIG TO FAIL."

MARRIAGE. For most people, the meltdown appears to be solidifying marriage relationships, not, as some would believe, leading to an increase in the divorce rate, which continues to fall—16.9 divorces per 1,000 married women in 2008 from 17.5 divorces in 2007, a decrease of 3 percent. It is assumed that debt increases the tension in marriage, but savings and/or spending less of one's assets is constructive and strengthening of a marriage.

MARRIOTT. The hotel chain posted a first-quarter 2009 loss on restructuring charges as revenue per room tumbled by 20 percent globally and 16 percent domestically.

On July 16, Marriott reported that its second-quarter earnings 2009 fell 76 percent. Its fiscal third-quarter loss resulted in part from its write-down of its time-share business. For the quarter ending September 11, Marriott posted a loss of $466 million. Revenue fell 17 percent to $2.47 billion.

Cf. ACCOR.

MASS TRANSIT. The Economic Stimulus package of 2009 provided $17.7 billion for mass transit, Amtrak, and high-speed rail, nearly a 70 percent increase over present spending levels.

The public took 10.7 billion trips on public transportation in 2008, a 4 percent increase over 2007.

MASTERCARD. Reported a third-quarter 2009 profit, with earnings of $452.2 million compared with a year-earlier loss of $193.6 million. Revenue increased 2 percent to $1.36 billion. At the same time cost-cutting operations were 13 percent.

Cf. VISA.

MATTEL. The major toy-making firm had a sharp 46 percent drop in profits as announced in February 2009. Mattel reported net income of $176.4 million, or 49 cents a share, compared with $328.5 million, or 89 cents, a year before.

In mid-July, Mattel reported an 82 percent jump in its second-quarter earnings, as cost cutting offset disappointing sales. The world's largest toy maker reported a profit of $21.5 million, up from $11.8 million from a year before. However, revenue declined 19 percent to $898.2 million.

Mattel's third-quarter 2009 earnings declined 3.5 percent. Earnings in the quarter were $229.8 million, down from $238 million a year before. Revenue dropped 8 percent to $1.79 billion.

MAZDA MOTOR CORP. Posted a net loss of $226.6 million in the three months ending June 30, 2009; sales dropped 4 percent .

MBS. *See* MORTGAGE-BACKED SECURITY.

MCCAIN, JOHN. U.S. senator and Republican Party candidate for president of the United States in 2008; lost to Barack Obama.
See also OBAMA, BARACK.

MCCARRAN-FERGUSON ACT OF 1945. The Supreme Court, in 1869, held that under the commerce clause of the Constitution, the federal government can't regulate insurance, setting the background for state insurance regulation.

The high court, in 1944, overturned its 1869 decision, holding that insurance is "interstate commerce" and thus subject to federal regulation.

The McCarran-Ferguson Act of 1945 returned regulatory jurisdiction over insurance to the states.

MCDONALD'S. The burger giant reported second-quarter 2009 profit of $1.09 billion, down 8.4 percent from $1.19 billion a year earlier. This was seen resulting from the recession, job losses around the country, and more people cooking at home.
See also STOCK MARKET.

MCGRAW-HILL. The publisher's first-quarter 2009 net income declined 22 percent to $66 million, down from $84.6 million a year earlier. Management predicted that revenue for 2009 would fall by between 4 and 5 percent.

McGraw-Hill plans to combine some of its educational publishing businesses and will trim, as announced in mid-July 2009, 550 jobs. The firm said it would restructure other parts of the business, which will make up 38 percent of the job reductions. McGraw-Hill employed 21,649 people.

In July, McGraw-Hill reported a 23 percent drop in second-quarter earnings with earnings of $164.1 million, down from $212.3 million a year earlier.

At the end of October 2009, McGraw-Hill posted a third-quarter profit of $336.1 million, down from $390.2 million a year before. Revenue fell 8.4 percent to $1.88 billion.

The company reported a 14 percent decline in its third-quarter 2009 earnings after announcing it had sold its *Business Week* magazine.

See also STANDARD & POOR'S.

MEDICAID. Medicaid rolls surged as the recession tightened its grip on the economy and Americans lost their employer-sponsored health coverage along with their jobs.

In some states, Medicaid populations grew by 5 to 10 percent in 2008. In many states, the growth rates were at least double what they had been in 2007.

See also AMERICAN RECOVERY AND REINVESTMENT ACT (OF 2009); OBAMA, BARACK.

MEDICAL RECORDS. *See* AMERICAN RECOVERY AND REINVEST-MENT ACT (OF 2009).

MEDICARE. *See* OBAMA, BARACK.

MEN'S WAGES. *See* WOMEN'S WAGES.

MEN UNEMPLOYED. The percentage of men ages sixteen and over who were working in December 2008 was at its lowest level since the government began keeping statistics in the 1940s.

The 2.3 percentage-point gap between men's June 2009 unemployment rate of 10.6 percent and women's of 8.3 percent is near the highest it has ever been since records started in 1948. A gap of 2.5 percent is the highest on record.

By the summer 2009 new figures indicated a worsening situation. Only 65 of 100 men aged twenty through twenty-four years old were working on any given day in the first six months of 2009. In the age group twenty-five through thirty-four years old, just 81 out of 100 men were working. For male teenagers, the numbers were even worse; only 28 of every 100 males were working among sixteen- through nineteen-year-olds. And for minorities teenagers the figures were far worse.

See also MEN WORKFORCE; OVERTIME; UNEMPLOYMENT; WOMEN UNEMPLOYED.

MEN WORKFORCE. Of the people losing their jobs in the Great Recession 78 percent were men. By October 2009, 10.7 percent of men had lost their jobs.

See also WOMEN WORKFORCE.

MERCEDES-BENZ. November 2008 sales were down 25 percent. *See also* AUTOMOBILE INDUSTRY; GERMANY.

MERCHANDISE (MERCHANDISING). *See* RETAILING.

MERGERS AND ACQUISITIONS. The volume of mergers and acquisitions fell about 35 percent in 2009 from an expected volume of $3.1 trillion in 2008, less than half of the previous year's record in deals.

Fees from mergers and acquisitions, a major source of revenue for investment banks, were down by one-third in 2008, after plunging globally. Merger and acquisition fee totals were down 40 percent in the United States, 34 percent in Europe, and 11 percent in Asia, excluding Japan. Projections for the first half of 2009 were equally dismal.

The value of global mergers and acquisitions fell 35 percent in the first six months of 2009 to $1,140 billion. The number of deals in the three months through June fell by more than 15 percent. By the summer of 2009, the number of mergers and acquisitions began to rise slowly.

MERKEL, ANGELA. *See* GERMANY; UN ECONOMIC COUNCIL.

MERRILL LYNCH. By April 2008, Merrill had posted a $1.96 billion loss on $6.6 billion in write-downs, and announced that it was cutting 4,000 positions.

As subprime lenders began toppling after record waves of homeowners defaulted on their mortgages, Merrill Lynch was left with $71 billion of eroding exotic mortgage loans on its books and billions in losses.

In mid-September 2008, torn apart by its CDO venture, Merrill Lynch was taken over by Bank of America. Its 16,090 brokers continued to worry about their employment destiny.

Fourth-quarter 2008 losses, disclosed on February 24, 2009, totaled $15.84 billion, more than $500 million higher than a prior estimate of $15.31 billion from its new owner. Larger-than-expected losses at Merrill forced Bank of America to accept an additional $20 billion in U.S. aid, bringing the total government assistance to Bank of America to $45 billion.

See also BANK OF AMERICA; BERNANKE, BEN; "TOO BIG TO FAIL"; UNEMPLOYMENT.

Cf. AMERICAN INTERNATIONAL GROUP; CITIGROUP.

METLIFE. The huge life insurance firm announced on April 12, 2009, that it wouldn't accept federal bailout funds, an indication of its strong position in an industry struggling with huge losses and shaky balance sheets.

MetLife had a second-quarter 2009 loss as the company recorded $3.83 billion in pretax investment losses. The firm lost $1.3 billion compared with one year before.

Cf. TRAVELERS.

METRO. The largest retailer in Germany, it announced in January 2009 that it would eliminate as many as 15,000 jobs as part of a plan to increase profit by €1.5 billion over four years. The reduction accounted for about 5 percent of its workforce.

METROPOLITAN OPERA. To offset their growing problems resulting from the economic meltdown and loss of revenue and contributions, the giant Marc Chagall tapestries in its lobby were placed as collateral on a bank loan. These works would remain in the Opera's lobby unless the Met defaulted on the loan.

See also ARTS, THE.

MEXICO. Economic growth fell well below potential in 2008 and 2009. The weak U.S. economy and fall in oil production will cut exports over the next several quarters, while the effects of the financial turmoil will depress domestic demand growth. Activity will recover through 2010 as global economic conditions improve. Inflation will return to near the target rate as commodity prices fall, activity slows, and monetary tightening keeps expectations anchored, although the recent sharp depreciation of the peso will put upward pressure on prices. Fiscal policy will be supportive in the near term, cushioning the shocks to demand. However, the balanced budget rule has resulted in spending too much of the oil windfall over the past years, and may now constrain fiscal policy if oil prices remain at lower levels. Gradual loosening of the monetary stance is justified unless the recent depreciation of the peso revives inflationary pressures. To boost longer term growth, reforms should focus on enhancing public spending efficiency, product and labor market flexibility, and competition (OECD).

On January 1, 2009, the North American Free Trade Agreement arrived at its fifteenth anniversary, with all of its positive and negative aspects.

By July, Mexican unemployment was at its highest level in eight years. The peso fell 25 percent. Exports, industrial production, and retail sales had fallen 17.3 percent.

Growth forecasts for 2009 were for 1.8 percent or less. The government would run its first budget deficit in five years as it increased spending to give the economy a push forward.

Its state oil monopoly, Pemex, saw its production fall 9.3 percent for the year through November 2008. Oil production fell to its lowest levels in thirteen years. Mexico pumped an average of 2.7 million barrels a day in 2008, down 9.2 percent from 2007 and the lowest annual average rate of production since 1995.

Mexican consumer prices rose at their fastest pace since 2001 in 2008, complicated by the effect of the global economic crisis on the country. The government pledged $150 million in spending to prevent layoffs, slashed household gas and electricity rates for some industries by as much as 20 percent, and froze gasoline prices until the end of 2009.

Mexico sends about 80 percent of its exports to the United States. The peso slipped more than 2 percent against the U.S. dollar to its weakest level since November 2001, as less export income entered Mexico. The central bank auctioned off $400 million in reserve in January 2009 to slow the slide.

To boost the country's slowing economy, Mexico's central bank cut interest rates for the first time since 2006 in mid-January as it inched toward recession. The bank lowered its benchmark lending rate an additional 50 basis points to 7.75 percent.

Unemployment in 2009 was at its highest level in eight years. The peso had fallen 25 percent, leading to a spike in the price of imports, and hurting consumers and businesses that depended on imported goods. Exports, industrial production, and retail sales had all fallen.

The recession of 2008 and 2009 was hitting Hispanic immigrants especially hard. Unemployment was 8 percent in the fourth quarter 2008. The number of people trying to sneak into the United States was at its lowest level since the mid-1970s. The unemployment rate for foreign-born Hispanics, estimated to be 1 million, was 8 percent in the fourth quarter 2008.

On March 16, due to its continuing arguments with the United States, Mexico announced that it would slap tariffs on ninety U.S. industrial and agricultural products, affecting some $2.4 billion in goods across forty U.S. states. Mexico argued that the tariffs were in retaliation for the cancellation of a pilot program allowing Mexican trucks to transport cargo throughout the United States.

The tariffs are based mostly on imported duties of 10 percent to 20 percent of their value. Fresh grapes would face a 45 percent tariff, the highest. Some of the U.S. items facing imports tariffs into Mexico included a 20 percent tariff on cherries, Christmas trees, coffee makers, curtain rods, mineral water, pears, peeled onions, potatoes, soy sauce, and statuettes; 15 percent tariffs included manicure/pedicure products, sunglasses, sunflower seeds, shampoo, and toothpaste.

The Mexican economy took another beating as Mexico's stocks fell sharply, 3.3 percent, and businesses shut down, following the impact of the H1N1 virus scare at the end of April.

Mexico saw exports collapse almost 29 percent in the first quarter 2009, while the Mexican economy contracted 21.5 percent at an annual rate, more than three times the rate of decline in the United States.

The amount of money sent back to Mexico in April by Mexicans working in the United States fell by almost one-fifth compared with a year earlier.

By the end of November 2009, Mexico finally pulled out of its recession, though its GDP shrank by 9.7 percent from January 1–June 30, a shocking number. Nevertheless Mexico's economic output fell about 7 percent in 2009.

See also NORTH AMERICAN FREE TRADE AGREEMENT; REMITTANCES.

MICHELIN. France's tire maker announced at the end of December 2008 that there would be a reduction in production at most plants as demand declined in all markets. Michelin shares closed 3.13 percent lower.

With falling demand, Michelin announced that it would eliminate about 2,900 jobs in three years.

In the first half of 2009, the tire maker had a net loss of €119 million, but generated an operating profit of €282 million on sales of more expensive tires. Revenue dropped 13 percent to €7.13 billion.

MICHIGAN. *See* STATES (U.S.).

MICRO-PRUDENTIAL PHILOSOPHY. When banks had numerous subsidiaries, regulators short of money and time tended to worry only about their own piece of the jigsaw.

Cf. MACRO-PRUDENTIAL PHILOSOPHY.

MICROSOFT. In mid-January 2009, Microsoft posted an unexpected 11 percent drop in quarterly profit and disclosed plans to slash 5,000 jobs. The job losses would occur over the next 18 months, representing about 5 percent of its total workforce of roughly 96,000.

On April 23, Microsoft reported the first year-over-year quarterly revenue decline since it became a public company in 1986. In its quarter, which ended March 31, its revenues fell 6 percent to $13.65 billion, from $14.45 billion. Microsoft posted a 32 percent drop in profit.

On July 23, Microsoft posted a 29 percent fall in quarterly profit and weak sales across all of its departments. The quarter was the company's first full year of declining sales since it went public more than twenty years before. The quarter results, ending June 30, show income of $3.05 billion, compared with $4.3 billion the year before. Revenue fell to $3.11 billion from the year before.

By the end of October 2009, the company's third-quarter profit was down 18 percent. Microsoft reported that fiscal first-quarter profit fell to $3.57 billion from $4.37 billion a year before. Revenue declined 14 percent to $12.92 billion from $15.06 billion.

On November 4 Microsoft announced that it was releasing another 800 workers. About 6.3 percent of its 91,000 employees will lose their jobs.

See also CHINA.

MIDDLE CLASS. In the past two decades, a growing middle-class population has evolved, especially in emerging market nations. These people now have about one-third of their income set aside for discretionary purchases. No longer are they simply limited only to search for food and shelter in order to survive.

Within this short period, the traditionally defined middle class has grown from one-third of the world's population to about one-half, or approximately 2.5 billion people. The developing nations are no longer primarily poor. The 2008–2009 meltdown may suddenly reverse their ambitions and goals of getting out of poverty. Their economic future and expectations are fogged by the turmoil in the present economy. Their reaction will likewise be unpredictable.

MIDDLE EAST. The year 2008 was an uneven one for the region. During the first half of the year, oil and other commodity prices rose rapidly, leading to huge increases in the revenue of oil- and gas-exporting countries. At the same time, all Arab and Muslim Middle Eastern states had to cope with rapidly rising food and raw material prices that threatened their economies and social stability.

Then, in August 2008, as the economic clouds thickened around the world, oil prices started to fall. Between August and December of 2008, they dropped by over 70 percent, and the income of the oil-producing states returned to their 2007 levels. With the meltdown, a shrinking of export markets for Middle East oil producers and non-oil producers alike became a reality.

Middle Eastern banks were not overly exposed to the U.S. mortgage or derivatives markets, but sovereign wealth funds and other holders of equities suffered significant losses. Moreover, a regional housing boom and bust contributed to local financial woes. Gulf Arab states extended assistance to banks that had particular problems, such as those hurt by the bursting of the real estate bubble in Dubai. In the twelve-month period ending in February 2009, the Saudi stock market fell by 49 percent, Dubai's by 72 percent, Egypt's by 61 percent, Qatar's by 29 percent, and Morocco's by 26 percent. These losses reduced consumption and discouraged investment in both financial and real assets.

Foreign investment, tourism revenues, and remittances had all declined. These are vital for Egypt, Jordan, Morocco, and other regional nations. The most important challenge facing Middle East countries in 2009–2010 is to reduce unemployment. The number of people joining the labor market is huge and is increasing at a much faster rate than the population as a whole. The slowdown in growth that is being experienced is expected to last at least a year, and will likely further reduce the level of employment. Greater socioeconomic and even political pressures in the region can be expected.

See also AUTOMOBILE INDUSTRY; Individual listed nations of the Middle East.

MIGRANT WORKERS. Migration tends to be slow during a recession; fewer people leave the urban cores to go to the suburbs. Migration throughout the United States barely happened in 2008, as a weak housing market and job insecurity forced many citizens to stay put.

The global recession is hitting immigrants around the world harder than native-born workers. In the United States, unemployment for immigrant workers in the summer of 2009 was about 10 percent, compared to 9.4 percent for the overall population. Prior to the recession, immigrant unemployment was lower than nonimmigrant employment.

The Great Recession has had a profound impact on migration patterns. Until July 2006, Florida and Nevada attracted net inflows of 141,448 and 41,640 people, respectively. By mid-July 2009, Florida, at one time a great attractor of migrant workers, lost more than 31,000 residents to other states; Nevada lost nearly 4,000.

See also CZECH REPUBLIC; IMMIGRATION; IRELAND; REMITTANCES.

MIGRATION. *See* MIGRANT WORKERS.

MILLIONAIRES. *See* WEALTH.

MINIMUM WAGE. In 2008 only 1.1 percent of Americans who worked 40 hours a week or more even earned the minimum wage. Therefore, 98.9 percent of 40-hour-a-week workers earn more than the minimum.

At the beginning of 2009, the 70-cent-per-hour increase in the minimum wage cost 300,000 jobs. Then, the mandated increase to $7.25 in July also led to a rapid disappearance of jobs for teenagers. The unemployment rate for teenagers reached 25.9 percent in September 2009.

See also UNEMPLOYMENT.

MINING. International mining companies have postponed or cancelled projects and locked the gates to mines as consumers have cut spending on cars, jewelry, and housing.

While in the past, coal firms have been more recession proof, now the average price per ton for Appalachian coal has fallen more than 35 percent since the summer 2008.

See also RIO TINTO.

MINNEAPOLIS STAR TRIBUNE. On January 15, 2009, the newspaper filed for bankruptcy protection.

MISERY INDEX. By adding together the unemployment rate and the budget deficit as a percentage of GDP an index is revealed. A high index indicates that a nation badly needs fiscal stimulus to spur economic growth, but may be in no condition to pay for it. For 2010, the nations with an overwhelming misery index are in descending order—Czech Republic, Italy, Germany, Hungary, Portugal, Estonia, France, United States, Iceland, Britain, Greece, Ireland, Lithuania, Latvia, and Spain.

MITSUBISHI (BANK). Japan's biggest bank by assets announced on March 23, 2009, that its main banking unit planned to close about fifty branches and cut 1,000 jobs over three years. Seventy branches had already been closed.

On April 27, Mitsubishi announced weaker results for the latest fiscal year, posting a net loss of $565 million, a significant decline from its net profit a year earlier.

See also JAPAN.

MITSUBISHI MOTORS. Reported a net loss of 26.64 billion yen in the second quarter 2009, compared with a net profit of 10.3 billion yen of a year earlier.

MOBILITY. The number of people who changed residences declined to 35 million from March 2007 to March 2008, the lowest number since 1962, when the population had 120 million fewer citizens. It suggested that people were unable or unwilling to follow job positions around the nation. On average it took a homeowner 10.5 months to sell a house in 2008, compared with 8.9 months in 2007. The impact was that it could further slow the U.S. economy or any subsequent recovery.

MODIFYING MORTGAGES. The nation's fourteen largest banks reported that more than half of the loans they modified in 2008 became delinquent again after just six months. Although banks and investors absorbed significant losses in foreclosures, some mortgage firms viewed foreclosures as more profitable and expedient than modifications because they could levy extra charges and they did not have to wait to see if the homeowner would continue on the payments.

The history of modifying mortgages was not positive. The number of loans modified in the first quarter that were thirty days delinquent was 37 percent after three months and 55 percent after six months. The number of loans modified in the first quarter that were sixty or more days delinquent was 19 percent at three months and nearly 37 percent after six months.

On March 5, the House of Representatives passed a bill that would allow bankrupt homeowners to have their loans modified in bankruptcy court, where the common solution was to reduce the principal.

By August 2009, 235,247 mortgages had been modified on a trial basis. That was not even 9 percent of the 2.7 million troubled loans deemed eligible.

See also CRAMDOWN; HOUSING BAILOUT PLAN; MAKING HOME AFFORDABLE PROGRAM; MORTGAGE MODIFICATION.

MOET HENNESSY LOUIS VUITTON. *See* LVMH.

MOLLER-MAERSK. In the first nine months of 2009, the world's largest shipping company posted a loss of $1 billion in the year, after posting a profit in 2008.

Prices fell on average 32 percent from 2008, along with volume at 3 percent.

MOLSON COORS BREWING COMPANY. Posted a 44 percent drop in fourth-quarter net income on February 10, 2009, reflecting sluggish demand in the economic downturn period.

MONACO. *See* TAX HAVENS; WEALTH.

MONETARY BASE. The notes and coins in the hands of consumers and corporate entities, plus the cash reserves that commercial banks hold with their central banks.

MONEY MARKET MUTUAL FUNDS. Funds that were usually low-risk investments in short-term debt, they have been troubled since the collapse of Lehman Brothers in September 2008. Around $500 billion was withdrawn from the market, which invested in commercial paper, certificates of deposit, and other financial instruments. The Federal Reserve facility created five "special-purpose vehicles" that would purchase instruments held by the funds.

The Federal Reserve Bank, in order to boost liquidity, provided up to $540 billion to support these money market mutual funds.

New proposed regulations, not requiring legislative approval, would require money market funds to retain a larger share of their assets in highly liquid investments like stocks, reduce their exposure to long-term debt, and limit their investments to securities with high credit ratings. By mid-September, the SEC had proposed the changes with expectations to go into effect in 2009.

See also FEDERAL RESERVE; FINANCIAL REGULATION PLAN (2009).

MONSANTO. The world's largest seed producer said that its third-quarter 2008 profit fell 14 percent and it planned to cut 900 jobs, or about 4 percent of its workforce.

On September 10, 2009, Monsanto announced that it would double previously stated job cuts to about 8 percent of its global workforce, some 1,800 jobs, from its earlier predicted 900 positions.

MONTENEGRO. Economy grew by 8.6 percent in 2007. In 2008, the government forecast 8 percent growth, but the actual figure was lower. In 2009, the government projected growth of 5 percent, while the IMF estimated only a 2 percent growth rate.

MOODY'S. A company that rates the creditworthiness of bond issuers. By 2009, the public and government were questioning the objectivity and reliability of rating services.

See also BUFFET, WARREN E.; GENERAL ELECTRIC.

Cf. STANDARD & POOR'S.

MOORE, MICHAEL. Just as the Great Recession neared its end in September 2009, the film director and writer released *Capitalism: A Love Story*. Its purpose was to entertain while at the same time inform the public of the growing debate about the nation's motivating principles of capitalism and free markets. The story accuses Washington politicians of favoring corporate decision makers over the welfare of the general public. Moore urges change as he examines a system that he calls "immoral" and "undemocratic."

See also CAPITALISM.

MORGAN. The fashion brand, founded forty years ago by two Parisian sisters, became the first French retailer to fall victim to the credit crisis after being forced in late December 2008 to file for bankruptcy protection.

See also RETAILING.

MORGAN BANK. *See* JP MORGAN CHASE.

MORGAN, J. P. *See* PECORA COMMISSION.

MORGAN STANLEY. On December 17, Morgan Stanley reported a quarterly loss of $2.36 billion. The quarterly loss, of $2.34 a share, was Morgan's first for the fiscal year. Nevertheless, the company reported a full-year profit of $1.59 billion, or $1.54 a share, down 49 percent from 2007.

In February 2009, it announced that 1,500 to 1,800 employees, or about 3 percent to 4 percent of its workforce, would lose their jobs. Morgan Stanley had previously announced in 2008 that it would cut 7,000 positions.

Morgan Stanley suffered its second consecutive quarterly loss in the first quarter of 2009 as it posted a net loss of $177 million, compared with quarterly profits of $1.41 billion one year earlier. This was the first back-to-back quarterly loss for the bank since it went public.

The company reported a $159 million second-quarter loss. It was the firm's third quarterly loss in a row. On August 6, Morgan Stanley agreed to pay $950 million to buy back a warrant it issued to the government.

See also CHINA; "TOO BIG TO FAIL."

Cf. GOLDMAN SACHS.

MOROCCO. *See* MIDDLE EAST.

MORTGAGE. A written conveyance of title to property, but not possession, to obtain the payment of a debt or the performance of some obligation, under the condition that the conveyance is to be void upon final payment; property pledged as security for payment of a debt.

By the beginning of 2009, 13.6 million Americans owed more on their mortgages than their homes were worth.

See also FORECLOSURE; HOUSING BAILOUT PLAN; MAKING HOME AFFORDABLE PROGRAM; MODIFYING MORTGAGES.

MORTGAGE AID. *See* HOME AFFORDABLE MODIFICATION PROGRAM.

MORTGAGE-BACKED CERTIFICATES. Certificates covering pools of conventional mortgages insured by private mortgage insurance companies. These certificates are issued in big denominations, so the market is limited mainly to institutions.

MORTGAGE-BACKED DEBT. *See* FEDERAL RESERVE.

MORTGAGE-BACKED SECURITY (SECURITIES) (MBS). A type of asset-backed security that is secured by a collection of mortgages; bond-type investment securities representing an interest in a pool of mortgages or trust deeds. Income from the underlying mortgages is used to make investor payments. By mid-September 2009, the Federal Reserve had bought $850 million of mortgage-backed securities.

MBSs backed by Fannie Mae, Freddie Mac, and Ginnie Mae rose to their highest level for the year on November 25, 2009.

See also BOND BUYING; FEDERAL HOME BANK; FEDERAL OPEN MARKET COMMITTEE; HOME MORTGAGES; MARK-TO-MARKET RULES; SECURITIZATION.

MORTGAGE BAILOUT. A program designed to assist one in nine homeowners who owe more than their homes are worth. President Obama announced details of the housing bailout plan on March 4, 2009.

By the end of November 2009, the government wanted banks and loan-servicing firms to amend hundreds of thousands of mortgages so they would be easier for borrowers to pay, usually without reducing the principal owed.

See also HOME AFFORDABLE MODIFICATION PROGRAM; HOUSING BAILOUT PLAN; MAKING HOME AFFORDABLE PROGRAM; MORTGAGE LEGISLATION; UNDERWATER.

MORTGAGE BANKER. A banker who specializes in mortgage financing; an operator of a mortgage financing firm. Mortgage financing companies are mortgagees themselves, as well as being mortgage agents for other large mortgages.

See also MORTGAGE BANKING.

MORTGAGE BANKING. The packaging of mortgage loans secured by real property to be sold to a permanent investor with servicing retained by the seller for the life of the loan in exchange for a fee. Activities include the origination, sale, and servicing of mortgage loans by a firm or individual.

See also MORTGAGE BANKER; MORTGAGE BROKER.

MORTGAGE BROKER. A firm or individual that brings the borrower and lender together, receiving a commission; does not retain servicing.

See also MORTGAGE BANKING.

MORTGAGE CERTIFICATE. An interest in a mortgage evidenced by the instrument, generally a fractional portion of the mortgage, which certifies as to the agreement between the mortgagees who hold the certificate and the mortgagor as to such as terms as principal, amount, date of payment, and place of payment. Such certificates are not obligations to pay money, as in a bond or note, but are merely a certification by the holder of the mortgage, generally a corporate depository, that he or she holds such mortgage for the beneficial and undivided interest of all the certificate holders. The certificate itself generally sets forth a full agreement between the holder and the depository, although in some cases a lengthier document, known as a depository agreement, is executed.

MORTGAGE CHATTEL. A mortgage on personal property.

MORTGAGE CREDIT. Money that is owed for the acquisition of land or buildings (frequently of a home) and that is paid back over an extended period of time; hence, long-term debt.

MORTGAGE DEBENTURE. A mortgage bond.

MORTGAGE DEBT. An indebtedness created by a mortgage and secured by the property mortgaged; it is made evident by a note or bond.

MORTGAGE-DELINQUENCY RATE. By November 2009 it was shown that one in ten borrowers were at least a month behind on their monthly mortgage payments, translating into about 5 million households. This figure was up from about one in fourteen mortgage holders in the third quarter of 2008.

See also SUBPRIME; UNDERWATER.

MORTGAGEE. The lender of funds used to purchase a house and/or property. The mortgagor retains possession and use of the property during the term of the mortgage (e.g., a bank—mortgagee—may hold the mortgage on your house, of which you are the mortgagor).

See also MORTGAGE LOAN.

MORTGAGE FINANCING. *See* MORTGAGE BANKER, MORTGAGE LENDING.

MORTGAGE GUARANTEE POLICY. A policy issued on a guaranteed mortgage.

MORTGAGE IN POSSESSION. A mortgagee creditor who takes over the income from the mortgaged property upon default of the mortgage by the debtor.

MORTGAGE INSURANCE POLICY. Issued by a title insurance firm to a mortgage holder, resulting in a title policy.

See also TITLE INSURANCE.

MORTGAGE INVESTMENT TRUST. A specialized form of real estate investment trust that invests in long-term mortgages and makes short-term construction and development loans.

MORTGAGE LENDING. Effective January 1, 2010, federal regulations require mortgage lenders and brokers to give consumers better estimates of the barrage of costs they incur when taking out home loans. Announced in November 2008, it was created to clarify the cost of mortgages.

MORTGAGE LEGISLATION. In mid-September 2009, one year after the collapse of Lehman brothers, various proposals were being deliberated in Congress. They would require lenders to make sure customers can repay loans, essentially banning loans that require little or no documentation and sharply restricting subprime and other exotic mortgages. Proposals would also ban "steering" of customers into subprime loans and ban certain hidden broker fees like "yield spread premiums."

By mid-September the House passed a predatory lending bill (May 7) that incorporates the proposals and requires lenders to keep 5 percent of mortgages they originate so they will be less likely to make bad loans. The

Federal Reserve adopted regulations in 2008 that sharply restricted subprime mortgages.

MORTGAGE LIEN. A mortgage given as security for a debt, serving as a lien on the property after the mortgage is recorded.

MORTGAGE LIFE INSURANCE. Insurance on the life of the borrower that pays off a specified debt if he or she dies.

MORTGAGE LOAN. A loan made by a lender, called the mortgagee, to a borrower, called the mortgagor, for the financing of a parcel of real estate. The loan is evidenced by a mortgage. The mortgage sets forth the conditions of the loan, specifies the manner of repayment or liquidation of the loan, and reserves the right of foreclosure or repossession to the mortgagee. In case the mortgagor defaults in the payment of interest and principal, or if he or she permits a lien to be placed against the real estate mortgaged due to failure to pay the taxes and assessments levied against the property, the right of foreclosure can be exercised.

See also UNDERWATER.

MORTGAGE MODIFICATION. The federal government had by November 2009 enrolled one in five eligible homeowners in a program to modify their mortgages to prevent foreclosure.

See also FORECLOSURE; MAKING HOME AFFORDABLE PROGRAM; MODIFYING MORTGAGES; MORTGAGE LEGISLATION; PUBLIC-PRIVATE INVESTMENT FUND.

MORTGAGE NOTE. A note that offers a mortgage as proof of indebtedness and describes the manner in which the mortgage is to be paid. This note is the actual amount of debt that the mortgage obtains, and it renders the mortgagor personally responsible for repayment.

MORTGAGE PREMIUM. An additional bank fee charged for the issuance of a mortgage when the legal interest rate is less than the prevailing mortgage market rate and there is a shortage of mortgage money.

MORTGAGE-PURCHASE PROGRAM. *See* HOME MORTGAGES.

MORTGAGER.
Synonymous with MORTGAGOR.

MORTGAGE RATES. Rates on a thirty-year, fixed-rate mortgage fell to a record low for the second straight week at the end of December 2008. This caused refinancing applications to surge to the highest level in more than five years, a month after the Federal Reserve pledged to channel billions to prop up the sinking U.S. housing market.

See also FEDERAL RESERVE; FREDDIE MAC; REFINANCING MORTGAGES.

MORTGAGE-REPLACEMENT LOANS. Concept of loans to prevent distressed homeowners from walking away from their debts. Under a plan in 2008, the government would provide low-cost loans to all mortgage holders, worth 20 percent of their outstanding mortgage debt. Homeowners would secure lower interest costs.

See also TROUBLED ASSET RELIEF PROGRAM.

MORTGAGE SECURITIES. *See* FEDERAL RESERVE; LEHMAN BROTHERS; MARK-TO-MARKET RULES; PUBLIC-PRIVATE INVESTMENT FUND.

MORTGAGE SERVICES. On July 28, 2009, the Treasury Department met with twenty-five mortgage servicer representatives, in part to order that more home loans be modified.

See also MAKING HOME AFFORDABLE PROGRAM.

MORTGAGOR. A debtor or borrower who gives or makes a mortgage to a lender, on property owned by the mortgagor.

Synonymous with MORTGAGER.

MOTOROLA. Motorola had 6,700 employee layoffs in 2008, as the economic downturn and a slump in cell phone demand increased pressure on the firm, which was already losing market share. It announced in January 2009 that it would eliminate another 4,000 jobs, or an estimated 6 percent of its workforce, and showed a fourth-quarter loss because sales of cell phones were weaker than expected. The plan would bring its cost cuts to $1.5 billion for 2009, $700 million in new savings on top of a previously announced plan for $800 million in expense cuts.

On February 3 Motorola reported that sales of its troubled cell phone unit plummeted in the fourth quarter 2008.

Motorola announced at the end of April that its total cash on hand had dropped to $6.1 billion from $7.4 billion at the end of 2008. The company posted a first-quarter net loss of $228 million, compared with a loss of $190 million a year before. Cell phone shipments worldwide dropped 13 percent in the first quarter of 2009.

The company had a third-quarter 2009 profit of $12 million, compared with a loss of $397 million a year before. Revenue fell 27 percent to $5.45 billion. Four years ago, its stock touched $55 billion; today it was just over $20 billion. Sales continued to fall, falling 27 percent in the third quarter 2009 to $5.5 billion, reporting $12 million of earnings.

Cf. NOKIA CORPORATION; VODAFONE.

MUNI BONDS. *See* MUNICIPAL BONDS.

MUNICIPAL BONDS (MUNI BONDS). In the United States, bonds that made up this market of $2.7 trillion were issued by local-government borrowers. By 2009, one-third of the buyers of muni bonds were gone. Banks became reluctant to get involved.

MUTUAL FUND ASSETS. For 2008, these assets had declined by $2.4 trillion, a fifth of their value, in the United States alone. In the United Kingdom, the drop was more than one-quarter, or almost $195 billion.

See also EUROPEAN PARLIAMENT; UNITED KINGDOM.

MUZAK. The maker of background music heard in elevators and offices filed for Chapter 11 bankruptcy protection on February 10, 2009. The firm listed its total debt at $100 million to $500 million, with assets of less than $50,000.

N

NAKED SHORT SELLING. A controversial trading practice using high-speed traders, accounting for nearly 40 percent of U.S. stock-trading volume today. Trading firms are usually unidentified, thereby reducing accountability.

See also SHORT SELLING.

NAME AND SHAME. As part of his program to restrict executive compensation for executives whose firms received bailout funds, President Obama, on February 4, 2009, introduced the name and shame provision, designed to make companies think twice about indulgent outlays. The intent was not to reward "executives for failure, especially when those rewards are subsidized by U.S. taxpayers."

See also CLAWBACKS; EXECUTIVE PAY; GOLDEN PARACHUTE.

NASDAQ COMPOSITE INDEX. A major American stock exchange with 3,700 companies and corporations. For 2008, fell 40.5 percent, the worst percentage decline in its thirty-eight-year history, surpassing its 39.3 percent plunge in 2000 after the tech-stock bubble burst.

See also STOCK MARKET.

NATIONAL BANK ACT OF 1863. Created a national banking system and established the Office of the Comptroller of the Currency, which charters, regulates, and examines all national banks.

NATIONAL BANK SUPERVISOR. Proposal that would eliminate savings and loans and close the Office of Thrift Supervision. Its responsibilities would fall under the new regulator, which would replace the Comptroller of the Currency and oversee all banks. By mid-September 2009, the Obama administration had submitted a draft bill to Congress. There have been no votes in the House or Senate.

See also FINANCIAL REGULATION PLAN (2009).

NATIONAL BUREAU OF ECONOMIC RESEARCH. A U.S. government data-collecting agency response for determining, among other matters, the official end of the recession 2008–2009. The group spent a year examining statistics before declaring that the recession had begun in December 2007. Its business cycle dating committee looks at output as well as other indicators such as employment to finalize their decision. It is the responsibility of this nonprofit research group to declare the beginning and end of U.S. recessions. The bureau defines recession as "a significant decline in economic activity spread across the economy, lasting more than a few months."

See also RECESSION OF 2007–2010.

NATIONAL DEBT. The debt about 40 percent of GDP in 2008, expected to rise to 60 percent by 2010 as a result of the recession and spending tied to the federal bank bailout and stimulus programs.

NATIONAL INSTITUTES OF HEALTH. *See* AMERICAN RECOVERY AND REINVESTMENT ACT (OF 2009).

NATIONALIZATION. The governmental takeover of a private firm. Nationalization usually means that the government buys big stakes in banks or other institutions/organizations to help them survive; other times it involves federal seizure of an insolvent institution. The government doesn't need to have 100 percent ownership. It is risky for a government to run the private sector; the government's record as a corporate manager is poor, and should the effort fail, taxpayers may lose billions of dollars they have spent; it also violates the spirit of its concept of free markets. The biggest problem for the government in nationalizing banks is that it is impractical and expensive to take over all 8,000 banks, or even the 314 institutions that described themselves as "banks" in order to receive government aid. It also would not solve the pressing problem of potential bank failures. Most specialists believe that nationalization should be used as an emergency method to prop up banks during difficult times. However, there is evidence that nationalization can cause market distortions. The longer banks remain in government hands, the more likely they will be used to further government policies. Assuredly, should banks lose large amounts of deposits or access to credit, they will need to be seized.

See also AUTOMOBILE INDUSTRY; "BAD BANKS"; ECONOMIC NATIONALISM; OBAMA, BARACK; TRUMAN, HARRY S.

NATIONAL SEMICONDUCTOR. Announced in mid-March 2009 its intent to eliminate 26 percent of its workforce, or more than 1,700 jobs, in one of the most severe cutbacks by a Silicon Valley firm during the current recession.

National Semiconductor's fiscal first-quarter profit 2009 dropped 63 percent as revenue fell by a third. For the quarter ending August 30, it reported a profit of $29.8 million, down from $79.6 million a year earlier.

NEC CORPORATION. The international IT company announced at the end of January 2009 that it would cut 20,000 jobs worldwide in response to mounting losses in the deepening global downturn. NEC's net loss for the October–December 2008 quarter swelled to $1.46 billion,

The job cuts, which included nearly 7 percent of the firm's permanent workforce, would be completed by March 2010.

NEGATIVE INFLATION RATE. *See* DEFLATION; SPAIN.

NEIMAN MARCUS. In January 2009, the upscale retailer announced it would cut about 375 jobs, or 2.3 percent of its workers. Then in mid-February it cut an additional 450 positions, its second round of layoffs in two months.

In mid-March, the company posted a $509.2 million quarterly loss compared with a loss of $44.3 million a year earlier.

For its fourth quarter ending August 1, 2009, Neiman Marcus posted a loss of $168.5 million, compared with a $35.6 million loss one year earlier. Sales declined 25 percent to $768 million from $1.03 billion in the year-ago quarter.

Neiman enlisted designs in cost-cutting plans.

See also RETAILING.

NETHERLANDS, THE. The Dutch economy contracted starting in the third quarter of 2008 into the first three months of 2009, resulting in its first recession since 1982.

See also FORTIS BANQUE.

"NEW BANKS." Not saving bad banks, but creating and/or supporting existing banks to become good banks would be a major means for solving the banking crisis and bringing other, usually smaller banks, to provide the new lending that the economy needs.

With a minimum of $350 billion in assets, the government encouraged these institutions to enter the market.

Cf. AGGREGATOR BANK; "BAD BANKS."

NEW COMPANIES. These business start-ups are crucial to any economic recovery. In their first ninety days of life, businesses accounted for 14 percent of hiring in the United States between 1993 and 2008. At the beginning of 2000 new companies fell 9 percent between the third quarter of 2000 and the first quarter of 2003. Business starts fell 14 percent from the third quarter of 2007 to the third quarter of 2008. The 187,000 businesses created in that quarter were the fewest in a quarter since 1995.

NEW DEAL. *See* G-20; ROOSEVELT, FRANKLIN DELANO.

NEW FOUNDATION. President Obama's approach to curb financial "risks built on piles of sand."

See also REGULATORS.

NEW HAVEN REGISTER. See JOURNAL REGISTER CO.

NEW HOME CONSTRUCTION. *See* HOME CONSTRUCTION.

NEW HOME SALES. *See* HOME SALES.

NEW JOB OPENINGS. *See* JOB OPENINGS.

NEW MONEY. Since September 2008, the Fed's balance sheet has ballooned to more than $2 trillion from about $900 billion as the central bank had created new money and loaned it out through all of its new programs. By the time the Fed completed its plans to purchase up mortgage-backed debt and consumer debt, the balance sheet was up to about $3 trillion.

See also FEDERAL RESERVE.

NEW PECORA COMMISSION. *See* FINANCIAL CRISIS INQUIRY COMMISSION.

NEW REGULATORY AGENCIES. Proposed agencies will require legislative approval.

See also CONSUMER FINANCIAL PROTECTION AGENCY; NATIONAL BANK SUPERVISOR.

NEWS CORPORATION. Owners of the *Wall Street Journal* took a large write-down on the value of its assets, pushing it to a $6.4 billion loss for the fiscal second quarter 2009.

The company's net income climbed 11 percent in the third quarter 2009. News Corporation reported a net income of $581 million.

NEWSPAPER ADVERTISING. *See* NEWSPAPERS.

NEWSPAPERS. Newspaper advertising, already in its worst slump since the 1930s Great Depression, suffered its sharpest drop during the first quarter of 2009, down 30 percent for many papers.

New figures, released at the end of April, indicated that U.S. newspapers continued their downward trend, with a 7 percent drop from the previous year. Of the most widely circulated twenty-five newspapers, all had declines, except for the *Wall Street Journal*, with a tiny 0.6 percent gain. For the others, the declines ranged from 20.6 percent to a slight 0.4 percent.

Average U.S. weekly newspaper circulation for the six months ending September 30, 2009, fell nearly 11 percent. Nearly two-thirds of the twenty-five largest newspapers posted circulation declines of 10 percent or more.

On October 26, 2009, the Audit Bureau of Circulations revealed that the *Los Angeles Times* had lost 11 percent of its paying readers in 2009. Circulation at the *Boston Globe* fell by 18 percent and at the *San Francisco Chronicle* it declined by 26 percent. Circulation at the *Wall Street Journal* climbed to 2 million, making it America's best-selling newspaper. Daily sales of the *New York Times* declined by 7 percent and *USA Today* saw circulation fall by 17 percent.

See also BALTIMORE SUN; *FINANCIAL TIMES*; GANNETT; HEARST CORPORATION; JOURNAL REGISTER CO.; *MINNEAPOLIS STAR TRIBUNE*; NEWS CORPORATION; NEWSPAPER WEBSITES; *NEW YORK TIMES; ROCKY MOUNTAIN NEWS; SUN-TIMES*; TRIBUNE; *WASHINGTON POST*.

NEWSPAPER WEBSITES. In the first quarter 2009, newspaper websites attracted more than 73 million hits, or visitors, every month on average. That was a 10.5 percent increase the first quarter of 2008.

See also NEWSPAPERS.

NEW YORK TIMES (*NY TIMES*). Revenues from print and online operations fell nearly 22 percent in November from the previous year. Its newspaper ad revenue declined 14.2 percent in 2008, for a drop of 19.5 percent in the last two years.

The Times Company has $1.1 billion in debt, $46 million in cash, and a substantial amount of debt maturing over the next couple of years. It continued to seek outside investors. In January 2009, company sold a portion of its midtown Manhattan headquarters. On February 19, it announced that it would suspend dividend payments to shareholders for the first time in four decades as a publicly trade company.

In mid-March, the company announced that it had raised $225 million in a sale of some of its assets.

Pay was cut in March by 5 percent for editors, and 100 workers, working on the business side, were dismissed, representing a cut of about 5 percent of its staff of about 2,000.

The newspaper posted a steep first-quarter 2009 loss amid worse-than-expected advertising results. Total revenue fell 19 percent to $609 million. It posted a loss of $74.5 million and a 28.4 percent decline in advertising revenue.

The New York Times Company sold its NY City radio station to Univision Communications in an arrangement that netted the publisher $45 million as it sought to stabilize its finances. WQXR-FM is among 275 of the nation's 13,000 radio stations carrying classical music.

On July 23, the New York Times Company reported a second-quarter profit of $39.1 million. Ad sales had fallen more than 30 percent in the quarter.

On October 14, 2009, the company scrapped efforts to sell the *Boston Globe*.

On October 19, the company announced its intention to shed another 100 jobs from its nearly 1,300-person newsroom by year's end. Buyouts were offered.

See also NEWSPAPERS.

Cf. TRIBUNE.

NEW ZEALAND. New Zealand's central bank cut rates by one and a half points to 5 percent on December 4, 2008.

NICHE BANKS. *See* INDUSTRIAL BANKS.

NIGERIA. *See* AFRICA.

NIKE. The world's largest maker of sportswear by sales announced on February 10, 2009, a 4 percent reduction in its workforce affecting about 1,400 employees as it realigns its operations amid the difficult economic times.

It announced on May 14 that it would cut another 1,750 jobs in its worldwide operations, comprising about 5 percent of its workforce.

Nike's fiscal second-quarter profit 2009 fell 4 percent on lower sales, with a profit of $375 million, and revenue fell 4 percent to $4.41 billion.

Fourth-quarter profits dropped 30 percent, with revenue declining 7.4 percent to $4.71 billion.

NIKKEI. A stock market index for the Tokyo Stock Exchange. Its 225-company index ended 2008 by recording a 42.1 percent fall, well above its last greatest annual loss of 38.7 percent in 1990.

See also JAPAN.

NINTENDO. In January 2009, the video game maker cut its full-year earnings estimate by 33 percent. The company said its net profit fell 18 percent to 212.5 billion yen ($2.35 billion) in the first nine months of its fiscal year ending March 31.

NISSAN. Japan's third-largest carmaker by sales, it posted a December 2008 drop in car sales of 31 percent. Then, on February 9, 2009, it announced plans to slash more than 20,000 jobs worldwide (it had 240,000 employees in March 2008), to shift production out of Japan, and to seek government assistance in Japan, the United States, and elsewhere.

The firm reduced monthly domestic production 59 percent in January 2009 to 47,477 vehicles. It was its lowest monthly output volume since at least 1971.

Nissan announced on May 12 that it had its first annual net loss in its history.

Nissan reported a loss of 16.53 billion yen in the three months ending in June, compared with a profit of 52.80 billion yen a year earlier.

See also AUTOMOBILE INDUSTRY.

NOBEL PEACE PRIZE. *See* OBAMA, BARACK.

"NO FIRING" PLAN. *See* GERMANY.

NOKIA CORPORATION. On January 22, 2009, Nokia posted a worse-than-expected 69 percent drop in fourth-quarter net profit, saying that the market would contract further in 2009 than what was earlier forecasted. The world's largest mobile phone maker noted that the economic downturn had led to a rapid decline in consumer demand for electronic goods.

Nokia's shares fell 9 percent, with net profits for the quarter dropping to $749.8 million, and sales declining 19 percent.

On February 24, Nokia announced a range of new job-cutting measures to lower costs and adapt to a weak market condition, including voluntary buyout packages for 1,000 workers, as well as wider use of short-term unpaid leaves and sabbaticals. Nokia employs nearly 130,000 workers worldwide.

On March 17, the company announced that it would eliminate as many as 1,700 jobs in order to reduce operating expenses by about $900 million in 2009. Nokia faced a 69 percent decline in its fourth-quarter net profit. Nokia posted a smaller-than-expected decline in second-quarter 2009 net profits. Sales and market share were down 15 percent.

Nokia reported a worse-than-expected third-quarter 2009 net loss. It expected industry volumes to fall 7 percent in 2009.

Cf. MOTOROLA; VODAFONE.

See also FINNAIR.

"NO NEW BAILOUT." *See* GEITHNER, TIMOTHY F.

NON-FARM UNEMPLOYMENT. *See* UNEMPLOYMENT.

NON-MANUFACTURING. *See* INSTITUTE FOR SUPPLY MANAGEMENT.

NONRESIDENTIAL CONSTRUCTION. *See* NONRESIDENTIAL PROPERTIES.

NONRESIDENTIAL PROPERTIES. Includes everything from hotels to factories; activity significantly declined at the end of October 2008. The U.S. commercial real estate bust reinforced the credit crunch, put added strain on taxpayers, and deepened the recession.

Cf. RESIDENTIAL PROPERTIES.

NORDSTROM. The upscale department store chain reported a 68 percent drop in fourth-quarter profit, hurt by falling sales and a lower profit margin. Income in the quarter fell to $68 million or 31 cents a share, from $212 million, or 92 cents a share, in the same quarter of 2007.

NORTEL NETWORKS. Toronto-based company, a one-time huge telecommunications equipment maker, it filed for bankruptcy protection in the United States and Canada on January 14, 2009, becoming the first major technology firm to take that step in the global meltdown. The filing came a day before Nortel was due to make a debt payment of $107 million.

At the time of filing, Nortel had $4.5 billion in debt and $2.4 billion in cash.

During the 1990s telecom and Internet boom, Nortel had more than 95,000 employees and a market capitalization of $297 billion. In 2000, it accounted for one-third of the market value of the Toronto Stock Exchange.

By January 2009, its market value was just $155 million, with about 26,000 employees. Then in February it was announced that Nortel would cut an additional 3,200 jobs. Once valued at $250 billion, Nortel sought chapter 11 protection in January.

NORTH AMERICAN FREE TRADE AGREEMENT (NAFTA). Effective January 1, 1994, a trade accord that created international marketing opportunities between the United States, Mexico, and Canada. Supplemental or side agreements on environmental cooperation and labor cooperation were signed in September 1993. Congress debated NAFTA in the fall of 1993; approval by a simple majority of both houses was needed for passage. On November 17, 1993, the House of Representatives, followed by the Senate on November 20, voted approval to the trade pact; NAFTA went into effect on January 1, 1994.

On January 1, 2009, NAFTA celebrated its fifteenth year of existence. Over this time period, exports accounted for almost a third of Mexico's GDP. More than 80 percent of Mexican exports went to the United States.

In mid-April 2009, the government concluded that it wasn't necessary to renegotiate NAFTA, despite a campaign promise by President Obama to strengthen the pact's labor and environmental provisions.

See also MEXICO; PROTECTIONISM.

NORTH CAROLINA. *See* STATES (U.S.).

NORWAY. The jobless rate rose to 1.8 percent in October 2008 from 1.7 percent the previous month.

Economic growth more than halved in November 2008 to 0.2 percent. Unemployment was expected to stay below 3 percent over 2009–2100.

The central bank in mid-December cut its benchmark interest rate by a larger-than-expected 1.75 percentage points, lowering the overnight deposit rate to 3 percent; two months later the central bank cut its main interest rate from 3 percent to 2.5 percent.

In early February 2009, the government unveiled a $14.8 billion plan to inject capital into the country's banks and lend directly to banks and other businesses by buying corporate bonds.

At the end of October 2009 Norway raised its main interest rate by 25 basis points to 1.5 percent, the first country in Europe to raise rates since the height of the global meltdown.

See also ICELAND.

NOVEMBER 4, 2008 SUMMIT. *See* SUMMIT OF NOVEMBER 15, 2008.

NY TIMES. See NEW YORK TIMES.

O

OBAMA, BARACK. From a campaign of promises to restore peace, Barack Obama became consumed by the need to restore the nation's prosperity. On November 4, 2008, Barack Obama won the presidential election, beating John McCain by 52 percent to 46 percent, subsequently declaring that "change has come to America."

Upon his becoming president on January 20, 2009, he pushed his economic agenda forward immediately. At the outset, he sought an economic stimulus package; direct mortgage relief to aid homeowners; new government regulations, including tightening reins on Wall Street; and automobile industry assistance and development.

Prior to his inauguration he had spoken of a recovery that would generate 2.5 million jobs in the first two years of his administration. That would require not just zero economic growth, but a fairly robust expansion, a swing, in effect, from the present 4 percent contraction to a growth rate of 2.5 percent, or 3 percent a year. This achievement would mean adding nearly $1 trillion in annual output to the economy. Shortly before taking office he called for the creation of an additional half million jobs, taking the total target to 3 million.

Obama planned to present a recovery plan soon after taking office that might cost $500 to $700 billion, soon raised to between $675 and $775 billion.

Besides new spending, he would provide tax relief for low-wage and middle-income workers of about $150 billion. The government would also lower the withholding of income or payroll taxes so that more employees received larger paychecks as soon as possible in 2009.

Over a two-day period, December 6 and 7, president-elect Obama pledged a recovery program "equal to the task ahead," with a vast public works plan built around bridge and highway projects, and the creation of green jobs and the spread of new technologies. He called for the largest infrastructure program since the federal highway system was built in the 1950s during the Eisenhower administration, under the Federal Aid Highway Act of 1956.

He planned to stimulate the economy through large direct government spending on infrastructure projects as well as through business and individual tax cuts.

He proposed prior to becoming president a plan that would permit those who lost jobs that did not come with insurance benefits to apply for Medicaid. He would also review existing programs, such as the Trade Adjustment Assistance Act and the Workforce Investment Act.

On February 26, the president proposed $634 billion in new taxes on upper-income Americans and reductions in government spending over the coming decade.

On April 1, one day before the G-20 summit, the president conceded U.S. culpability in starting the global financial crisis.

The president, in his warning of April 14, that tough months were ahead for the economy, laid out his five "Pillars" to build a lasting recovery: new regulations for Wall Street; education spending focusing on strengthening the work force; renewable energy investments to create jobs and lessen the nation's dependence on imported oil; health-care containment; and long-term deficit reduction based on controlling the growth of Medicare, Medicaid, and Social Security.

President Obama's first 100 days showed dramatic shifts in the economic conditions of the nation:

	Before	After
Unemployed Americans	Dec. 2008 11.1 million	March 2009 13.2 million
Value of the U.S. stock market, as a percentage of its Oct. 2007 peak	Jan. 20, 2009 51 percent	April 28, 2009 55 percent
Financial firms receiving bailout funds	Jan. 20, 2009 295	April 28, 2009 566

In summary, the major events of his first 100 days in office include:

a. January 26—Timothy Geithner becomes Treasury secretary following a confirmation delayed over problems with his personal tax payments.
b. January 28—House of Representatives passes $819 billion stimulus bill without a single Republican vote; regulators guarantee $80 billion in uninsured deposits at the financial institutions that service credit unions.
c. February 5–6—A bipartisan group works to craft a lower-cost stimulus plan after Senate amendments swell package to $920 billion.
d. February 10—Treasury secretary outlines plan to examine banks and get credit flowing; Dow declines nearly 5 percent.
e. February 11—Congress and White House reach a stimulus deal.
f. February 17—President signs $787 billion stimulus bill.

g. February 18—President pledges as much as $275 billion in programs for homeowners.

h. February 26—President releases budget blueprint, signaling shift in U.S. policy by expanding government activism and raising taxes on the rich.

i. March 6—Labor Department announces 651,000 job losses in February and an unemployment rate of 8.1 percent.

j. March 19—House passes bill to recoup bonuses paid by American International Group.

k. March 30—President announces restructuring measures for General Motors and Chrysler, including the ousting of GM's chief executive, Rick Wagoner.

l. April 2—G-20 leaders conclude summit by agreeing to pump up the IMF's financial capacity to $1 trillion to help handle crises in developing countries.

m. April 10—President says economy shows "glimmers of hope."

n. April 23—President steps up pressure on banks and credit card issuers that are boosting fees and tightening lending.

The president lost his first big legislative fight on April 30, when his measure that would have allowed bankruptcy-court judges to reduce the value of some mortgages, called cramdowns, was defeated.

On September 14, 2009, at Federal Hall on Wall Street, commemorating the first anniversary of the demise of Lehman Brothers, President Obama sternly admonished the financial industry and members of Congress to accept his proposals to reshape financial regulations. Expectations of passage of most of his suggestions remained doubtful as the markets slowly recovered.

At the G-20 summit in Pittsburgh, Pennsylvania, President Obama urged a reshaping of the global economy: "We have achieved a level of intangible, global economic cooperation that we've never seen before. . . . Our financial system will be far different and more secure than the one that failed so dramatically this year."

Meeting with top executives from the twelve biggest banks on December 14, 2009, the president pressured them to "take extraordinary" steps to revive lending from small businesses and homeowners. He declared that it was their obligation, considering that the taxpayers were behind the bailout. It is becoming increasingly clear that with these banks paying off their government obligation they now have a stronger hand to do as they wish.

On October 9, 2009, President Obama won the 2009 Nobel Peace Prize.

See also AMERICAN RECOVERY AND REINVESTMENT ACT (OF 2009); AUTOMOBILE INDUSTRY; FEDERAL AID HIGHWAY ACT (OF

1956); GREEN JOBS PROGRAM; G-20; KRUGMAN, PAUL; MAKING WORK PAY; MCCAIN, JOHN; NEW FOUNDATION; PELOSI, NANCY; PUBLIC WORKS; "SHOVEL READY"; TARP 2.0; TAX BREAKS; TAXES; TRADE ADJUSTMENT ASSISTANCE ACT; WORKFORCE INVESTMENT ACT.

OECD. *See* ORGANIZATION FOR ECONOMIC COOPERATION AND DEVELOPMENT.

OFFICE DEPOT. Showed a $1.5 billion net loss for the fourth quarter of 2008 as sales fell 15 percent to $3.3 billion.

In April 2009, Office Depot announced a first-quarter net loss of $55.3 million amid $120 million of restructuring charges.

Office Depot's second-quarter 2009 loss widened, with a sales decline of 22 percent to $2.82 billion. The company had by now closed five stores, opened three, and relocated one.

OFFICE OF FEDERAL HOUSING ENTERPRISE OVERSIGHT. A government agency responsible for regulating Fannie Mae and Freddie Mac.

See also FANNIE MAE; FREDDIE MAC.

OFFICE OF MANAGEMENT AND BUDGET. *See* DEFICIT (BUDGET, U.S.).

OFFICE OF THE COMPTROLLER. *See* HOUSE (U.S.) FINANCIAL OVERHAUL PLAN; NATIONAL BANK ACT OF 1863; NATIONAL BANK SUPERVISOR.

OFFICE OF THRIFT SUPERVISION. U.S. thrifts reported a slight quarterly profit of $4 million in the second quarter 2009, the first positive result since mid-2007. This profit compared with a first-quarter loss of $1.62 billion.

See also FINANCIAL INSTITUTIONS REFORM RECOVERY AND ENFORCEMENT ACT OF 1989; FINANCIAL REGULATION PLAN (2009); HOUSE (U.S.) FINANCIAL OVERHAUL PLAN; NATIONAL BANK SUPERVISOR.

OFFICE RENTS. Office rents fell 2.7 percent in the second quarter of 2009 from a year before, the largest single-quarter decline since the first quarter of 2002.

Rents continued to decline. By October 2009, rent for office space fell 8.5 percent, the fastest pace in more than a decade. The fall came as companies returned a net 19.6 million square feet of space to landlords in the third quarter, slightly more than in the second quarter. The vacancy rate hit 16.5 percent, a five-year high.

OFFSHORE-BANKING HAVENS. *See* TAX CURBS; TAX HAVENS.

OFFSHORE TAX HAVENS. *See* TAX CURBS; TAX HAVENS.

OIL. Oil briefly reached $100 a barrel on January 3, 2008, for the first time. Prices of oil then reached a peak in July 2008 of $147 a barrel before turning downward again. By the end of October 2008, oil had dropped to $62 a barrel. Following a quarter of a century of growth, 2008 global oil consumption had its first annual drop since 1983. In the United States oil demand fell 5 percent in 2008.

The demand for oil declined in 2008 by 1.1 million barrels per day, or 5.4 percent, the first time annual oil consumption declined by more than a million barrels since 1980. For 2009, U.S. oil demand was projected to decline by another 250,000 barrels per day, or 1.3 percent.

On December 2, the price of a barrel of oil slipped below $47, the lowest level since May 2005 and less than a third of the peak reached in July 2008. Oil prices continued to decline in December, sliding to $38.85 per barrel, as the widening global recession showed no sign of relenting soon.

The demand for oil by was now expected to fall 1.2 percent in 2009, the biggest annual drop in 27 years.

On October 21, 2009, oil prices went above $81 a barrel for the first time in twelve months; by December 28 it was above $79 a barrel.

See also BRITISH PETROLEUM; CHEVRON; CONOCOPHILLIPS; EXXON; HALLIBURTON; OIL EXPLORATION; OPEC; REFINERS; ROYAL DUTCH SHELL; SCHLUMBERGER; TOTAL.

OIL COMPANIES. In July 2009, oil firms reported lower profits because of falling prices and weaker demand. Royal Dutch Shell's net profit fell by 67 percent to $3.8 billion. ConocoPhillips's profit fell by 76 percent and BP by 53 percent.

OIL EXPLORATION. By December 2008, oil exploration had been meaningfully reduced; dozens of major oil and natural gas projects had been put on hold or cancelled as firms scrambled to adjust to the collapse in energy markets. Such postponements would likely lower future energy supplies and could set the stage for another rapid climb in prices once the global economy recovered.

Oil demand growth had weakened throughout the industrial world. The International Energy Agency projected that worldwide demand would actually drop in 2008, for the first time since 1983.

See also OIL.

OLYMPIC GAMES. *See* UNITED KINGDOM.

100 DAYS. *See* OBAMA, BARACK.

ONLINE. *See* RETAILING; WOOLWORTHS.

OPEC (ORGANIZATION OF PETROLEUM EXPORTING COUNTRIES). A group comprising thirteen members, concentrated in the Middle East, but also including countries in Africa, South America, and the Far East. By virtue of their large exports, Saudi Arabia and Iran have been the most powerful influences.

During the summer of 2008, the OPEC cartel could not prevent oil prices from surging to record levels. At the end of the year, the producers seemed equally unable to stop prices from collapsing as the global economy cooled down.

Accounting for 40 percent of the world's oil exports, OPEC officials were also puzzled how oil topped $147 a barrel in July, and then rapidly prices dropped by more than $90, ostensibly due to lower economic growth around the world. Prices could keep falling in 2009, analysts say, with some predicting new lows of around $30 a barrel.

OPEC members need prices of $60 to $90 a barrel to balance their budgets, so the prospect of lower prices and crimped revenues is daunting for them.

At the December 18 OPEC meeting, members agreed to the largest ever production cut—2.2 million barrels a day—in an effort to put a floor on falling oil prices as demand waned. It was the third time OPEC had reduced its output in three months. The new target set OPEC's production at 24.85 million barrels a day, starting on January 1, 2009.

The cartel had not faced such a situation since the early 1980s. Oil consumption had declined for the first time in twenty-five years because of the economic crisis. Indicative of the meltdown, OPEC collectively postponed thirty-five oil-drilling projects in various stages of development.

See also MIDDLE EAST; OIL; OIL EXPLORATION.

OPEL. GM, which owns Opel and Vauxhall operations in Europe, in August 2009 reconsidered whether to sell these units. Then, on November 1, 2009, GM reversed its earlier decision and backed out of the deal to sell the automobile makers to Magna International.

See also MAGNA.

OPTION ADJUSTABLE-RATE MORTGAGES (OPTION ARMS). Nearly $750 billion in these mortgages were issued from 2004 to 2007. Option ARMs were usually made to borrowers with higher credit scores than those getting subprime mortgages. But many of these borrowers were stretched thin by the global economic decline and rising unemployment. Borrowers faced payment shock when they had to begin making payments of full interest and principal.

ORACLE CORPORATION. At the beginning of 2009 posted a revenue decline for the first time since 2002. Profits dropped 7.2 percent to $1.89 billion and revenue fell 5.2 percent to $6.86 billion.

Oracle's first-quarter 2009 profit climbed 12 percent. Revenues rose 4 percent from the year before, which followed two straight periods of revenue declines amid a greater slowdown in tech spending.

ORGANIZATION FOR ECONOMIC COOPERATION AND DEVELOPMENT (OECD). Created in 1948, an organization of seventeen European nations (including the German Federal Republic), known until 1960 as the Organization for European Economic Cooperation (OEEC). Initially, the group developed and implemented economic recovery programs following World War II. It was enlarged to twenty-one members with the change of its name to OECD. Headquartered in Paris, France, it promotes the economic growth of member nations, the expansion of world investment and trade, and the economic development of emerging countries.

By the end of November 2008, OECD called for aggressive economic stimulus measures. OECD claimed the number of unemployed people in their now thirty member nations could rise to 42 million over two years from a current 34 million.

At the same time, they said the U.S. economy would shrink 0.9 percent in 2009, after posting growth of 1.8 percent in 2008.

The OECD concluded in March 2009 that large emerging economies were being dragged down by the recession in richer countries.

The OECD had set standards on transparency and information exchange in tax matters, demanded cooperation from tax haven nations.

In an updated forecast at the end of March, the OECD predicted that 2009 GDP would drop 4.2 percent in their thirty countries. This dramatic deterioration from its forecast in November, when they predicted contraction of just 0.4 percent, indicated the huge shift in decline.

The combined GDP of the OECD nations fell 2.1 percent in the January–March period from the previous year. It is the largest drop since 1960, when the organization began collecting such data. The GDP of member countries fell 2 percent in the final quarter of 2008.

OECD economies, which accounted for 71 percent of the world GDP in 2007, shrank 4.2 percent in the first quarter 2009 from a year earlier.

At the end of June 2009 the OECD revised upward its assessment of the world's economy, saying that the worst would soon be over in the current recession. The OECD forecast that the combined output of its member nations would contract 4.1 percent in 2009 and expand 0.7 percent in 2010.

The OECD showed in mid-November that economic output in its members in the third period was up 0.8 percent from the second quarter, although it was 3.3 percent lower in annual terms. The combined GDP of the OECD nations, accounting for 61.3 percent of world GDP, increased for the first time since 2008 first quarter.

See also G-20; PENSION FUNDS; TAX HAVENS; and listings by country.

ORGANIZATION OF PETROLEUM EXPORTING COUNTRIES. *See* OPEC.

ORSZAG, PETER. President Obama's White House budget director. He had been director of the Congressional Budget Office for nearly two years.

OTIS ELEVATORS. *See* UNITED TECHNOLOGIES.

OUTPUT PER HOUR. *Synonymous with* PRODUCTIVITY.

OVERSEEING. *See* REGULATORS.

OVERSIGHT. *See* TIER 1 FINANCIAL HOLDING FIRM; TRANSPARENCY.

OVERSIGHT OF EXECUTIVE PAY. *See* EXECUTIVE PAY.

OVER-THE-COUNTER DERIVATIVES. *See* FINANCIAL REGULATION PLAN (2009).

OVERTIME. Enables firms to increase productivity to meet rising customer orders without adding fixed costs such as health care benefits for new hires. Should business suddenly slow, firms choosing increased overtime expenses can withdraw workers without having to make costly layoffs. For example, during the gradual recovery in the economy in the fall 2009, overtime increased 6.5 percent to 3.2 hours per week in October over September's level of 3 hours and 14 percent from the 2.8 hours of overtime averaged in the second quarter. The downside of using overtime is that the process does not create new jobs.

Also, it helps to provide a middle-class lifestyle for many hourly workers. *See also* UNEMPLOYMENT.

P

PACE. *See* PROMOTE AMERICA'S COMPETITIVE EDGE.

PACIFIC INVESTMENT MANAGEMENT COMPANY. The world's biggest bond fund.

PAKISTAN. In August 2009, the IMF added $3.2 billion to a loan it extended to Pakistan in 2008, bringing the total value of aid offered the country to $11.3 billion.

Pakistan's central bank cut its benchmark rate by half a percentage point to 12.5 percent in November 2009.

See also INTERNATIONAL MONETARY FUND.

PANASONIC. Reported on February 4, 2009, that it was shedding 15,000 jobs, the second significant layoff in Japan's electronics industry in less than one week. The company projected a net loss of 380 billion yen, or $4.2 billion, for the year ending March 31, 2008.

On August 3, 2009, Panasonic posted a fiscal first-quarter loss of about $460 million for the April–June period. Revenue during this period fell 26 percent from a year earlier.

By the end of October the company announced that it had a decline in revenue, and would be eliminating 15,000 jobs in a turnaround effort.

See also SANYO ELECTRIC.

PANDIT, VIKRIM. *See* CITIGROUP.

PARTNERING. *See* PUBLIC-PRIVATE INVESTMENT FUND.

PART-TIME WORKERS. Under the Economic Stimulus Plan of 2009, $7 billion was made available to states for workers, such as part-timers and people in training programs. While the vast majority of workers contributed directly or indirectly to the unemployment insurance pot, just 36 percent of people out of work actually collected benefits.

By February 2009, the number of people working part-time, because they couldn't secure full-time work or because their hours had been cut back, rose by 787,000 to 8.6 million; up 3.7 million over the past year.

See also PRIVATE-SECTOR PAYROLLS; SPENDING; UNDEREM-PLOYED.

PAULSON, HENRY (HANK). President George W. Bush's Treasury secretary. Criticized on February 28, 2008, for his promoted rescue plans for homeowners, branded by many as bailouts for reckless lenders and speculators; predicted the administration's market-based approach would keep a foreclosure crisis under control.

Attended Harvard University and after a brief stint in Washington worked at Goldman Sachs and in 1982 became a partner and then co-chief executive in June 1998. He became sole chief executive and in 2005 was the highest-paid CEO on Wall Street, with $38.3 million in compensation. After thirty-two years of Goldman service, he returned to Washington, D.C.

Hank Paulson's $700 billion plan in October created quite a stir. Many on the left accused him of ripping off taxpayers to save banking inefficiencies and mismanagement, while those on the right argued that it was approaching socialism. Paulson misread the severity of the economic meltdown and problems in the housing sector. He was seen as a hero for taking decisive action to back up the U.S. banking system but was criticized for confusing markets.

See also BANK BAILOUT (PLAN) OF 2008; EMERGENCY ECONOMIC STABILIZATION ACT OF 2008; TARP; "TOO BIG TO FAIL."

PAY. By December 2008, pay across the United States hadn't significantly fallen, as had been projected by many experts. For the year, the weekly pay of rank-and-file workers, who make up roughly 80 percent of the workforce, had risen 2.8 percent.

The meltdown kept salary growth to a minimum in 2009, and predictions for 2010 weren't better. Employers have increased salaries in 2009 by the smallest percentage in decades. Median pay increases for 2009 ranged between 2 percent and 3 percent. The government announced that pay for the average worker increased 2.2 percent in the first quarter 2009, down from 3.2 percent in the year before. Firms are projecting an average of 3 percent increase in 2010, making it the smallest forecast increases in the twenty-nine years that these figures have been collected.

By mid-September, the Federal Reserve and the U.S. Treasury were preparing broad new rules to force banks to rein in practices that made multimillionaires. Under the proposal, banks would have wide leeway in how they structure their rewards, and it would not prohibit million-dollar pay packages or address issues of fairness. The Fed program would affect roughly 5,000 bank holding companies as well as state-chartered banks.

See also G-20; OVERTIME; PAY CZAR; TARP.

PAY CZAR. Kenneth Feinberg, who oversaw the federal government's compensation fund for victims of September 11, 2001, was appointed to serve as the pay czar for the Treasury Department. Feinberg will focus on pay restrictions related to firms receiving TARP bailout funds, aiding firms in interpreting the rules and ensuring that they are being followed. The pay czar will review, reject, and even set pay levels, with no appeal.

By October 2009, Feinberg was planning to clamp down on compensation at firms receiving significant sums of government stimulus funding by reducing annual cash salaries for many of the top employees, expected to be 175 people at the firms he oversees. He wants to shift a portion of an employee's annual salary into stock that cannot be touched for several years, thus reducing take-home pay.

Kenneth Feinberg oversees seven firms that accepted bailout packages. American International Group, Citigroup, Bank of America, General Motors, GMAC Financial Services, Chrysler Group, and Chrysler Financial. The Treasury Department gave him responsibility of tying more compensation at these firms to long-term performance and cutting pay deemed "excessive." By the end of October 2009, Feinberg cut total compensations by half, and at the same time increased regular salaries. According to some legal experts, one of the lingering issues is the constitutionality of having Feinberg make these decisions, as he was never properly appointed an officer of the United States.

The U.S. Treasury Department's pay czar plans to cap salaries of top employees under his jurisdiction. He also plans to expand the $500,000 salary cap.

PAY FOR SUCCESS. *See* HOUSING BAILOUT PLAN.

PAYROLLS. *See* PRIVATE-SECTOR PAYROLLS.

PAYROLL TAX CUTS. By the end of February 2009, the Treasury Department had begun to direct its employees to lower taxes withheld from the paychecks of workers, effective April 1; this increased take-home pay for an average family by at least $65 a month.

See also AMERICAN RECOVERY AND REINVESTMENT ACT (OF 2009).

PC MARKET. *See* DELL INC.; INTERNATIONAL BUSINESS MACHINES CORPORATION; PERSONAL COMPUTERS.

PECORA COMMISSION. The Pecora inquiry began on March 4, 1932, by the U.S. Senate Committee on Banking and Currency. These Depression-era hearings sought to expose banking practices deemed "detrimental to the public welfare" and to reveal "unsavory and unethical methods" used in the sale of securities. Ferdinand Pecora served as chief counsel. The hearings ended on May 4, 1934, after which Pecora was appointed as one of the first commissioners of the SEC.

Pecora was a Sicilian immigrant and a former assistant district attorney for New York County before President Herbert Hoover appointed him in 1929 to the Senate Committee. During the hearings he met with President Roosevelt and was instrumental in helping the president enact sweeping changes to the law. Pecora's fame spread during the hearings, and he had his photograph on the cover of *Time* magazine in May 1933, with an accompanying article "Wealth on Trial."

The Pecora Commission was intended to lay the foundation for remedial legislation. The investigation uncovered a wide range of abusive practices on the part of banks and bank affiliates. During the inquiry, J. P. Morgan stated that he had not paid personal income taxes in 1930, 1931, and 1932. Several National City Bank executives cushioned their stock losses by tapping interest-free loans from a special bank fund; others made millions selling short bank shares.

While the investigation proceeded, Congress enacted the Glass-Steagall Banking Act of 1933, the Banking Act of 1933, the Securities Act of 1933, and the Securities Exchange Act of 1934.

Pecora ended his autobiography with "Laws aren't a panacea and they're not self-executing."

Cf. FINANCIAL CRISIS INQUIRY COMMISSION; GREAT DEPRESSION (OF THE 1930S).

PEE-PIPS. *See* PUBLIC-PRIVATE INVESTMENT FUND.

PELL GRANTS. *See* AMERICAN RECOVERY AND REINVESTMENT ACT (OF 2009); BUDGET (U.S.); STUDENT LOANS.

PELOSI, NANCY. U.S. House of Representatives Speaker, she differed from Barack Obama on at least two issues—tax increases and investigating the Bush administration. After Obama's inauguration, the speaker wanted Congress to consider repealing President Bush's tax cuts for those who make more than $250,000 well before they expired at the end of 2010. The president had promised to repeal the tax cuts but then backed off that pledge, signaling that he would be willing to simply let them expire in 2010.

See also OBAMA, BARACK.

PEMEX. *See* MEXICO.

PENSION BENEFIT GUARANTY CORPORATION. *See* DELPHI.

PENSION FUNDS. The meltdown of 2008 significantly impacted pension funds. By October 2008, total assets had dropped by nearly 20 percent since the beginning of 2008. In the United States, these funds accounted for two-thirds of the $3.3 trillion in losses.

In OECD countries, pension funds lost over 20 percent of their values during the Great Recession.

PERSIAN GULF. *See* KUWAIT.

PERSONAL BANKRUPTCY. *See* BANKRUPTCY FILINGS.

PERSONAL COMPUTERS. Worldwide shipment of personal computers dropped 4.5 percent in 2009, as the economy continued to deteriorate. Shipments in the fourth quarter of 2008 fell 1.9 percent and during the first half of the year declined by more than 8 percent.

PEUGEOT-CITROEN. On June 23, 2009, the French carmaker announced that it would lose as much as $2.75 billion in 2009.

Peugeot-Citroen announced at the end of July 2009 that its sales plunged into the red in the first half of the year with a net loss of €962 million, down from net profit of €733 million a year before.

See also FRANCE.

PFIZER. The world's largest drug organization announced it was laying off up to 800 scientists in 2009, reducing its global research staff of about 10,000 by 5 to 8 percent. The company also announced that it planned to lay off nearly a third of its 8,000 salespeople.

Sales, reported on July 22, were $2.26 billion for the second quarter, down from $2.78 billion. Revenue declined 9.4 percent to $10.98 billion. Pfizer's second-quarter profit dropped 19 percent.

Pfizer's third-quarter 2009 profit rose 26 percent despite a drop in sales, with revenue falling 2.9 percent to $11.62 billion. Pfizer planned to eliminate a total of 19,500 jobs.

By mid-December 2009, Pfizer raised its quarterly dividend 13 percent.

PHILIPPINES, THE. The Philippines' economy contracted in the first quarter 2009, for the first time since 2001. GDP shrank a seasonally adjusted 2.3 percent in the first quarter from the fourth quarter 2008.

See also SOUTHEAST ASIA.

PHILLIPS-VAN HEUSEN. Announced in January 2009 that it would cut jobs and close 175 stores over the coming two to three years. It planned to cut 250 salaried positions and about 150 hourly neckwear-manufacturing positions.

See also RETAILING.

PHISHING. *See* IDENTITY THEFT.

"PILLARS" OF RECOVERY. *See* OBAMA, BARACK.

PLAIN-VANILLA FINANCING. Mortgages and credit cards with simple standard terms.

PLEDGED-ACCOUNT MORTGAGE. A variation on graduated-payment mortgages, where a portion of the borrower's down payment is used to fund a pledged savings account, which is drawn on to supplement the monthly payment during the first years of the loan. The net effect to the borrower is lower payments at first. Payments gradually rise, slightly above those on conventional mortgages.

See also GRADUATED-PAYMENT MORTGAGE.

POLAND. The European Central Bank opened in November 2008 a €10 billion credit line to Poland, which saw its currency fall sharply at the beginning of the month.

On November 30, the government of Poland was prepared to spend about $31 billion to help the country weather the global economic crisis. It also lowered its 2009 economic forecast to 3.7 percent growth from 4.8 percent. For the month of November, unemployment increased to 9.1 percent, rising 0.3 percentage point from October, the first increase after five years of steady declines. Poland's jobless rate previously peaked at 20.7 percent in February 2003.

The IMF set up a $20.5 billion credit line with Poland in April 2009. The zloty had fallen by 30 percent since its peak; the central bank reduced interest rates from 6 percent in October 2008 to 3.75 percent in April 2009.

The government of Poland projected a 2010 budget with a growing deficit and heavy borrowing. Its treasury needs to raise $12.8 billion by the year's end through the sale of state-owned assets. Poland avoided formal recession, with a GDP increase of 0.8 percent in the first quarter from a year before, and 1.1 percent in the second quarter.

See also EUROPEAN BANK FOR RECONSTRUCTION AND DEVELOPMENT.

POLO RALPH LAUREN. Net income fell 6.6 percent for its fiscal third quarter 2008 on slumping sales and margins. For the period ending December 31, the company posted net income of $105.3 million, with retail sales declining 71 percent.

Profits in August fell 19 percent in its fiscal first quarter 2009. Sales fell 9 percent in the quarter.

See also RETAILING.

POOR, THE. *See* FOOD STAMPS; POVERTY; WEALTH.

PORSCHE. Porsche and Volkswagen agreed on May 3, 2009, to merge corporations, uniting ten auto brands, including Porsche's sports cars, into a single company. At that point, Porsche had already owned a 51 percent stake in VW.

On May 17, Porsche indefinitely postponed talks with VW. Almost as suddenly, a few days later VW and Porsche agreed to continue discussions toward a potential merger.

By mid-June, Porsche announced that its vehicle sales had fallen nearly 30 percent in the first nine months of its fiscal year. From August 2008 to April 2009, Porsche sold 53,635 cars, down 28 percent from the year before. Revenue fell 15 percent to $6.44 billion.

Porsche's request for a $2.5 billion loan from a state-controlled German bank was rejected. The carmaker continues to seek an "alternative financing possibility," which may include an investment from Qatar. Porsche garnered nearly $13 billion in debt when it accumulated a stake in Volkswagen.

On December 18, 2009, Porsche report that revenue fell 31 percent in its fiscal first quarter. Revenue was $1.6 billion and sales fell 40 percent from a year before to 11,385 cars in the three months ending October 31.

See also AUTOMOBILE INDUSTRY; VOLKSWAGEN.

PORTUGAL. Unemployment in Portugal in the second quarter 2009 was 9.2 percent and the economy shrank by 3.7 percent in 2009.

POUND (BRITISH). In July 2008 the British pound was trading around $2 against the U.S. dollar, and dropped to around $1.80 by September and $1.55 on October 27. It fell in late October 2008 to a five-year low against the dollar. Most specialists argued that the sterling had been overvalued at $2.

The pound tumbled on January 21, 2009, to a 23-year low against the U.S. dollar.

See also DOLLAR (U.S.).

POVERTY. In 2005, just over a quarter of the world's population, or 1.4 billion people, were living in extreme poverty, according to the World Bank. That compares with 42 percent in 1990. In China, the share of people below the threshold of $1.25 a day fell from 60.2 percent to 15.9 percent between 1990 and 2005. But the poverty rate fell much more slowly in India, to 41.6 percent in 2005 from 51.3 percent in 1990. South Asia has the most very poor people of any region in the world. But the fraction of the population that lives in extreme poverty is highest, at 50.9 percent in sub-Saharan Africa, though it has fallen there from 57.6 percent in 1990.

In 2009, the UN calculated that the 500 richest people in the world earned more than the 416 million poorest people. As many as 222 million workers run the risk of joining the ranks of the working poor, earning less than $1.25 a day. In addition, remittance flows, which reached $328 billion in 2008, dropped by 7.3 percent in 2009. In the United States the poverty rate rose to 13.2 percent in 2008, the highest level since 1997, and a significant increase from 12.5 percent in 2007, suggesting that some 40 million U.S. citizens are living below the poverty line, defined as an income of $22,205 for a family of four. Median household income fell in 2008 to $50,300 from $52,200 in 2007, the steepest year-to-year declines in forty years.

The recession's impact on low-income families brought more children into poverty as family incomes shrank. On September 29, 2009, the government reported an increase in poverty across the United States, especially among children. The percentage of children living in poverty increased in twenty-six states, compared with seventeen states in 2007. The highest concentration of poor was in Southern states, with 21.2 percent poverty rates in Mississippi, while Kentucky, West Virginia, and Arkansas each had a poverty rate about 17 percent.

See also FOOD AID; FOOD STAMPS; LIVING STANDARDS.

PPIP. *See* PUBLIC-PRIVATE INVESTMENT FUND.

PPP. *See* PURCHASING-POWER PARITY.

PRATT & WHITNEY. *See* UNITED TECHNOLOGIES.

PREFORCLOSURE SALE. *Synonymous with* REAL ESTATE OWNED.

PREP SCHOOLS. Along with most institutions of education, prep schools also faced significant losses in their endowments, resulting in large cutbacks in student aid.

Some endowments fell 20–21 percent during the meltdown at many independent private schools.

See also EDUCATION.

PRESIDENTIAL TASK FORCE ON AUTOS. Overseeing the reorganization of General Motors and Chrysler.

See also AUTO TASK FORCE.

PRINCETON UNIVERSITY. One of the nation's wealthiest colleges reported on September 29, 2009, that its endowment shrank 23 percent over the past year, losing $3.7 billion.

Cf. HARVARD UNIVERSITY; STANFORD UNIVERSITY; YALE UNIVERSITY.

PRIVATE-EQUITY FIRMS. By 2009 private-equity companies saw declines of 15 percent to 50 percent amid the deep economic recession.
See also BUYOUT FIRMS.

PRIVATE-EQUITY FUNDS. *See* FINANCIAL REGULATION PLAN (2009).

PRIVATE-SECTOR PAYROLLS. Fell in February 2009 in almost 80 percent of the followed 271 major industries. One year before, payrolls were shrinking in only 45 percent of industries.
See also SPENDING.

PROCTER & GAMBLE. The world's largest consumer-goods firm, it reported in August 2009 that its profit of $2.5 billion was down 18 percent; sales of its paper towels and detergents were down 11 percent.

On October 29, 2009, the company reported the quarter ending September 30 had a profit of $3.31 billion, down from $3.35 billion a year earlier, with sales falling 6 percent to $19.81 billion.
Cf. COLGATE-PALMOLIVE CO.

PRODUCTIVITY. Output per hour, jumped in fourth quarter 2008, rising at a 3.2 percent seasonally adjusted annual rate.

American worker productivity grew in the second quarter 2009 at the fastest rate in almost six years, as employers slashed payrolls to bolster profits. Productivity rose at an annual rate of 6.4 percent.

Productivity surged in the third quarter 2009 as the economy resumed growing. When taken together with the second quarter's 6.9 percent rise, it was the strongest productivity growth rate over a six-month period since 1961.

November's production figures rose 0.8 percent, the largest increase since August, outpacing expectations.
Synonymous with OUTPUT PER HOUR.

PROFITS. Corporate profits posted their third consecutive gain in the third quarter 2009 as the U.S. economy grew by 2.8 percent. But the 10.6 percent annualized gain over the second quarter to a seasonally adjusted $1.3 trillion came at the expense of employees.

PROMOTE AMERICA'S COMPETITIVE EDGE (PACE). A coalition of business associations and corporations founded in the spring 2009 to confront the government's advancing new rules on the conduct of business.

Specifically, this not-for-profit organization confronts President Obama's program to curb corporations' ability to park their overseas business earnings indefinitely outside the United States and avoid U.S. taxes, a practice known as deferral.

In addition, PACE looks to confront the government's plan to right an imbalance created by U.S. tax policy between multinationals and the small businesses that generate the bulk of American jobs but generally don't qualify for these tax breaks.

PROPERTY TAXES. *See* FORECLOSURE.

PROTECTIONISM. The imposition of high tariffs and quotas on imports that are presumed to compete with domestic items, with the objective of giving the domestic manufacturer an advantage.

Advancing protectionism threatened the global economy in concert with the current recession. Following the Group of 20's meeting in mid-November 2008, when the signers to the meeting said they would not create barriers to trade, several countries turned around and raised tariffs to protect domestic industries.

The belief appears to be that this style of protectionism, reminiscent of the Smoot-Hawley Act of the 1930s, would be an antidote to the current recession. The Smoot-Hawley Act raised duties on more than 20,000 items imported into the United States. The result was that U.S. international trade declined by 42 percent, while world trade fell 60 percent, measured in dollars. Needless to say, it was a disaster.

An often unnoticed part of the stimulus package is one provision that discourages federal bailout companies from hiring skilled foreign workers.

By 2009, in response to the economic meltdown, nations around the globe were involved in more trade disputes, and were pondering protectionist policies in response to the deepest global downturn since World War II. In fact, in early March, seventeen members of the Group of 20 had adopted forty-seven measures aimed at restricting cross-border trade.

See also BUY AMERICAN; BUY LOCAL; FINANCIAL PROTECTIONISM; GENERAL AGREEMENT ON TARIFFS AND TRADE; GLOBAL UNEMPLOYMENT; MEXICO; SMOOT-HAWLEY ACT OF 1930; WORLD TRADE ORGANIZATION.

PROTESTORS. *See* G-20.

PUBLIC COMPANY ACCOUNTING OVERSIGHT BOARD. *See* SARBANES-OXLEY ACT OF 2002.

PUBLIC DEBT (U.S.). *See* CHINA; DEBT, FEDERAL (U.S.).

PUBLIC-PRIVATE INVESTMENT FUND. The Treasury secretary on February 10, 2009, called for an investment fund to "provide government capital and government financing to help leverage private capital to help get private markets working again." With this fund, the government was trying to help private investors to buy toxic bank assets.

The U.S. Treasury's public-private effort to rid banks of toxic assets, building on existing financial rescue plans included:

a. Stress tests for major banks, with new capital requirements for those in need of it.
b. A Treasury/Fed program to spur auto, credit card, and other consumer lending.
c. Government purchasing of securities backed by Small Business Administration loans to encourage lending.
d. A mortgage-loan modification plan to reduce foreclosures.

The Public-Private Investment Program (PPIP) aimed to spur purchases of soured loans and real estate–related securities. The two-part plan would use up to $100 billion of bank-rescue funds from the Treasury, as well as financial guarantees from the Fed and Federal Deposit Insurance Corporation. Funds would be established to purchase and manage mortgage securities, and the government would provide financing to private investors to purchase the loans.

TALF (Term Asset-Backed Securities Loan Facility), which presently sought to jump-start the market for newly issued securities by a range of consumer and small-business loans, would also be expanded. The expansion extended TALF to existing securities, not only new ones. "PEE-pips" is the insider's name for public-private investment partnerships.

The Legacy Loans Program purported to clear bank balance sheets of distressed loans. A bank holding a mortgage loan with face value of $100 informs the FDIC that it wants to rid itself of the loan and faces the following steps:

a. The bank will take a loss on a portion of the original value.
b. FDIC will decide how much it is willing to guarantee in financing for a purchaser. The amount of financing could be more than half the loan's face value.
c. The highest bidder at auction purchases the loan and pays for half the equity position. This private owner services the loan using asset managers approved by the FDIC.
d. Treasury finances the other half of the equity.

Under the Legacy Securities Program, one of the aims is to set prices for hard-to-value securities backed by commercial and residential mortgages. Up to five managers will assist the government manage pools of assets that will be created by the plan:

   a. Asset managers raise private funds and present a plan to purchase eligible securities from banks and financial firms.
   b. Treasury approves plans and matches the amount raised privately.
   c. Treasury provides a loan of 100–200 percent of the private financing, turning that $100 into a potentially $400 fund. Banks can accept or reject bids for their securities.

By mid-October 2009, five investment funds that raised $1.94 billion in private capital to purchase troubled assets began buying. With the PPIP program, the Treasury pledges to match the funds raised by approved money-management firms. It would also provide leverage, or loans to the fund, equal to the full amount of the fund, doubling its spending power.

See also BAILOUT RESCUE PLAN (OF 2009) (U.S.); HEDGE FUNDS; STRESS TESTS; TOXIC ASSETS.

PUBLIC-PRIVATE INVESTMENT PROGRAM (PPIP). *See* PUBLIC-PRIVATE INVESTMENT FUND.

PUBLIC WORKS. Upon being sworn in on January 20, 2009, President Obama urged the spending of $500 billion to $700 billion over two years to help pull the country out of its economic downslide. His plan included funds for infrastructure rebuilding around the nation, including rebuilding new hospitals and schools, with more to come.

PUERTO RICO. At the beginning of January 2009, the governor of Puerto Rico declared a fiscal emergency, forecasting a towering deficit of $3.2 billion. "The present deficit is the greatest, in percentage terms, of all the U.S. states."

More than 30,000 government workers, about 14 percent of the public workforce in Puerto Rico, would be fired, according to a March 2009 report.

See also LATIN AMERICA.

PULTE. One of the two largest home builders in the United States, it reported in August 2009 that its second-quarter loss widened to $189.5 million. Revenue dropped 58 percent to $678.6 million. New orders fell 34 percent to 3,367 homes.

Cf. D.R. HORTON.

PURCHASING-POWER PARITY (PPP). The concept that in the long run, exchange rates should equalize prices across nations.

Q

QATAR. Qatari shares soared on March 9, 2009, after the government said it would purchase investment funds from banks to help shield the financial system from the global credit crisis.

See also BARCLAYS; MIDDLE EAST; PORSCHE.

QUANTAS AIRWAYS. Australia's largest airline, it posted a 66 percent decline in profit for the fiscal first half of 2008. Its net profit for the first half fell to AZ$210 million from AZ$617.7 million a year earlier.

Management forecast in April 2009 that it would need to cut as many as 1,750 jobs as it extended efforts to reduce costs.

Quantas said its fiscal-year net profit fell 88 percent to $96.2 million as revenue continued to slide.

On December 21, 2009, the airline management reported that it expected to return to profitability shortly as passenger listings increased.

QUANTITATIVE ANALYSTS. People employing mathematical models in quantitative financing.

See also LONG-TERM CAPITAL MANAGEMENT.

Synonymous with QUANTS.

QUANTITATIVE EASING. Incorporates various measures for pumping money into the economy. It is considered an unconventional monetary policy because its effect is felt through the quantity rather than the costs of credit. The newly printed money is used to buy assets.

See also FEDERAL RESERVE (U.S.).

QUANTS. *Synonymous with* QUANTITATIVE ANALYSTS.

R

RACE TO THE TOP PROGRAM. The federal government's attempt to overhaul school systems with stimulus funding of $4.35 billion in education grants serving as an incentive. Under this program, states will be rewarded for promoting one of the federal government's top aims—the adoption of common educational standards and testing assessments. Under a point system the government intends to reward states that band together in adopting the same testing standards.

RADIOSHACK. The electronics retailer's profits dropped 39 percent in its fourth-quarter earnings for 2008, as reported on February 24, 2009. In the fourth quarter 2008, sales at stores open at least one year dropped 9.2 percent compared with a year earlier. Profits dropped $62 million, from $101 million a year before.

Third-quarter 2009 earnings fell 24 percent. The company reported a profit of $37.4 million, compared with $491 million a year earlier. Revenue fell 3.1 percent to $990 million as same-store sales fell 2.9 percent.

RAIL INVESTMENTS. *See* AMERICAN RECOVERY AND REINVESTMENT ACT (OF 2009).

RAIL HAULERS. *See* FREIGHT HAULERS.

RAIL SERVICE. On April 16, 2009, it was announced by the government that it planned to spend $8 billion in stimulus funds on high-speed passenger-rail service.

RAT BOARD. Charged with sniffing out waste, fraud, and abuse in the $787 billion stimulus plan.

Synonymous with RECOVERY ACCOUNTABILITY AND TRANSPARENCY BOARD.

RATERS. The SEC was given authority over credit-rating firms in 2006, then named ten of them as "nationally recognized." On August 28, 2009, the SEC indicated serious concerns about one firm. Some rating firms have been accused of exacerbating the meltdown in giving overly positive ratings to certain types of debt, including some backed by subprime mortgages.

See also SECURITIES AND EXCHANGE COMMISSION.

RATTNER, STEVEN. President Obama's top auto industry troubleshooter; one of fourteen people on a committee that was charged with orchestrating the rescue of the giant U.S. automakers.

Rattner, the chief architect of the GM and Chrysler bailouts, left the administration after less than six months on the job, just days after completion of the GM return from bankruptcy

See also AUTO TASK FORCE; CHRYSLER; GENERAL MOTORS.

RAW MATERIALS. *See* RIO TINTO.

RBS. *See* ROYAL BANK OF SCOTLAND.

READER'S DIGEST. Announced on January 29, 2009, that it would lay off close to 300 people, about 8 percent of its workforce, putting employees on unpaid furloughs and suspending contributions to their 401(k) plans. On August 17, *Reader's Digest* announced that it would seek bankruptcy protection to restructure $2.2 billion in debt.

"READY TO GO" PROJECTS. Under the Economic Stimulus Plan, funds would flow quickest to identifiable projects that could start within a couple of months.

Cf. "SHOVEL READY."

REAL ESTATE. *See* COMMERCIAL REAL ESTATE; COMMERCIAL REAL ESTATE LOANS; FARM REAL ESTATE.

REAL ESTATE OWNED. *See* REO.

REBATES. *See* AMERICAN RECOVERY AND REINVESTMENT ACT (OF 2009).

RECESSION. The International Monetary Fund (IMF) defines a global recession as growth below 3 percent, because that is far too weak to keep up with the demands of a growing population in emerging markets for jobs. The National Bureau of Economic Research defines recession as "a significant decline in economic activity spread across the economy, lasting more than a few months."

Likewise, recovery from a recession can take many shapes. Some of them are:

1. A V-shaped recession. Cases when the economy snaps back as quickly and steeply as it fell. Few economists are predicting a V-shape now, since consumers and job seekers are still facing difficulties.
2. A W-shaped recession. Downturns that become upturns but then revert to downturns again. Some economists fear that this type of recession may be ahead of the nation.

Synonymous with DOUBLE-DIP RECESSION; ROLLER-COASTER RECESSION; SECOND-LEG-DOWN RECESSION.

3. An L-shaped recession. Probably the most worrisome of all. It suggests that once the economy plunges, it stays down for a long period. Because the current meltdown was triggered by an asset bubble, this form of recession is likely.

   Synonymous with HOCKEY STICK RECESSION.

4. A U-shaped recession. Somewhere between a V- and an L-shape recession. Describes a long, tedious recession with a bottom that is difficult to determine. Some economists believe this could now happen if the economy stagnates.

RECESSION OF 1972. Several months of a stagnant labor market were followed by a violent contraction over the next year. After the worst month, December 1974, the job market turned around.

Cf. RECESSION OF 1982; RECESSION OF 2007–2010.

RECESSION OF 1982. Employment suffered a major contraction in December 1981 and January 1982, and workers did not see a stable market for about ten months, including another big round of layoffs in July 1982. The first big blow to the economy was the 1979 revolution in Iran, which sent oil prices skyrocketing. The larger blow was a series of sharp interest-rate increases by the Federal Reserve, meant to snap inflation. Home sales plummeted. At their worst, they were 30 percent lower than in 2008. Nationwide, the unemployment rate rose above 10 percent in 1982.

See also RECESSION; UNDEREMPLOYED; UNEMPLOYMENT.

Cf. RECESSION OF 1972; RECESSION OF 2008.

RECESSION OF 2001. *See* RECESSION OF 2007–2010.

RECESSION OF 2007–2010. The U.S. economy went into a recession in December 2007, although it wasn't announced by the National Bureau of Economic Research until December 2008. This was the first recession in the United States since 2001, when the economy suffered after the bursting of the technology bubble and the economic repercussions of the 9/11 attacks on the World Trade Center. The period of expansion lasted seventy-three months, from November 2001 to December 2007. The 2008–2009 meltdown was the worst since 1982. Unofficially, the Great Recession ended on October 29, 2009, awaiting an official statement from the National Bureau of Economic Research for an official declaration.

Evidence of a downturn had been widespread for months with slower production, stagnant wages, and hundreds of thousands of lost jobs.

The current recession had become the second-worst in the last half century and was close to surpassing the severe 1973–1975 downturn. The Conference Board's March figures indicated a decline of 5.6 percent from the high set in November 2007. The drop in the 1970s recession was 6 percent.

In April 2009, the U.S. recession became the longest since the Great Depression. It marked the seventeenth month of the recession beginning in December 2007.

On July 15, a commission was created to examine the causes of the financial crisis. The panel was to issue its report no later than the end of 2010.

On July 31, the Commerce Department announced that the current recession turned out to be worse than previously thought, while the 2001 recession was milder than earlier reported. Revisions indicated that from the fourth quarter of 2007 to the first quarter 2009, inflation-adjusted GDP fell at a 2.8 percent annual rate, compared with the 1.8 percent drop earlier reported. The decline continued in 2009's second quarter, producing the worst recession since World War II.

A comparison of the recessions for the past eighty years indicates:

2007–2009: duration eighteen months; decline in real GDP 3.8 percent; decline in industrial production 16.9 percent; unemployment of 9.5 percent.

1937–1938: duration thirteen months; 18.2 percent decline in real GDP; decline in industrial production 32.4 percent; unemployment of 20.0 percent

1973–1975: duration sixteen months; 4.9 percent decline in real GDP; decline in industrial production 15.3 percent; unemployment 9.0 percent.

1981–1982: duration sixteen months; 3.0 percent decline in real GDP; decline in industrial production 12.3 percent; unemployment 10.8 percent.

By the end of September 2009, most economists believed that statistically the Great Recession had come to an end. Then, on October 29, 2009, the government announced that the country's GDP had grown at an annual rate of 3.5 percent in the quarter ending in September, matching its average growth rate of the last eighty years. Unofficially, the United States had emerged from the longest economic contraction since World War II. The stock market reacted favorably, as the people remained gloomy over a projected sluggish growth and the near 10 percent workforce unemployment. (After the 2001 recession, output rose for six quarters before the economy added jobs.)

See also ACCOUNTANTS; CONFERENCE BOARD; ECONOMY (U.S.); FEDERAL RESERVE; FINANCIAL CRISIS INQUIRY COMMISSION; NATIONAL BUREAU OF ECONOMIC RESEARCH.

Cf. GREAT DEPRESSION (OF THE 1930S); RECESSION OF 1972; RECESSION OF 1982.

Synonymous with GREAT RECESSION.

RECONSTRUCTION FINANCE CORPORATION (RFC). Former U.S. government agency, created in 1932 by the administration of Herbert Hoover. Its purpose was to facilitate economic activity by lending money during the depression. At first it lent money only to financial, industrial, and agricultural institutions, but the scope was widened during President Roosevelt's administration.

It financed the construction and operation of war plants, made loans to foreign governments, provided protection against war and disaster damages, and other activities.

In 1939 RFC merged with other agencies, forming the Federal Loan Agency. The Federal Loan Agency was abolished in 1947, and RFC was abolished as an independent agency by act of Congress in 1953 and was transferred to the Department of the Treasury to wind up its affairs, effective June 1954. It was totally disbanded in 1957, after having made loans of approximately $50 billion since its creation.

See also HOOVER, HERBERT.

RECOVERY. Recovery from the 2008–2009 recession is expected to take years. The evidence was abundant. From the 2001 recession to the present, the economy advanced at an average annual rate of 2.5 percent. That would amount to roughly $350 billion a year, demanding three years to restore the $1 trillion in lost capacity.

The stimulus package of $787 billion is to be consumed in two years. Therefore, should every dollar of spending restore a dollar of output, more than three years would be needed before output approached the level achieved just before the start of the recession in December 2007.

Examining 122 recessions in rich economies since 1960, the IMF found that in the aftermath of a financial bust, private investment tends to fall even after the downturn approaches stability, whereas private consumption grows more slowly than in other recoveries. Recoveries from global recessions take 50 percent longer than other recoveries.

The initial step to recovery is for output to stop shrinking. Then one of three types of recovery may occur—V, U, or W. A V-shaped recovery is strong and vigorous, with significant demand released. A U-shaped recovery is flatter and tends to be weaker. A W-shaped recovery has a return of growth for a few quarters, only to return to another slump.

RECOVERY ACCOUNTABILITY AND TRANSPARENCY BOARD. *See* FRAUD.

Synonymous with RAT BOARD.

RECOVERY ACT. *Synonymous with* AMERICAN RECOVERY AND REINVESTMENT ACT (OF 2009).

REDCORP VENTURES. A Canadian gold and silver mining firm, it filed for bankruptcy in March 2009, in the United States and Canada, citing cost overruns and a lack of financing.

REFINANCE. *Synonymous with* DEBT PAYBACK.

REFINANCING MORTGAGES. Six of ten homeowners at the end of December 2009 with mortgages had rates that exceed the 4.8 percent rate currently available on 30-year fixed mortgages. However, only half as many refinancing applications were reported in the month than were reported in January 2009. The total volume of refinancing activity in 2009 was about $1 trillion. In 2003, it was $2.8 trillion. Mortgage rates are at their lowest since the end of World War II, but banks continue to balk at refinancing, and the shortage of credit continues to slow the nation's economic recovery.

See also HOUSE (U.S.) FINANCIAL OVERHAUL PLAN; HOUSING BAILOUT PLAN.

REFINERS. On February 11, 2009, U.S. gasoline refiners announced that they would cut production to the lowest level since 2003 as higher prices and fears of recession decreased demand.

See also OIL.

REFLATION. The expectation that the world economy will rebound, driving up interest rates and commodities prices.

Cf. DEFLATION; INFLATION; STAGFLATION.

REGIONAL BANKS. *See* STANDARD & POOR'S; STRESS TEST.

REGULATION. Under President Obama's proposed 2010 budget, enforcement was high on his agenda. Closer government scrutiny was called for, and specially allocated funds were to be available to hire regulators to discharge responsibilities of transparency, accountability, and fulfilling the laws of the nation. For example:

a. Department of Agriculture—$26 billion to improve food-safety monitoring and nutrition education and promotion.
b. Army Corps of Engineers—Management reforms to lower project costs, improve accountability, and maximize returns on waterway projects.
c. Internal Revenue Service—About $890 million to fight fraud and improve enforcement, resulting in "a $5 return for every $1 spent."
d. Department of Defense—Money to monitor military contracting through improved reporting and scrutiny of no-bid contracts.

e. SEC—Budget increase of more than 13 percent for "risk-based, efficient regulatory structure that will better detect fraud and strengthen markets."
f. CFTC—A 44 percent increase in part for "filling gaps in regulatory oversight of energy and over-the-counter derivative trading," as well as foreign exchange.

By the end of August 2009, new financial and banking regulations were few. Changes that were adopted are:

a. Credit cards—Legislation passed requires card companies to inform consumers before raising rates, limits credit card fees, and restricts card ownership among people under 21. Few changes have resulted.
b. Short selling—Legislation prohibits "naked" short selling, that is, selling shares of stock without borrowing them first, and requiring short-selling trades to be reported daily. The SEC instituted a temporary ban in April 2009, made permanent in July 2009.

See also ACCOUNTABILITY; REGULATORS; TRANSPARENCY.

REGULATORS. Regulators in 2009 were to play an increasing role in the future of the banking industry. The Financial Stability Forum (FSF) brought together central banks, financial regulators, and treasuries from the big Western economies. They were charged with and have successfully closed loopholes that banks previously took advantage of. The issue of violations and enforcement was left to other global agencies.

The primary financial regulators in the federal government are:

a. Securities and Exchange Commission—regulates financial markets, sets disclosure rules, and oversees accounting rules for corporations that trade on U.S. exchanges.
b. Federal Reserve—the central banking entity, which oversees monetary policy, bank-holding companies, and some state-chartered banks.
c. Federal Deposit Insurance Corporation—insures bank deposits at more than 8,000 banks nationwide. It also supervises most state-chartered banks.
d. Office of the Comptroller of the Currency—division of the Treasury Department that oversees and charters all national banks.
e. Office of Thrift Supervision—division of the Treasury Department that regulates and oversees federal thrifts and thrift-holding companies.

f. Commodity Futures Trading Commission—oversees commodity futures and options markets in the United States.
g. Federal Housing Finance Agency—oversees Fannie Mae, Freddie Mac, and the twelve Federal Home Loan Banks.
h. National Credit Union Administration—charters and supervises federal credit unions.

See also BANK BUYOUTS; CONSUMER FINANCIAL PROTECTION AGENCY; DODD, CHRISTOPHER J.; FINANCIAL REGULATION PLAN (2009); HOUSE (U.S.) FINANCIAL OVERHAUL PLAN; NATIONAL BANK SUPERVISOR; REGULATION; SECURITIES AND EXCHANGE COMMISSION; STRESS TESTS.

RELOCATING. *See* MOBILITY.

REMITTANCES. Funds sent back to one's native country from another nation where there is employment. The U.S. government started tracking cross-border flows of money from migrants after the September 11, 2001, terrorist attacks. The World Bank estimates that foreign workers sent $328 billion from developed and richer nations to poor and developing ones in 2008. For example, $52 billion was sent by Indian foreign workers back to India.

Since the meltdown in 2008, remittances to Latin America, and primarily to Mexico, fell by 4.2 percent between January and August 2008 compared with the same period in 2007. In the poor, rural communities, remittances from migrant workers would often account for 12 or more percent of local income.

Migrant workers, initially lured by the building boom and other opportunities for work, were losing jobs and were struggling to send cash home.

The amount of money that Mexicans working in the United States sent back home dropped 3.6 percent in 2008, as the rising U.S. jobless rate took a toll on immigrants. It was the first decline in remittances recorded since Mexico began tracking money flows from abroad thirteen years ago. The drop to $25 billion from $26 billion was twice what the government forecast.

Migrant workers in the United States sent home a record $69.2 billion in 2008, nearly 1 percent more than in 2007. That would change during the meltdown. Mexico had a 12 percent drop in remittances in January 2008; Colombia suffered a 16 percent decline, Brazil saw a 14 percent drop, and Ecuador, the hardest hit, had a drop of 22 percent on remittances in the fourth quarter of 2008.

By mid-2009, remittances by Mexicans had fallen 8.7 percent over the first four months in 2008. Migrants sent $1.8 billion in April 2009, 18.7 percent less than in April 2008.

By the end of the summer 2009, remittances to Mexico fell by 11 percent, to $62 billion in 2009 from $69 billion in 2008. This was the first decline in global remittances to the region since records were kept. While remittances reached $328 billion in 2008, they fell by 7.3 percent in 2009.

By the fall 2009 unemployment among Mexicans in the United States was sharply increasing. Therefore, a strong reverse remittance concept is developing, sending funds to members of families in the United States.

See also ARMENIA; IMMIGRATION; MEXICO; SOUTHEAST ASIA.

RENAULT. The French carmaker's first-quarter 2009 revenue slid 31 percent from a year earlier to $9.3 billion, with unit sales declining 22 percent.

See also AUTOMOBILE INDUSTRY; FRANCE.

RENEGOTIABLE-RATE MORTGAGE. Authorized by the Federal Home Loan Bank Board; requires home buyers to renegotiate the terms of the loan every three to five years, a distinct advantage if interest rates drop, but a poor hedge against inflation if they go up.

See also FLEXIBLE-PAYMENT MORTGAGE; VARIABLE-RATE MORTGAGE.

RENEGOTIATING MORTGAGES. *See* HOUSING BAILOUT PLAN.

RENEWABLE ENERGY SOURCES. *See* ENERGY EFFICIENCY.

RENTAL CARS. *See* AVIS; ENTERPRISE; HERTZ.

RENTERS. *See* APARTMENT VACANCIES.

REO (REAL ESTATE OWNED). Distressed or foreclosed properties purchased through a preclosure sale. With the REO, the bank typically clears any title issues before it puts the house on the market. Most REOs are sold as is, so buyers should make their offers contingent on a home inspection and buyers who pay in cash do best. Often all short sales, where homeowners, under pressure, sell a property for less than their mortgage.

See also FORECLOSURE; SHORT SALES.

Synonymous with PREFORECLOSURE SALE.

REPAYMENT OF BAILOUT FUNDS. *See* "TOO BIG TO FAIL"; TROUBLED ASSET RELIEF PROGRAM.

REPOSSESSIONS. *See* UNITED KINGDOM.

RESET ECONOMY. Term coined by General Electric CEO, suggesting the concept that business needs to adjust its expectations and behavior to a new, post-recession world.

RESIDENTIAL PROPERTIES. Improved real property used or intended to be used for residential purposes, including single-family homes, dwellings for from two to four families, and individual units of condominiums and cooperatives.

Cf. NONRESIDENTIAL PROPERTIES.

RESIDENTIAL SPENDING. *See* CONSUMER SPENDING.

RESOLUTION TRUST CORPORATION (RTC). A savings and loan bailout of the 1990s, this U.S. government agency administered the last federal bailout. The RTC was set up by the government in 1989 to sell off what ultimately grew to $450 billion worth of real estate and other assets assembled from 747 collapsed savings banks.

As a model for the 2008–2009 bank crises, the U.S. government has rejected the creation of a new RTC. Instead, it was relying upon financial institutions to find their own ways to sell off bad debts or assets they ended up with as a result of foreclosures.

See also BANK BAILOUT (PLAN) OF 2008, EMERGENCY ECONOMIC STABILIZATION ACT OF 2008.

RESPONSIBLE HOMEOWNERS. *See* HOUSING BAILOUT PLAN.

RESTAURANT WORK. *See* UNEMPLOYMENT.

RETAILING. The activity of purchasing for resale to a customer, including all activities undertaken by intermediaries. The primary function is to sell goods and services to ultimate consumers. The four functions of retailing are: (a) buying and storing merchandise; (b) transferring title of those items; (c) providing information on the nature and uses of those goods; and (d) in some situations, extending credit to buyers.

On February 8, 2008, figures indicated the worst monthly sales in five years as big retail chains prepared for a prolonged slowdown with plans to close stores and cut jobs.

American consumers clearly had lost their appetite to shop starting in October 2008. Numerous retailers witnessed an approximate 50 to 80 percent drop in their stock value.

November sales through December 4, the days following Thanksgiving, were dismal. Discount stores also suffered. November sales were down by about 2 percent from 2007. Many department stores had double-digit declines. Major sectors like apparel, luxury goods, and electronics all suffered steeper declines in November than in September and October. Sales in November tumbled to the weakest level in more than 35 years.

For 2008, electronic equipment and appliances fell a combined 26.7 percent versus a 2.7 percent gain in 2007. Women's apparel slid 22.7 percent compared with a 2.4 percent drop a year before.

The International Council of Shopping Centers estimated that 148,000 stores closed in 2008, the most since 2001. It predicted that there would be an additional 73,000 closures in the first six months of 2009.

Customer traffic during Christmas week of 2008 fell 4.9 percent compared to 2007, and for the entire holiday season plummeted 16 percent. Total retail sales sank 2.3 percent.

For the entire 2008 year, retail sales were down 0.1 percent, a sharp decline after a 4.1 percent gain in 2007. It was the first time the annual retail sales figures had fallen based on government records going back to 1992.

Retail sales took another monthly tumble of 1.1 percent, in March 2009, as job losses and tight credit left consumers cautious and constrained. It would dampen hopes for a rapid economic turnaround, as consumer spending represented 70 percent of the U.S. economy. Retail sales were down more than 9 percent from the same month a year earlier.

In June retail sales climbed 0.6 percent from a month earlier on a seasonally adjusted basis to $342.1 billion.

July 2009 was the worst month since January for retailers, with a decline of 5.1 percent.

Retailers had their worst sales performance of school items in more than a decade. One analyst found that summer sales of school supplies fell 3 to 4 percent, compared to a 1 percent increase one year earlier. Overall shopping center sales were off 8.3 percent. Another firm found clothing purchases for school was down 5.4 percent, footwear down 4.4 percent, and electronics, down 1.8 percent.

In stores that specialize in selling only clothing, sales peaked in 2007. In the summer of that year, stores sold $13 billion worth of goods. In July and August 2009, sales fell to $11.9 billion. Specialty clothing sales were back to 2005 levels.

There were signs of shoppers beginning to return to retailing operations, as stores, especially in malls, reported a 2.9 percent sales decline in August 2009, small by comparison with past months.

Department store sales had dropped an average of 8.9 percent each month since the start of 2009.

September 2009 store sales indicated the first monthly gain in more than a year, climbing 0.6 percent. These results compare to a 0.9 percent drop in September 2008. Caution remains. Retail sales declined 1.5 percent in September with the termination of the cash for clunkers program.

On November 16, the government reported that retailers saw sales improve, climbing 1.4 percent from the prior month to a seasonally adjusted $347.5 billion.

At the end of November 2009, Cyber Monday, the Monday following Thanksgiving, online shopping sites reported a surge in sales and traffic. Web shoppers spent, in total, 11 percent more than they did a year before, although the average size of each sales ticket fell nearly 14 percent from the previous year. Sales grew about 5 percent, with shoppers spending $887 million online.

Holiday sales in 2009 were sluggish at retailers, encouraging larger price discounts. While most experts expected a 2.2 percent increase during this holiday period, sales were up less than 1 percent from last year. Retailers added 321,000 jobs in November. That was more than a year earlier, but far below November 2007's 465,000.

Sales for the week ending December 5, 2009, declined 18 percent from the prior week. For the same period in 2008, these sales fell only 14 percent. Nine of ten people waited to complete their holiday 2009 shopping to get discounts of at least 50 percent. A third were holding off purchases until they could receive a 70 percent discount.

November sales climbed 1.3 percent from October. Excluding autos, auto parts, and gasoline, retail sales were up 0.4 percent, the first gain in thirteen months. However, such sales were 3.7 percent lower than those of November 2007, just prior to the official beginning of the Great Recession. By year's end, 2009 sales at traditional stores were about flat compared with 2008. Online retailing grew 4 percent from the beginning of November through December 18, 2009, to $24.8 billion.

The good news appeared on December 27, 2009. Holiday shoppers spent a little more in 2009 than the previous year. Retail sales rose 3.6 percent from November 1 to December 24 compared with a 3.2 percent decline in 2008.

See also ABERCROMBIE AND FITCH CO.; ADVERTISING; BEST BUY; BURBERRY; CARREFOUR; CASH FOR CLUNKERS; CHICO'S FAS; CHRISTMAS SALES; COSTCO WHOLESALE; EDDIE BAUER HOLDINGS; ESCADA; ESPRIT HOLDINGS; FUR INDUSTRY; GENERAL GROWTH PROPERTIES; GOODY'S FAMILY CLOTHING; HOME DEPOT; INVENTORIES; IRELAND; J.C. PENNEY; JONES APPAREL GROUP; LIMITED BRANDS; LIZ CLAIBORNE; LOWE'S COMPANIES; LUXURY GOODS; MACY'S; MARKS & SPENCER; METRO; NEIMAN MARCUS; NORDSTROM; PHILLIPS-VAN HEUSEN; POLO RALPH LAUREN; RADIOSHACK; SAKS; SEARS HOLDING CORPORATION; SHOPLIFTING; TARGET; TIFFANY; UNEMPLOYMENT; UNITED KINGDOM; WILLIAMS-SONOMA; WOOLWORTHS.

RETAIL SALES. *See* RETAILING.

RETENTION BONUS. A corporate bonus given or promised to pay certain executives for staying in their jobs. The payments, in the form of cash, stock, or both, are usually given over a period of a few years, in some cases regardless of how the executives or their firms perform.

See also CITIGROUP.

RETIREES. *See* RETIREMENT.

RETIREMENT. The percentage of workers who claimed that they were confident about having sufficient funds to retire comfortably declined to 13 percent in 2009, down from 18 percent in 2008, and from its all-time high of 27 percent in 2007. Confidence was particularly low among households with annual incomes of $75,000 or higher, in large part because these people had more money at risk in the stock market.

Current retirees, 20 percent today as contrasted to 41 percent in 2007, were very confident of being able to afford a financially secure retirement. Twenty-five percent of workers indicated that they planned to postpone retirement, with the median age of retirement rising from an expected 62 in 1991 to 65 since 2004.

One of the primary reasons that firms weren't hiring by summer's end 2009 was due to many older workers being unable, reluctant, or fearful of retiring. The contrast is impressive: In the United States in 2008, almost a third of people aged 65 to 69 were still in the labor force; in France, just 4 percent in this bracket were still working or seeking employment.

See also CONSUMER CONFIDENCE.

RETIREMENT BENEFITS. U.S. firms needing to conserve cash began to trim their contributions to workers' retirement plans, especially the so-called 401(k) plans, placing a new strain on workers' safety net at the same time that many were seeing their accounts fall along with the stock market.

Retirement plans such as 401(k) accounts allow employees to opt in or out and require them to invest their own funds, bearing the market risk on their own. By contrast, employers had greater freedom to stop making matching contributions to the plans, especially during difficult financial times.

RETIREMENT SAVINGS. As of February 2009, U.S. citizens' retirement savings were down more than $2 trillion in about one year's time.

REVULSION STAGE. Indiscriminate and contagious selling of distressed assets that lead banks to stop lending on the collateral of such assets.

See also EMERGENCY ECONOMIC STABILIZATION ACT OF 2008; SUBPRIME.

RICH, THE. *See* WEALTH.

RIEGLE-NEAL INTERSTATE BANKING AND BRANCHING EFFI-CIENCY ACT OF 1994. Repealed ban on interstate banking in the United States.

RIO HEDGE. The idea of a trader who is facing financial or legal troubles to hedge his or her position with a ticket to a tropical location (such as Rio de Janeiro). If the investment goes bad (either legally or through financial loss) the investor will use the ticket to escape, preferably to a non-extraditing country, depending on the circumstances.

RIO TINTO. On December 10, 2008, the Anglo-Australian mining company announced that it would cut 14,000 jobs and sharply lower spending as demand for raw materials slowed dramatically. Rio Tinto would release 12.5 percent of its workforce of 112,000.

The company had a net debt of $39 billion, and a market capitalization of $32 billion, with record debts since its acquisition of Alcan. Rio abandoned plans to raise $10 billion from asset sales in 2008.

Rio Tinto announced that iron ore production, used to make steel, tumbled 18 percent in the fourth quarter 2008, and that its aluminum subsidiary would double previously announced production costs.

In mid-August 2009, Rio Tinto posted a 65 percent fall in first-half profit. First-half net profit fell to $2.4 billion from $6.95 a year earlier.

See also MINING.

RISK. *See* SYSTEMATIC RISK.

ROAD BUILDING. *See* AMERICAN RECOVERY AND REINVEST-MENT ACT (OF 2009).

ROCHE HOLDING. The Swiss drug maker saw profits decline, with projected slow sales growth in 2009. Profits, announced on February 4, 2009, were 8 percent lower than in 2008.

ROCKWELL AUTOMATION. A maker of industrial-automation products. On February 2, 2009, it reported a 24 percent slump in its fiscal first-quarter profit and lowered its 2009 forecast as customers closed factories and reduced capital outlays. Its stock fell 11 percent.

ROCKY MOUNTAIN NEWS. On February 27, 2009, this 150-year-old Denver, Colorado, newspaper printed its last edition. Falling revenues, lower advertising, and big debts caused the paper's downfall.

See also NEWSPAPERS.

ROLLER-COASTER RECESSION. *See* RECESSION.

ROMANIA. Had a current-account deficit of only 14 percent of GDP in 2009, a floating currency that gave it more flexibility, and was less dependent on exports to the slowing eurozone.

However, its projected growth rate in 2009 was just 0.9 percent and its banking system was minimally profitable. Its interbank rates had nearly doubled in 2008 to 15 percent. Foreign reserves were minimal and the IMF believed that its currency was overvalued by 19 percent.

By mid-March 2009 Romania sought aid from the EU and the IMF to save it from a possible financial crisis. By March 25, Romania reached an agreement with the IMF for a financial-aid package valued at about $25.9 billion. Two-thirds of the package would come from the IMF in the form of a standby loan. The funds would be used to support Romania's central bank reserves and its ability to manage local liquidity, while the other funds would be used to cover public financing and other needs.

See also EASTERN EUROPE.

ROOSEVELT, FRANKLIN DELANO. In 1933, when Roosevelt became president, unemployment stood at a staggering 26 percent; the Dow Jones Industrial Average was down 75 percent from its 1929 peak. There were many more bank failures, and many more devastating foreclosures, especially among farmers, than in the 2008 meltdown. To this day, experts argue that his economic policies were too cautious. However, his New Deal placed millions of Americans on the public payroll via the Works Progress Administration and the Civilian Conservation Corps.

After winning a smashing election victory in 1936, the Roosevelt administration cut spending and raised taxes, precipitating an economic relapse that drove the unemployment rate back into double digits. What saved the New Deal was the enormous effort and activity of World War II, which finally provided a fiscal stimulus adequate to the economy's needs. The single biggest cause of the Depression of the 1930s was that the Federal Reserve let the money supply fall by one-third, causing deflation. Banks were allowed to fail, causing a credit crisis. The worst years of the New Deal were 1937–1938, immediately after the Federal Reserve increased reserve requirements for banks, thus curbing lending and moving the economy back to dangerous deflationary pressures. The president instituted a disastrous legacy of agricultural subsidies and sought to cartelize industry, backed by force of law. Neither helped the economy to recover. Government spending increased significantly, but taxes climbed also.

New Deal fiscal policy didn't do much to promote recovery. World War II did help the American economy, especially before the U.S. entry in 1941. Expansionary monetary policies and wartime orders from Europe, not the policies of the New Deal, did more to drive the U.S. recovery and bring it out of the depression. Roosevelt was inaugurated on March 4, 1933. The next day, he declared a national bank holiday, and set the Federal Reserve and the Treasury to work on a phased program to sort good banks from bad ones, provide finance, and restore confidence in the banking system.

See also BANKING ACT OF 1933; GREAT DEPRESSION (OF THE 1930S); HOOVER, HERBERT; RECONSTRUCTION FINANCE CORPORATION.

ROYAL BANK OF SCOTLAND (RBS). On January 20, 2009, the British government took an almost 70 percent stake in the bank, the second major British bank bailout in two months. It also offered to insure other banks against large-scale losses on risky assets in exchange for binding agreements to lend out more money. RBS's 2008 losses reached $41.3 billion, the biggest ever for a British corporation.

This arrangement would save the bank about $862 million a year in interest charges, but it ignited fear in the market that the bank would soon be fully nationalized.

On February 26, 2009, the British government moved toward nationalization by agreeing to place as much as $36.64 billion and insure £300 billion in the bank's assets as RBS reported the largest loss in British corporate history. The move gave the UK a stake of as much as 95 percent in the bank, up from 70 percent, and also indicated the lack of other bailout options available.

On April 7, RBS, following the government's claim to a stake of 70.3 percent ownership of the bank, announced that it would trim its staff by 9,000. Some 4,500 jobs are in the UK.

On August 7, RBS posted a $1.7 billion loss for the first half of 2009, with forecasts for improvement in 2011.

See also ASSET PROTECTION SCHEME; BARCLAYS; UNITED KINGDOM.

Cf. LLOYDS.

ROYAL CARIBBEAN CRUISES. In July 2009, the company swung to a second-quarter loss.

The cruise company reported a 44 percent decline in third-quarter 2009 earnings. Net yields or revenue per available passenger cruises days fell 17 percent. The firm showed a profit of $230.4 million, down 15 percent from the year before.

Cf. CARNIVAL.

ROYAL DUTCH SHELL. Europe's largest oil firm announced that its second-quarter 2009 profit tumbled by 67 percent.

Since July it cut 20 percent of its top management positions, reducing them to 600 from 750. It expects further reductions of 24,000 out of its total workforce of 102,000. In the second quarter 2009, profit fell by 67 percent to $3.82 billion from a year before.

See also OIL COMPANIES.

RTC. *See* RESOLUTION TRUST CORPORATION.

RUBLE. *See* BELARUS; RUSSIA.

RUSSIA (RUSSIAN FEDERATION). In October 2008, the Russian stock market plunged by two-thirds from its peak in May.

With $1.3 trillion in oil and gas reserves from the past eight years, Russia had a pile of cash and liquid assets, in excess of $500 billion.

With plummeting oil prices in November, a 70 percent drop in stock markets, a global credit crunch, and a slow-motion run on private banks, Russia had to spend its reserves faster than anybody imagined.

On August 8, reserves peaked at just under $600 billion; by November they had dropped to $484 billion.

Russian investment banks cut jobs as a deepening crisis threatened to stall a ten-year economic boom. Russian banks in November had seen trading, investment banking, and asset management revenues plunge, and bonuses were cut.

On November 18, the World Bank halved its forecast for Russian economic growth in 2009 as the global financial crisis pushed down the price of oil and companies cut investments. Predictions were also that inflation would reach 13.5 percent.

On November 24, Russia's central bank allowed the ruble to weaken by widening its trading bank against other currencies, the second time it had done so in two weeks. The central bank allowed the ruble to weaken about 1 percent against the dollar and the euro while raising interest rates by a full percentage point on November 28. The central bank raised its refinancing rate to 13 percent, an increase of one percentage point.

Russia's chief macroeconomic planner announced on December 11 that a recession had started in the country. Growth in the third quarter of 2008 was the slowest in three years, and the October trade surplus hit a thirteen-month low.

The central bank devalued the ruble again, on December 15, for the second time in one week as signs appeared that despite spending $161 billion defending its currency, it would be forced to let it decline even further. The central bank supported the ruble that was 45 percent euros and 55 percent dollars, but the bank had been allowing it to notch down by about 1 percent a week in six devaluations, starting in November. The bank spent $17.9 billion defending the ruble in the week that ended on December 5, when it had $437 billion remaining. Still, the ruble had declined 16 percent against the dollar since oil prices peaked in the summer of 2008.

Russian industrial output shrank 10.8 percent in November from the previous month and wage arrears doubled, raising the fear of recession for the once-buoyant economy. Economic growth, which had averaged 7 percent a year, had come to an abrupt halt.

On the first trading day in 2009, Russia had its thirteenth ruble devaluation in two months. The ruble had weakened around 1.5 percent with a euro/dollar basket trading at thirty-five/thirty rubles. The dollar rose to thirty rubles for the first time in more than five years.

Russian authorities announced in February that they would slash spending and expand bank bailouts as their economic troubles prompted a new cut to its debt rating.

The government pledged more than $1 billion in state support in March to support its ailing car industry in order to avoid heavy job losses and potential social unrest, as the once-booming industry contracted 60 percent in 2009.

On April 6, the prime minister presented his economic recovery program to generate domestic consumer demand as a substitute for decreasing oil exports. The program offered $90 billion in stimulus spending, including $17.6 billion in new spending, emphasizing tax reductions and social welfare spending for the elderly and young families. Soon after, the central bank cut its key lending rate by a half percentage point and increased its reserve requirements.

The World Bank projected that Russia's recession will run deeper and longer than originally estimated. The Bank indicated that the Russian economy would shrink by 7.9 percent in 2009, and not recover to pre-crisis levels until 2012.

Russian consumer prices were flat at the end of December 2009, up 8.8 percent since January, compared with a rise of 13.3 percent in the year before. Inflation was projected to be below 9 percent in 2009, one of the lowest readings in the nation's post-Soviet history. A 6 percent growth in 2010 was predicted.

See also HYUNDAI MOTOR COMPANY; RUSSIAN RTS INDEX.

RUSSIAN RTS INDEX. An index of Russian stocks trading on the Russian Trading System. For 2008, it fell 72 percent.

S

SAAB. Saab, the Swedish automaker, filed for bankruptcy protection on February 20, 2009. It is owned by General Motors. GM had taken a 50 percent stake in Saab in 1990 and full control in 2000.

In a Swedish court, Saab sought protection from its creditors, and said it would, with Swedish government help, reorganize to pave the way for private investors to purchase all or part of the firm.

Saab was General Motors' smallest brand in the United States, selling 21,383 cars in 2008, down 34.7 percent from 2007.

On March 12, Saab management announced that it would lay off nearly one-fifth of its workforce, giving notice to 750 staff people. It had employed 4,100 workers prior to this announcement.

The government of Sweden, in response to pleas for assistance from Saab, said no. Reports from Saab management noted that the firm sold just 93,295 vehicles worldwide in 2008, with 21,383 of them in the United States.

In mid-June, Saab's creditors approved the proposal for settling its debts by paying a quarter of what it originally owed. General Motors subsequently sold its Saab division to Koenigsegg, a small, quality carmaker based in Sweden. The firm received a $600 million loan from the European Investment Bank, guaranteed by the Swedish government, and approximately $500 million from General Motors. With a workforce of 45 people, Koenigsegg presently sells less than twenty cars a year, at a cost of more that $1.2 million per automobile. Saab had lost abut $343 million in 2008.

Saab declared the Swedish equivalent of Chapter 11 bankruptcy on August 21, one day after General Motors formally agreed to sell the carmaker to Koenigsegg.

Koenigsegg declared on November 24, 2009 that it was withdrawing from the GM deal, citing costly delays with no promise of high-volume sales. The future of 4,000 workers was in question.

Beijing Automotive Industry Holding Company, in mid-December 2009, reached a tentative deal to acquire some of the assets of GM's Saab unit. This would allow the Chinese firm to integrate the Saab technology into its own vehicles.

Then on December 18 GM, with little choice left, announced that it would shut down Saab. A potential buyer, Spyker Cars, a small Dutch maker of high-end sports cars, failed to bailout Saab. If closed, Saab's 3,500 workers would lose their jobs and it would significantly impact on Sweden's economic base.

See also GENERAL MOTORS; SWEDEN.

Cf. VOLVO.

SABMILLER. The brewer of several global beers, SABMiller reported in January 2009 that its underlying volumes fell 1 percent with signs that drinkers in emerging markets, which accounted for more than 80 percent of its profits, were cutting back amid the economic slowdown.

SAKS. An upscale retailer, Saks said in February 2009 that it would cut 1,100 jobs, or about 9 percent of its workers. Saks announced that they had a fourth-quarter 2008 loss.

The company reported a fiscal first-quarter 2009 net loss of $5.1 million. Saks reported a 15.5 percent drop in same-store sales in the quarter ending August 1, 2009.

See also RETAILING.

SALARIES. *See* PAY.

SALARY CAPS. *See* TROUBLED ASSET RELIEF PROGRAM.

SALES. *See* CONSUMER CONFIDENCE.

SALES-TAX REVENUES. *See* STATES (U.S.).

SAMSONITE CORPORATION. The luggage maker filed for bankruptcy-court protection on September 2, 2009. The company plans to close as many as 84 of its 173 stores. As of July 31, it had $233 million in assets and $1.5 billion in debts.

SAMSUNG (ELECTRONICS). In mid-January 2009, Samsung announced a major restructuring, consolidating business operations into two divisions as South Korea's most powerful and iconic corporation dealt with the slowing global economy.

The world's largest manufacturer of flat-screen televisions, memory chips, and liquid crystal displays posted its first-ever quarterly loss as the global economic slump hit both prices and demand for mainstay products. Samsung lost $14.4 million in the three months ended December 31, 2008.

Samsung's first-quarter 2009 net profit fell 72 percent to $460 million. Samsung's second-quarter profit climbed 5.1 percent, with a net profit of $1.8 billion.

The company's third-quarter 2009 profit more than tripled from a year before to $3.14 billion, its highest quarterly profit ever. Revenue was $20.9 billion.

S&P. *See* STANDARD AND POOR'S.

SAN FRANCISCO CHRONICLE. See NEWSPAPERS.

SANYO ELECTRIC. Set to be acquired by Panasonic in 2009, the company cut its annual net profit outlook as losses climbed in its chip business and announced that it would eliminate 1,200 jobs. Sanyo is the world's top producer of rechargeable batteries.

Sanyo announced a fiscal full-year net loss in 2009. The company posted a net loss of $978.5 million for the year ending March 31, 2009, compared with a year-earlier net profit. Sales fell 12 percent. By the end of October Samsung reported that its profit tripled to $3.14 billion from a year before.

See also PANASONIC.

SARBANES-OXLEY ACT OF 2002. Created a new regulator for the auditing profession, the Public Company Accounting Oversight Board. It required greater disclosure, heightened standards for auditor independence, and increased penalties for certain white-collar crimes.

See also REGULATORS.

SARKOZY, NICOLAS. *See* FRANCE.

SAS. *See* SCANDINAVIAN AIRLINES.

SAUDI ARABIA. *See* MIDDLE EAST.

SAVINGS AND LOAN HOLDING COMPANY ACT OF 1967. Authorized the Federal Reserve to monitor nondepository-related businesses of savings and loan holding companies.

SAVINGS RATE. On average, U.S. consumers from 1950 to 1985 saved 9 percent of their disposable income. That rate then steadily declined, to around zero early in 2008.

As the recession deepened, American consumers and businesses were embarking on an era of thrift, saving money as they cut spending on purchases. The personal savings rate, which indicates what we collectively spend from what we make expressed as a percentage, in the last three months of 2008 rose to its highest level in six years. This rate of 2.9 percent was the highest since early 2002.

One concern, should this trend continue, is that it would increase the worries of deflation spreading throughout the global economy.

Savings jumped to 5 percent of disposable income in January 2009, the highest level in fourteen years. Then, in March, the national savings rate was at 4.2 percent from 4.0 percent in February.

The savings rate climbed to 6.9 percent in May 2009, to its highest level in fifteen years as consumers tried to build a buffer against the threat of job losses and more economic instability.

By June, Americans were saving more of their paychecks than at any time since February 1995. In October 2009 the savings rate for U.S. citizens was 4.4 percent.

SCAMS. *See* FORECLOSURE-PREVENTION PLAN.

SCANDINAVIAN AIRLINES (SAS). Announced on August 12, 2009, that it would cut as many as 1,500 more jobs and reduce salaries as it posted a wider second-quarter net loss. In total, about 9,000 workers would lose their jobs. The carrier's net loss was $143 million from a year earlier.

See also AIRLINES.

SCANIA. This Swedish truck maker reported a 93 percent decline in its first-quarter 2009 profit. Net profits fell $22.1 million, while revenue fell 28 percent. Orders for its trucks and buses declined 70 percent to 6,061.

SCHAPIRO, MARY L. President Obama's head of the Securities and Exchange Commission. She called for tighter regulation of hedge funds and credit rating agencies. She proposed greater federal oversight of insurance companies, and of the credit-default swaps markets.

SCHLUMBERGER. In January 2009, the oilfield services giant painted a bleak picture of the oil patch, reporting a 17 percent drop in fourth-quarter earnings for 2008, and announcing that it planned to cut 5,000 jobs worldwide. These reductions amounted to about 5 percent of its global staffing.

Schlumberger's first-quarter 2009 net income fell 30 percent, with net income falling to $940.4 million compared to $1.34 billion the year before. Revenue dropped 4.5 percent to $6 billion.

See also OIL.

SCHOOL SALES. *See* RETAILING.

SDRS (SPECIAL DRAWING RIGHTS). *See* INTERNATIONAL MONETARY FUND.

SEARS HOLDINGS CORPORATION. Posted a $94 million loss on August 20, 2009, dropping $94 million.

The company's third-quarter 2009 loss narrowed, with a loss of $127 million compared to the year before when its losses were $146 million. Revenue declined 4.4 percent to $10.19 billion.

SEBELIUS, KATHLEEN. President Obama's secretary of health and human services was sworn in on April 28, 2009.

SEC. *See* SECURITIES AND EXCHANGE COMMISSION.

SECOND-LEG-DOWN RECESSION. *See* RECESSION.

SECOND MORTGAGES. *See* MORTGAGES.

SECURITIES ACT OF 1933. The first major federal securities law, still in effect, prohibits securities fraud and requires registration or an exemption of registration of securities offered for public sale. It also requires that investors receive financial and other significant information.

See also PECORA COMMISSION.

SECURITIES AND EXCHANGE COMMISSION (SEC). Agency of the U.S. government created by the Securities Exchange Act of 1934, charged with protecting the interests of the public and investors in connection with the public issuance and sale of corporate securities. The five members of the SEC are appointed by the president and confirmed by the Senate for five years.

By 2008, the U.S. Treasury secretary had convinced Christopher Cox, chairman of the SEC, to begin a crackdown on improper short selling in the shares of Fannie Mae and Freddie Mac, as well as seventeen other financial companies, including Lehman Brothers. Cox would be present at the Lehman collapse meeting and its eventual bankruptcy.

The SEC chairman was directly involved, along with the U.S. Treasury, in attempting to get Barclays Bank in Britain to take over Lehman. All attempts failed.

On December 16, 2009, the SEC voted 4 to 1 to expand the disclosure requirements for public firms. The SEC also changed a formula that critics say permitted firms to understate how much their senior executives are paid. The new requirements include information on how a firm's pay policies might encourage too much risk taking.

See also DERIVATIVES LEGISLATION; EXPAND REGULATORY POWERS LEGISLATION; FINANCIAL REGULATION PLAN (2009); FLASH ORDERS (TRADING); MONEY MARKET MUTUAL FUNDS; RATERS; SECURITIES EXCHANGE ACT OF 1934; SHORT SELLING.

SECURITIES EXCHANGE ACT OF 1934. Created the Securities and Exchange Commission and granted it broad authority over the nation's securities markets, brokerage firms, transfer agents, clearing agencies, and self-regulatory organizations.

See also PECORA COMMISSION; SECURITIES AND EXCHANGE COMMISSION.

SECURITIES REGULATIONS. *See* CREDIT RATING AGENCY RE-FORM ACT OF 2006; INVESTMENT ADVISERS ACT OF 1940; IN-VESTMENT COMPANY ACT OF 1940; SARBANES-OXLEY ACT OF 2002; SECURITIES ACT OF 1933; SECURITIES EXCHANGE ACT OF 1934.

SECURITIZATION. The process of taking an illiquid asset, or group of assets, and through financial engineering, transforming them into a security. Pooling loans with others as securities, which are then sold into a secondary market, where investors buy them. Includes the packaging and selling of bundles of debts from credit cards to mortgages. It helped fuel the massive expansion of consumer finance over the past fifteen years. A typical example is the mortgage-backed security.

Most of the tightness or lack of accessibility to credit in 2008–2009 was due to the collapse of securitization. A significant amount of taxpayers' money would be needed to overcome this huge problem.

See also BEAR STEARNS; MORTGAGE-BACKED SECURITY (MBS).

SECURITIZED LENDING. Beginning March 17, 2009, large investors, including hedge funds and private-equity firms, could secure cheap credit from the Federal Reserve and utilize these funds to purchase newly issued securities backed by such loans. It was originally designed for markets for things such as credit card debt, student loans, car loans, and loans guaranteed by the Small Business Administration.

TALF (Term Asset-Backed Securities Loan Facility) was the appropriate outlet for this program, which was announced on March 3, and was set up to finance up to $1 trillion in new lending to consumers and businesses.

See also TALF.

SEMICONDUCTORS. Sales fell almost 10 percent in November 2008, as the economic slowdown shook the chip sector. Sales fell to $20.8 billion in November, from $23.1 billion a year earlier.

SENIOR DEBT ISSUE. *See* EMERGENCY ECONOMIC STABILIZA-TION ACT OF 2008.

SETTLEMENT SYSTEMS. *See* FINANCIAL REGULATION PLAN (2009).

"SHADOW BANKS." Finance firms, investments banks, off–balance sheet vehicles, government-sponsored enterprises, and hedge funds that fueled the credit boom, all were aided by less regulation and more leverage than commercial banks.

By 2008, shadow banks moved as a herd, helping to inflate the bubble and worsen the bust. Losses at shadow banks knocked holes in the balance sheets of the ordinary banks that had lent to them.

See also HEDGE FUNDS; "TOO BIG TO FAIL."

SHADOW MARKET. *Synonymous with* DERIVATIVE MARKET.

SHANGHAI COMPOSITE INDEX. For 2008, fell 65.4 percent.

SHARP. The electronics company reported on April 27, 2009, its first annual loss in more than fifty years. Revenue declined 17 percent.

SHARPER IMAGE. Filed for Chapter 11 bankruptcy on February 21, 2008.

SHEDDING DEBT. *See* DELEVERAGE.

SHIPPING. Container shipping firm profits fell amid softer container demand. A.P. Moller-Maersk, a Danish shipping line—the world's largest, reported a 4.8 percent decline in 2008 net profit. By mid-2009, the company announced a first-half loss as freight rates fell sharply.

Almost 10 percent of the world's merchant ships are unused during this economic meltdown. It is projected that shipping capacity would exceed the needs of the market by between 50 percent and 70 percent in the near future.

Container shipping remains in turmoil. Since the second half of 2008, the industry has experienced a spectacular fall as charter rates fell alongside the rest of the global economy. Container-shipping rates fell to zero in January on the Asia-to-Europe route as brokers waived fees and charged only for fuel costs.

See also MOLLER-MAERSK.

SHOPLIFTING. Since the fall of 2008, retailers have had to reduce the number of employees in their stores who were responsible for preventing the theft of merchandise. With the meltdown, shoplifting has increased, with shoplifting arrests 10 to 20 percent higher in 2008 than in 2007. More than $35 million in merchandise is stolen in the United States every day.

SHORTCUT FORECLOSURE. A method of foreclosure in which a power of sale clause in the mortgage allows the lender to sell a property if it goes into default. The borrower must be informed, but the issuing of a public statement need not be carried out. Upon property foreclosure, the junior mortgage holders' positions are wiped out, unless the sale yields more than the outstanding first mortgage.

SHORT SALES. In real estate, sales involving homeowners under duress selling a property for less than their mortgage.

See also REO.

SHORT SELLING. Borrowing a security and selling it with the intent of buying it back at a lower price to return to the lender. A proposal, not requiring congressional approval, was made by the Obama administration that would ban "naked" short selling—selling shares of stock without borrowing them first—and require short-selling trades to be reported daily. In mid-September 2008, the SEC instituted a temporary ban on short selling but it was lifted in October.

See also NAKED SHORT SELLING; REGULATION; SECURITIES AND EXCHANGE COMMISSION.

"SHOVEL READY." Describes projects already designed and ready to be launched within 90 to 120 days of being funded by President Obama's proposal to provide funds to states.

Cf. "READY TO GO" PROJECTS.

SHRINKING INVENTORIES. *See* INVENTORIES.

SICHUAN TENGZHONG HEAVY INDUSTRIAL MACHINERY COMPANY. *See* HUMMER.

SIGURDARDOTTIR, JOHANNA. *See* ICELAND.

SIKORSKY HELICOPTERS. *See* UNITED TECHNOLOGIES.

"SILENT KILLER." *Synonymous with* INFLATION.

SINGAPORE. Plunged deeper into recession in the fourth quarter of 2008, as its GDP marked its biggest quarterly decline on record, which substantially demanded a revision of its 2009 forecast. The economy contracted at a seasonally adjusted, annualized pace of 12.5 percent in the fourth quarter, accelerating from a 5.4 percent decline in the third quarter.

Sharply cut its 2009 economic outlook; revised to an expectation for its economy to shrink by 2 percent to 5 percent in 2009.

Singapore's economy had a significant rebound in the third quarter 2009. GDP expanded 14.9 percent.

See also SOUTHEAST ASIA; TAX HAVENS.

SINGLE CURRENCY. *See* EURO.

SIX FLAGS. The U.S. amusement park company with twenty locations filed for Chapter 11 bankruptcy protection in mid-June 2009. It needs $2 billion of debt restructuring.

SKF. Based in Sweden, the world's largest maker of ball bearings said on December 10, 2008, that it would cut 2,500 jobs after a steeper-than-expected decline in demand from automakers and industrial customers. This was equal to about 6.3 percent of its total workforce.

See also SWEDEN.

SKIING. *See* SWITZERLAND.

SLOVAK REPUBLIC. *See* EASTERN EUROPE.

SMALL BANKS. As contrasted with the giant U.S. banks, these community banks became more visible during the meltdown. Of the more than 8,000 such banks in the United States, most have less than $10 billion in assets. Since January 2009 165 banks failed by year's end 2009. Small banks represent 95 percent of the total assets within the banking system.

Synonymous with COMMUNITY BANKS.

SMALL BUSINESS ADMINISTRATION. *See* SECURITIZED LENDING.

SMART BRIDGES. *See* SMART INFRASTRUCTURE.

SMART ELECTRIC GRIDS. *See* ENERGY EFFICIENCY; SMART INFRASTRUCTURE.

SMART INFRASTRUCTURE. With passage of the Economic Stimulus Plan in mid-February 2009, funds would be moving into the infrastructure area. Tens of billions of dollars will be pouring into building or rebuilding smart roads, smart bridges, smart electric grids, and so on.

SMART ROADS. *See* SMART INFRASTRUCTURE.

SMOOT-HAWLEY ACT OF 1930. Had a significant impact on the creation of the Great Depression of the 1930s. The tariff act increased nearly 900 American import duties. Willis Hawley, a congressman from Oregon, and Reed Smoot, a U.S. senator from Utah, both projected an isolationist flair, which was popular at the time. What began as an agricultural program spread throughout the economies of the nation. The average rate on dutiable goods rose from 40 percent to 48 percent, with dutiable import rates down to 17–20 percent. U.S. imports dropped by 15 percent following its passage. The Tariff Act of the 1930s effectively raised duties by 20 percent. The 2008–2009 recession has reinvigorated calls for greater U.S. protectionism. Some have even called for a reinvention of a new Smoot-Hawley Act.

See also BUY AMERICAN; BUY LOCAL; FISHER, IRVING; PROTECTIONISM; WORLD TRADE ORGANIZATION.

Synonymous with TARIFF ACT OF 1930.

SOCIAL SECURITY. *See* OBAMA, BARACK.

SOLIS, HILDA. President Obama's labor secretary.

SONY CORPORATION. In December 2008, the electronics maker announced cuts of 8,000 jobs, or 4 percent of its workforce. It planned to reduce investments in response to the global financial crisis and the severe drop in spending by consumers around the world. Sony was aiming to save $1.1 billion annually, which included the shutdown of several manufacturing sites. The number of production sites was reduced by about 10 percent from 57.

In mid-January 2009, Sony announced an operating loss of $29 billion, recording an annual loss for the first time in fourteen years as plunging LCD television prices hit the biggest name in the consumer-electronics sector.

Crippled by a global economic downturn, Sony announced that it would cut 16,000 jobs from its electronics division and close as many as six factories in order to save over $1 billion in annual costs.

On July 30, Sony reported a 37.1 billion yen first-quarter net loss. Sony's net income fell to 1.6 trillion yen; revenue fell 19.2 percent from a year earlier.

The company posted its fourth consecutive quarterly loss on October 30, 2009. During this period Sony had a net loss of $289 million. Sales for the period, which ended September 30, fell 20 percent.

SOTHEBY'S. The world's largest auction house swung to a fourth-quarter net loss, hurt by charges and a 52 percent drop in the auction house's sales. A net loss of $8.45 million was shown for the fourth quarter of 2008, compared with the previous year's net income of $102.4 million. Revenue fell 52 percent to $166.2 million as auction sales declined 46 percent.

Sotheby's profit plunged 87 percent in the second quarter 2009, and earnings dropped to $12.2 million from $95.3 million a year before.

Sotheby's reported a third-quarter 2009 loss as sales slumped; its revenue fell 41 percent to $44.9 million. The loss for the quarter was $57.8 million, compared with the 2008 loss of $47 million.

SOUTH AFRICA. The South African Reserve Bank cut its benchmark interest rate by a half point to 11.5 percent in the fourth quarter of 2008. The move was intended to help economic growth in the global economic downturn.

Its trade deficit widened to 12.1 billion rand, or $1.3 billion in November 2008, as the global economic recession cut demand for exports of platinum and ferrochrome.

On February 5, 2009, the central bank predicted that the country would go through "a rough patch for the next three to four years."

South Africa's economy contracted for the first time in a decade in the final three months of 2008, with declining demand for the country's commodities exports. GDP for the largest economy in Africa shrank an annualized 1.8 percent on the fourth quarter, compared with essentially flat growth of 0.2 percent in the third quarter.

Matters did not improve in 2009. Output declined by an annualized 3 percent in the second quarter, its third quarterly contraction in a row. This was, however, half the 6.4 percent decline from the first three months in the year.

Nearly half a million jobs were lost in the first half of 2009, out of a workforce of 17 million.

By October 2009 the annual rate of inflation fell by 0.2 percentage points to 5.9 percent.

See also AFRICA.

SOUTH AMERICA. *See* ARGENTINA; BRAZIL; LATIN AMERICA; WORLD TRADE.

SOUTHEAST ASIA. By 2009, export orders throughout Southeast Asia declined. Factories slowed down as the main motor of these economies sputtered, according to government officials.

Thailand, Indonesia, the Philippines, and Vietnam depend heavily on exports to power economic growth. For Malaysia and Singapore, overseas markets are even more crucial to domestic prosperity.

In November 2008, the World Bank predicted that countries that rely heavily on remittances from foreign workers, such as the Southeast Asian countries, would be severely affected.

See also REMITTANCES; THAILAND.

SOUTH KOREA. Economy shrank a seasonally adjusted 5.6 percent in the fourth quarter of 2008 from the previous three months.

South Korean exports tumbled a record 32.8 percent in January 2009 as shipments of products including cars and wireless communication equipment fell. The drop in exports to $21.7 billion was the steepest since South Korea began collecting monthly tallies of exports and imports in 1980.

The Bank of Korea cut its benchmark interest rate to 2 percent, a record low, to aid the plunging economy.

By 2009, corporate leaders were proposing ways of avoiding layoffs by convincing workers and union officials to reduce wages, often by about 20 percent, in a strategy referred to as job preservation.

Exports fell 19 percent in April, and imports fell 35.6 percent.

South Korea's economic output grew 2.9 percent in the third quarter 2009. In October, South Korea had a larger-than-expected $3.79 billion trade surplus. Exports for the month fell 8.3 percent from a year before at $34.03 billion, less than the 12 percent decline projected by market observers, while imports were down 16.3 percent at $30.23 billion versus a forecast for a 15.7 percent fall.

See also HYUNDAI MOTOR COMPANY; LG; SAMSUNG.

SOUTHWEST AIRLINES. Reported in mid-January 2009 that although it had strong revenue growth, it also had a second consecutive quarterly loss after years of steady profits. The company posted a net loss on January 22 of $56 million.

The airline booked its third straight quarterly loss and provided a down forecast as it laid plans to reduce its staff.

In July, the airlines returned to a profit after three straight quarterly losses.

Southwest's third quarter 2009 showed a slight loss of $16 million, compared to a $120 million the year before. Revenue fell 7.8 percent to $2.67 billion.

See also AIRLINES.

SOVEREIGN FUND. A portfolio of investments in foreign markets funded from current account surpluses.

SOYBEAN PRICES. In six months, this farm commodity had plunged about 40 percent since July 2008.

SPAIN. In November 2008, the number of people filing jobless claims in Spain rose 7.3 percent and was at the highest level since 1996. The jobless rate stood at 11.3 percent in October, the highest rate among the twenty-seven countries in the EU. As a beginning strategy, the government announced a program that may have been the first of its kind to allow out-of-work homeowners to defer mortgage payments.

The government announced on November 27 that a $14.3 billion stimulus package would be put in place, aimed at creating 300,000 jobs and attempting to cushion the Spanish economy from the global crisis. It would cost the equivalent of about 1 percent of the nation's GDP. It included about $10 million for public works and an additional $1 billion to help the ailing automobile industry.

In addition, the government said it would buy $10 billion of debt at its second purchase of bank assets and urged the financial sector to use the proceeds from the sale to provide credit to businesses and families.

Spain created more jobs and drew more immigrants than any country in Europe over the past decade, largely because of a construction boom. The foreign population had risen to 5.2 million in 2008, out of Spain's total population of 45 million, from a foreign population of 750,000 in 1999. As the economy shrank, firms were releasing workers at an alarming rate. Unemployment soared 11 percent in the third quarter of 2008 and immigrants in low-skilled jobs were the hardest hit, with job losses estimated to be 17 percent. The government encouraged immigrants to return home on lump-sum welfare payments.

From 1999 to 2007, Spain's GDP grew at 3.7 percent a year, 1.5 percentage points over the average of nations using the euro. Over the past decade, Spain created more jobs than any other European nation. Now it was eliminating them just as fast. The jobless rate was 13 percent, which was equated to over 3 million people. The construction bust was central, and Spain's large immigrant population needed for the building boom had risen eightfold in 10 years to over 5 million.

Spain's GDP shrank by 1 percent in the fourth quarter of 2008, its worst performance in fifteen years.

The government instituted a €33 billion public-works program that it hoped would lead to 25,000 new building projects by May 2009.

Spain's automobile sales plummeted in 2009. Registrations fell 42 percent in January to 59,385 cars.

Nearly 50 percent of Spain's lending institutions were in the hands of unlisted savings banks largely controlled by the regional governments, and were demanding state aid.

In March, Spain became the first of the sixteen countries that use the euro to record a negative inflation rate of 0.1 percent, the first time since the government began tracking inflation in 1961. Combining rising unemployment and decreasing prices, Spain may be in the early grip of deflation, resulting in a downward spiral. As unemployment in Spain, which is 15.5 percent, continues to climb, consumers cut their spending.

By the end of April, Spain's unemployment had jumped to 17.4 percent from 13.9 percent in the previous quarter. Unemployment was predicted to reach 19.3 percent by the end of 2009.

By July, Spain's unemployment rose to 18 percent, the highest within the 27 member nations of the European Union. It shed 1.2 million jobs in one year, and would soon have as many jobless as Italy and France combined. Spain's budget deficit was nearly 12 percent of its GDP.

On July 24, the government announced that more than 1 million households had no working members. The nation's unemployment rate more than doubled on the year to 17.92 percent in the second quarter, by far the highest rate of the thirty countries within the OECD.

Spain's economy contracted in the second quarter 2009 with GDP falling 4.1 percent. The prime minister of Spain, in early September, announced tax increases and spending cuts to reverse a ballooning budget deficit. With a soaring unemployment rate of 18.5 percent, the tax burden rose as much as 1.5 percent of GDP. Spain's economy shrank for the sixth quarter in a row.

By December 10 Spain became the latest eurozone country to face a possible downgrade of its government debt. The nation's deficit was expected to top 11 percent of GDP in 2009.

See also AUTOMOBILE INDUSTRY; DEFLATION.

SPECIAL DRAWING RIGHTS (SDRS). *See* INTERNATIONAL MONETARY FUND.

SPECIAL-PURPOSE VEHICLES. *See* MONEY MARKET MUTUAL FUNDS.

SPENDING. As the unemployment rate rose, people with jobs were increasingly fearful of spending, which only made the economy's problems worse. In the last three months of 2008, consumer purchases accounted for 69.9 percent of GDP, compared with 70.5 percent in the same period a year earlier.

By summer's end 2009, transportation spending fell 1.8 percent and apparel outlay dropped 4.3 percent. Families spent 8.1 percent more on home dining, or $279 a family.

See also PART-TIME WORKERS; SAVINGS RATE.

SPRINT NEXTEL. Announced the cutting of 8,000 jobs, with most to be completed by March 31, 2009, as it sought to reduce labor costs by $1.2 billion.

On October 29, 2009, the company reported that during its third quarter, it lost 801,000 customers, while 991,000 customers defected in the second quarter and 1.25 million customers left in the first quarter of the year. Sprint lost $478 million in the third quarter compared with $326 million one year earlier. Revenue fell by 9 percent to $8.04 billion.

At the beginning of November the company was eliminating up to 2,500 jobs, or 6 percent of its workforce, thereby cutting expenses by at least $350 million.

SPYKER CARS. *See* SAAB.

STABILIZATION FUND. Under the Economic Stimulus final package, and designed to help states avoid budget cuts, it was increased to $53.6 billion from $44 billion.

See also AMERICAN RECOVERY AND REINVESTMENT ACT (OF 2009).

STAGFLATION. Stagnation in the economy accompanied by a rise in prices. Combining high inflation and high unemployment results in stagflation. Individual earning power evaporates and the standard of living declines.

Cf. DEFLATION; INFLATION; REFLATION.

STANDARD & POOR'S (S&P). A stock index and bond rating organization, it gave a rating action on more than 8,000 residential mortgage bonds and collateralized debt obligation on January 31, 2008. It forecast financial firms' losses would reach $265 billion.

Standard & Poor's stock index had fallen at the end of November 2008 by 50 percent, lower than at any point since 1997. It had lost more than a third of its value in a calendar year only twice before, both times during the Great Depression of the 1930s. It fell 41.9 percent in 1931, and 38.6 percent in 1937. The worst post-depression year, until now, was 1974, when the index fell 29.7 percent amid the worst postwar recession the United States had yet seen.

In 2009, the public and government were questioning the objectivity and reliability of S&P and the other rating companies in making recommendations. For example, S&P failed to predict the bankruptcy of Iceland in 2008, a nation that had a very high rating up until it suddenly collapsed.

On June 17, S&P cut the credit ratings and outlooks of twenty-two banks, most of them regional ones, and downgraded five of them to junk status.

Between March 9, 2009, to September 9, 2009, the S&P's 500 stock index rose 53 percent. By the end of the summer, the S&P 500 remained 35 percent below its 2007 high.

See also STOCK BUYBACKS.

Cf. MOODY'S.

STANDARD & POOR'S 500 STOCK INDEX. *See* STANDARD & POOR'S.

STANFORD UNIVERSITY. Laid off 412 employees by summer 2009 and planned another 60 layoffs by the year's end, attempting to offset a significant fall in the value of its endowment, which was expected to fall 30 percent for the year. In addition, the university froze salaries and faculty hiring, eliminated unfilled positions, and suspended campus construction.

In addition, following the university's loss of one-quarter of its original endowment of $12.6 billion, the administration put on the block as much as $1 billion of hard-to-sell investments ranging from private equity to real estate as it sought cash.

Cf. HARVARD UNIVERSITY; PRINCETON UNIVERSITY; YALE UNIVERSITY.

STAPLES. The office supply retailer reported a 14 percent profit decline for its fiscal fourth quarter 2008.

Staples' fiscal second-quarter 2009 earnings fell 38 percent. For the quarter ending August 1, the firm posted a profit of $92.4 million, down from $150.2 million a year before.

The management reports its fiscal third-quarter 2009 earnings rose 72 percent from a year before. Profit climbed to $269.4 million from $156.7 million the year before.

STARBUCKS. Posting a 69 percent drop in quarterly (2008) profit, the company announced in January 2009 that it would close another 300 stores and cut 6,700 workers.

After reporting a 77 percent decline in first-quarter 2009 profit, the company declared on April 29, 2009, that it would adjust its pricing in some markets and lower prices on basic drinks.

Starbucks posted a small profit in its fiscal third quarter 2009. Net revenue fell 6.6 percent to $2.40 billion from $2.57 billion a year before.

In November 2009, Starbucks Corporation reported a profit in its fiscal fourth quarter, earning $150 million.

START-UPS. *See* VENTURE CAPITAL.

STARWOOD. Operating more than 900 properties in 100 countries, it posted a 46 percent drop in fourth-quarter 2009 net income amid anemic consumer demand, offering the first detailed look at the dimming prospects for the global hotel industry. Starwood's net income declined to $79 million from $146 million in the year-earlier quarter.

First-quarter 2009 profit tumbled 82 percent, with a net income of $6 million, down from $32 million a year earlier.

STATES (U.S.). Twenty of the fifty American states have cut their budgets for the 2009 fiscal year. Many are having trouble paying for health care for the poor or disabled. Forty-six states were bracing for budget shortfalls by the end of 2008. These states were running deficits, forcing governors to raise taxes and trim spending while postponing urgent repairs to roads, bridges, hospitals, and ports.

Jobless rates rose in nearly every state in January 2009, indicating that no region was immune to the recession. The February American Recovery and Reinvestment Act provided $150 billion in state relief.

State tax revenues fell by $5.4 billion compared with the same period in 2007, a decline of 3.6 percent, the steepest drop since the second quarter of 2002. Of forty-seven states involved in a study, thirty-five reported declines.

By March/April 2009, the decline in tax revenues was pushing state lawmakers to reconsider increasing taxes in a bid to close widening budget gaps. While many states had managed to cope with dwindling cash by reducing spending and raising fees, it was probably insufficient to cover the needs of the public. Sales tax revenues had declined more sharply than at any other time in fifty years, and income tax and sales tax increases were considered by more states.

State sales-tax revenues tumbled in the fourth quarter of 2008 and continued to fall into 2009. The decline in tax revenue had forced cities and towns to cut back local services. State and local taxes fell 6.1 percent in the fourth quarter of 2008; revenue from personal income taxes was down 1.1 percent in the fourth quarter, and corporate income taxes fell 15.5 percent, reflecting weaker profits. In the first two months of 2009, the forty-one states that had reported tax revenues saw total receipts decline 12.8 percent, versus the same time a year earlier.

In March, California and North Carolina posted their highest jobless rates in at least three decades. California's unemployment rate jumped to 11.2 percent, while North Carolina's rose to 10.8 percent, the highest since records of state joblessness began in 1976. Eight states posted double-digit unemployment rates in March, with the highest level being 12.6 percent in Michigan. In nineteen states, rates were higher than the national rate. In twenty states, unemployment grew faster than the national rate since the beginning of the recession.

State tax collections continued to fall in the first quarter of 2009. Forty-seven states reported first-quarter revenues dropped by 12.6 percent, about $20 billion, compared with the first three months of 2008. The steepest drops were in income taxes. Corporate income taxes declined 16.2 percent, personal income taxes fell 15.8 percent, and sales taxes were down 7.6 percent. Forty-five of the forty-seven reporting states saw revenues decline.

By summer's end 2009, many states began to "shut down" to preserve cash, with furloughs, leaves, and other means to save money. States with the highest budget gaps of more than $4 billion and their cost-cutting measures include:

California—$45.5 billion: Layoffs (some 210,000 state workers are affected by furloughs the first three Fridays of each month through June 2010)
New York—$20 billion: Layoffs
Illinois—$13.2 billion: Layoffs
New Jersey—$8.8 billion: Furloughs (the enacted budget requires ten unpaid furlough days for state workers)
Florida—$5.9 billion
Massachusetts—$5.0 billion
Pennsylvania—$4.8 billion: Layoffs
North Carolina—$4.6 billion: Layoffs
Connecticut—$4.2 billion
Oregon—$4.2 billion: Layoffs

Georgia—$4.1 billion: Furloughs
Arizona—$4.0 billion: Layoffs and furloughs (the state has implemented employee furloughs of one or two days per month, depending on salary)

By mid-September 2009, California's jobless rate reached a 70-year high of 12.2 percent (it was 14.7 percent in 1940). While the average in the nation was 9.7 percent, other states with higher than California's unemployment were Michigan (13.2 percent), Nevada, and Rhode Island (12.8 percent).

In fourteen states and the District of Columbia at least a tenth of the workforce was unemployed in August 2009.

State tax revenues in the second quarter 2009 fell 17 percent from a year earlier, the sharpest decline since at least the 1960s. The largest fall was in state income taxes, down 28 percent from a year before. Sales-tax revenues fell 9 percent. About two-thirds of state revenues come from sales and income taxes.

By November 2009 states had filled 30 percent to 40 percent of their budget gaps with federal stimulus money, being given about $250 billion of the $787 billion stimulus package, most disbursed by the end of 2010. States still face a combined deficit of $142 billion for 2011, up from $113 billion for 2009.

By the third quarter 2009, tax collection fell 11 percent across forty-four states, resulting in increasingly low government revenues. All forms of tax revenue from sales and corporate and personal income taxes declined. The largest fall was in corporate-income taxes, down 19.4 percent. Personalized income taxes fell 11.4 percent, while sales taxes fell another 8.2 percent. Approximately 80 percent of states' total tax collection comes from state and personal income taxes.

On December 16, 2009, the House of Representatives passed a separate $154 billion package that included $23 billion for states to pay teachers' salaries.

New reports at year's end 2009 indicated a third-quarter 7 percent decline in state and local tax revenues. Sales taxes were down 9 percent to $70 billion in the third quarter 2009 compared to the year before. Income taxes fell 12 percent to about $58 billion. Together, sales and income taxes make up roughly half of state and local tax revenue.

Twenty-two states saw third-quarter revenues fall more than 10 percent.

See also AMERICAN RECOVERY AND REINVESTMENT ACT (OF 2009); GAMBLING; UNEMPLOYMENT.

STATE STREET. Profits for the bank's first quarter of 2009 fell 10 percent on a loan-loss provision tied to mortgages from the previous quarter of 2008. Net income fell from $530 million to $476 million.

STATE SUBSIDIES. *See* EUROPEAN COMMISSION.

STEEL. *See* ARCELORMITTAL; US STEEL.

STEERING. *See* MORTGAGE LEGISLATION.

STERLING. *See* POUND (BRITISH).

STIMULUS PLAN. By July 2009, the loss of an additional 467,000 jobs for the month indicated that the meltdown continued to have a significant impact on the economy as a whole. Average hours worked per week fell to thirty-three, the lowest level in at least forty years. Because people worked less, wages fell by 0.3 percent for the first half of 2009. Factories operated at only 65 percent capacity, while the overall jobless rate hit 9.5 percent. Including discouraged workers who want full-time work, the labor underutilization rate climbed to 16.5 percent.

Most U.S. citizens saved their 2008 stimulus checks, and a mere one-third of consumers spent them. Most of the $96 billion that was put aside for one-time stimulus payments designed to encourage consumer spending was not used to purchase goods or services.

See also AMERICAN RECOVERY AND REINVESTMENT ACT; OVERTIME.

STIMULUS PLAN (EUROZONE). By early December 2008 a variety of substantial stimulus plans had been introduced by several European governments. In Spain, €11 billion, €31 billion in Poland, €80 billion in Italy, €32 billion in German, €20 billion in Britain, and €20 billion in France.

See also EUROPEAN COMMISSION; UNITED KINGDOM.

STIMULUS SPENDING (G-20). *See* G-20; LENDING.

STOCK BROKERS. In April 2009, more than 2,800 people registered as brokers left the securities industry. The total number of departures from January to the end of April stood at 11,600, a loss of about 35 percent of brokers, by the end of 2009.

STOCK BUYBACKS. Tumbled 66 percent in the fourth quarter of 2008, from a year earlier on the benchmark S&P 500 stock index. Buybacks fell 42 percent in all of 2008 from the record $589.1 billion index members spent on buybacks in 2007.

STOCK MARKET (DOW JONES). On January 18, 2008, the Dow Jones Industrial Average declined 306.95 points, or 2.5 percent, to 12,159.21, on fears of more damage from the subprime mortgage crisis.

On November 4, 2008, the United States recorded its biggest election-day gain in twenty-four years. The Dow Jones Industrial Average and the NAS-DAQ indices both closed more than 3 percent higher. Nevertheless, the 2008 fall in the marketplace has been so steep that it has erased all the gains made in the rally from 2003 to 2007.

Meanwhile, $30 trillion of global stock market value was wiped out in 2008.

The Dow Jones Industrial Average ended 2008 at 8,776.39, down 4,488.43 points, or 33.8 percent from its high, the weakest year since 1931. Stocks lost 42 percent of their value in 2008, erasing more than $29 trillion in value and all of the gains made since 2003. The year 2008 was the stock market's third-worst year in more than a century. The only two Dow stocks to rise in 2008 were Wal-Mart Stores, with an 18 percent gain, and McDonald's, up nearly 6 percent.

On February 10, 2009, the day Treasury Secretary Geithner announced his bank rescue plan, the Dow Jones dropped nearly 400 points, the worst performance since President Obama took office.

On February 23, the stock market dropped to 50 percent of its peak that was achieved only sixteen months prior. It lost 3.4 percent on that day. Then on March 2, the Dow dropped 4.2 percent to 6,763.29, its lowest close since April 1997. It had lost almost one-quarter of its value in 2009 and more than half since its high in October 2007.

By mid-March, the share prices for some prime companies had sunk to or near the level of penny stocks. For example, AIG was $0.35, Citigroup was $1.02, General Motors was $1.86, Bank of America was $3.17, and General Electric was $6.66. On March 23, the day that the Treasury secretary announced plans for a public-private program to purchase up to $1 trillion in toxic assets and securities, the stock market soared 6.8 percent, or 497.48 point, to 7,775.86, in its biggest gain since October 2008. Also, bank stocks jumped sharply in the hope that the plan would rid them of much of the soured debt and securities weighing on their balance sheets.

Throughout June, the stock market kept rising based on hopes of a rapid economic recovery. By mid-June resurgent fears about a longer downturn and an anemic recovery impacted severely on financial markets. A World Bank report indicated that recovery would be the slowest since World War II. The World Bank predicted a 2.9 percent decline until 2010, as the world was "entering an era of slower growth." On June 22, the stock market Dow lost 200.72 points, or 2.35 percent, to close at 8,339.01.

By June 30, the stock market completed its best quarter in years, with a gain of 35 percent. Nevertheless, it is still a long way from the 14,000 mark it was at before the current economic recession.

Fear that rising unemployment would prolong the recession sent stocks tumbling on July 2, pushing the broad market into the red again for the year.

Then on July 7, following a three-month rise, the DJIA fell 161.27 points, or 1.94 percent, to its lowest close since April 28, 2009. Part of this fall was based on concerns about second-quarter corporate losses or gains about to be reported.

By September 1, 2009, the stock market completed its best six months since 1933 and ended the year with a comeback of historic proportions.

See also BAILOUT RESCUE (PLAN) OF 2009; DOW JONES INDUS-TRIAL AVERAGE; LIBOR; NASDAQ COMPOSITE INDEX; PUBLIC-PRIVATE INVESTMENT FUND; STOCK MARKET (FOREIGN); UN-EMPLOYMENT; WINDOW DRESSING; WORLD BANK.

STOCK MARKET (FOREIGN). During 2008 foreign markets also tumbled, erasing more than $29 trillion in value and all of the gains made since 2003, percentage changes for select stock markets around the world included:

Argentina Merval—49.8 percent
Brazil Bovespa—41.2 percent
France CAC 40—42.7 percent
Germany Dax—40.4 percent
Hong Kong Hang Seng—48.3 percent
India BSE Sensex—52.4 percent
Japan Nikkei 225—42.1 percent
Mexico IPC—24.2 percent
United Kingdom FTSE 100—31.3 percent

See also STOCK MARKET.

STOCK MARKET CRASH. *See* GREAT DEPRESSION; PECORA COM-MISSION.

STRAUMUR-BURDARAS INVESTMENT BANK. *See* ICELAND.

STRESS TESTS. As part of the new bailout plan announced on February 10, 2009, many U.S. banks would be subjected to rigorous examinations to see if they were sufficiently healthy to lend to before receiving further financial aid. The secretary of the Treasury used this approach to determine if the big banks were adequately capitalized; if not, new funds may or may not be provided.

The stress test would use computer-run "what if" situations to estimate what would happen to each bank under Depression-like conditions—unemployment surging to 10 to 12 percent, for example, or home prices dropping by 27 percent over two years. The nineteen largest banks (those with more than $100 billion in assets) were asked to undergo the stress test to make certain that they would remain adequately capitalized even if the economic recession became substantially worse than expected.

Under the rules of the stress test, a bank that could not cover a projected shortfall by raising funds from private investors would have to accept it from the government. In exchange, the government would take a potentially large ownership stake.

Stress tests were being applied under the Capital Assistance Program and began on February 25.

On April 24, regulators began briefing banks about how they fared in their stress test, before the results were to be made public on May 7. While the April 24 announcement of the condition of the nineteen largest banks appeared to present a strong picture, regional banks were preparing for huge losses. They were among the hardest hit by the housing collapse, and remained saddled with piles of commercial real estate and corporate loans expected to sour throughout 2009.

The Bank of America and Citigroup were informed by regulators on April 27 that the banks would probably have to raise more capital based on early results of the stress test.

The stress tests revealed that many of the nineteen banks studied would need more money. The banks were expected to plug some of the shortfalls by selling assets or raising new funds from investors. But the banks were also able to use bailout money that they had already received by converting some of the government's preferred stock into common stock, increasing the government's stake but diluting existing shareholders. Stress test results were as follows:

Bank (Ranked by Assets)	Money Needed (Billions)	TARP funds (Billions)
JP Morgan Chase	0	$25.0
Citigroup	$50.0–$51.0	$45.0
Bank of America	$33.9	$45.0
Wells Fargo	$15.0	$25.0
Goldman Sachs	0	$10.0
Morgan Stanley	$1.0–$2.0	$10.0
MetLife	0	0
PNC Financial Services	—	$7.6
US Bancorp	—	$6.6
Bank of New York Mellon	0	$3.0
GMAC	$11.5	$5.0
SunTrust	—	$4.9
State Street	—	$2.0
Capital One Financial	0	$3.6
BB&T	—	$3.1
Regions Financial	—	$3.5
American Express	0	$3.4
Fifth Third Bancorp	—	$3.4
KeyCorp	—	$2.5

On May 6, 2009, the Federal Reserve directed at least seven of the nation's largest banks to reinforce their capital levels by $65 billion. Six others were found to be stable.

See also CITIGROUP; EUROPEAN UNION; FEDERAL RESERVE; LEMON SOCIALISM; PUBLIC-PRIVATE INVESTMENT FUND; "TOO BIG TO FAIL."

STRUCTURED BANKRUPTCY. A procedure in which a government convenes creditors, unions, shareholders, and the firm's management and assigns a share of the hit to each of them.

STUDENT LOANS. President Obama's proposed 2010 fiscal budget included making the government the sole provider of federal student loans, ending the participation of private lenders in the program. Private lenders would be eliminated, and the government would use the savings, estimated at $47.5 billion over the coming ten years, to help bolster the Pell Grant program for low-income students.

By mid-April 2009, defaults on student loans were rapidly climbing. Default rates for federally guaranteed student loans reached 6.9 percent for fiscal year 2007. That was up from 4.6 percent two years earlier and was the highest rate since 1998.

See also BUDGET (U.S.) (FISCAL YEAR 2010); PELL GRANTS.

SUBARU. Subaru's U.S. sales were higher in 2008, making the Japanese firm the only major automaker with a yearly sales increase. Sales rose by 0.3 percent to 187,699 vehicles from 187,208 in 2007. The company announced on December 26, 2008, that it would reduce output by a further 10,000 vehicles in the business year ending in 2009, bringing the total reduction to 70,000. In addition, it shed 300 temporary jobs.

See also AUTOMOBILE INDUSTRY.

SUBPRIME. The designation of a loan typically having relatively unfavorable terms, made to a borrower who does not qualify for other loans because of a poor credit history.

The mortgage-delinquency rate among subprime borrowers reached 25 percent in the first quarter 2009, with the pace of delinquencies accelerating. Since prime loans account for 80 percent of U.S. bank exposure to mortgages and credit cards, these losses may ultimately exceed those from weaker borrowers.

See also BEAR STEARNS; EMERGENCY ECONOMIC STABILIZATION ACT OF 2008; STOCK MARKET.

SUBPRIME MORTGAGE. *See* EMERGENCY ECONOMIC STABILIZATION ACT OF 2008; OPTION ADJUSTABLE-RATE MORTGAGES; RATERS.

SUBSIDIES. The bankruptcy of both Chrysler and General Motors has had an impact on the idea of subsidies, usually from governments. U.S. trade experts claim that the country could be accused by foreign nations of unfairly subsidizing manufacturing and production.

See also AUTOMOBILE INDUSTRY; EUROPEAN COMMISSION; UNFAIR TRADE SUBSIDIES.

SUICIDES. Throughout the Great Recession the number of U.S. suicides increased. Data from nineteen states indicated in 2008 a total of 15,335 suicides, up about 2.3 percent from a year earlier. Traditionally, 90 percent of those committing suicide had issues from beyond unemployment, job failure, or economic downturns. The suicide rate in 2007, prior to the meltdown, was 10.8 per 100,000 citizens.

SUMMERS, LAWRENCE. President Obama's senior economic adviser. He is director of the White House's National Economic Council. At Harvard University, he remains the Charles W. Eliot University Professor. As Treasury secretary in 2000, he championed the law that deregulated derivatives, the financial instruments that have spread the financial losses from reckless lending around the globe.

Summers was on the staff of the Council of Economic Advisers from 1982 to 1986.

In 1991, he left Harvard University and served as chief economist for the World Bank until 1993.

He left the Treasury Department in 2001 and returned to Harvard University as its twenty-seventh president, serving from July 2001 until June 2006.

Summers backed the law in 1999 that removed barriers between commercial and investment banks, and continued to back it despite recent criticism.

SUMMIT OF NOVEMBER 4, 2008. The November 4 session of the twenty-seven EU finance ministers was one of two gatherings to prepare a common European position for the G-20 summit meeting, described as a new Bretton Woods. The governments watered down a French call for speedy international agreement on a range of specific measures regarding the credit crisis, lowering expectations for the summit meeting. By convening the G-20 rather than the closed, rich club of G-7, the old order had in effect acknowledged that the rest of the world had become too important to bar from the room.

See also BRETTON WOODS II; EUROPEAN UNION; FRANCE; G-20.

SUN-TIMES. The Chicago newspaper filed for Chapter 11 bankruptcy on April 1, 2009.

SUPER-REGULATOR. *See* DODD, CHRISTOPHER J.

SUPER-RICH. *See* WEALTH.

SUZUKI. *See* VOLKSWAGEN.

SWAP. The simultaneous purchase and sale of a currency for different maturity dates that closes the gaps in the maturity structure of assets and liabilities in a currency.

SWAP AGREEMENTS. *See* FUTURES TRADING PRACTICES ACT OF 1992.

SWAP CONTRACT. A derivative contract that involves exchanging cash flow streams.

SWAP FUND. A fund into which many investors put their own investments and receive a share in the pooled investment portfolio. The purpose of this exchange of investments is to obtain a diversified portfolio without selling stock and paying capital gains.

SWAP RATE. The loss rate for exchanging units of currencies at a future date.

SWATCH GROUP. Sales fell 6 percent in the second half of 2008.

SWEDEN. The Swedish government took over the struggling investment bank Carnegie on November 10, 2008, following a series of actions that drained the bank of liquidity and prompted regulators to revoke its license.

The takeover was the government's first nationalization of a major bank since a financial crisis in the early 1990s. The national debt office would own Carnegie after it extended the bank loans of up to 5 billion kronor, or $645 million, to replace loans that the central bank had previously provided to keep the bank liquid.

On December 4, the Swedish central bank reduced its key-lending rate by 1.75 percentage points to 2 percent.

The government introduced stimulus measures worth the equivalent of $1 billion in December. On December 11, the government said it would provide credit guarantees and emergency loans to its ailing automobile industry but that it had no plans to buy stakes in Volvo or Saab. The government said it would provide up to $2.5 billion in collateral-backed credit guarantees, directed toward the manufacture of more environmentally friendly vehicles, as well as rescue loans of up to approximately $600 million.

Its benchmark interest rate dropped from 2 percent to 1 percent on February 11, 2009. Sweden's economy was expected to shrink by 1.6 percent in 2009.

See also AUTOLIV; "BAD BANKS"; ELECTROLUX; GENERAL MOTORS; SAAB; SKF; VOLVO.

SWISS FRANC. *See* DOLLAR (U.S.); EXCHANGE RATES.

SWISS RE. The world's second-largest reinsurer stated in early April 2009 that it would cut 10 percent of its global staff over the coming months.

SWITZERLAND. On November 12, 2008, the government announced a stimulus plan of up to 1.55 billion francs, or $1.31 billion, to help the Swiss economy as the global outlook worsened. The government released about 550 million francs from a fund for small and midsize firms. In addition, an additional 1 billion francs were tapped from the federal budget to revive the stalling economy.

It was clear to Switzerland's government that tourism would decline over the next two years. Overnight stays were expected to drop 3 percent the first year and 1.4 percent the following year. Ski-lift operators braced for a 6.3 percent decline in 2008 after an 18 percent increase in 2007.

On Thursday, November 20, the Swiss central bank lowered its benchmark interest rate by a percentage point, after the economic outlook worsened. It reduced its target for the three-month Libor to 1 percent and promised a "generous and flexible" supply of Swiss francs.

By December 1, the Swiss market index lost 31 percent of its value. UBS, the flagship Swiss bank, amassed the biggest losses in Europe in the credit crunch, forcing the government and central bank to offer $59 billion in support. UBS shares fell 67 percent in 2008.

The Swiss economy was predicted to shrink 0.2 percent in 2009, after expanding 1.9 percent in 2008. Manufacturing contracted in November, the most since at least 1995.

The Swiss franc tumbled against the dollar. The central bank cut its main interest rate three times since early October. Since October 20, the bank had been forced to team up with the European Central Bank to supply francs to borrowers outside Switzerland in an effort to bring three-month rates in line with its target.

The Swiss National Bank cuts its benchmark interest rate in half to 0.5 percent on December 11, citing the worsening situation in financial markets and a deterioration of the global economy. The decision was the fourth cut by Switzerland since October.

UBS, the world's biggest manager of money for the wealthy, and the country's largest bank, had eliminated 9,000 positions companywide, or 11 percent of the workforce.

Then in early February, 2009 UBS announced more staffing cuts at its investment-banking operation, cutting more than 2,000 jobs as it reported the largest annual loss ever by a Swiss firm.

On March 12, the Swiss National Bank announced steps for fighting deflation by cutting interest rates and intervening to weaken the Swiss franc as it forecast a deep recession.

See also TAX HAVENS; UBS.

SYSTEMATIC RISK. The domino effect of one business's failure on the rest of the economy.

T

TAA. *See* TRADE ADJUSTMENT ASSISTANCE ACT.

TAIWAN. The government announced that its exports in January 2009 plunged a record 44 percent from the same month last year, pushing them down to a level unseen since 2005.

By February, Taiwan ranked as the country impacted hardest by the global slump. Output plummeted by 32 percent in 2008; in the fourth quarter it plunged at an annual rate of 62 percent.

Taiwan's exports fell by a record 44 percent over the year. Averages wages had fallen 5 percent.

Taiwan's exports fell 34 percent from a year ago to $14.9 billion, the eighth consecutive month of decline and steeper than the 28.2 percent forecast. April 2009 was the first time in 2009 when exports decreased on a month-on-month basis. The country recorded $15.5 billion in exports in March.

TALF (TERM ASSET-BACKED SECURITIES LOAN FACILITY). Created in November 2008, TALF lends as much as $200 billion to investors in securities backed by credit card debt, auto loans, and student loans. It provides financing to investors so they can buy new securities backed by loans.

The Federal Reserve extended TALF, even as it allowed other recovery programs to expire. TALF was set to expire at the end of 2009, but was extended to March 31, 2010.

See also PUBLIC-PRIVATE INVESTMENT FUND; SECURITIZED LENDING; TROUBLED ASSET RELIEF PROGRAM.

TARGET. In January 2009, the retailer announced a 4.1 percent decline in same-store sales; net income fell 41 percent in the fourth quarter 2008. Target posted a net of $609 million, or 81 cents a share, down from $1.03 billion, or $1.23 a share, a year earlier. Revenue dropped 1.6 percent to $19.56 billion.

Target's fiscal first-quarter earnings 2009 fell 13 percent. Target reported that sales at stores open at least a year were down 6.2 percent from a year before in the quarter ended August 1, 2009.

See also RETAILING.

TARIFF ACT OF 1930. *Synonymous with* SMOOT-HAWLEY ACT OF 1930.

TARIFF BARRIERS. Tariff barriers can once again become the protectionist's barrier of choice, despite limits agreed upon by members of the World Trade Organization. Should all nations raise tariffs to the maximum permitted, the average global rate of duty would be doubled.

See also GLOBAL TRADE; PROTECTIONISM; WORLD TRADE ORGANIZATION.

TARP. *See* TROUBLED ASSET RELIEF PROGRAM.
Synonymous with TARP 1.0.

TARP-FUNDED WARRANTS. *See* TROUBLED ASSET RELIEF PROGRAM.

TARP 1.0. *See* TROUBLED ASSET RELIEF PROGRAM.

TARP 2.0. Use of remaining TARP funds not as a stimulus plan for the rescue of financial and banking institutions but for job creation.
See also BAILOUT RESCUE (PLAN) OF 2009.
Synonymous with FINANCIAL STABILITY (AND RECOVERY) PLAN.

TATA MOTORS LTD. India's biggest automaker by sales showed fiscal third-quarter 2008 net losses amid declining auto sales and foreign exchange losses. It reported an unconsolidated net loss of $53.8 million (2.63 billion rupees) for the quarter ended December 31, 2008, compared with a net profit of 4.99 billion rupees a year earlier. Tata Motors acquired Jaguar and Land Rover in 2008.

The company's earnings doubled in its fiscal second quarter 2009 as raw-material costs dropped and sales in India increased, marking Tata Motors' second consecutive quarter of profit growth.

The company's sales declined in the quarter ending June 30, 2009, indicating a loss of $67 million, compared with a profit of $147 million for the same period in 2008. The company posted profit of $156.8 million for the quarter ending September 30. Sales rose 13 percent.

On November 26, 2009, Tata Motors turned to a consolidated net profit for its second quarter from a net loss a year before. The automaker posted a consolidated net profit of $4.6 million in the three months ended September 30. Net sales fell 8.5 percent

Cf. HUMMER.

TATA STEEL. India's Tata Steel, with a net debt of $11 billion and a market capitalization of $3 billion, was burdened by the leveraged takeover of a giant competitor. Tata has until 2010 sufficient liquidity to cover maturing debt.

Tata posted a 39 percent drop in fiscal third-quarter consolidated net profit. Profits in the last three months of 2008 declined to $159.6 million (8.14 billion rupees), from 13.25 billion rupees a year before. On February 9, 2009, Tata Steel shares were down 76 percent, compared to a year earlier.

TAX BREAKS. Fears of raising taxes might worsen the economic crisis in 2009, according to President Obama. However, he believed that eliminating Bush's tax cuts would make it possible to generate much larger immediate increases in total spending. It would pay for larger temporary tax cuts for low- and middle-income families. These people tended to spend most or all of their post-tax income, roughly equal to the additional revenue from repealing the Bush tax cuts. Or the extra revenue could be used to raise benefits, such as unemployment insurance, and extend them more broadly. That would lift total spending by almost the full amount of the additional revenue.

See also DEFICIT; OBAMA, BARACK; PELOSI, NANCY; TAX BREAKS.

TAX COLLECTIONS. *See* STATES (U.S.).

TAX CREDITS. In early October 2009, in an attempt to encourage more hiring, the government floated the idea of a tax credit for firms that create new jobs, last done in the 1970s. The proposal would give employers a two-year tax credit if they increased the size of their work force or added significant hours of work. Employers would then receive a credit worth twice the first-year payroll tax for each new hire, amounting to several thousand dollars, depending on the new worker's income.

See also HOME SALES.

TAX CURBS. President Obama detailed on May 3 a far-reaching crackdown on offshore tax avoidance, targeting U.S.-based multinational corporations and wealthy individuals. His proposal is to curb the practice of leaving foreign earnings parked in offshore tax havens indefinitely. It is estimated that as much as $700 billion or more of U.S. corporate earnings sit in overseas accounts.

The proposal also seeks to curb other tax avoidance by U.S.-based firms by changing the legal treatment of offshore subsidiaries and structures they have used to avoid not only U.S. taxes but also taxes in other nations. Additionally, the president seeks to tighten rules that have encouraged thousands of U.S. citizens to open offshore bank accounts in order to avoid U.S. taxes.

See also TAX HAVENS.

TAX CUTS. *See* PELOSI, NANCY; TAX BREAKS.

TAX DATA. *See* TAX HAVENS.

TAXES. President Obama proposed on February 26, 2009, the spending of $634 billion in new taxes on upper-income Americans and cuts in government spending over the coming ten years. The tax increases were projected to raise an estimated $318 billion over ten years by lowering the value of such longstanding deductions as mortgage interest and charitable contributions for people in the highest tax brackets.

TAX GAP. The difference between taxes owed and taxes collected.

In 2008, the tax gap was $300 billion, of which more than $100 billion was believed to be collectible.

TAX HAVENS. Countries that shield the holdings of its clients, mostly rich people.

Switzerland is the world's biggest offshore-banking haven with about $2 trillion of foreign assets under its management. Switzerland also announced that it would relax its bank secrecy laws to cooperate with international tax probes.

See also G-20; TAX CURBS.

TAX PAYERS. As the nation sank deeper into recession in 2009, the Internal Revenue Service offered to waive late penalties, negotiate new payment plans, and postpone asset seizures for delinquent taxpayers who are financially strapped but make a good-faith effort to settle their tax debts.

See also DEFICIT (BUDGET, U.S.); UNEMPLOYMENT.

TAX REVENUES. *See* STATES (U.S.).

TBTF. *See* "TOO BIG TO FAIL."

TECHNOLOGY COMPANIES. By mid-November 2008, purchases of computer hardware, software, and services had been affected by the global credit crisis. Specifically, software firms and semiconductor companies, some with high debt loads, were negatively impacted. Bankruptcies were climbing by the end of the year.

TECHNOLOGY INVESTMENT. Tailoring of technology systems according to what is needed and the condition under which the technology will be used. Technology investment is increasingly being used in President Obama's strategy for his economic stimulus plan. His approach is to minimize waste and the spending of huge sums of funds for "things that people don't need or can't use."

TECH-STOCK BUBBLE BURST. *See* NASDAQ COMPOSITE INDEX.

TEENAGE UNEMPLOYMENT. *See* UNEMPLOYMENT.

TELECOMMUNICATIONS. Any transmission, emission, or reception of signs, signals, writing, images, and sounds or intelligence of any nature by wire, radio, optical, or other electromagnetic systems. In varying ways, both positive and negative resulted from the meltdown; some telecommunication companies providing these services have prospered, while others have suffered.

See also ALCATEL-LUCENT.

TELEVISION ADVERTISING. *See* ADVERTISING.

TEMPORARY HIRINGS. *See* UNEMPLOYMENT; U.S. CENSUS.

TEMPORARY LAYOFFS. *Synonymous with* FURLOUGHS.

TEMPORARY WORK. Employment with hours that are usually less than full-time and often short term. Temporary workers in 2009, especially in Europe, are losing jobs faster than permanent ones.

See also OVERTIME; UNEMPLOYMENT.

TERM ASSET-BACKED SECURITIES LOAN FACILITY. *See* TALF.

TERM AUCTION FACILITY. Intended to provide cash-short banks with funds to reduce the pressure on the banking system; created in December 2007.

See also FEDERAL RESERVE.

TERM SECURITIES LENDING FACILITY. Permits banks to borrow money using mortgage-backed securities and other hard-to-sell assets as collateral.

TERM STRUCTURE. The difference between near-term and long-term options prices.

TEXAS INSTRUMENTS. The technology firm announced in January 2009 that it would eliminate 3,400 jobs, or 12 percent of its workforce.

On April 20, 2009, it announced that its first-quarter net profit declined 97 percent. The firm posted first-quarter net income of $17 million, or 1 cent a share, compared with a net profit of $662 million, or 49 cents a share, a year earlier. Revenue fell 36 percent to $2.1 billion from $3.3 billion. Texas Instruments' second-quarter 2009 profit dropped 56 percent on lower sales.

Texas Instruments reported third-quarter 2009 profit declined 4.4 percent on lower sales. Profit dropped to $538 million from $563 million a year before. Revenue fell 15 percent to $2.88 billion.

THAILAND. A contraction in Thailand's quarterly economic growth in 2009 confirmed fears that the country, until recently a brighter spot in the world economy, was sinking into a potentially deep recession. The government reported on February 23, 2009, that the GDP contracted 4.3 percent in the fourth quarter. The government's forecast for the year was 0 percent to minus 1 percent contraction, down from earlier projections of 3 percent to 4 percent growth.

In early April, Thailand's central bank cut its benchmark interest rate by 0.25 percentage point to 1.25 percent, its lowest since June 2003, to boost its worsening economy.

Thailand's economy contracted by 2.8 percent in the year to the third quarter 2009, an improvement over the 4.9 percent decline in the previous three-month period.

See also SOUTHEAST ASIA.

THATCHER, MARGARET. *See* UNITED KINGDOM.

3M. After posting a 37 percent drop in quarterly net income, the company announced in January 2009 plans to reduce capital spending by about 30 percent in 2009.

It reported sharply lower profit and sales for the first quarter 2009, with net falling 47 percent. Revenue fell 21 percent to $5.09 billion. Second-quarter earnings for 3M fell 17 percent, to $783 million from $945 million the year before. Revenue dropped 15 percent to $5.7 billion from a year earlier.

THRIFTS. *See* OFFICE OF THRIFT SUPERVISION.

TIER 1 FINANCIAL HOLDING COMPANIES. Usually a bank that is so big and systematically important that it is subject to especially thorough scrutiny and tight controls. Under the government's proposal financial-regulatory plan, certain firms would face much stricter oversight from the Federal Reserve. The Fed would have the power to examine all data from the company's domestic parent to its smallest overseas subsidiary.

TIFFANY. For the 2008 holiday season, sales slid 24 percent. Total sales for the November–December period dropped 20 percent, while worldwide sales fell 21 percent to $687.4 million. This followed more than two decades of price increases and rising demand.

On May 29, 2009, Tiffany announced a 62 percent drop in fiscal first-quarter earnings as its jewelry sales plunged. Sales fell 22 percent to $523.1 million from a year earlier as sales at its New York City flagship store dropped 42 percent.

The firm reported on August 28 that its second-quarter profit fell when it earned $56.8 million, down 30 percent from $80.8 million a year before. Sales at stores open at least one year in the United States fell 27 percent. At its flagship store in New York, sales dropped 30 percent.

See also LUXURY GOODS; RETAILING.

TIME **MAGAZINE.** *See* PECORA COMMISSION.

TIME WARNER. The media giant reported in February 2009 a $16 billion fourth-quarter loss and expected its 2009 profit to be essentially flat. On February 4, it announced that a quarterly loss of $16 billion occurred, the worst results since at least 2001. Advertising revenue fell 20 percent in the fourth quarter 2008.

Time Warner's second-quarter 2009 profit fell 34 percent, with its operating income falling just 2 percent.

Time Warner's third quarter 2009 fell as advertising sales continued to drop. Quarter sales fell 22 percent, with operating income falling 40 percent. The company reported a profit of $661 million.

Third-quarter 2009 earnings declined 11 percent to $268 million. Revenue climbed 3.6 percent to $4.5 billion.

See also AOL.

TITLE. In real estate, proper and rightful ownership.

TITLE GUARANTY COMPANY. A firm that examines real estate files and conducts title searches to determine the legal status of a property and to find any evidence of encumbrances, faults, or other title defects. Once a search has been completed and the property found sound, the company receives a fee from the property purchaser who needed to determine that his or her title was clear and good. The property purchaser receives an abstract of the prepared title, and the title is verified by an attorney of the company, who gives an opinion but does not guarantee the accuracy of the title.

The company agrees to indemnify the owner against any loss that may result from a subsequent defect, with costs based on the value of the property and the risk involved as determined by the condition of the title.

TITLE INSURANCE. An insurance contract from a title guaranty company presented to owners of property, indemnifying them against having a defective or unsalable title while they possess the property. This contract is considered to be a true indemnity for loss actually sustained by reasons of the defects or encumbrances against which the insurer agrees to indemnify; it includes a thorough examination of the evidences of title by the insurer.

See also TITLE GUARANTY COMPANY.

TOLL BROTHERS. The largest U.S. builder of luxury homes reported a significant loss of $472.3 million for its third quarter 2009.

Tolls Brothers reported a fiscal fourth-quarter 2009 loss of $111.4 million, compared with a loss of $78.8 million a year earlier.

"TOO BIG TO FAIL" (TBTF). A concept, still unproven, suggesting that the largest U.S. financial and banking institutions must survive in order to protect against a collapse of the economy, both domestically and internationally. The argument is that these organizations are so interconnected, so leveraged, or so complex that the government cannot let them collapse for fear of endangering the whole economic system.

By mid-September 2008 the country's financial system was in free fall. Lehman Brothers had filed for bankruptcy and Merrill Lynch was forced to sell itself to Bank of America. Days later, the world's largest insurance company, AIG, would be nationalized while Goldman Sachs and Morgan Stanley voluntarily turned themselves into highly regulated banks. The federal government in turn rushed in to save some of the most prized financial institutions to save the world economy from collapse.

See also AMERICAN INTERNATIONAL GROUP; BANK OF AMERICA; GOLDMAN SACHS; LEHMAN BROTHERS; MERRILL LYNCH; MORGAN STANLEY; TROUBLED ASSET RELIEF PROGRAM.

TOSHIBA. Projecting the biggest annual loss in the firm's history from a sharp decline at its computer chip division, Toshiba announced on January 29, 2009, to slash costs by 15 percent, shift semiconductor production to cheaper markets, and cut 4,500 temporary jobs in Japan.

TOTAL. France's biggest oil company by market value reported on May 6, 2009, a 36 percent drop in first-quarter net profit. Total's management said that net profit fell to $3.05 billion in three months ending March 31.

TOURISM. Declined in 2008 and then in 2009, for the first time since the 9/11 terrorist attacks. People cancelled vacations, a strong dollar kept foreigners away, and businesses slashed travel budgets.

Spending declined at a 22 percent annualized rate in the October–December 2008 quarter. The decline was the greatest since the government's quarterly records began in 2001, topping the 19 percent drop after the terrorist attacks that year.

Ten million jobs would be lost over 2009–2011 as the recession led to a slump in spending on travel. The industry contracted by 3.6 percent in 2009 and was expected to expand by less than 0.3 percent in 2010.

By the summer 2009, European tourism was down 10 or more percent, outpacing an already 8 percent worldwide slump. In the Mediterranean region, 10 million fewer tourists arrived for a loss of about $20 billion in income.

Tourist volume in Italian airports fell by 13.4 percent in the first quarter of 2009. Spain reported a 19.1 percent drop in tourist arrivals. Nice airport reported a drop of 8 percent in passengers during the first half of 2009.

Tourism spending increased slightly in the third quarter 2009. Spending increased 6.4 percent to $587 billion compared to the $619 billion spent in the third quarter of 2007, before the official start of the Great Recession.

See also airlines by name; SWITZERLAND.

TOXIC ASSET FUND. An investment concept of purchasing shares in closed-end funds. The fund would permit people or retail investors to buy toxic assets from banks.

TOXIC ASSETS. The federal government announced on March 23, 2009, its three-pronged program to rid the financial system of toxic assets, hoping that investors would be attracted to the combination of discount prices and government aid. It would create an entity, backed by the Federal Deposit Insurance Corporation to purchase and hold loans.

In addition, the Treasury Department expanded a Federal Reserve facility to include older so-called *legacy assets*, a term used interchangeably with toxic assets. Originally, TALF was created to purchase newly issued securities backing all manner of consumer and small-business loans. But some of the most toxic assets were securities from before 2006, which TALF was now able to absorb.

The government would establish public-private investment funds to purchase mortgage-backed and other securities. These funds would be run by private investment managers but be financed with a combination of private money and capital from the government, which would share in any profit or loss.

The term, since it has a negative connotation, is frequently replaced with *legacy assets* or *legacy securities* to reflect a more positive approach for the federal bank-rescue plan.

See also FEDERAL DEPOSIT INSURANCE CORPORATION; FEDERAL RESERVE; PUBLIC-PRIVATE INVESTMENT FUND; TROUBLED ASSET RELIEF PROGRAM; U.S. TREASURY.

TOXIC MORTGAGE ASSETS. *See* "BAD BANKS"; BAILOUT RESCUE (PLAN) OF 2009 (U.S.); LEGACY ASSETS; PUBLIC-PRIVATE INVESTMENT FUND; TOXIC ASSETS; TROUBLED ASSET RELIEF PROGRAM.

TOYOTA. On December 22, 2008, Toyota Motor announced that it expected its first loss in seventy years. With about $18.5 billion in cash and little debt, Toyota was still in far better shape to weather the meltdown than most other global carmarkers.

Losses during the fiscal year were $1.66 billion, its first operating loss since 1938, a year after the firm was founded. Toyota's sales in the United States dropped 33.9 percent in 2008. It sold 141,949 vehicles in the United States in December, down from 224,399 a year earlier. Sales of the Prius hybrid dropped 45 percent as gas prices fell from their record highs in July.

Toyota lowered its worldwide forecast for its current fiscal year, ending March 31, 2009, to 7.54 million cars, down from 8.9 million sold the previous year. For 2008 fiscal year, Toyota expected to sell 2.17 million vehicles in the United States, down from 2.9 the previous year.

Toyota suspended production at all twelve of its Japan plants for eleven days over February and March 2009.

On January 16, the company announced cuts at North American plants where its auto sales in 2009 would be its lowest in twenty-seven years. Toyota expected a first-ever annual operating loss in 2009, as its inventory of vehicles building in North America covered eighty to ninety days of sales, having doubled in the past year. Sales were falling 30 to 40 percent each month.

On February 12, Toyota announced that it would offer job buyouts to its U.S. workers for the first time and cut the workweek at some of its American plants by 10 percent. It also announced that it would eliminate bonuses or approximately 3,000 executives and salaried employees and reduce executive pay, part of an emergency cost-cutting program.

The world's largest carmaker announced on February 25 that its Japanese factories now produce 40.3 percent fewer automobiles, its biggest drop in sales since 1988.

By March, Toyota saw its worldwide production fall to about 12 percent in the fiscal year, its lowest level in seven years, from 7.08 million cars down to 6.2 million. Toyota, the world's largest carmaker by volume, planned to scale back production in Japan by 54 percent.

Toyota on May 8 posted a $7.74 billion fiscal fourth-quarter net loss, leading the world's largest automaker to its first annual loss in fifty-nine years.

On August 27, 2009, it was announced that Toyota topped the list for purchases made in the cash-for-clunkers program.

Toyota Motor Corporation reported a quarterly profit on November 5, 2009, citing a net profit of $241.1 million in its fiscal second quarter ended September 30, down 84 percent from a year earlier. Sales fell 24 percent, leading to a net loss for the fiscal year.

On November 26, Toyota announced that it was reducing bonus pay by 20 percent for 8,700 managers as it tackled an enormous recall program due to defective accelerators and deep losses for the second consecutive fiscal year.

In the summer 2008 Toyota displaced General Motors as the world's biggest carmaker. Those glory days have faded. In the financial year that ended in March 2009 the worst sales slump in the history of the automobile took hold. Toyota had a net loss of $4.3 billion, its first since 1950, and it lost in the three months to March alone the equivalent of $2.5 billion more than

GM did in the same time. In 2007, Toyota's sales had reached almost 9 million cars, 13.1 percent of the world total, and in 2009 it fell to 11.8 percent. Toyota's sales in the United States have fallen by 23.8 percent in 2009, while in Europe Toyota's share is the lowest since 2005.

See also AUTOMOBILE INDUSTRY; CASH FOR CLUNKERS; GENERAL MOTORS; JAPAN.

TRADE. In January 2009, U.S. imports and exports slumped for the sixth month in a row, creating the biggest collapse in global trade activity since the end of World War II. Imports fell 6.7 percent to $160 billion, having plunged by nearly a third since August 2008. There was a similar drop in exports of 5.7 percent.

See also GLOBAL TRADE; PROTECTIONISM; SMOOT-HAWLEY ACT OF 1930.

TRADE ADJUSTMENT ASSISTANCE ACT (TAA). To be considered by President Obama as part of a model to assist the unemployed. TAA serves those who have lost their jobs because of changing patterns of trade, giving eligible workers counseling, training, income support, and other services. But TAA relieves only a fraction of the displaced.

See also UNEMPLOYMENT; WORKFORCE INVESTMENT ACT.

TRADE BARRIERS. Were on the increase in late 2008 and more evident in 2009. For example:

- Russia raised import tariffs on dozens of products, including cars and combine harvesters.
- The European Union put anti-dumping duties on imports of Chinese screws.
- The United States announced it would increase tariffs on French cheese and Italian water.
- Egypt increased tariffs on sugar imports.
- Brazil and Argentina have asked Mercosur, the Latin-America free-trade area, for tariff increases on numerous goods.

See also PROTECTIONISM; TRADE; WORLD TRADE ORGANIZATION.

TRADE DEFICIT (U.S.). The U.S. trade deficit widened in October 2008 for the first time in three months. It rose 1.1 percent to $57.2 billion from $56.6 billion in September. It was the first widening of the deficit since July.

The trade deficit with China widened to $28 billion from $27.9 billion in September. For 2008, the trade deficit ran at an annual rate of $709.11 billion, up slightly from $700 billion in 2007.

The deficit for November plunged by 28.7 percent to $40.4 billion. As of November 30, China held $682 billion in U.S. currency, a sharp rise from $459 billion a year earlier. Japan had reduced its holdings, to $577 billion from $590 billion a year earlier.

Government figures, released in February 2009 indicated that the U.S. trade deficit shrank for the second consecutive month, to $35 billion from $40 billion in November 2008. Oil prices fell nearly 27 percent in December, pushing the dollar value of oil imports lower, while the end of a Boeing strike bolstered exports.

At the end of the first quarter 2009, the U.S. trade deficit fell to 2.4 percent, the smallest deficit in a decade and less than half of the deficit in the first quarter of 2008.

The deficit widened for the second consecutive month in April, as exports dropped more than imports. The U.S. deficit in international trade in goods and services rose to $29.2 billion from a revised $28.5 billion in March. The drop in exports accelerated in April, falling 2.3 percent to $121.1 billion from March's $123.9 billion. Imports fell 1.4 percent to $150.3 billion. The spread between what the U.S. imports and exports grew in June 2009.

On August 12, the government said that the trade deficit widened as imports rose ($3.5 billion) for the first time in nearly one year, and U.S. exports increased from the month before, though not as much as imports. The gap between the import and export of goods and services grew 16.3 percent to $31.96 billion, up from $27.49 billion in June 2009. Imports surged 4.7 percent to $159.55 billion, while exports grew 2.2 percent to $127.59 billion.

After widening in September, the trade deficit narrowed again in October 2009 to $32.9 billion, as exports climbed 2.6 percent—the sixth straight monthly gain. Imports rose 0.4 percent. In October manufactured goods exports were 2.8 percent higher than in September, but still 20 percent below July 2008.

See also DEFICIT; UNEMPLOYMENT.

TRADE FINANCING. Financing of cross-border purchasing and selling. Roughly, 90 percent of global trade requires financing.

In the economic meltdown of 2008–2009, trade financing became more expensive and more difficult to secure, thereby accelerating an already large downturn. Banks hesitated to allocate scarce capital to trade financing. Banks were wary about being caught short by defaults by other banking institutions that write letters of credit or by the importers and exporters themselves.

TRADE GAP. *See* TRADE DEFICIT (U.S.).

TRADE SUBSIDIES. *See* AUTOMOBILE INDUSTRY; UNFAIR TRADE SUBSIDIES.

TRADE WAR. *See* MEXICO.

TRADING DESKS. *Synonymous with* DARK POOLS.

TRANSIT IMPROVEMENTS. *See* AMERICAN RECOVERY AND RE-INVESTMENT ACT (OF 2009); MASS TRANSIT; RAIL SERVICE.

TRANSPARENCY. The extent to which agreements and practices are open, clear, measurable, and verifiable.

The Obama administration pledged to make the bank bailout program more transparent, demanding that banks report publicly how they were spending funds from the bailout. True transparency would require putting specific details of government expenditures before the public, a difficult and perhaps overwhelming challenge.

The government had promised to disclose how much it gives to a state, and the state must report how the funds are distributed. But no requirements exist to disclose where the money actually ends up.

Under the Emergency Economic Stabilization Act and the Financial Stability Oversight Board, transparency is studied for all programs.

See also ACCOUNTABILITY; EMERGENCY ECONOMIC STABILIZATION ACT OF 2008; FINANCIAL STABILITY OVERSIGHT BOARD; G-20; REGULATION.

TRAVEL. *See* AIRLINES; CLUB MED; TOURISM.

TRAVELERS. The commercial and personal insurance provider's second-quarter 2009 profit fell 21 percent on lower revenue and high claims costs.
Cf. METLIFE.

TREASURY DEPARTMENT (U.S.). *See* U.S. TREASURY.

TREATY OF MAASTRICHT. *See* EUROPEAN UNION.

TRIBUNE. The U.S. newspaper chain that owns the *Chicago Tribune* and the *Los Angeles Times* filed for bankruptcy protection on December 8, 2008. The Tribune Corporation's assets included twenty-three television stations and twelve newspapers, including two of the largest in the United States by circulation. It also owned the Chicago Cubs baseball team and Wrigley Field.

The Tribune Corporation maintained a $13 billion debt.
See also NEWSPAPERS.
Cf. NEW YORK TIMES.

TROUBLED ASSET RELIEF PROGRAM (TARP) (TARP 1.0). The bailout plan of 2008 is also called TARP. It could slow the resolution of the crisis by stopping property prices and home ownership falling to sustainable levels. Some homeowners who were up-to-date with payments but whose home was worth less than their mortgage could cease paying, betting the federal government would be a more forgiving creditor.

The Treasury considered using TARP funds to write down mortgages to levels that squeezed homeowners could afford.

If TARP assisted banks and investors established reliable prices for mortgage securities, it could restart lending and help to bring the housing crisis to an end.

However, the $700 billion government program, passed by Congress on October 3, was adding to the U.S. deficit. As of December 5, the Treasury had allocated a total of $335 billion to TARP and disbursed $195 billion to institutions under its various parts. About forty-eight employees were assigned to TARP; only five were permanent staffers, the rest coming from other Treasury offices, U.S. government agencies and organizations providing temporary assistance. For them, critical questions remain: What are the bank's assets really worth? How much can it earn? And how much capital would the bank require to operate profitably?

The decision by the U.S. Treasury not to buy toxic mortgage assets with TARP money after it said it would do so produced paper losses for the banks that held these securities. The value of those securities rose when TARP was announced but fell significantly when the mortgage purchase program was abandoned.

The U.S. deficit for the full year would top $1 trillion.

Just over half of the Treasury Department's $700 billion TARP was committed—$379.8 billion—during the George W. Bush administration. On February 10, the new Treasury secretary unveiled some details about how the new administration would use the fund's remaining $320.2 billion.

The Congressional Budget Office in April quietly changed its estimate of the ultimate cost to taxpayers for the $700 billion TARP, concluding that the initiative would be more expensive. In January, CBO estimated the cost to taxpayers for TARP at $189 billion: now in late March it was reassessed at $356 billion.

Banks that benefited from funds received from TARP included:

Bank of America, $45 billion
JP Morgan Chase, $25 billion
Citigroup, $50 billion
Morgan Stanley, $10 billion

Goldman Sachs, $10 billion
Wells Fargo, $25 billion
PNC Financial Services, $8 billion
American Express, $3 billion
State Street, $2 billion

By April, the banking industry was lobbying the Treasury Department to make it less costly for them to get out of TARP. At issue were "warrants" the government received when it bought preferred stock in roughly 500 banks, permitting the government to buy common stock in the banks at a later date so taxpayers could receive more of a return on their investment. Many banks wished to return their TARP funds and wanted to expunge the warrants. To do this, the banks must either purchase them back from the government or allow the Treasury to sell them to private investors.

To buy back TARP-funded warrants, the bank had to provide the Treasury with an independent valuation of the warrants. Then the Treasury and the bank had to agree on the price. If they could not, the Treasury had to try to sell the warrants in the private market.

Those banks wishing to return TARP funds had to demonstrate their ability to wean themselves off another major federal program—a guarantee of debt issuance by the Federal Deposit Insurance Corporation that allows firms to borrow money relatively inexpensively.

The Treasury Department announced on June 8 that they received an initial payback from the nation's largest banks of at least $50 billion in bailout funds, an indication of improvement in the banking sector. These banks, and the government's TARP investment, in billions, are:

American Express, $3.38
BB&T, $3.13
Bank of New York Mellon, $3
Capital One, $3.55
Goldman Sachs, $10
JP Morgan, $25
KeyCorp, $2.5
State Street, $2
US Bancorp, $6.59

The government dropped its plans to cap salaries at firms receiving federal bailout funds, leaving them subject to congressionally imposed limits on bonuses. A pay czar to monitor the firms receiving the greatest government aid was announced in mid-June.

Then, on June 17, the government received $68 billion from ten financial firms eager to leave the curbs that came with taxpayer-funded capital infusions. By returning these funds, the banks were now to be left alone on their own to wrestle with the recession and financial meltdown. Some of these banks announced that they planned to immediately begin the tricky task of negotiating to repurchase warrants that the government received in return for the infusions.

The special inspector general for the TARP testified on July 21, before a House committee, that "the total potential federal government support could reach up to $23.7 trillion." The figure was considered not realistic or plausible, but became a point of political debate.

By September 1, 2009, the U.S. government, and thereby the U.S. taxpayers began to profit from many of its largest investments. For example:

Goldman Sachs received $10 billion in TARP funds, and the government has already received in return $1.418 billion plus the original investment; American Express received $3.389 billion in TARP funds; the government has already gotten back $414 million plus the original investment

Morgan Stanley received $410 billion in TARP funds; the government has already profited by $1.268 million plus received the original investment back.

By November 2009 about $210 billion in TARP funds remained unspent, including about $70 billion returned from financial firms. An additional $50 billion is expected to be repaid in the coming twelve to eighteen months. Also, it was found that more than twenty-seven U.S. banks that received TARP funds had been taken over by federal regulators, putting taxpayers at risk of losing as much as $5.1 billion invested in the banks since TARP was launched in October 2008.

By December 2009 the government was discussing the possibility of using unspent and repaid TARP funds to help offset additional spending to create jobs and aid the long-term unemployed. TARP's long-term cost was reported lower by more than $200 billion and the president would use this money to pay for a new jobs program. Now the Treasury Department expects to recover all but $42 billion of the $370 billion it has lent to ailing financial institutions. The Treasury estimated that over the next ten years TARP will cost $141 billion at most, down from the $341 billion projected in August 2009.

The government extended the $700 billion financial-sector bailout until October 2010.

Citigroup and Wells Fargo announced on December 14, 2009, that they were about to pay back a total of $45 billion in aid from TARP. The Treasury Department expects $19 billion in total profits from its infusions and other investments in financial institutions, reversing the agency's initial projection of a $76 billion net loss.

The top-tier banks announced by the end of 2009 that they had or were prepared to pay back TARP. However, of the other sixty-nine banks receiving TARP funds only seventeen of the other banks that received at least $100 million from TARP have repaid the funds.

See also AUTO PARTS; AVIS; BANK BAILOUT (PLAN) OF 2008; BANK OF AMERICA; CITIGROUP; DEBT CEILING; ENTERPRISE; EXECUTIVE PAY; FEDERAL DEPOSIT INSURANCE CORPORATION; FINANCIAL STABILITY OVERSIGHT BOARD; FRAUD; GEITHNER, TIMOTHY F.; GOLDMAN SACHS; HERTZ; INSURERS; JOB CREATION; JP MORGAN CHASE; LENDING; LIFE INSURERS; MORGAN STANLEY; PAY CZAR; TOXIC ASSETS; WELLS FARGO BANK.

Synonymous with BAILOUT; FINANCIAL STABILITY (AND RECOVERY) PLAN; HOTEL GEITHNER; TARP 1.0.

TROUBLED ASSETS. *See* "BAD BANKS"; BANK BAILOUT (PLAN) OF 2008; TROUBLED ASSET RELIEF PROGRAM.

TRUCKING DISPUTE. *See* MEXICO.

TRUCKING INDUSTRY. Following a few years of doubling their output, truck manufacturers began to retrench. It was predicted that through 2009, the global demand for heavy trucks of more than fifteen tons would drop by 29 percent. A 24 percent decline in developed markets would accompany a 32 percent decline in emerging nations.

Prior to 2009, it seemed that the trucking industry was having difficulty recruiting new drivers. Into the new year, the industry suddenly found that it had more applicants than positions. In January, the industry, which employed about 1.32 million people, lost 25,000 jobs. In 2008, more than 3,600 trucking firms went out of business, with roughly 7 percent of its capacity disappearing.

Sales of heavy trucks in Europe fell about 40 percent in 2009, but demand for trucks globally was expected to start recovering before the end of the year. Between 180,000 and 200,000 trucks were to be sold in Europe in 2009, down from 318,000 in 2008.

See also AUTOMOBILE INDUSTRY; FREIGHT HAULERS; SCANIA; VOLVO.

TRUMAN, HARRY S. President Truman seized U.S. steel mills in 1952 rather than allow a strike to imperil the conduct of the Korean War. He was on the edge of nationalizing the industry and told his staff, "The president has the power to keep the country from going to hell."

See also NATIONALIZATION; OBAMA, BARACK.

TURKEY. A deal with the IMF for $20 billion to $40 billion was announced at the end of November 2008.

Foreign investors, who held as much as 70 percent of the Istanbul Stock Exchange, had been pulling out, and the Turkish lira tumbled by more than a third against the U.S. dollar in 2008. Growth of GDP had dipped sharply, to below 2 percent. Turkey's huge current-account deficit made it more vulnerable than many other emerging markets.

Officials released figures on December 15, indicating that the country's GDP was contracting and that unemployment was increasing. The IMF returned to Turkey in January 2009 to assist in restoring the economy, which was plagued by a current account deficit. The jobless rate rose to 10.3 percent in September from 9.3 percent the year earlier.

At the end of December, Turkey's parliament cut the budget allocations of most ministries by as much as 16 percent as the country prepared for a loan arrangement with the IMF.

See also INTERNATIONAL MONETARY FUND.

TYSON FOODS. The company posted a net loss of $455 million in its fiscal fourth quarter 2009 compared to a year-earlier profit of $48 million. Revenue climbed slightly to $7.21 billion from $7.20 billion.

U

UAL. *See* UNITED AIRLINES.

UBS. UBS, the world's largest private bank, agreed on February 18, 2009, to pay fines of $780 million and to hand the American authorities the names and account details of up to 300 clients accused of tax fraud.

The offshore banking business of UBS gathered some $20 billion in assets from more than 20,000 U.S. clients, earning the bank huge sums of money each year. The U.S. government concluded that some 17,000 of these clients omitted to mention their numbered Swiss accounts on their tax returns.

With a big loss in the first quarter 2009, UBS announced 8,700 layoffs and a 15 percent cut to its operating costs. The bank employed 83,800 people at its peak in 2007, and with its latest cuts, 11 percent of its workers, the figure fell to 67,500.

On August 4, 2009, UBS posted a $1.3 billion quarterly loss, its third.
See also SWITZERLAND.

UKRAINE. Since October 2008, Ukraine's stock market plunged by nearly 80 percent. The hryvnia, the national currency, hit a seven-year low against the dollar. Economic growth plunged, and inflation was 25 percent.

The IMF provided an emergency loan of $16.5 billion—around a fifth of the $55 billion that Ukraine needed to raise by 2009 in order to roll over short-term loans, pay interest on other debts, and finance the rest of its current-account deficit.

The World Bank announced at the end of November it would provide Ukraine with a $500 million loan to battle a crippling economic crisis.

The IMF reached an agreement with Ukraine in mid-April 2009 paving the way for resuming disbursement of a $16.4 billion loan. Ukraine would receive $2.8 billion of the loan by mid-May. Its economy, by now, was contracting at an annual rate of 9 percent. Then on December 30 the IMF reworked a loan agreement with the government, freeing up about $2 billion.
See also INTERNATIONAL MONETARY FUND.

UN. *See* POVERTY.

UNDEREMPLOYED. People working part-time for lack of full-time positions, also includes so-called labor force reserve, workers who have abandoned their job searches but who would work if employment became available.

In October 2008, this rate jumped to 12.5 percent from 8 percent. Most of the underemployed are people working part-time, want to work full-time, but cannot find positions. The 12.5 percent figure is the highest level of under-employment since the statistic was first compiled in 1994.

By 2009, this pool of underutilized labor had risen above 24 million, with expectations that it would continue to grow.

The peak underemployment rate was higher in the recession of 1981–1982 than it is today, largely because the last big wave of the baby boom generation was entering the job market in the early 1980s. Those boomers who couldn't find work were officially counted as unemployed. In the first thirteen months of the 2008–2009 meltdown, the number of jobs lost was a staggering 4 million.

Nearly 2.2 million young people, ages sixteen through twenty-nine, lost their jobs in 2009. About 1.7 million people were working part-time in January because they could not secure full-time employment, a 40 percent increase from when the recession officially began in December 2007.

Even with the end of the recession, about 10 percent of the workforce will remain unemployed, unable to find gainful employment. By the summer of 2009, there were more than five unemployed workers for each job opening in the country. The numbers of the poor and on welfare rolls continue to rise.

Back in November 2007—before the official start of the Great Recession—about 7 million Americans were unemployed. By mid-year 2009, it had doubled to about 14 million. One should add to this figure people who are working part-time who would prefer working full-time and those who have become disillusioned and have stopped seeking employment. It is estimated that nearly 30 million people were underutilized in May 2009, the largest number in the country's history. The overall labor underutilization rate that month rose to 18.2 percent, its highest in twenty-six years.

Cf. UNEMPLOYMENT.

UNDEREMPLOYMENT RATE. *See* UNDEREMPLOYED.

UNDERUTILIZATION. *See* UNDEREMPLOYED.

UNDERWATER. The condition of a home being worth less than the mortgage taken out on it due to declining prices. This creates an incentive for the mortgage borrower to walk away and allow the home to be foreclosed on. At the end of 1991, 6.4 percent of households were underwater and were eventually foreclosed upon.

In February 2009, it was estimated that 10 million households fit into this category.

By mid-November 2009, the proportion of homeowners owing more on their mortgages than their properties are worth jumped to 23 percent. Nearly 10.7 million households had negative equity in their homes in the third quarter 2009. Thus, one out of four borrowers is underwater.

Roughly 588,000 borrowers defaulted on mortgages in 2008, more than double the number in 2007.

See also FORECLOSURE; HOME PRICES; HOUSING BAILOUT PLAN; MODIFYING MORTGAGES.

UNDERWATER MORTGAGES. *See* UNDERWATER.

UN ECONOMIC COUNCIL. A proposal, made by German Chancellor Angela Merkel in February 2009 to form an internationally funded institution within the United Nations as a possible replacement for the International Monetary Fund.

See also INTERNATIONAL MONETARY FUND.

UNEMPLOYMENT. At the end of 2007, the jobless rate reached 5 percent, its highest level in more than two years.

By March 2008, 63,000 jobs were lost, the most in five years, adding to January's unexpected decline of 17,000 jobs. The U.S. economy lost an additional 240,000 jobs in October 2008. The unemployment rate jumped 6.5 percent from 6.1 percent, the highest level since 1994. The economy had shed 1.2 million jobs since the beginning of the year.

By the end of November, new claims for unemployment benefits stood at a 16-year high.

Losses cut across all industries, but appeared to begin within the financial and banking communities, and then rapidly spread to other industries.

About 90,000 jobs were cut at major global banks since September 2008. Of these, more than 50,000 had been at Citigroup. Bank of America, which acquired Merrill Lynch, cut about 10,000 investment jobs at the combined banks. On December 4, Credit Suisse announced plans to eliminate 5,300 of its jobs, or 11 percent of its workforce. Commerzbank announced plans to eliminate 1,200 jobs in London.

AT&T, the biggest telephone company in the United States, announced plans to cut 12,000 jobs, or 4 percent of its workforce. DuPont, the chemicals company, said it would lay off 2,500 employees equaling about 4 percent of its workforce, and Viacom, the media/film firm, eliminated 850 jobs.

While financial firms had the most job cuts in November, with a 91,356 reduction, the retail industry showed the second-worst performance, with 11,073 losses, and this was before the Christmas season.

Headlines of newspapers around the country on December 6–7 revealed that November's job losses were the worst in thirty-four years, reaching more than 1.5 million, which at 0.4 percent of the workforce, was the worst showing since 1980. The unemployment rate rose to 6.7 percent in what was the eleventh consecutive monthly fall in employment, arguably making the recession the longest since the Great Depression.

In addition, 70 percent of the jobs lost were in the service sector, notably in retailing, temporary work, and hotel and restaurant employment. The only sectors adding jobs in November 2008 were health care and education.

The manufacturing sector had been particularly hard hit, losing more than 600,000 jobs in 2008.

The nation lost 524,000 jobs in December 2008. The unemployment rate jumped to a sixteen-year high of 7.2 percent, nearly 50 percent larger than at the start of the recession in December 2007.

There were 1.9 million U.S. layoffs in 2008. There were 3.3 unemployed individuals for every vacancy, a ratio that worsened in 2009. Job hunting took on average about four months before finding a position, which often carried a 20 percent to 30 percent cut in salary.

In mid-January 2009, the Labor Department reported that first-time requests for unemployment insurance jumped to a seasonally adjusted 524,000 in the week ending January 10 from an upwardly revised figure of 470,000 the previous week. By the start of 2009, unemployment had risen in every state.

The Labor Department announced on February 6, that 598,000 jobs were lost in January. The contraction in jobs was steeper than in any other recession since at least the early 1980s. The unemployment rate rose from 7.2 percent in December to 7.6 percent, which worked out to 11.6 million unemployed workers. If the rate had included part-time workers who need full-time jobs and jobless workers who had given up seeking because their prospects were so poor, the figure would have reached 13.9 percent, or 21.7 million workers, up from 13.5 percent in December. As reported on February 26, the number of Americans filing new claims for unemployment insurance rose to 667,000.

In February alone, the economy shed 651,000 jobs, and the government revised some recent months to include more losses than previously thought, for a total of 4.4 million jobs lost since December 2007.

During the current downturn, more jobs had been lost faster than in any period since 1974, as measured from peak employment. The economy had now lost 3.2 percent of its jobs since December 2007. It dropped 3.1 percent between the summer of 1981 and the end of 1982.

The losses pushed the unemployment rate to 8.1 percent, its highest level since March 1983. But this did not take into account those who had given up looking for work or those who were working part-time but wanted full-time work.

Manufacturing and overtime hours declined, leading to more job cuts in the future. A quarter of a million construction and manufacturing jobs disappeared; the service sector lost 375,000 positions. (Only health services and government showed a slight increase.)

Claims for jobless benefits added 12,000 to reach 669,000 in the last week of March, hitting a new high for the current recession. Claims for unemployment benefits rose to a record 5.7 million ending March 21.

March figures indicated the unemployment rate at its highest level since 1983, with job losses at 5.1 million, with two-thirds of the cuts coming since November 2008. The jobless rate climbed to 8.5 percent from 8.1 percent a month earlier. The number of jobs lost in March was 663,000. Almost one in twelve adult males was now jobless. Almost every private industry lost jobs; construction 126,000; manufacturing 161,000; business services 133,000; and retailing 48,000.

Workers ages forty-five and older had a disproportionate share of the long-term unemployment, those out of work for six months or longer. On average, laid-off workers in this group were out of work 22.2 weeks in 2008, compared with 16.2 weeks for younger workers. The unemployment rate for workers ages forty-five and older was 6.4 percent, the highest since at least 1948.

Initial jobless claims tumbled 53,000 to 610,000 in the week ending April 11. The decline brought the four-week average for claims down 8,500 to 651,000, the first decline since the beginning of 2009. Continuing claims for unemployment benefits jumped 172,000 to 6.02 million in the week ending April 4, underscoring the difficulty in finding new work.

Initial jobless claims fell 14,000 to 631,000 in the week ending April 25. That raised hopes that job losses could moderate over the coming months.

Unemployment in April, although reaching 8.9 percent, showed signs of a slowdown. The month's figures were 539,000 people without full-time work. This jobless number indicated that those receiving benefits would rise to 6.35 million.

Nonfarm payrolls fell by 345,000 in May, less than April's 504,000 drop and the smallest decline since September. Yet more jobs were lost in May than in any month of the prior three recessions, and the economy had now lost 6 million jobs since the recession began in December 2007. The unemployment rate rose a half point to 9.4 percent, its highest level since February 1983.

The jobless rate in June continued to inflict damage, reaching its highest level in twenty-six years. Challenging visions of an economic recovery, the

Labor Department released its May unemployment figures on July 2. The U.S. economy had lost 467,000 more jobs in June, and the unemployment rate edged up to 9.5 percent. These numbers make a compelling case for further government stimulus funds. The economy falls short by some 8.8 million jobs since the recession began; 6.5 million jobs have been lost and 2.3 million new jobs that were needed just to keep up with population growth never materialized. New figures confirmed that unemployment was highest for teenagers (24 percent), African Americans (14.7 percent), and Hispanics (12.2 percent). Of the 14.7 million jobless workers, 4.4 million, nearly 30 percent, have been out of work for twenty-seven weeks or more. Unemployment benefits will begin to expire in September for nearly 650,000 jobless workers.

On July 16, the government reported that claims for unemployment benefits fell sharply for the second consecutive week. Newly filed jobless claims fell 47,000 in one week on a seasonally adjusted 522,000, the lowest level since January.

In the one and a half years since the meltdown began, the unemployment rate had doubled and one out of six construction workers was out of work. Labor hoarding sometimes occurs during recessions, as companies retain their workers even as business declines, a form of stockpiling for the future, but this recession appears to be working inversely, where hoarding has reversed its course and layoffs continue in greater number. This suggests that companies are not optimistic about their future growth. At the same time, wages are also declining. By the end of the first half of the year, overall wage growth was zero.

The U.S. unemployment rate fell in July to deliver the labor market's best performance in a year. Nonfarm payrolls fell by 247,000 jobs in July, far fewer than the 443,000 shed in June. The jobless rate slipped to 9.4 percent from 9.5 percent one month before, the first decline since April 2008.

Unemployment of people sixteen to nineteen fell to 23.8 percent, the highest since record keeping began in 1954. Among African American teens it was 35.7 percent, nearly four times the national average of 9.4 percent.

By the summer 2009, the national employment population ratio was 59.4 percent. For teenagers it was 28.9 percent, the lowest on record.

Never in the 61 years of record keeping by the government has one-third of the unemployed, currently 14.5 million people, been out of work for twenty-seven weeks or more. Thirty million citizens—19 percent of the overall workforce—are either unemployed, no longer seeking work, or employed at a considerably lower pay level.

Jobless benefit claims climbed in mid-August, rising 15,000 to 576,000, the highest level in three weeks. The El Centro metropolitan area in Imperial

County, California, had America's worst unemployment, 27.5 percent as of June 2009, almost three times the then national rate of 9.7 percent.

In July, the unemployment rates in 372 U.S. cities continued to climb. Nineteen metropolitan areas had unemployment rates above 15 percent, with eight in California. Detroit's unemployment rates were the highest in the country at 17.7 percent.

Job losses in August 2009 indicated a small improvement. Employment declined by 146,000 in the month, while goods-producing jobs including construction and manufacturing fell by 152,000. This combined loss of 298,000 positions was an improvement from July's revised drop of 300,000, and was less than half the pace of declines seen at the beginning of the year.

Even though August 2009 job cuts were at their slowest rate for the year, a climb in unemployment to a twenty-six-year high of 9.7 percent does not forecast the recession end. Nonfarm payrolls dropped by 216,000 in August, fewer than the 276,000 of July according to a government announcement on September 4. The construction and manufacturing sectors together accounted for more than half of August's losses, while retail and business services narrowed. The largest gain was in health care, with nearly 28,000 new positions. Teenage unemployment rose to 25.9 percent, the highest since government records began in 1948 and up from 23.8 percent in July. The jobless rate for men rose to 10.1 percent, well above the 7.6 percent rate for women. People who have stopped looking for employment and those working part-time but who desire full-time positions rose half a percentage point to 16.8 percent.

In August, temporary payrolls fell by 6,500, far fewer than the average monthly drop of 51,000 during the first half of 2009. Since December 2007, the official beginning of the recession, temporary employees fell from 2.6 million to 1.7 million. One of every eight jobs lost during the meltdown has been a temporary position. In addition, the proportion of people who had been searching for work for longer than six months climbed to 35.6 percent of the unemployed, from a third of the work force in August. With a poor job market there was a 571,000 drop in the labor force.

The International Monetary Fund predicted that U.S. unemployment would average 10.1 percent in 2010 and forecast that the jobless rate would not drop to 5 percent until 2014.

As the recession was bottoming out, job losses continued to slow in September 2009 as the private sector shed fewer jobs than in August. GDP decreased at a 0.7 percent annual rate in the second quarter, better than the 6.4 percent fall in the first quarter. September's unemployment was the smallest since July 2008. Nevertheless, employers laid off another 263,000 people in the month, and the unemployment rate climbed to a twenty-six-year high of 9.8 percent. The nation was facing twenty-one consecutive months of job losses. The 15.1 million unemployed was greater than the population of all but four states.

On October 2, 2009, the government stated that the jobs picture was far worse than it had previously claimed. It was found that during the twelve months ending in March 2009, the economy lost 5.6 million jobs, 824,000 more than the 4.8 million earlier given. During the first half of 2008 job losses averaged 146,000 per month. That is three times the average of 49,000 jobs indicated in the initial estimated.

The largest declines in civilian employment since 1940 are:

Last Month of Decline	Percentage Decline	Decline in Employment in Millions	Months the Decline Lasted	Months Recovery Took
Sept. 1945	−10.1	−4.3	22	12
Oct. 1949	−5.2	−2.3	13	9
Aug. 1954	−3.4	−1.7	13	10
June 1958	−4.4	−2.3	14	10
Feb. 1961	−2.3	−1.3	12	10
Nov. 1970	−1.5	−1.0	8	10
April 1975	−2.8	−2.2	9	10
Dec. 1982	−3.1	−2.8	17	11
May 1991	−1.5	−1.6	11	21
Aug. 2003	−2.0	−2.7	30	18

Private-sector employment declined 203,000 in October 2009, the seventh straight month of moderating job losses and the smallest decline since July 2008. Job cuts declined for the third straight month, down 16 percent from September 2009 to 55,679.

The government reported that the jobless rate in October 2009 hit 10.2 percent. More than one out of every six workers, 17.5 percent, were unemployed or underemployed that month, probably the highest since the Great Depression of the 1930s. In October, nearly 16 million people were unemployed and more than 7 million jobs had been lost since the start of the Great Recession in December 2007.

By mid-November 2009, the jobless rate was up in twenty-nine states, hitting records in four of them. The unemployment rate fell in thirteen states.

Then, by early December the government reported that after a two-year climb the jobless rate had dropped to 10 percent in November, from 10.2 percent earlier. Employers shed 11,000 jobs, the fewest number since December 2007. Temporary hiring picked up 52,400 jobs in November, and workers received more hours in November: 33.2 per week, or 0.2 percent.

The number of workers who had been without work for more than twenty-six weeks rose to 5.9 million in November, the highest ever, and more than double the number in January. And the median duration of unemployment was up to 20.2 weeks.

See also APARTMENT VACANCIES; AUTOMATIC STABILIZERS; COBRA; CONSTRUCTION; ELDERLY, THE; FLEXICURITY; FOOD AID; FOOD BANKS; FOOD STAMPS; FURLOUGHS; GLOBAL UNEMPLOYMENT; ICELAND; IMMIGRATION; JOB CREATION; JOBLESS CLAIMS; JOB OPENINGS; KEYNES, JOHN MAYNARD; MEN UNEMPLOYED; MINIMUM WAGE; MISERY INDEX; OBAMA, BARACK; OVERTIME; ROOSEVELT, FRANKLIN DELANO; SPAIN; SPENDING; STATES (U.S.); SUICIDES; TAX CREDITS; TEMPORARY WORK; TRADE ADJUSTMENT ASSISTANCE ACT; UNEMPLOYMENT BENEFITS; UNITED KINGDOM; WELFARE; WOMEN UNEMPLOYED; WORKFORCE INVESTMENT ACT.

Cf. UNDEREMPLOYED.

UNEMPLOYMENT BENEFITS. U.S. unemployment benefits rolls rose to a twenty-six-year high in the last week of December 2008. Extending unemployment benefits through 2010 would cost about $100 billion. The number of people still on jobless rolls after drawing an initial week of aid jumped 101,000 to 4.61 million. That was the highest since November 1982 and higher than analysts' expectations of 4.5 million.

By the end of September 2009, there was a push by Democrats in Congress to extend unemployment coverage that would provide four more weeks of benefits to all states, while states over the 8.5 percent threshold would get twelve additional weeks.

On October 29, the Labor Department reported that initial claims for unemployment insurance fell by 1,000 to a seasonally adjusted 530,000.

In Europe, unemployment benefits provide a better cushion against financial collapse than in the United States. For example, Belgian and Norwegian workers take home almost three-quarters of what they earn when employed. France and Sweden both pay an unemployed worker around two-thirds of his previous income in the first year of joblessness. Such benefits are less generous in the United States and usually expire after one year.

The government reported that the jobless rate hit 10.2 percent in October 2009. If statistics were available, but aren't, the measure would be at its highest level since the Great Depression of the 1930s. More than one out of every six workers, 17.5 percent were unemployed or underemployed. The previous high was 17.1 percent, in December 1982.

On November 6, the president signed into law the Worker, Homeownership and Business Assistance Act (2009), extending unemployment benefits by twenty weeks and renewing the first-time homebuyer tax credit until April 2010. About 1 million laid-off workers will see their unemployment benefits extended for another fourteen weeks of federally paid aid to unemployed people who had exhausted state and federal limited benefits that already lasted up to seventy-nine weeks in many states. And for the majority of states with especially high unemployment, it added six more weeks of payments, bringing the total to ninety-nine weeks.

By November the unemployment rate had fallen in thirty-six states, while only eight states saw a rise in unemployment rates.

Most economists don't expect unemployment to fall below 6 percent until 2013.

See also JOBLESS CLAIMS; UNEMPLOYMENT.

UNEMPLOYMENT COVERAGE. *See* UNEMPLOYMENT BENEFITS.

UNFAIR TRADE SUBSIDIES. The discriminatory commercial exchange activities of goods that are either unfairly subsidized or dumped, or are otherwise illegitimate, as with counterfeit items.

A huge debate ensued following George W. Bush's announcement in the fall of 2008, of the use of $17.4 billion of taxpayers' money to prevent the collapse of General Motors and Chrysler. European and Asian carmakers had been hard-pressed to refrain from using their government funds to assist failing companies, but now chose to reexamine their positions.

See also AUTOMOBILE INDUSTRY.

UNILEVER. The Anglo-Dutch consumer-goods company reported that its first-quarter 2009 sales volume dropped 1.8 percent, with revenue falling to $974.5 million. That was down 45 percent from the year before.

The world's third-largest consumer-goods firm by sales reported in August that its profits in the second quarter were down 17 percent.

Unilever's third-quarter 2009 profit fell. Revenue fell 2 percent.

UNIONS. *See* AUTO TASK FORCE; EMPLOYEE FREE CHOICE ACT.

UNITED AIRLINES (UAL). The airline planned to reduce its mainline capacity by as much as 9.5 percent in 2009, on top of a 4.2 percent reduction in 2008. UAL reported a net loss of $1.3 billion for the fourth quarter 2008, for an annual net loss of $5.35 billion. There were plans to cut another 1,000 salaried and management positions by the end of 2009, bringing the reduction in ranks to 30 percent, after previous cuts of 1,500 positions.

On June 17, 2009, UAL declared that the second-quarter traffic was to fall as much as 10.5 percent.

In September 2009, United reported a 5.8 percent decline in its mainline service, with capacity down 8.9 percent.

See also AIRLINES.

UNITED ARAB EMIRATES. In mid-May 2009, the UAE, the second-largest Arab Gulf economy, informed the Gulf Cooperation Council that it was withdrawing from plans to join a monetary union with the GCC, damaging hopes for economic integration planned for thirty years. The program was intended to improve relations between oil-rich Arab states straddling the Persian Gulf. A projected central bank for five GCC nations also was put on hold.

The collapse in November 2009 in Dubai has put considerable pressure on the government of the United Arab Emirates to step in with fresh financial support.

See also DUBAI; MIDDLE EAST.

UNITED AUTO WORKERS. *See* AUTOMOBILE INDUSTRY; CHRYS-LER; FIAT; FORD; VEBA.

UNITED KINGDOM. In 2001, large British banks lent about the same amount to their corporate and consumer clients as they took in deposits, but by the end of June 2008, they were lending out $1.16 trillion.

It was projected that by the end of 2009, from the peak of 353,000 in 2007 roughly 62,000 financial services jobs in London would be lost, which would return financial industry employment to its 1998 levels.

The British economy contracted by 0.5 percent in the three months through September 2008, ending a string of sixteen years without a negative quarter.

Prime Minister Gordon Brown, on September 3, unveiled the first in a series of measures to prop up the collapsing housing market.

The number of people in Britain receiving jobless payments increased at the fastest pace in sixteen years in October, reaching 980,000. The Bank of England predicted that the economy was likely to shrink through much of 2009, and the total unemployment rate for the third quarter rose to 5.8 percent, the highest in eleven years.

On November 24, the British government announced a large sales tax cut as part of a package of measures to stimulate the struggling national economy. The government attempted to spend its way out of its first recession in seventeen years by cutting taxes and increasing public spending despite a budget deficit that was already among the largest of any developed nation. As part of the $30 billion fiscal package presented to Parliament, the government planned to reduce the value-added tax to 15 percent from 17.5 percent for a year, help homeowners struggling with mortgage payments, and further support retirees and small businesses.

As a result, Britain's budget deficit was projected to climb to 8 percent of GDP in 2010. To cover for the tax cuts, the government increased national insurance payroll deductions and raised income taxes for those earning more than £150,000 a year. The tax rate rose to 45 percent from 40 percent, which was the highest bracket for the past twenty years, to take effect beginning in 2011.

On December 3, the British government announced that it would guarantee interest payments worth up to £1 billion owed by homeowners struggling to keep up with mortgages, in an effort to prevent home repossessions.

Only 32,000 mortgages were approved for house purchases in October. The number matched August's record low and was almost two-thirds below the level of a year earlier.

Housing prices in England registered their largest decline in sixteen years during November. This decline, the tenth in a row, was the largest since 1992 when house prices fell a monthly 3 percent. As banks reined in mortgage lending and buyers were deterred by the economic slowdown, house prices were projected to decrease 10 percent in 2009 and 3 percent in 2010, after a 9 percent decline in 2008. Repossessions were expected to reach a near record high of 70,000 in 2009. That number would be up from 45,000 in 2008 and close to the highest level ever recorded, 75,500 in 1991, when the UK was last in a recession.

The UK's bank rescue plan, considered the global model of what to do right, ran into trouble by mid-December. Domestic banks were resisting pressure to lend more as they sought to protect themselves in the harsh meltdown. In October, when Gordon Brown presented the plan to inject capital into banks in exchange for a substantial shareholding, he promised he would not only attempt to stabilize the British banking system, but to jump-start the stalled lending markets.

British retail sales posted a 0.6 percent drop for November, following October's 0.1 percent dip.

The government, on December 15, increased the amount that they would make available for lending to first-time home buyers by a third in an effort to help the struggling construction industry. The funds were lent to first-time homebuyers, interest free for five years, and could be used as a deposit for up to a third of the price of a home. This increase brought the total to about $600 million. The Exchequer sought support of the biggest British banks for a £1 billion mortgage program aimed at preventing home repossessions.

Unemployment climbed to 6 percent in the three months to October, from 5.5 percent in the previous same period. New benefit claimants numbering 75,700 were listed in November, the biggest one-month increase since 1991.

In the third quarter of 2008, the British economy shrank by more than previously thought, as Britain headed into a deep recession. GDP fell 0.6 percent in the quarter, compared with a 0.5 percent decline earlier. The drop was the steepest since 1990. Manufacturing shrank 1.6 percent, the largest decline since 2001, while the distribution, hotels, and catering sector contracted 2.1 percent, the biggest decline since 1980.

The British economy officially sank into recession in January 2009, with output falling 1.5 percent in the fourth quarter 2008, as the financial crisis ravaged banks, retail, and manufacturing. Britain was officially in recession, based on the standard definition of a recession of two consecutive quarters of negative growth.

It was the biggest decline since the early days of Margaret Thatcher's government nearly thirty years ago and prompted a further bout of selling of the pound, which slumped to a new twenty-three-year low against the dollar.

The government released $642 million in public funds to bail out two key venues for the 2012 London Olympics in the face of the global economic downturn.

The UK lost a record number of jobs in the closing months of 2008, with unemployment claims rising for the eleventh straight month, increasing 77,900.

In January 2009, Prime Minister Brown pledged to create 100,000 jobs through a public works program and announced that he would press banks to resume normal lending.

Britain announced on January 27 a $3.2 billion aid package loan guaranteed from the European Investment Bank, and another £1 billion from its Treasury.

By January 2009, luxury home prices fell 3.7 percent. In the year, the average price of homes that cost more than $1.4 million slumped 21 percent.

The declining British pound pushed up prices for food and other imported items.

Consumer price inflation rose to 3.2 percent in February on an annualized basis, from 3 percent in January. The 26 percent decline of the pound against the U.S. dollar and 16 percent decline against the euro over a twelve-month period failed to encourage demand for British exports.

The UK's fourth-quarter GDP contracted 1.6 percent in 2008, more than the 1.5 percent reported in January.

The Bank of England's Monetary Policy Committee, in early April, kept its key interest rate at 0.5 percent and agreed to pump $110 billion in new money into the economy through June 2009.

By mid-April Britain's budget deficit was 11 percent of its GDP, compared with 13 percent forecast for the United States in 2009. Without large spending cuts it would jump to 80 percent of the overall economy in coming years, from today's level of about 40 percent.

A drop in UK retail prices, their first fall in nearly half a century, fueled fears that shook up the government's forecasts. By the end of April, it was feared that the country's economy would contract by 3 percent to 3.5 percent in 2009.

On April 22, the government laid out plans for more than $1 trillion in deficit spending over the next five years, and ordered a five-percentage-point increase, to 50 percent, in the top marginal rate of income tax for the nation's highest earners.

By the end of April, the government stated that it would run its largest peacetime budget deficit on record—about 12 percent of GDP in both of the next two years. Should the economy return quickly to growth after shrinking by 3.5 percent in 2009, the deficit would remain above 5 percent of GDP in 2013. That would push the government's debts up to more than 75 percent of GDP, from about the present 43 percent.

The UK's economy took its worst drop in three decades, shrinking by 1.9 percent in the first quarter 2009, from the previous quarter. By June, Britain's unemployment rate rose to 7.2 percent in the three months to April, from 6.5 percent in the previous quarter. The number of claimants for unemployment benefits more than doubled in the twelve months ending in May to 1.54 million, the highest level since 1997.

By the end of June, weak lending was predicted to contribute to a 4.3 percent fall in the UK's GDP, more pessimistic than an earlier forecast for a 3.7 percent decline.

The UK's GDP fell by 0.8 percent in the second quarter from the first, and dropped 5.6 percent year-over-year, the largest annual decline since quarterly records began in 1955.

On August 28, the government reported that the nation's GDP contracted 0.7 percent from April to June 2009. Many experts expected economic growth to resume in the third quarter, after bottoming out in a 2.4 percent contraction in the first three months. Any return to expansion in the third quarter would be the first quarterly rise since early 2008 and would be the official end of the 2008–2009 meltdown.

The nation's manufacturing output rose in July 2009, the best monthly manufacturing data in three years, with output climbing 0.9 percent. The UK's GDP edged up 0.2 percent over the period, following a 0.3 percent decline in the three months to July 2009.

Unemployment in the UK jumped to 7.9 percent in the three months through July 2009, lowering hopes of a speedy economic recovery.

The British economy remained in recession during the third quarter 2009. GDP contract by 0.4 percent from July to September from the earlier three months, and it shrank by 5.2 percent compared to a year before. The

British economy contracted for six successive quarters, making this the longest downturn since 1955, lagging behind other EU nations.

By October 2009, housing prices rose for the third straight month, as a low supply of suitable properties continues to push prices upward. House prices increased 0.2 percent from September, though they fell 4.2 percent for the year.

To offset the recent gloomy news on the UK's economy, the European Commission announced on November 1, 2009, that the UK's GDP would expand 0.9 percent in 2010 and 1.9 percent in 2011, outpacing growth of 0.7 percent in 2010 and 1.5 percent in 2011 for the sixteen nations of the eurozone.

On December 9, 2009, the government said that it would return money from banks to taxpayers by placing a 50 percent tax on banker bonuses of more than $40,700.

See also ASSET PROTECTION SCHEME; BANK OF ENGLAND; BARCLAYS; EUROPEAN CENTRAL BANK; FTSE; LLOYDS; MANUFACTURING; ROYAL BANK OF SCOTLAND; WATERFORD WEDGWOOD; WINDFALL TAX; WOOLWORTHS.

UNITED NATIONS (UN). *See* POVERTY.

UNITED PARCEL SERVICE (UPS). UPS's second-quarter 2009 income fell 49 percent, with its export volume falling 7.3 percent.

Profits in the third quarter 2009 fell 43 percent from a year earlier.

UNITED STATES. The U.S. economy is facing extremely difficult conditions. The financial crisis has intensified at a time when growth had already been weakened by the prolonged housing downturn. A credit crunch is likely to result in a pronounced contraction in activity over the near term and a further deterioration of the labor market. Once financial conditions normalize, GDP growth should resume but at a slower pace than in past recoveries, in part because of negative wealth effects. In response to lower commodity prices and the opening of a large output gap—that is, a shortfall between actual and potential output—inflation should recede significantly to around 1.5 percent in 2010. Once the crisis has passed, the focus will be to restore fiscal sustainability by reducing the budget deficit and tackling the challenge of rising entitlement spending. The unfolding events since mid-2007 have highlighted the need for a major overhaul of financial regulation and supervision, a process that should boost investor confidence and thus help to revive the economy (OECD).

See also STATES (U.S).

UNITED STATES STEEL CORPORATION. *See* US STEEL.

UNITED TECHNOLOGIES. UTC makes Otis elevators, Carrier air conditioners, Pratt & Whitney jet engines, Sikorsky helicopters, Hamilton Sundstrand aerospace components, and various fire and security products. Hard hit by a simultaneous downturn in the building and aerospace industries, it cut 5 percent of its work force, or 11,600 jobs, in early 2009.

Their first-quarter net income, announced on April 21, slid 26 percent as the firm moved to cut costs because of slipping demand. Its net income of $499 million dropped from $1.08 billion a year before.

The company reported a decline of 17 percent sales in its third-quarter profit.

UNIVERSITY ENDOWMENTS. *See* HARVARD UNIVERSITY; STANFORD UNIVERSITY; YALE UNIVERSITY.

UNIVISION COMMUNICATIONS. *See NEW YORK TIMES.*

UNPAID FURLOUGHS. *See* FURLOUGHS.

UPS. *See* UNITED PARCEL SERVICE.

U.S. *See* STATES (U.S.); UNITED STATES.

US AIRWAYS. Reported second-quarter 2009 profit of $58 million, compared to a $568 million loss a year earlier.

In early September 2009, US Airways reported that its August passenger traffic fell 3.9 percent, about in line with the airline's 3.8 percent in capacity.

On October 28, 2009, the airlines disclosed its retrenchment program, cutting back on a number of routes so it can focus on its main hubs, losing 1,000 jobs.

USA TODAY. See NEWSPAPERS.

US BANCORP. Posted a 65 percent drop in fourth-quarter 2008 net income as it took a $253 million securities write-down and boosted credit-loss provisions. It had received $6.6 billion in November 2008 from the U.S. Treasury under TARP. It reported a net income of $330 million, or 15 cents a share, compared with $942 million, or 53 cents a share, the year before.

U.S. CENSUS. Preparing for the 2010 census will employ 1.2 million people and a $2.3 billion injection into the job market.

U.S.-CHINA TRADE. China and the United States are each other's second-largest trading partner; the value of the two-way trade in goods exceeds $300 billion.

Since 2003, U.S. exports to China have doubled. The U.S. trade surplus with China in services had growth 36 percent each year and the overall value of American exports services to China exceeded $16 billion in 2008.

U.S. businesses invested more than $60 billion in 57,000 projects in China. In 2007, American-funded companies in China enjoyed a 17 percent profit, while domestically the profit of U.S. businesses dropped by 3 percent on average. A possible new trade war between China and the United States began in September 2009, with the United States placing tariffs on imported Chinese tires, and China in response imposing tariffs on U.S. chickens and auto parts.

See also G-2.

U.S. COMMERCE DEPARTMENT. A federal agency established in 1913 to promote domestic and foreign trade. The agency has a $19 million annual budget and fewer than twenty grant officers. Under the Stimulus Plan of 2009, the department is now in charge of $7 billion in grants to expand Internet access in rural areas.

See also U.S.-CHINA TRADE.

U.S. DEFICIT. In the 2008 fiscal year, the budget deficit approached $1 trillion, roughly equal to the combined budgets of the U.S. military and Medicare, the government health care program for the elderly and disabled.

See also CHIMERICA; DEFICIT (BUDGET).

U.S. ENERGY DEPARTMENT. A federal agency, established in 1977 to control oil prices and allocations, to coordinate energy research and development efforts, to set rates for oil and oil-product appliances, and to design conservation standards.

In 2009, the Energy Department's annual budget was approximately $25 billion. With $40 billion in new funds from the Stimulus Plan of 2009, some programs will grow.

For example:

	Current Funding	Stimulus Funds
Efficient electricity grids	$140 million	$11 billion
Low-income home weatherization	$250 million	$5 billion
Fossil-energy research/development	$311 million	$3.4 billion
Aid for advanced vehicle batteries	$215 million	$2.0 billion

U.S. GOVERNMENT DEBT. The world's safest investment. It lowers the cost of borrowing for the U.S. government, but slows down the recovery. If investors remain reluctant to put money into stocks and corporate bonds, that could choke off funds that businesses require to keep financing day-to-day activities.

See also CHIMERICA; ZERO-RATE.

U-SHAPED RECESSION. *See* RECESSION.

U.S. LABOR DEPARTMENT. A federal agency created in 1913 to advance workers' welfare, working conditions, and in general, employment opportunities.

See also UNEMPLOYMENT.

US STEEL. Had a $439 million first-quarter 2009 loss. US Steel reported at the end of April that its sales fell 47 percent to $2.75 billion from $5.2 billion one year earlier.

US Steel reported at the end of July 2009, a second-quarter loss of $392 million. Nevertheless it recalled about 800 workers at its huge flat-rolling mill, suggesting a forecast by them of a brighter future.

The company swung to third-quarter 2009 losses.

U.S. SUPREME COURT. *See* CHRYSLER.

U.S. TREASURY. A federal agency created in 1789 to impose and collect taxes and customs duties, to enforce revenue and fiscal laws, to disburse federal funds, to manage the public debt, and to coin and print money.

The Treasury was and remains a central player in the meltdown. The Treasury led the way for the $700 billion bank bailout plan passed during the George W. Bush administration.

On September 8, the Treasury announced plans to replace the CEOs of both Fannie Mae and Freddie Mac and buy $1 billion of preferred shares in each without providing immediate cash.

Treasury initially turned down a request by General Motors for as much as $10 billion to help finance a merger with Chrysler.

On December 31, the Treasury drafted broad guidelines for aid to the auto industry that would allow them to provide bailout funds to any firm they deemed important to making or financing cars.

On May 26, 2009, the Treasury laid out details of its proposal for dealing with bank stock warrants it received in return for cash injections into troubled banks.

See also ASSET GUARANTEE PROGRAM; AUDITORS; AUTOMOBILE INDUSTRY; BANK BAILOUT (PLAN) OF 2008; EMERGENCY ECONOMIC STABILIZATION ACT OF 2008; FINANCIAL REGULATION PLAN (2009); FINANCIALSTABILITY.GOV; GEITHNER, TIMOTHY F.; GMAC; INTERNAL REVENUE SERVICE; LEHMAN BROTHERS; LIFE INSURERS; PAULSON, HENRY; PAY; TOXIC ASSETS; TROUBLED ASSET RELIEF PROGRAM; VEBA.

UTILITY CUTOFFS. During the Great Recession utility shutoffs rose 5 percent in 2009 and 4.3 million households were disconnected for nonpayment.

V

VACANCIES. *See* APARTMENT VACANCIES; OFFICE RENTS.

VARIABLE-RATE MORTGAGE. A type of mortgage that permits the interest rate on the loan to rise or fall automatically in accordance with a predetermined index, for instance, an index of banks' cost-of-funds, such as the London Interbank Offered Rate (LIBOR). The interest rate can fluctuate every six months, but cannot be raised by more than two and a half percentage points over the life of the mortgage. In addition, banks must offer customers a choice between variable-rate and other conventional mortgages.
   See also FLEXIBLE-PAYMENT MORTGAGE; LIBOR; RENEGOTIABLE-RATE MORTGAGE.

VAUXHALL. *See* MAGNA; OPEL.

VEBA (VOLUNTARY EMPLOYEE BENEFICIARY ASSOCIATION). U.S. Treasury Department protection for the United Auto Workers union pension fund that controls 55 percent of the equity in the new Chrysler Corporation, since it emerged from bankruptcy. The Treasury's contribution is a $4.6 billion note, payable over thirteen years at a 9 percent interest rate, helping to fund roughly $10 billion in liabilities.
   See also CHRYSLER.

VENEZUELA. In the winter of 2007–2008, $100 million of free heating oil was supplied to poor people throughout the United States by the government of Venezuela. Then, on January 5, 2009, President Chavez announced that he was suspending the program. This temporary action resulted from the sharp drop in oil prices, which forced the country to reduce government spending.
   Oil accounts for 93 percent of the government's export income and about 50 percent of its overall income. Venezuela also sold 15,000 barrels a day of subsidized oil to Central American nations. The government provided nearly 100,000 barrels a day of oil and oil products to Cuba, a close ally, free of charge.
   With oil being the source of 93 percent of Venezuela's export income, President Chavez announced on March 21 a lowering of 2009's federal budget, offsetting a drop in the government's oil revenues. Growth slowed to its most

sluggish rate in five years. The new measures included a plan to expand the government's domestic debt by roughly $10 billion. The budget would be lowered by 6.7 percent, while the minimum wage would rise in 2009 by 20 percent from its current level of about $372 per month. An annual inflation rate of 29.5 percent in the capital was a major reason for the wage adjustment.

As most emerging nations of the world were improving their economies by the fall of 2009, Venezuela's third-quarter output declined 4.5 percent compared with the year before. This fall followed a second-quarter drop of 2.4 percent, the second consecutive quarter of economic decline, which officially placed the nation into recession. Imports are down 29 percent and retail sales fell 11.5 percent. Inflation remains high, at nearly 30 percent for 2009.

By December 2009, the president of Venezuela threatened to nationalize the nation's entire private banking system, even though its ten largest banks, which control about 70 percent of deposits, are in good shape. By mid-month with its economy shrinking and inflation soaring, Venezuela began nationalizing its banks, stoking fears that a full-blown banking crisis was fast approaching. Venezuela's economy is falling deeper into recession, even as the rest of the region recovers.

VENTURE CAPITAL. Venture capitalists had a dismal 2009 resulting from the decline in investment activity. They invested just $14.6 billion into start-ups through the first three quarters of 2009, down from more than $25 billion the year before. It does not appear that the venture industry in 2010 will match the $31 billion invested for all of 2008.

VERIZON. As businesses cut back, and unemployed people no longer needed cell phones and laptop data cards, the company announced on July 27, 2009, a 21 percent decline. Management announced that it would eliminate 8,000 jobs in the landline unit, all by the end of the year 2009.

Verizon Communications posted a 30 percent drop in its third-quarter 2009 profit. The company added 1.3 million new wireless subscribers in the quarter, down from 2.1 million a year before.

VIACOM. By February 2009, Viacom reported a 69 percent drop in quarterly profit, resulting from the recession.

On April 30, Viacom posted a 34 percent slide in first-quarter net income to $177 million.

See also UNEMPLOYMENT.

VIETNAM. Vietnam's central bank devalued the dong by 5.4 percent against the U.S. dollar, and raised its benchmark interest rate by one percentage point to 8 percent.

See also SOUTHEAST ASIA.

VISA. Reported fourth-quarter 2009 earnings of $514 million.
Cf. MASTERCARD.

VODAFONE. A giant telecommunications firm, it declared in February 2009 that it would cut 500 jobs in the UK as part of a $1.45 billion cost-reduction program.
Cf. MOTOROLA; NOKIA.

VOLCKER, PAUL. Appointed by President Obama to chair a newly formed Economic Recovery Advisory Board.

In 1952 he joined the staff of the Federal Reserve Bank of New York as a full-time economist and in 1962 returned to become the director of financial analysis within the U.S. Treasury Department. In 1963 became deputy under-secretary for monetary affairs, and from 1969 to 1974 served as undersecre-tary of the Treasury for international monetary affairs.

He was the chairman of the Federal Reserve under presidents Carter and Reagan, from August 1979 to August 1987. He is credited with ending the U.S. stagflation crisis of the 1970s. Inflation, which peaked at 13.5 percent, was lowered to 3.2 percent by 1983.

President Obama appointed him to the chairman of the White House's Economic Recovery Advisory Board. On September 16, 2009, Volcker said that banks should operate in a much less risky fashion, including not making trading bets with their own capital. He also believes that banks should be restricted to trading on their clients' behalf instead of making bets with their own funds through internal units that often act like hedge funds.

VOLKSWAGEN. By December 2009, Volkswagen made public its ap-plication for financial assistance from Germany's $650 billion bank bailout program. The carmaker's affiliated bank and financial services units both wanted state loan guarantees.

Volkswagen said on January 20, 2009 that it would put about two-thirds of its employees in Germany, about 60,000 workers, on shorter hours for five days in the last week of February.

Following a 20 percent fall in fourth-quarter 2008 profit, the automaker forecast lower earnings and vehicle sales in 2009.

In the first quarter 2009, Volkswagen sold 1.39 million cars worldwide. It reported a 74 percent drop in first-quarter net profit, which was $314.4 mil-lion. Revenue fell 11 percent from one year earlier.

On May 17, VW announced that it was indefinitely postponing talks over a possible merger with Porsche. Days later, Porsche and VW affirmed that they would continue talks.

On August 13, 2009, VW announced that they had reached a broad agree-ment to merge the premium sports-car maker Porsche into VW, paying as much as $4.7 billion. VW would take a 42 percent stake in Porsche's business by the end of 2009, with a full merger projected for 2011.

The company reported an 86 percent fall in third-quarter 2009 profit. Net income at Europe's largest carmaker fell $253 million, as sales slumped 10 percent from a year earlier.

On December 9, 2009 Volkswagen reported that it would purchase a 20 percent stake in Suzuki Motor for $2.5 billion.

See also AUTOMOBILE INDUSTRY; GERMANY; PORSCHE.

VOLUNTARY EMPLOYEE BENEFICIARY ASSOCIATION. *See* VEBA.

VOLVO. New truck deliveries fell by more than half in January 2009, delivering 10,232 vehicles, down 51 percent from 20,856 in 2008. Deliveries to Eastern Europe and North America were hardest hit, down 78 percent and 67 percent respectively. Volvo makes trucks under the Mack, Renault, Eicher, and Nissan Diesel brands, as well as their own.

On March 12, Volvo management announced that it was freezing salaries and scaling back production. To avoid further layoffs, Volvo signed a deal with its unions to lower personnel costs.

Truck deliveries in February 2009 fell 51 percent globally, and 63 percent in Europe from a year before. By April, it swung to a first-quarter 2009 loss of $510 million. Revenue declined 27 percent.

In April, truck deliveries plunged 63 percent from a year earlier. Volvo delivered 9,196 vehicles, down from 24,616 in April 2008. In Europe and North America, deliveries fell 69 percent to 4,052 and 1,128 trucks, respectively. Deliveries in Eastern Europe dropped 87 percent to 382 trucks.

On July 21, Volvo posted its worst-ever quarterly net loss as sales fell in the wake of the economic downturn. It had a net loss of $718.5 million for the three months ending June 30.

On October 28, 2009, Ford Motor Company announced that it had chosen China's Zhejiang Geely Holding Group as the preferred bidder for its Volvo subsidiary. For the entire year, Volvo is expected to sell about 325,000 cars, made by 20,000 employees. By year's end 2009, Ford agreed to terms for Volvo's sale, with a formal agreement to be signed in the first quarter of 2010.

See also SWEDEN.

VOUCHERS. *See* GERMANY.

V-SHAPED RECESSION. *See* RECESSION.

W

WACHOVIA. In late October 2008, Wachovia suffered a $23.7 billion quarterly loss, the biggest ever for an American bank. Sold to the Wells Fargo Bank.

See also WELLS FARGO BANK.

WAGE GROWTH. *See* UNEMPLOYMENT.

WAGES. By December 2009 the average weekly wage for most of the country's workers rose by nearly two-thirds of a percentage point in a single month, to $622.

WAGONER, RICK. Became president of GM on October 5, 1998, and in June, added chief executive to his title. On February 26, 2009, GM announced a $9.6 billion loss in the fourth quarter of 2008, bringing its loss for the year to $30.9 billion and raising new concern about its viability.

On March 27, the U.S. government asked Wagoner to agree to resign as part of an agreement for new federal aid. He accepted.

See also GENERAL MOTORS.

WALL STREET JOURNAL (WSJ). On October 14, 2009, the *Wall Street Journal* announced that its average weekday circulation rose to 2.02 million printed copies and online subscriptions, making it the nation's largest newspaper by weekday circulation.

See also NEWS CORPORATION; NEWSPAPERS.

WAL-MART STORES. The largest retailer in the United States said on February 10, 2009, that it would cut 700 to 800 jobs at its headquarters in Arkansas.

Wal-Mart same-store sales reported a 5.1 percent sales increase in February compared with a 2.7 percent increase for the period a year before.

The company's fourth-quarter profit was $3.25 billion, up 3.2 percent from $3.14 billion a year before. Net sales increased 1.1 percent to $98.67 billion.

See also STOCK MARKET.

WALT DISNEY COMPANY. *See* ABC.

WARS IN AFGHANISTAN AND IRAQ. "A troop withdrawal may not bring budget relief. The economic payoff may be in the nation's psychology." On February 27, 2009, President Obama announced that the troops would be coming home from Iraq. The annual budget of the United States would be significantly altered.

The war had already cost an estimated $860 billion. The cost in Afghanistan and Iraq followed a simple progression in the president's budget plan: $144 billion in fiscal year 2009, $130 billion in 2010, and possibly $50 billion for 2011 and beyond.

In October 2008, a government agency estimated that in 2006 (the last year of available numbers) it cost $390,000 a year to sustain each American soldier overseas. Then in January 2009, the Congressional Budget Office estimated that between 2010 and 2019 the costs would be based on two alternatives. In the first, the number of soldiers deployed in both nations draws down fairly quickly, to about 30,000 by 2011. In the second option, levels drop to 75,000 by 2013. Both are significantly lower than the present 180,000 troops. The cost would be $388 billion for the first case, or nearly double, at $867 billion for the second option.

WASHINGTON MUTUAL. On September 26, 2008, federal regulators seized Washington Mutual and struck a deal to sell the bulk of its operations to JP Morgan in the largest bank failure in U.S. history.

WASHINGTON POST. First-quarter 2009 losses were $18.7 million, compared with a profit of $39.3 million a year earlier. Revenue for the quarter dropped 0.8 percent to $1.05 billion.

By August 1, 2009, the *Washington Post* showed a profit for the second quarter.

Effective December 31, 2009, the newspaper closed its remaining U.S. news bureaus outside of Washington, D.C.

WASTE. *See* TECHNOLOGY INVESTMENT.

WATERFORD WEDGWOOD. Makers of classic china and crystal, the company filed for bankruptcy protection in January 2009. Founded 250 years ago, this iconic British firm succumbed to the global economic slowdown and credit squeeze.

Sales for the year that ended in April 2008 were €672 million, down 9.4 percent from the previous year. The firm posted a loss of €231 million, up from €71 million. About 1,900 workers would lose their jobs in Britain alone.

On February 27, 2009, it was announced that KPS Capital Partners would purchase the Irish and UK operations of Waterford Wedgwood.

WATER INFRASTRUCTURE. *See* AMERICAN RECOVERY AND RE-INVESTMENT ACT (OF 2009).

WEALTH. The wealth of American families dropped nearly 18 percent in 2008, erasing years of sharp gains on housing and stocks. It was the largest loss since World War II.

The number of U.S. millionaires fell from 9.2 million to 6.7 million between 2007 and 2008, and it was also estimated that the number of global billionaires in 2008 fell to 793 from 1,125. The 400 richest people in 1982 had a combined net worth of $92 billion; by 2006, they owned $1.25 trillion. (To get on the list in 1982 you needed a net worth of $5 million, by 2006 it had to be $1 billion.) The gap between rich and poor had been widening for thirty years; now it was narrowing.

For example, in 2008, Monaco was the most expensive residential property location in the world. Ending in 2007, prices for property reached £100,000 per square meter. By April 2009, it had fallen back to $50,000. Also, in New York's Hamptons, where the rich often own large estates, offers were presented at 40 percent off of the peak bids from the previous year.

By the end of June, the world population of millionaires fell 15 percent, with the superrich losing the most. The number of millionaires fell to 8.6 million from 10.1 million in 2008. The wealth held by the world's millionaires plunged nearly 20 percent to $32.8 trillion from $40.7 trillion. The ultra-wealthy—those with $30 million in investable assets—saw their ranks tumble 25 percent, with their wealth declining 24 percent. There were 2.5 million millionaires in the United States at the end of 2008, down from 3 million in 2007. The wealthiest people are referred to as high-net-worth individuals (HNWIS).

After nearly two years, American households grew a bit wealthier in the second quarter 2009. Net worth grew by 3.9 percent to $53.1 trillion in the April–June period from the first quarter. Yet, it was still down almost 19 percent from the $65.3 trillion peak in the third quarter of 2007.

WEATHERIZATION. *See* AMERICAN RECOVERY AND REINVESTMENT ACT (OF 2009); ENERGY EFFICIENCY.

WEBSITE. *See* HACKING.

WELFARE. By 2009, despite soaring unemployment and the worst economic crisis in decades, eighteen states had cut their welfare rolls. Nationally the number of people receiving cash assistance remained at or near the lowest in more than forty years.

Twenty-three of the thirty largest states, which account for more than 88 percent of the country's population, indicated on June 22 that welfare caseloads were higher than the previous year. The largest increases are in states with the worst jobless rates.

The total number of welfare recipients is climbing. Paralleling this increase, the number of Americans receiving food stamps has risen sharply, from 24.9 million in September 2007, to 33.2 million in March 2009.

See also FOOD STAMPS; POVERTY; SPAIN.

WELLPOINT. The nation's largest health insurer reported a 61 percent drop in fourth-quarter profit on January 28, 2009. The insurer announced in mid-January 2009 that it would cut about 1,500 jobs, or 3.5 percent of its staff.

The company's third-quarter 2009 profit declined 11 percent, with a profit of $730 million. Revenue climbed 3.1 percent to $15.43 billion.

See also HEALTH INSURERS.

WELLS FARGO BANK. Posted a $2.55 billion loss in the fourth quarter 2008, becoming the first quarterly loss for the San Francisco–based bank since 2001.

In March 2009, the bank became the latest large U.S. firm to sharply cut its dividend—by 85 percent to a nickel a share—amid growing scrutiny of its once-strong balance sheet. The move looked to save $5 billion a year.

Management announced on April 9 that its profit in the first quarter 2009 rose to roughly $3 billion. This triggered a jump in shares of banks.

Wells Fargo posted a $3.2 billion profit for the second quarter 2009, up from $1.75 billion a year before.

By September 2009, Wells Fargo announced its intention to return $25 billion in federal bailout funds.

On December 14, 2009, Wells Fargo became the last of the big bank lenders to rush through a repayment of $25 billion before year's end. It first had to secure $10.4 billion by selling shares.

See also WACHOVIA.

Cf. CITIGROUP.

WEYERHAEUSER. The timber industry-building products firm announced in March 2009 that it would close two lumber mills as demand for wood products continued to decline with the slump in home construction.

Nearly 300 employees, or 1.5 percent of the firm's workforce, were affected. Weyerhaeuser had already closed ten plants making wood products.

It had losses in the first quarter of $264 million from a loss of $148 million the year earlier.

On July 31 Weyerhaeuser reported that its second-quarter 2009 loss had widened. The company lost $106 million, with sales dropping 36 percent to $1.39 billion from $217 billion a year earlier.

Cf. LOUISIANA-PACIFIC CORPORATION.

WHIRLPOOL. Fourth-quarter 2008 net income fell 76 percent for the world's largest appliance company by revenue. Management projected that its North American appliance sales would drop around 10 percent in 2009, after a 16 percent decline in the fourth quarter. They forecast sales in Europe to drop 8 percent in the same period, while Asia and Latin America were projected down 5 percent.

Whirlpool's first-quarter 2009 net income declined 27 percent on lower global sales and production. The world's largest appliance maker by revenue posted a first-quarter net income of $73 million, down from $100 million.

The company's third-quarter 2009 earnings fell 47 percent, with sales in North America—its largest market—slipping 9 percent from the previous year.

WHITE-COLLAR WORKERS. Usually those working in the service sector. Unlike most union workers, salaried workers have no safety net of health care or guaranteed income for a year.

WHOLESALE INVENTORIES. Wholesalers reduced their inventories in December 2008 by the largest amount in nearly seventeen years. This reduction would encourage wholesalers to order fewer new goods, leading to reduced production and potentially more job layoffs.

Wholesale inventories plunged by 1.4 percent, which was double analysts' expectations. It also was the fourth consecutive monthly decline.

Inventories at the wholesale level were reduced for a record eleventh consecutive month by July 2009, more than the 1 percent decline expected.

WIA. *See* WORKFORCE INVESTMENT ACT.

WILLIAMS-SONOMA. Facing difficult sales trends, the retailer of kitchenware cut 1,400 jobs as part of an effort to trim fiscal 2009 overhead costs by $75 million before taxes.

Sales plunged 24 percent over the eight-week Christmas period, dropping 24 percent as consumers curbed discretionary spending.

The firm's fourth-quarter 2008 net income dropped 90 percent on declining sales.

The company posted a first-quarter 2009 loss and a 22 percent decline in sales.

WINDFALL TAX. For significant bonuses being given, the United Kingdom slapped on a hefty windfall tax. The government expects to make nearly $1 billion from a 50 percent tax on bonuses above $40,000.

See also UNITED KINGDOM.

WINDOW DRESSING. The act of selling the month's losers and purchasing strong performers so that those names show up on clients' quarterly statements.

WINE MARKET. In the first six months of 2009, luxury wine sellers saw both an increase in sales and lower profits as Americans continued to consume a greater amount of wine but purchase less expensive brands.

WOMEN'S WAGES. Wages of the average woman who had a position during 2008–2009 climbed faster than those of the typical male. Over this time period, the median wages of women rose 3.2 percent after adjusting for inflation. For men, wages rose 2 percent. Minority men were especially hard hit, while minority women and highly educated women of all races did better.

WOMEN UNEMPLOYED. The share of women with jobs in December 2008 had fallen almost two percentage points from the peak it reached in 2000; at no other point in the past fifty years had the share of employed women fallen so much from its peak.

By October 2009, 8.1 percent of working women became unemployed.

See also MEN UNEMPLOYED; OVERTIME; UNEMPLOYMENT; WOMEN'S WAGES; WOMEN WORKFORCE.

WOMEN WORKFORCE. In early 2009, U.S. women surpassed men on payrolls, capturing the majority for the first time. The proportion of working women has not significantly changed, but a full 82 percent of the job losses have been borne by men.

The Great Recession has driven women who had left the work force to return. By September 2009 women held nearly half (49.9 percent) of all U.S. jobs, excluding farm workers and the self-employed, a rise of 1.2 percent from the 48.7 percent when the Great Recession began in December 2007 (in 1970, women held 35 percent of positions). Unemployment among women is lower than men at 8.8 percent.

See also WOMEN UNEMPLOYED.

WOOLWORTHS. In mid-December 2008, all Woolworths in the United Kingdom would be shut down. It closed its 807 stores, with the last one shutting its doors on January 5, 2009, putting 27,000 people out of work. Woolworths terminated U.S. operations in 2001.

Woolworths, the largest retail casualty during the British recession, was reborn on June 25, 2009, as an online brand selling children's wear, toys, and party goods.

See also RETAILING.

WORKER, HOMEOWNERSHIP AND BUSINESS ASSISTANCE ACT (2009). *See* UNEMPLOYMENT BENEFITS.

WORKFORCE INVESTMENT ACT (WIA). Enacted in 1998, the act sought to replace jumbled federal schemes with a streamlined system for workers and employers. States have some flexibility, with help for job searches, career counseling and, for some, money for training, often at community colleges.

Its funding is confused and declining, down 10 percent since 2002 to about $3.2 billion for the whole country in 2008. Only about 40 percent of WIA money is spent on training.

WORK OPENINGS. *See* JOB OPENINGS.

WORKS PROGRESS ADMINISTRATION. *See* ROOSEVELT, FRANKLIN DELANO.

WORLD BANK (THE BANK). Commenced operation in June 1946 to provide funds and technical assistance to facilitate economic development in its poorer member countries. Funds come from capital provided by member nations, sales of its own securities, sale of parts of its loans, repayments, and net earnings.

In December 2008, the Bank declared that the global financial meltdown was a heavy burden on developing economies, forecasting 4.5 percent growth in 2009, down from 6.3 percent in 2008.

The Bank argued that net private capital flows to emerging economies in 2009 was likely to be only half the record $1 trillion of 2007, while global trade volumes would shrink for the first time since 1982. The World Bank plans to increase lending over the next three years, to $100 billion to emerging countries to help them in dealing with the 2008–2009 economic meltdown.

The World Bank predicted that in 2009, global trade would shrink by 2 percent, the first time in twenty-seven years.

In mid-June, the World Bank reported that developing nations' net private capital inflows fell 41 percent in 2008 and will be reduced nearly in half in 2009. The Bank offered little hope that the nations would provide the spark for the global economic engine. GDP growth in emerging nations was projected to grow only 1.2 percent in 2009, as rich countries contracted by 4.5 percent.

See also BRETTON WOODS; BRETTON WOODS II; CHINA; GLOBAL TRADE; G-20; POVERTY; RUSSIA; TRADE.

Synonymous with INTERNATIONAL BANK FOR RECONSTRUCTION AND DEVELOPMENT.

WORLDCOM. *See* GENERAL MOTORS.

WORLD TRADE. Shrank in 2009 for the first time since 1982. Capital flows to emerging markets fell to $165 billion, from a 2007 high of $929 billion.

World trade in 2009 continued to shrink rapidly. Japan found that its exports in January were worth $47.2 billion, the lowest monthly total in more than four years and down 34 percent from the same month in 2008.

China's overall exports were down 17 percent in January.

The three largest economies in South America—Argentina, Brazil, and Chile—reported declines of 27 percent to 42 percent.

By June 2009, world trade volume increased 2.5 percent from May, the largest increase in a single month since July 2008.

See also EXPORTS; GLOBAL TRADE; PROTECTIONISM.

WORLD TRADE ORGANIZATION (WTO). Replacing the General Agreement on Tariffs and Trade (GATT) in 1995, its multilateral trade rules are a bulwark against protectionism. Headquarters are in Geneva, Switzerland. After two decades of unilateral tariff cutting, most countries' tariffs have fallen below their "bound" rates, the ceilings agreed on in the trade group. In the period of meltdown and increased protectionism, nations will be able to increase, sometimes tripling their import levies without breaking WTO rules.

On March 23, 2009, the WTO predicted that global trade would drop 9 percent, or more, in 2009. It issued its most negative report on global trade in its sixty-two-year history.

On March 26, its 153 members were told that there was a significant slippage in the global commitment to free trade, with increases in tariffs, new nontariff measures, and more resort to trade defense measures such as antidumping actions.

See also CHINA; GENERAL AGREEMENT ON TARIFFS AND TRADE; GLOBAL TRADE; G-20; PROTECTIONISM; SMOOT-HAWLEY ACT OF 1930; TRADE BARRIERS.

WORLD WAR II. *See* ROOSEVELT, FRANKLIN DELANO.

WQXR-FM. *See NEW YORK TIMES.*

W-SHAPED RECESSION. *See* RECESSION.

WSJ. *See WALL STREET JOURNAL.*

WTO. *See* WORLD TRADE ORGANIZATION.

X

XEROX. Reported in April 2009, a small first-quarter profit as revenue fell 18 percent.

On July 23, Xerox reported a profit decline, with earnings down 35 percent to $140 million. Revenue declined 18 percent to $3.73 billion.

XSTRATA. An international mining company, it had a net debt in 2008 of $15 billion and a market capitalization of $9 billion. It planned a 50 percent cut in jobs.

Y

YAHOO! Posted a 76 percent quarterly profit decline as the recession hit. The firm said on April 21, 2009, that it would eliminate about 675 more jobs, or 5 percent of its work force. Yahoo!'s revenue fell 13 percent in the first quarter to $1.58 billion, from $1.81 billion a year before.

Yahoo! saw sales decline again in the second quarter 2009. The company's overall revenue fell 13 percent from a year earlier, and made a profit gain of 7.6 percent.

From December 25, 2009, through January 1, 2010, Yahoo! shut down its offices, except essential functions as one way of cutting expenses during the meltdown.

Cf. APPLE.

YALE UNIVERSITY. Yale University estimated its endowment had fallen by mid-December 2008 25 percent, to $17 billion, since the end of June because of the global financial crisis, leading the university to restrict pay raises and cut spending to close a projected $100 million budget deficit. Yale's endowment fell to $16 billion on June 30 from $22.9 billion a year earlier. In 2009–2010 Yale cut staff and non-salary expenses by 7.5 percent. The university projected an annual deficit of $150 million each year from 2010–2011 through 2013–2014.

Cf. COLUMBIA UNIVERSITY; HARVARD UNIVERSITY; PRINCETON UNIVERSITY; STANFORD UNIVERSITY.

YEN. By the end of October 2008, the Japanese yen rose up against most major currencies, surging as much as 10 percent against the dollar. This rise was another signal of weakness in the world's economy.

The U.S. dollar weakened 19 percent against the yen in 2008, the biggest winner in the currency markets. By February 2009, the yen was 23.2 percent higher than last year's low point against the dollar, 46.7 percent higher against the euro, and 65 percent up against the British pound.

See *also* JAPAN.

YIELD CURVE. The difference between short-term and long-term interest rates on government bonds. Indicating growing investor optimism, this measure hit a record on December 21, 2009, suggesting that the economic recovery is growing.

YIELD SPREAD PREMIUMS. *See* MORTGAGE LEGISLATION.

YOUTH UNEMPLOYMENT. *See* UNEMPLOYMENT.

YUAN. *See* CHINA.

Z

ZALES. The second-largest jewelry retailer's sales declined to $658.7 million in the third quarter 2009, from $679.4 million a year before. Zales closed hundreds of its branches in 2008. On November 24, 2009, it posted a loss of $57.6 million for the fiscal first quarter, ending October 31. The figures compared with a year-before loss of $48.4 million. Sales fell 18.6 percent in November 2009.

See also JEWELRY.

ZAMBIA. *See* AFRICA.

ZERO-RATE. For some people who have lost vast amounts on stocks, bonds, and real estate, making an investment that offers security but no gain is tantamount to coming out ahead. With no apparent, acceptable option, a zero percent rate of return appealed to many people.

Often shortened to ZIRP—zero interest rate policy.

See also U.S. GOVERNMENT DEBT.

ZHEJIANG GEELY HOLDING GROUP. *See* VOLVO.

ZIRP (ZERO INTEREST RATE POLICY). *See* ZERO-RATE.

ZOMBIE BANKS. Banks that are failing but allowed to linger on.

See also BANK RESCUE (PLAN) OF 2009 (U.S.); ZOMBIES.

ZOMBIES. Debtors that have little hope of recovery and manage to avoid being wiped out thanks to support from their lenders or from the government. They consume tax monies, capital, and labor that could be better used in growing companies. By lowering prices to generate sales, zombie firms can draw healthier rivals into insolvency. Zombies are financial institutions that are effectively bankrupt but are kept alive by government assistance.

Japan was confounded during its lost decade of minimal growth in the 1990s. Weak Japanese borrowers used the proceeds from new loans to pay interest on old ones, a process called evergreening that kept banks from having to acknowledge losses.

Protecting zombies stunts long-term growth by blocking the needed reallocation of resources from declining firms and sectors to rising ones.

Sectors that could spawn them are:

a. Finance—The government props up weak banks that may never be capable of normal lending.
b. Homeowners—Assistance for homeowners may keep them out of foreclosure but still leave them with significant debt.
c. Automakers—Assistance to U.S. carmakers could tie up billions, supporting firms that are unable to compete successfully.

See also LEMON SOCIALISM; ZOMBIE BANKS.

INDEX

ABOUT THE AUTHOR

Jerry M. Rosenberg, a 2008 Fulbright Specialist recipient and a 2006 Marshall Foundation Fellow, is professor of management and global business at the Rutgers Business School and member of the faculty of the Division of Global Affairs, Rutgers University, Newark, New Jersey.

He is author of thirty-six books, including eight business dictionaries, and has been the business terminology consultant for twenty-five years to the *Oxford English Dictionary*. The *New York Times* has acclaimed him as "the leading business and technical lexicographer in the nation."

Breinigsville, PA USA
11 June 2010
239538BV00004B/2/P